# Instructor's Guide and Test Bank

FOR

# Environment

## THE SCIENCE BEHIND THE STORIES

Scott Brennan • Jay Withgott

INSTRUCTOR'S GUIDE
by
Dawn Ford
*University of Tennessee, Chattanooga*

TEST BANK
by
Sherri Morris
*Bradley University*

PEARSON
Benjamin Cummings

San Francisco Boston New York
Cape Town Hong Kong London Madrid Mexico City
Montreal Munich Paris Singapore Sydney Tokyo Toronto

Acquisitions Editor: Chalon Bridges
Project Editor: Susan Minarcin
Editorial Assistant: Alissa Anderson
Senior Production Editor: Corinne Benson
Copy Editor: Anna Reynolds Trabucco
Proofreader: Martha Ghent
Compositor: The Left Coast Group

(ISBN) 0-8053-4431-4

www.aw-bc.com

1 2 3 4 5 6 7 8 9 10—TCS—07 06 05 04

# Contents

## Instructor's Guide/Test Bank

# About the Authors

## Dawn Ford

Dawn M. Ford is an Assistant Professor of the Biological and Environmental Sciences at the University of Tennessee at Chattanooga (UTC). She holds the B.S. degree in Biology from Western Kentucky University and the M.S. degree in Botany from Miami University. Professor Ford has eight years of teaching experience, during which she has taught field botany, introductory geology, environmental science, conservation biology, tropical marine ecology, and tropical biology. Dawn Ford teaches international field courses in the Bahamas and Costa Rica during which students experience coral reefs, seagrass beds, mangrove swamps, tropical rainforests, and cloud forests. Her research focuses on the community ecology of seaweeds in tropical coastal zones.

Professor Ford has been very active in curriculum development and recently was awarded a National Science Foundation grant to develop, integrate, and assess field-based group research projects in the environmental science laboratory courses at UTC. She is a 2003–2004 Teaching, Learning & Technology Faculty Fellow during which she serves as a model to other UTC faculty on the use of effective teaching and learning strategies. Dawn Ford has spent many years developing laboratory activities for environmental science courses and recently published the laboratory manual *Investigations in Environmental Science* through the Kendall/Hunt Publishing Company.

Professor Ford lives with her husband, Robert Lathrop, and young son, Nathan, in Chattanooga. As a family, they enjoy a variety of outdoor pursuits in the beautiful Southern Appalachian mountains.

## Sherri Jeakins Morris

Dr. Morris received both her B.S. and masters degrees in Biology from San Diego State University. She received a Ph.D. in Plant Biology from Ohio State University and then went on to do postdoctoral work as a researcher in the Crop and Soil Sciences Department at Michigan State University. Currently, Dr. Morris is an assistant professor in the Biology Department at Bradley University, where she teaches ecology to biology majors and environmental science to nonmajors.

Dr. Morris's research interests focus on terrestrial carbon and nitrogen dynamics, which she integrates into an inquiry-based curriculum for her students. In October 2003, Morris received the Caterpillar Inc. New Faculty Achievement Award for Scholarship from Bradley University. She has authored or co-authored more than a dozen journal articles that have been published in journals such as *Soil Science Society of America Journal, Forest Ecology and Management, Landscape Ecology,* and *Soil Biology and Biochemistry* and has several more in press or review. Morris has also authored or co-authored book chapters in eight different edited volumes.

Professors Ford and Morris would like to thank Christine Freeman for her contribution to this text writing the answers to the *Weighing the Issues* questions.

# 1 An introduction to environmental science

## Chapter Objectives

**This chapter will help students understand:**

- What environmental scientists mean by the term *environment*
- The interdisciplinary nature of environmental science
- The scientific method and how science operates
- Some of the pressures on the global environment
- Natural resources and their importance to human life
- How population pressures and natural resources interact
- The concepts of sustainability and sustainable development

## Lecture Outline

I. Our Island, Earth
   A. Our environment is the sum total of our surroundings.
      1. It includes both biotic factors and abiotic factors.
      2. People most commonly use the term in the sense of a natural or nonhuman world that is outside of and apart from the human world.
      3. Understanding our interactions with the environment is important for several reasons.
      4. Topics studied by environmental scientists are today's most centrally important issues to our world and its future.
   B. Natural resources are vital to our survival.
      1. Natural resources are the various substances and forces we need in order to survive.
      2. Renewable natural resources are virtually unlimited or can be replenished by the environment over short periods of time.

3. Nonrenewable natural resources are in limited supply and are not replenished or are formed much more slowly than we use them.
4. Some renewable resources may turn nonrenewable if we deplete them too drastically.

C. Human population growth has shaped our relationship with natural resources.
1. The human population has grown to over 6 billion as a result of two events.
a. The transition from a hunter-gatherer lifestyle to an agricultural way of life took place 10,000 years ago.
b. The industrial revolution brought a shift from rural life to an urban society powered by fossil fuels.

D. Thomas Malthus and population growth
1. Malthus claimed that unless population growth was controlled, the number of people would outgrow the food supply.
2. He argued that a growing population would eventually be checked by famine, disease, or war.

E. Paul Ehrlich and "The Population Bomb"
1. Ehrlich predicted that a rapidly increasing human population would bring widespread famine and civil strife.
2. He claimed that population control was the only way to avoid starvation and war.
3. Although his predictions have not come true yet, many who support his ideas predict a global food crisis in the near future.

F. Garrett Hardin and "The Tragedy of the Commons"
1. Hardin analyzed how people approach resource use.
2. He disputed economic theory that individual self-interest, in the long term, serves the public.
3. According to Hardin's essay, a public pasture that is open to unregulated grazing will eventually be destroyed.

G. Environmental science can help us avoid mistakes made by past civilizations.
1. Easter Island is an example of a great civilization falling after depleting its resource base and devastating its island environment.
2. Environmental science is a multifaceted field that brings together many disciplines to make decisions and solve problems.

II. The Nature of Environmental Science

A. Environmental problems are perceived differently by different people.
1. An environmental problem is any undesirable change in the environment.
2. A person's age, gender, class, race, nationality, employment, and educational background can all affect whether he or she considers an environmental change a "problem."
3. In other cases, different types of people may vary in their awareness of problems.

B. Environmental science provides interdisciplinary solutions to environmental problems.
    1. Environmental science is especially broad because it encompasses not only the natural sciences, but also many social sciences.
    2. An interdisciplinary approach to addressing environmental problems can produce effective and lasting solutions.
C. Environmental science is not the same as environmentalism.
    1. Environmental science is the pursuit of knowledge about the workings of the environment and our interactions with it.
    2. Environmentalism is a social movement dedicated to protecting the natural world.
    3. Although environmental scientists may study many of the same issues environmentalists care about, they attempt to take an objective approach.

III. The Nature of Science
A. Science has many definitions.
    1. Modern scientists describe science as a systematic process for learning about the world and testing our understanding of it.
    2. Environmental science is a dynamic yet systematic way of studying the world, and it is also the body of knowledge accumulated from this process.
B. Scientists test ideas by weighing evidence.
C. The scientific method is the key element of science.
    1. It is a technique for testing ideas with observations and involves several assumptions and a more-or-less consistent series of interrelated steps.
    2. The steps of the scientific method are: Make observations, ask a question, develop a hypothesis, make predictions, test the predictions, analyze and interpret results, and make conclusions.
        a. A hypothesis is an educated guess that explains a phenomenon or answers a scientific question.
        b. A prediction is a specific statement that can be directly and unequivocally tested.
        c. An experiment is an activity designed to test the validity of a hypothesis; it involves manipulating variables.
        d. An independent variable is the variable that the scientist manipulates, while the dependent variable is the one that depends upon the other variable.
        e. Scientists collect data from experiments; quantitative data is information that can be expressed using numbers.
D. There are different ways to test hypotheses.
    1. A manipulative experiment is an experiment in which the researcher actively chooses and manipulates the independent variable.
    2. When variables cannot be manipulated, a natural experiment is performed.

3. The social sciences often involve less experimentation than the natural sciences and depend more on careful observation and interpretation of patterns in data.
4. Observational studies and natural experiments can show correlation between variables, but cannot demonstrate that one variable causes a change in another variable.

E. The scientific process does not stop with the scientific method.
1. Peer review is an essential part of the scientific process.
2. Scientists frequently present their work at professional conferences.
3. A large portion of a research scientist's time is spent writing grant applications requesting money for research from private foundations or from government agencies.
4. Sound science is based on doubt rather than on certainty, and on repeatability rather than on one-time occurrence.
5. If a hypothesis survives repeated testing by numerous research teams, it may be modeled and potentially be incorporated into a theory.
6. A theory is a widely accepted, well-tested explanation of one or more cause-and-effect relationships that has been extensively validated by a great amount of research.

F. Science may go through "paradigm shifts."
1. Thomas Kuhn argued that science goes through periodic revolutions in which one dominant view is abandoned for another.
2. Understanding how science works is paramount to comprehending how scientific ideas and interpretations change through time as new information accrues.

IV. Environmental Science and the State of the World

A. Human population growth lies at the root of many environmental changes.
1. The ways we modify the environment have been influenced by the sudden rise in human population.
2. The rate of population growth is slowing, but the absolute numbers continue to increase, impacting the environment.

B. Increased agricultural production has been a triumph, but also entails serious costs.
1. Advancing technology has enabled us to grow more food per unit of land.
2. Massive use of chemical fertilizers and pesticides and widespread conversion of natural habitats are the environmental costs of conventional agriculture.
3. In response to agricultural problems, people have developed and promoted environmentally friendly farming techniques and genetically engineered crops.

C. Pollution comes in many forms, with diverse consequences.
1. Scientists in the field of toxicology study the impacts of synthetic chemicals on humans and other organisms.
2. Artificial chemicals pollute land, water, and air.

3. Political will is crucial if we are to address the looming specter of climate change.

D. Aquatic resources have been neglected, but are now receiving more attention.

1. The socioeconomic impact of El Niño and La Niña has given ocean science heightened relevance.
2. Both oceans and freshwater systems face serious pollution problems.
3. Even worse than pollution for ocean life is overfishing.
4. Approximately 20% of freshwater fish species are either endangered or extinct.

E. Earth's biodiversity is gravely threatened.

1. Biodiversity, the cumulative number and kind of living things, is declining dramatically.
2. Many biologists say that we are in the midst of one of the greatest mass extinctions in Earth's history.
3. E. O. Wilson has warned that the loss of biodiversity is our most serious and threatening environmental dilemma.

F. We need to use resources, but we can use them in better ways.

1. Mining and mineral processing causes severe environmental problems.
2. Recycling is one way to minimize harm to the natural environment.
3. Global consumption of fossil fuels has quadrupled since 1950, causing air and water pollution.
4. Suburban sprawl and loss of natural space are problems seen worldwide.

G. Solutions to environmental problems must be global and sustainable.

H. Are things getting better or worse?

1. Some people maintain that the general conditions of human life are getting better, not worse.
2. Furthermore, some say that human ingenuity and Earth's vast natural resources will meet all of our needs indefinitely.

V. Sustainability

A. The primary challenge in our increasingly populated world is how to live within the planet's means, such that Earth and its resources can sustain us and the rest of Earth's biota for the foreseeable future.

B. Development is a term economists and scientists use to describe the use of natural resources for economic purposes alone.

C. Sustainable development is the use of resources in a manner that satisfies our current needs without compromising future availability of resources.

VI. Conclusion

A. The sustainable use of resources and the relationship between resource use and population are themes that you will encounter every day.

B. Finding effective ways of living peacefully, healthily, and sustainably on our diverse and complex planet will require a thorough scientific understanding of both natural and social systems.

C. It is important to keep in mind that identifying a problem is the first step in devising a solution to it.

## Key Terms

abiotic factors
agricultural revolution
alternative hypotheses
biodiversity
biotic factors
built environment
controlled experiment
correlation
DDT
dependent variable
Easter Island
ecology
Ehrlich, Paul
environment
environmental problem
environmental studies
environmentalism
experiment
fossil fuels
globalization
Hardin, Garrett
historical sciences
hypothesis
independent variable
industrial revolution
interdisciplinary
Malthus, Thomas
manipulative experiment
natural experiment
natural resources
natural sciences
neo-Malthusian
nonrenewable natural resources
organisms
paradigm
peer review
prediction
probability
qualitative data
quantitative data
renewable natural resources
repeatability
science
scientific method
social sciences
sustainable development
theory
toxicology
variables

## Teaching Tips

1. Begin class by asking the students to define the term "environment" in their own words. Ask students to respond on a notecard to be submitted. At the end of the semester, return the notecards to the students and ask them to redefine the term based on what they learned during the course. Lead a discussion about how their definitions changed.
2. To teach the scientific method, present a situation to the class and ask students to work in groups to address the issue using the scientific process. For example:

   A farmer in South Carolina notices that the pond on his property has an unusually high amount of algae in it. Because of the algal growth, his cattle will not drink from the pond. What is happening and what could he do?

   Based on this information (the observation), ask students to formulate a hypothesis, make a prediction, and design an experiment.
3. To make environmental science more appealing to students, present information about *local* environmental issues. When students are faced with environmental problems where they live, they see how it relates to them personally, and realize that they can make a difference.
4. Ask students to conduct Internet research on Easter Island. What is it like today? How many people live on the island? What are the main resources?

# Additional Resources

## Websites

1. "Agricultural Biotechnology," United States Department of Agriculture, www.usda.gov/agencies/biotech/index.html

   This website provides information about genetically engineered crops that are used for pest management and food.

2. "NASA Spacelink Curriculum Support," NASA, http://spacelink.nasa.gov/Instructional.Materials/Curriculum.Support

   This Web page provides educator guides for life science activities that integrate the scientific method.

3. "Sustainable Development Issues A to Z," United Nations Division of Sustainable Development, www.un.org/esa/sustdev/sdissues/sdissues.htm

   Information, documents, and publications related to sustainable development and Agenda 21 can be accessed from this Web page.

4. "World POPClock Projection," U.S. Census Bureau, www.census.gov/cgi-bin/pc/popclockw

   This website provides the current total population of the world.

## Audiovisual Materials

1. *Earth on Edge,* Bill Moyers Reports, distributed by Films for the Humanities and Sciences (www.films.com).

   In collaboration with the World Resources Institute, Bill Moyers assesses the state of the environment in interviews with scientists from around the world.

2. *Paul Ehrlich and the Population Bomb,* distributed by Films for the Humanities and Sciences (www.films.com).

   This program presents interviews with Ehrlich and his critics about his belief that an unchecked population would upset the balance of nature.

3. *Scientific Methods and Values,* distributed by Hawkhill Video (www.hawkhill.com)

   This 35-minute program describes the history of the scientific method and explains how the technique is used by scientists.

4. *State of the Planet: A Biosphere in the Balance,* 2001, produced by BBC Worldwide and distributed by Films for the Humanities and Sciences, (www.films.com).

   This video, narrated by David Attenborough, is the first in a three-part series that describes worldwide biodiversity and the human activities that are destroying it.

# *Weighing the Issues:* Suggested Answers

## Tragedy of the Commons

***Facts to consider:*** *If everyone who grazed cattle in the shared pasture added animals to their herds, eventually the quality of the resources in the pasture—grass, soil, water—would degrade. The cattle would eat the grass faster than it could regrow. They would trample the soil faster than it could recover. And they would consume or pollute the water faster than it could be diluted with clean water from other natural sources. In the long run, this degraded environment could support fewer cattle, perhaps even fewer than are grazing there before people add more cattle to the pasture.*

*Individual responses will vary about whether government regulation or private ownership would be more appropriate solutions.*

## Replicates and Data Analysis

***Facts to consider:*** *If seven, eight, or nine of the treatments grew more algae, one might conclude that treatment increased the likelihood of heavier algae growth, but it would also have to be noted that treatment evidently was not the only factor in determining whether algae growth would be heavier. Either some other unidentified factor must also be present for growth to be heavier, or some factor reduced the likelihood of algae growth. Further research would have to explore possible differences between the treatment ponds that had heavier growth and those that did not, in order to try to identify the possible factor and then establish a more refined set of treatment and control ponds that take that factor into account.*

*The more complex possible outcome, in which either eight treatment ponds showed 10 percent more growth than the control ponds, and two control ponds showed 300 percent more than their paired treatments, indicated that the algae growth doesn't correlate well with fertilizer use, so something else could turn out to be a much more significant factor. This would suggest looking at commonalities among the ponds that had algae growth, regardless of the fertilizer use.*

*Replicates are important because a small set of results may not reveal enough of the range of results that would be revealed if a larger set were used. The smaller the set of results, the more likely that some significant data would not be included. The larger the set of results, the more likely that differences in results are statistically significant.*

## Genetically Engineered Crops to Feed the World

***Facts to consider:*** *This question requires an individual response. Advantages to feeding more people include lower levels of starvation and hunger; higher ability of well-nourished populations to be production and economically prosperous; and reduced tensions because of resource competition. Disadvantages might include the environmental costs of raising more food for more people (such as increased use of chemical fertilizers and pesticides, soil degradation, and poorly managed irrigation), even with "super-crops"; other environmental costs created by a larger population (such as increased use of fossil fuels; degradation of air, soil, and water); and social costs of having more people competing for similar economic and physical resources.*

## Additional Questions

1. It was stated in this chapter that the human population is the root of many changes in the environment. What do you think causes a greater environmental impact: a fast-growing population that uses few resources or a slow-growing population that uses many resources?

   *It is important for students to realize that even though the annual growth rate in the United States is relatively low, the environmental impact we make is great because of our consumption of resources. In fact, the United States has only 5% of the world's population, but consumes more than 30% of its natural resources. Countries with high growth rates, in general, consume few resources. In the end, we all make impacts on the environment; but it is not a solution in itself to try to slow population growth in other parts of the world. There are actions we can take as individuals to reduce our own environmental impacts.*

2. Many people confuse environmental science with environmentalism. Imagine you are interested in starting an environmental education program in the local school system. You must present your proposal to the school board and convince board members that environmental activism is not a component, only environmental education. Develop your proposal to include the following: What is environmental science? How is it different from environmentalism? Why is it important to teach environmental science in the local schools?

   *This activity provides an opportunity for students to think about the importance of environmental education. As stated in the chapter, environmental science is the interdisciplinary study of the workings of the natural world and how we affect it. In contrast, environmentalism is a social movement dedicated to protecting the environment from certain human activities. Unfortunately, some people think that environmental scientists are "tree huggers" fighting for a certain cause.*

   *Environmental education in schools is extremely important for the future of the environment. It is crucial that people become aware of environmental issues at a young age so that they can make sound environmental decisions as adults.*

3. Assign students to read the online case study, "The L.A. of the South: Atlanta's Urban Sprawl." Why is "smart growth", as exemplified by the development of Atlantic Station, considered a type of sustainable development?

   *Sustainable development is the use of renewable and nonrenewable resources in a way that satisfies our current needs without jeopardizing the future availability of the resources. With Atlantic Station, developers are filling vacant downtown space that was contaminated with pollution from Atlantic Steel Mill. Cleaning up and reusing that space is a perfect example of using resources in a sustainable manner. As a result, less natural land is converted to urban land use.*

# 2 Environmental ethics and economics: Values and choices

## Chapter Objectives

**This chapter will help students understand:**

- The influences of culture and worldview on the choices people make
- The history and evolution of major schools of thought in environmental ethics
- Precepts of classical and neoclassical economic theory and their implications for the environment
- Concepts of environmental economics and ecological economics
- Concepts of economic growth, economic health, and sustainability
- The relationships between ethics, economics, and environmental science

## Lecture Outline

I. Central Case: The Mirrar Clan Confronts the Jabiluka Uranium Mine

   A. The remote Kakadu region of Australia's Northern Territory is home to several groups of Australian Aborigines and the Kakadu National Park.

      1. The region's land contains large amounts of uranium, and uranium mining is a key part of the Australian national economy.

      2. Many of Australia's uranium deposits occur on Aboriginal lands, giving rise to conflicts between mining corporations and the Aboriginal people.

   B. The Mirrar clan has been fighting the development of the Jabiluka mine because of threats to human health and the environment.

   C. On September 5, 2002, the CEO of the corporation that holds the rights to the Jabiluka ore announced the cancellation of mining plans at Jabiluka.

II. Culture, Worldview, and Our Perception of the Environment

   A. Ethics and economics are sources of values.

   B. Values, culture, and worldview influence a person's perception of the environment.

      1. Our decisions about how we meet our needs and how we use the environment to do so are heavily influenced by our culture and worldview.

      2. Culture can be defined as the overall ensemble of knowledge, beliefs, values, and learned ways of life shared by a group of people.

      3. A worldview reflects a person's beliefs about the meaning, operation, and essence of the world.

      4. People with different worldviews can study the same situation and draw very different conclusions.

   C. Many factors can shape our worldview and perception of the environment.

      1. The traditional culture and worldview of the Mirrar clan have played a large role in its view of the proposed Jabiluka mine.

      2. Aborigines believe that they descended from "sky heroes," spirit ancestors that left important signs and lessons in the landscape.

      3. A given social group may share a particular view of its environment because its members have lived through similar experiences.

      4. A person's political ideology can also shape his or her attitudes toward the environment.

      5. Economic factors also sway how people perceive their environment and how they make decisions regarding it.

III. Environmental Ethics

   A. The field of ethics involves the study of good and bad, of right and wrong.

      1. Ethics overlaps in its standards with both religion and law, but is distinct from both.

      2. Ethical standards may be viewed as tools for decision making, as criteria that help differentiate right from wrong.

   B. Environmental ethics is the application of ethical standards to environmental questions.

   C. We have extended ethical consideration to more entities through time.

      1. Ethical consideration has expanded to include more people and nonhuman entities.

      2. Some people have suggested that all of nature should be ethically represented.

      3. This expansion of ethical consideration pertains mainly to modern European-based culture; many non-Western cultures have long held expanded ethical domains.

      4. Anthropocentrism is a human-centered view of our relationship with the environment.

   5. Biocentrism ascribes relative values to actions, entities, or properties on the basis of their effects on all living things or on the integrity of the biotic realm in general.
   6. Ecocentrism considers actions in terms of their damage or benefit to the integrity of whole ecological systems.

D. Environmental ethics has . . . roots.
   1. People have contemplated our relationship with Earth for thousands of years.
   2. Some ethicists and theologians have pointed to the Judeo-Christian religious tradition as a source of anthropocentric hostility toward the environment.
   3. Although humans have held differing views of the ethical relationship with the environment for millennia, the developments leading to the rise of modern environmental ethics occurred much more recently.

E. The industrial revolution inspired environmental philosophers.
   1. The industrial revolution amplified the intentional and unintentional impacts of human activities on the environment.
   2. John Ruskin, a British art critic, poet, and writer, criticized industrialized cities as "little more than laboratories for the distillation into heaven of venomous smokes and smells."
   3. Transcendentalism was a philosophical movement started in the United States by Ralph Waldo Emerson and Henry David Thoreau in the 19th century.

F. The conservation and preservation movements arose around the turn of the 20th century.
   1. John Muir was an advocate for the preservation of untouched wilderness.
   2. Gifford Pinchot is associated with the conservation ethic that emphasizes that humans should put natural resources to use, but should manage them wisely.

G. Aldo Leopold's land ethic arose from the conservation and preservation ethics.
   1. Aldo Leopold came to see that healthy ecological systems depended on the protection of all their interacting parts, including predators as well as prey.
   2. He argued that humans should view themselves and "the land" as members of the same community and that humans are obliged to treat the land in an ethical manner.

H. Deep ecology is a recent philosophical extension of environmental ethics.

I. Ecofeminism draws parallels between male attitudes toward nature and toward women.

J. Environmental justice seeks equal legal treatment for all races and classes in environmental matters.
   1. A protest in the early 1980s by African Americans in North Carolina against a toxic waste dump in their community is widely seen as the beginning of the environmental justice movement.

2. The movement was fueled by the perception that environmental hazards are inequitably distributed, with poor people and people of color bearing a greater share of pollution than richer people and whites.
3. Uranium mining in Australia and in North America has been a source of environmental justice concerns.
4. Cases of lung cancer began to appear among Navajo miners in the early 1960s, but scientific studies of the effects of radiation on miners at the time excluded Native American workers.

IV. Economics: Old Approaches, New Approaches, and Environmental Implications

A. Is there a trade-off between economics and the environment?

B. Economics is the study of our use of scarce resources for competing purposes.

C. Several types of economies exist today and have borrowed from one another.

1. An economy is a social system that converts resources into goods and services.
2. The oldest type of economy is the subsistence economy in which people meet most or all of their daily needs directly from nature.
3. In the capitalist market economy, buyers and sellers interact to determine the types and amounts of goods and services to produce.
4. In a centrally planned economy, a nation's government determines how to allocate resources.

D. The environment and the economy are intricately linked.

1. Human economies are open systems, connected with the larger environmental system of which they are a part.
2. Earth is a closed system, so the inputs Earth can provide to human economies are limited.
3. Economic activities utilize resources from the environment.
4. We obtain resources from the environment, but the environment also naturally functions in a manner that supports economies.
5. The environment enables economic activity by providing so-called ecosystem goods and services, and economic activity can affect the environment in return.

E. Adam Smith and other philosophers founded classical economics.

1. Economics and ethics share a common intellectual heritage.
2. Adam Smith, the father of classical economics, believed that when people are free to pursue their own economic self-interest in a competitive marketplace, the marketplace will behave as if guided by "an invisible hand" that ensures their actions will benefit society.

F. Neoclassical economics incorporates human psychology and behavior.

1. Neoclassical economics focuses on consumer choices and the psychological factors underlying these choices.
2. The conflict between buyers and sellers results in a compromise price being reached and the "right" quantity of commodities being bought and sold.

G. Several aspects of neoclassical economics contribute to environmental problems.
    1. Resources are considered infinite or substitutable.
    2. Long-term effects are discounted.
    3. Costs and benefits are internal.
        a. The market does not take the costs of pollution into account.
        b. By ignoring external costs, economies create a false idea of the true costs of particular choices.
    4. Growth is considered good.

H. Is the growth paradigm good for us?
    1. The world economy is seven times bigger today than it was 50 years ago.
    2. Many observers today worry that growth has become an end in itself and is no longer necessarily the best tool with which to pursue human happiness.
    3. Defenders of traditional economic approaches argue that most economies are still expanding despite predictions that limited resources would doom them.
    4. Technological innovation has enabled us to push back the limits on growth.

I. Economists disagree on whether economic growth is sustainable.
    1. Cornucopians believe technology can solve everything.
    2. Ecological economists argue that history has shown us that civilizations do not overcome environmental limitations in the long run and we must undergo reform to achieve sustainability.
    3. Environmental economists maintain that we can attain sustainability within our current economic systems by modifying the principles of neoclassical economics to address environmental challenges.

J. A steady-state economy is a revolutionary alternative to growth.
    1. A steady-state economy does not grow and shrink but remains stable.
    2. Modern proponents of a steady-state economy believe that we will need to fundamentally change the way economic transactions are conducted.
    3. Attaining long-term sustainability will certainly require the reforms that environmental economists advocate, and may well require fundamental shifts in thinking, values, and behaviors.

K. Ecosystem goods and services can be given monetary value.
    1. Our society often mistreats the very systems that keep it alive and healthy in large part because the market assigns these entities no quantitative monetary value or, at best, assigns values that underestimate their true worth.
    2. Environmental economists have tried to assign nonmarket values to ecosystem services, values that are not usually included in the price of a good or service.

3. One technique of assigning nonmarket value is contingent valuation, which involves using surveys to determine how much people would be willing to pay to protect a resource or to restore it.
4. Critics point out that surveys produce inflated values that people would not actually pay.
5. An alternative approach is to calculate the overall economic value of all services that an ecosystem provides.

L. Markets can fail.
   1. Markets fail when they do not reflect the full costs and benefits of actions.
   2. Traditionally, market failure has been countered by government intervention.

M. Ecolabeling and permit trading are two of several ways to address market failures.
   1. Ecolabeling informs consumers of which brands use processes believed to be environmentally beneficial, and which do not.
   2. Another technique is to create markets in permits for environmentally harmful activities, thereby allowing companies to buy and sell the rights to conduct such activities.

V. Conclusion
   A. Permit trading, ecolabeling, and valuation of ecosystem services are some of many recent developments that have brought economic approaches to bear on environmental protection and resource conservation.
   B. Sustainability is the key to ethical treatment of future generations of humans, as well as the nonhuman environment.
   C. The convergence of science, ethics, and economics plays a role in the resolution of important human and environmental problems.

## Key Terms

Aborigines
anthropocentrism
biocentrism
capitalist market economy
categorical imperative
centrally planned economies
conservation ethic
contingent valuation
culture
deep ecology
demand
ecocentrism
ecofeminism
ecolabeling
ecological economics
economics
economy
ecosystem services
ecosystem valuation
Emerson, Ralph Waldo
environmental economics
environmental ethics
environmental justice
ethics
external cost
externalities
financial resources
genuine progress indicator
goods
gross domestic product
human resources
Leopold, Aldo
manufactured resources
market failure
Mill, John Stuart
Mirrar Clan
Muir, John
Nash, Roderick
neoclassical economies
nonmarket values
permit trading
Pinchot, Gifford
preservation ethic
Ruskin, John

services
Smith, Adam
steady-state economy
subsistence economy
supply
Thoreau, Henry David
transcendentalism
utilitarian principle
vested interest
virtue
worldview

# Teaching Tips

1. Present a local situation to your students that is similar to the Jabiluka uranium mine issue. Are there public movements in your area against a development (logging, mining, road building) because of its environmental impacts? How do the students feel about it?
2. Assign outside readings from books that are mentioned in the chapter:
   - *Walden* by Henry David Thoreau
   - *A Sand County Almanac* by Aldo Leopold
   - *The Rights of Nature* by Roderick Nash
3. Ask the students to research the Jabiluka Mine issue on the Internet for updates on the story.
4. Assign an ethical perspective to each student (anthropocentrism, biocentrism, or ecocentrism) and ask them to defend that worldview in a class discussion. They should do research on that perspective before the next class. If you have a large class, ask students to be involved in an online discussion.
5. Describe to the class how Aldo Leopold, Gifford Pinchot, John Muir, and Theodore Roosevelt were instrumental in how federally protected lands are managed.

# Additional Resources

## Websites

1. "Environmental Ethics Resources on WWW," Center for Applied Ethics, www.ethics.ubc.ca/resources/environmental

   This website provides links to environmental ethics information, publications, and organizations.
2. The International Society for Ecological Economics, www.ecologicaleconomics.org

   The ISEE provides information that "facilitates understanding between economists and ecologists and the integration of their thinking into a transdiscipline aimed at developing a sustainable world."
3. "John Muir Exhibit," Sierra Club, www.sierraclub.org/john_muir_exhibit

   This online exhibit features the life of John Muir, renowned naturalist and founder of the Sierra Club.

## Audiovisual Materials

1. *Crossing the Stones: A Portrait of Arne Naess,* distributed by Bullfrog Films (www.bullfrogfilms.com).

   This video is an intimate biography of the Norwegian founder of deep ecology.
2. *The Nature of Business: Partnering with the Environment,* distributed by Films for the Humanities and Sciences (www.film.com).

   This program shows corporate leaders who are planning for a sustainable future by incorporating social responsibility and environmental protection into all processes and decisions.
3. *The Wilderness Idea—John Muir, Gifford Pinchot and the First Great Battle of Wilderness,* distributed by Direct Cinema Ltd. (Ph. 310-636-8200).

   This documentary focuses on the Hetch Hetchy battle.

# *Weighing the Issues:* Suggested Answers

### Uranium Mining in Bethlehem

***Facts to consider:*** *It is probable that any plans for mining such a religious site in these regions would be met with fierce opposition despite any claims of minimal environmental impact. These situations may have many similarities including the disturbance of lands considered by the inhabitants to be sacred. In both examples, the people involved have strong cultural values drawn from the stories surrounding the sites. The resulting pollution could contaminate local habitats, including air and water. Some differences might include the distinct socioeconomic status of the inhabitants of the regions in question. The Mirrar Clan number 27 people in all, while the populations in Jerusalem and Mecca are much higher. The size of these populations would have many ramifications in terms of political power, economic resources, and political power. The mine would also have a greater impact in terms of social consequences in a more heavily populated region.*

### Preservation, Conservation, and the Jabiluka Uranium Mine

***Facts to consider:*** *Preservationalists would likely argue against the mine overall. Answers will vary but questions that might be asked would focus on the inherent value of the land itself and would seek to determine whether or not the value of the land would be destroyed by development. Another likely question would be to ask which option would play a larger role in overall human happiness: a uranium mine that scarred the land or "a place to play and to pray."*

*Conversationalists would be more likely to support the mine. Again, individual student answers will vary but may include a focus on what use of the land constitutes the greatest good for the greatest number of people. Conversationalists would likely seek to manage the resources to make them available to the largest number of people for the longest time possible.*

*Which ethic students identify with will require a personal response.*

## Environmental Justice

***Facts to consider:*** *In the United States, a federal order issued by President Clinton already requires federal agencies to make sure that their environmental actions do not discriminate on the basis of income. This sets the precedent for expanding this to actions of state and local governments. People may disagree about whether such restrictions should also apply to private entities, but other procedures can be followed that will reduce this inequality even without such changes. For instance, public agencies can provide more vigorous enforcement of existing anti-pollution laws, including levying of fines and other punishments for violators. Also, both public and private studies could be required, not only to predict environmental consequences of proposed projects but also to assess the effect of existing facilities. Making public the results of what is known would help control unwanted negative effects on communities. Other ways may also suggest additional ways to reduce this inequality, such as increases in regulations, fines, compensation, and public education.*

## Environmental Ethics and Political Decisions

***Facts to consider:*** *Responses will vary. The politician might begin by asking whether one use of the land is more ethical than the other and what use of the land constitutes the greatest good for the greatest number of people. To do this effectively, the politician would need to put measures in place to minimize negative impacts and maximize benefits. Positive aspects would include focusing on the mine as a source of jobs in the region, bringing both economic growth and energy reserves, thereby contributing to the betterment of the community and to a better quality of life overall. The emphasis then would be on the numbers of people put to work by the mine, the economic costs of their productivity, the development of geographic regions, and the social good that can come with increased services like health care and social services.*

*The politician would also need to develop a strategy for minimizing negative effects. Some ways to do this would be to gather and consider information about potential consequences and ways of minimizing such effects like taxes and penalties on the mine owners for violations. The politician would also need to evaluate how other factors like the possibility of increased levels of radiation might effect the population and the environment and put measures in place to preempt such problems. The politician might also ask what the consequences of not opening the mine would be and emphasizing long-term benefits.*

## Adam Smith and the Invisible Hand

***Facts to consider:*** *The Tragedy of the Commons tells us that unfettered self-interest harms the community and that a public pasture (or commons) will eventually be destroyed because each person whose animals graze there will be motivated to maximize personal profit by increasing the number of this or her animals that graze until the pasture's ability to provide food collapses. Because no one owns the resource no one has the incentive to expend effort taking care of it.*

*However, an environmental economics view would identify the pasture as part of an "open system" and see it as a "scarce resource." Under this view the individuals that graze animals in the pasture would recognize that their economic advantage is dependent on environmental resources, thus, for continued survival, those resources would have to be maintained.*

*Adam Smith's concept of the invisible hand, then, would support the development of the Jabiluka mine by supposing that, in a free-market economy, what benefits the mine would in turn benefit society. The reality, however, might be somewhat different because in a capitalist marketplace social values like preserving natural resources have not typically been taken into account. That is, the mine benefits by minimizing its expenses and maximizing its profits, unless there is recognition that the economic advantage is dependent on scarce environmental resources, then there is no vested interest in protecting them.*

## Sustainability and the Environment

***Facts to consider:*** *The precautionary principle might be applied to many different environmental issues. Topics mentioned will depend on student awareness, but might include genetically modified food, genetic engineering in other contexts (such as farm animals), endocrine-disrupting chemicals, release of nanotechnology and micromachines in the environment, other aspects of biotechnology, fuel-cell vehicles, and irradiation of foods. The precautionary principle would add costs to the development of new products, certainly higher costs for research, exploration of alternatives, and testing. Then, in the early stages of application, both developers of such products and the governmental entities regulating them would have costs associated with compliance, insurance, and human resources such as training, monitoring, enforcement, and communication.*

*Such efforts might also reveal alternatives to potentially hazardous new areas, and might also spur development of refinements that create more benign results. For example, alternative chemicals or processes might be developed that reduce the impact of endocrine-disrupting chemicals.*

## Natural Gas Pipeline Across Peru

***Facts to consider:*** *To weigh economic gains against environmental and social disruptions would involve questions such as the following. What is the purpose of the pipeline—to provide a cleaner and cheaper form of energy for Peru or to provide an export for world trade? If the energy will be used in Peru, what will it facilitate—greater industrial expansion, commercial agriculture, or urban infrastructure? Who would own and control the pipeline—a private firm or the Peruvian national government and what would happen to profits from this enterprise? Would the projected economic improvement cover the cost of the loan repayment without requiring reduction in government expenditures for other needs or increasing Peru's international indebtedness? What kinds of jobs would be brought by the building of the pipeline? By its maintenance? What is the long-term outlook for such employment?*

*How broad a range of disturbances would such a pipeline have as it runs through a rainforest? How many tribes and people would be disturbed? In what ways would they be disturbed—their food gathering and hunting, religious and cultural sites, and boundary definitions? What kinds of methods have been planned to minimize degradation of rainforest soils, since rainforests are prone to erosion once plants are removed? Are animals and plants in the affected areas threatened or endangered? Could other locations for the marine terminal also work, even if they require additional funding? What provisions for environmental protection does the project include?*

*An ethical standard focusing on virtue might emphasize whether this project was fair to the indigenous people, whose lives would be much more disturbed than those of other Peruvians. Kant's categorical imperative might focus on whether the results would feel acceptable if they were applied to oneself. Finally, a utility-oriented ethic would focus on the costs and benefits to the overall Peruvian economy and society.*

## Additional Questions

1. The following quote is from Aldo Leopold's *A Sand County Almanac* (1948):

   > "The first ethics dealt with the relation between individuals; the Mosaic Decalogue is an example. Later accretions dealt with the relation between the individual and society. The Golden Rule tries to integrate the individual to society, democracy to integrate social organization to the individual.
   >
   > "There is as yet no ethic dealing with man's relation to land and to the animals and plants which grow upon it. Land, like Odysseus' slave-girls, is still property. The land relation is still strictly economic, entailing privileges but no obligations."

   Since 1948, do you think that society has developed a land ethic? Why or why not? Describe your land ethic.

   *Answers will vary. Some students may argue that a land ethic has been developed as shown by the protection of land by private, state, and federal agencies. Other students may argue that there is still no land ethic as evidenced by loss of natural habitat and rapid development.*

2. The central case study of this chapter focuses on the proposed Jabiluka uranium mine in Australia's Northern Territory and the concerns of the Mirrar Clan. Imagine that members of the Mirrar Clan requested that the health department speak to them about uranium, radiation, and its health effects. Conduct Internet research on these topics and develop a short presentation for the Mirrar Clan.

   *The Environmental Protection Agency provides basic information about radiation at www.epa.gov/radiation/students/what.html. Students will find that uranium is an unstable metal that gradually decays at the atomic level, causing it to be radioactive. Radiation is the energy given off by the nucleus of an atom in the form of particles or waves. There are different types of radiation: nonionizing and ionizing. Ionizing radiation has enough energy to change atoms chemically and can be harmful to living organisms. There is alpha, beta, and gamma ionizing radiation, with gamma radiation being the most destructive. Small doses of radiation can cause burns, loss of hair, nausea, loss of fertility, and cancer. Massive doses can cause death.*

3. As mentioned in this chapter, there are market-based strategies to improve the environment, such as permit trading. One such strategy, called the "Clear Skies Initiative," has recently been introduced by the Bush Administration to address air pollution.

   The online case study "Lake Acidification in the Adirondacks" describes the initiative and provides a hyperlink to the EPA Clear Skies Web page. Assign students to read the case study and linked Web page and answer the following question:

How will the Clear Skies plan reduce overall sulfur dioxide and nitrogen oxide emissions? How is this strategy different from "command-and-control" approaches?

*If approved, the Clear Skies Initiative will be a mandatory program for power producers. It will use a cap and trade program for three air pollutants: sulfur dioxide, nitrogen oxides, and mercury. The EPA will limit the amount of pollution that can be emitted by power plants to meet specific environmental goals by distributing "allowances." Electricity generators must hold one "allowance" for each ton of pollution they emit. The numbers of allowances that are distributed by EPA are reduced over time. The allowances can be traded freely, so a power plant can reduce its emissions to the allowable amount or buy allowances from another generator. This plan is different from the command-and-control approach that limits each power plant to a certain level of emissions without flexibility. For more information about the cap and trade system of Clear Skies, go to http://epa.gov/air/clearskies/captrade.html.*

# 3 Environmental policy: Decision-making and problem-solving

## Chapter Objectives

**This chapter will help students understand:**

- The origins, history, and societal role of environmental policy
- The relationship between science, ethics, economics, and policy
- The institutions important to U.S. environmental policy
- The environmental policy process, including the role of citizens and interest groups
- Selected U.S. environmental laws
- The nature and institutions of international environmental policy
- How nations handle transboundary issues

## Lecture Outline

I. Central Case: San Diego's Sewage Pollution Problems and Policy Solutions
   A. In 1996, officials closed all public beaches in San Diego, California, due to stormwater runoff that contaminated local rivers and coastal waters.
   B. This problem also occurred across the border in the Mexican city of Tijuana, with raw sewage overflowing into streets and beaches.
   C. The international watershed of the Tijuana River covers 1,750 square miles, with 70% in Mexico, where urban development has boomed in recent years.
   D. The problem is worse on the Mexican side because most Mexican residents of the Tijuana River watershed live in poverty and the pollution of their river directly affects their day-to-day lives.
   E. Many people in the San Diego and Tijuana areas have worked with policy-makers to address this problem.

II. Environmental Policy: An Introduction

A. Science, ethics, and economics all influence the problem-solving process of environmental policymaking.

B. When a society reaches broad agreement that an environmental problem exists, its leaders may often be persuaded to address the problem through the making of policy.

C. A policy is a rule or guideline that directs individual, organizational, or societal behavior; environmental policies primarily regulate the behavior of individuals, corporations, and government agencies.

D. Environmental policy addresses issues of equity and resource use.

1. One goal of environmental policy is to protect resources, held and used in common by the public, from depletion and degradation.

2. Environmental policy is also developed to ensure that some people do not benefit from common resources in ways that harm others.

E. Many factors can hinder implementation of environmental policy.

1. In the United States, much environmental policy has come in the form of regulations handed down from the federal government, which businesses and individuals may view as restricted, bureaucratic, and unresponsive to human needs.

2. Another reason for resistance to environmental policy involves the nature of environmental problems, which often develop slowly and gradually.

III. U.S. Environmental Policy: An Overview

A. U.S. policy results from participation by the three branches of government.

1. Legislation is enacted or vetoed by the President, who heads the executive branch.

2. The legislative branch of government is made up of Congress and government agencies.

3. The judicial branch, or judiciary, consisting of the Supreme Court and various lower courts, is charged with interpreting the law, which is necessary due to changing social factors and new technologies.

a. Decisions made by the courts make up a body of law known as case law.

b. Grassroots environmental advocates and nongovernmental organizations have used lawsuits, or requests for judicial action, as tools to level the playing field somewhat with large corporations and agencies.

4. Administrative agencies are the "fourth branch" of government.

a. The enforcement and elaboration of statutory laws is assigned to an administrative agency.

b. Regulations are specific rules that are based on the more broadly written statutory law.

B. State and local policy also affects environmental questions.

C. Some constitutional amendments bear on environmental law.
    1. One of these is the clause from the Fourteenth Amendment prohibiting states from denying "equal protection of its laws" to any person.
    2. The Fifth Amendment ensures, in part, that private property shall not "be taken for public use without just compensation"; this prohibition is known as the takings clause.

D. The first laws shaping U.S. environmental policy addressed public-land management.
    1. The early environmental laws were the General Land Ordinances of 1785 and 1787, which gave the federal government the right to manage Western lands and create a grid system for surveying them.
    2. Other laws addressing public-land management were The Homestead Act of 1862, The Mineral Lands Act of 1866, and The Timber Culture Act of 1873.

E. The second wave of U.S. environmental policy sought to address impacts of the first.

F. The third wave of U.S. environmental policy responded largely to pollution problems.
    1. The publication of Rachel Carson's *Silent Spring* awakened the American public to the negative impacts of pesticides and industrial chemicals.
    2. The burning of the Cuyahoga River moved the public to prompt Congress to do more to protect the environment.
    3. Earth Day, first celebrated on April 22, 1970, continues to be supported by millions of people worldwide.

G. The National Environmental Policy Act (NEPA) guarantees citizen input into environmental policy decisions.
    1. NEPA was signed in 1970 and requires that an environmental impact statement (EIS) be prepared for any major federal action.
    2. The EIS process forces government agencies to evaluate the impacts on the environment before building a new dam or highway.

H. The creation of the Environmental Protection Agency (EPA) marked a shift in U.S. federal environmental policy.

I. Other key laws followed, including the Clean Water Act.

J. The social context for environmental policy changes over time.

IV. Approaches to Environmental Policy

A. The command-and-control approach has resulted in some definite successes, as evidenced by the cleaner air and water U.S. residents enjoy today.

B. Green taxes offer financial rewards and punishments.
    1. Green taxes are charges on environmentally harmful activities and products.
    2. In levying a green tax, a government must first assess the monetary value of a given reduction of pollution, and then set a tax rate per unit emission.

3. Using market-based incentives can protect the environment while minimizing overall costs to industry and easing concerns about the intrusiveness of government regulation.

C. Creating markets in permits saves money and produces results.

D. Market incentives are being tried widely on the local level.

E. Many subsidies are harmful.

1. A subsidy is a government giveaway of cash or publicly owned resources or a tax break that is intended to encourage a particular activity.

2. Subsidies judged to be harmful to the environment and the economy total roughly $1.45 trillion yearly across the globe and include those of the Hardrock Mining Act, coal subsidies, and the U.S. Forest Service road-building subsidies.

V. The Environmental Policy Process

A. The environmental policy process begins with the identification of a problem.

B. The second step in the policy process is identifying specific causes of the problem.

C. Envisioning a solution is the third step.

D. The fourth step in the policy process is getting organized.

E. Once organized, gaining access to political powerbrokers is the fifth step.

1. Lobbying is spending time or money trying to change an elected official's mind.

2. Making campaign contributions is another way to get our voices heard.

3. The movement of powerful officials between the private sector and governmental agencies helps gain political influence and is called the revolving door.

F. Shepherding a solution from concept into law is the sixth step in the process.

G. For the policymaker, the enactment of a law or issuing of a regulation is not the end of the policy process.

VI. International Environmental Law

A. Mexico and the United States are working together to improve water management in the Tijuana River.

B. International environmental law includes conventional law and customary law.

1. Conventional law arises from conventions, or treaties, that nations agree to enter into.

2. Customary law arises from long-standing practices, or customs, held in common by most cultures.

C. Several organizations shape international environmental policy.

1. The United Nations sponsors large and active environmental agencies.

2. The World Bank holds purse strings for development projects.

3. The European Union is active in environmental affairs.
4. The World Trade Organization has recently attained surprising power with the authority to impose financial penalties on nations that do not comply with its directives.
5. Nongovernmental organizations attempt to shape policy directly or indirectly through their work.

VII. Conclusion

A. Environmental policy is a problem-solving tool that requires science, ethics, economics, and the political process.

B. The political process has produced solutions for the Tijuana River sewage problem.

## Key Terms

administrative agency
bill
Carson, Rachel
case law
command and control
conventional law
customary law
Cuyahoga River
due diligence
Earth Day
emission charges
Environmental Impact Statement
Environmental Protection Agency
equitable resources
executive branch
executive orders
external costs
federal supremacy
federalism
Fifth Amendment
Fourteenth Amendment
good neighborliness
green tax
Hardin, Garrett
injunction
judicial branch
lawsuits
legislative branch
lobbying
maquiladoras
marketable emissions permits
NEPA
policy
policy cycle
precedent
regulations
regulatory taking
revolving door
*Silent Spring*
statutory law
subsidy
takings clause
tort law
tragedy of the commons
transboundary
treaties
watershed

## Teaching Tips

1. The chapter briefly describes three major impacts of raw sewage on humans and the environment: pathogens that cause illness, lowered dissolved oxygen levels, and economic impacts caused by reduced tourism and recreation. Discuss these impacts in more detail in class and ask the students to rank those impacts in order of importance to them. Is human health most important? The economy? The environment?

2. Assign students to read Garrett Hardin's paper, "The Tragedy of the Commons," published in *Science* 162:1243–1248. The article can be found on the *Science* magazine website at www.sciencemag.org. Ask them to answer the following questions:
   a. Why does the "economic man" behave differently in a commons than on his own property?
   b. What are the implications of this behavior on public lands?
3. Ask students to conduct Internet research for updates on San Diego's sewage problem. Is the Tijuana River Valley Estuary and Beach Sewage Cleanup Act being implemented? What has been done so far? Has it been successful?
4. Discuss some of the environmental laws that were passed in the late 1960s and early 1970s to emphasize that the "third wave of U.S. environmental policy responded largely to pollution problems." The Clean Water Act; the Clean Air Act; the Federal Insecticide Fungicide, and Rodenticide Act; and the Wilderness Act are just a few. Summaries of the major environmental statutes are available on the U.S. EPA website (www.epa.gov/epahome/laws.htm).
5. Ask the students to create a concept map that illustrates the three branches of the federal government and the components of each. Concept maps graphically illustrate relationships between pieces of information. Maps can be drawn by hand or designed using computer software such as *Inspiration*. For more information about concept mapping, see www.inspiration.com.

# Additional Resources

## Websites

1. "Tijuana River Watershed," Department of Geography, San Diego State University, http://trw.sdsu.edu/English/indexEng.htm

   This website provides information about the physical and human characteristics of the watershed.
2. "Major Environmental Laws," U.S. Environmental Protection Agency, www.epa.gov/epahome/laws.htm

   This Web page provides full text and summaries of the major environmental laws.
3. "NEPA: Project Development Process," U.S. Department of Transportation Federal Highway Administration, www.fhwa.dot.gov/environment/00001.htm

   This Web page is an overview of NEPA and its impacts on projects planned by the Federal Highway Administration.

## Audiovisual Materials

1. *Motor* video distributed by Bullfrog Films (www.bullfrogfilms.com).

   This video is a summary of the controversy surrounding the use of off-road vehicles on public lands.

2. *The God Squad and the Case of the Northern Spotted Owl,* video distributed by Bullfrog Films (www.bullfrogfilms.com).

   In this video, the God Squad investigates the Endangered Species Committee proceedings that selected economic interests over the survival of a species.

3. *Greenplans,* video produced by John de Graaf and distributed by the Video Project (www.videoproject.net).

   This program, hosted by CNN's Jack Hamann, takes viewers to the Netherlands and New Zealand to see how national plans for sustainable development have been developed using a national environmental policy called a Green Plan.

## *Weighing the Issues:* Suggested Answers

### Do We Really Need Environmental Policy?

*This question requires an individual response.*

### The Takings Clause and Land Use Laws

*This question requires an individual response.*

### Boomer v. Atlantic Cement and the End of the Tort Era

*This question requires an individual response.*

### The Lobbying Power of Environmental Organizations

*This question requires an individual response.*

### Pros and Cons of the Revolving Door

*This question requires an individual response.*

## *The Science behind the Stories:* The Scientific Method

### Investigating Sewage via Satellite

**Observation:** Despite clean-up efforts, San Diego's bacterial contamination from sewage in ocean water remained mysteriously high in the late 1990s.

**Hypothesis:** There were undetected sources of sewage pollution along the border, and a type of airborne imaging technology known as synthetic aperture radar (SAR) could be used to detect them.

**Experiment:** In 1999, satellite-based SAR scanned coastal waters for signs of large sewage pollution, while at the same time ongoing water tests looked for high bacteria levels from sewage.

**Results:** SAR images, made public in 2000, showed a large, little-known sewage source dumping pollution into coastal waters just south of the U.S.-Mexico border. The sewage then flowed north along the San Diego coast, the images showed. Water tests confirmed high levels of bacteria in the same area. Policymakers used the findings to develop new environmental laws, tracking efforts and cleanup plans.

## Additional Questions

1. A goal of environmental policy is to recognize nonmarket values that people hold for a good or service. Describe some nonmarket values of trees. In other words, besides the monetary value of trees, what do trees provide that are valuable to you?

   *Trees provide lots of environmental benefits that people value. Trees provide habitat for wildlife, provide shade and oxygen, filter water, prevent erosion, and are aesthetically pleasing. It is important for students to recognize that components of our environment have important ecological functions in addition to commercial value.*

2. Imagine that you want a law passed that addresses the environmental problem in your community as described below. Describe the process that you would go through to see the problem solved.

   Your family has lived on a farm in Iowa for many years. Recently, the next-door neighbor built an animal feeding operation (AFO) to raise chickens. There are two buildings that house 20,000 chickens each. The waste from the chicken houses is spread on the adjacent field. When it rains, the waste is washed into the creek behind your house. The waste is a source of nitrates, causing oxygen depletion and fish kills.

   *Answers will vary. The students should describe the environmental policy process as related to the problem above:*

   1. *Identify the problem.*
   2. *Identify specific causes of the problem.*
   3. *Envision a solution.*
   4. *Get organized.*
   5. *Gain access to the political process.*
   6. *Prepare a bill that can potentially become a law.*

3. In this chapter, the difference between a statutory law and a regulation was described. For example, the Clean Air Act is a law, and the EPA (the administrative agency) enforces the law with regulations. Why do you think it is important for agencies to have the power to set specific rules about what's legal and what's not?

   *It is extremely important for agencies, specialized in certain fields, to have the power to develop specific rules for compliance with a law. For example, the EPA employs scientists who are experts in environmental fields and are qualified to develop specific regulations to help the public comply with environmental laws.*

# 4 From chemistry and energy to life

## Chapter Objectives

**This chapter will help students understand:**

- The fundamentals of environmental chemistry
- The fundamentals of energy and matter
- The molecular building blocks of living organisms
- Photosynthesis, respiration, and chemosynthesis
- Hypotheses on the origin of life on Earth
- The theory of evolution by natural selection

## Lecture Outline

I. Central Case: Bioremediation of the *Exxon Valdez* Oil Spill

   A. The tanker *Exxon Valdez* struck a reef on March 24, 1989, in Alaska's Prince William Sound and spilled 11 million gallons of crude oil.

   B. Thousands of workers employed by Exxon tackled the spill with conventional methods.

   C. Scientists used the opportunity to test a new way of cleaning up the spill by enlisting bacteria to naturally break down the oil in a process called bioremediation.

      1. Although the bacteria were presented with an abundant new food source, they were not immediately able to consume it because the oil contained too much carbon.
      2. Scientists applied a fertilizing mixture containing nitrogen and phosphorus that seemed to work.
      3. Because there were many complicating factors, experts have debated how much the treatments sped up degradation.

II. Chemistry and the Environment

A. Chemistry is often central to developing solutions to environmental problems such as the oil spill in Prince William Sound.

B. Atoms and elements are the chemical building blocks.

1. An element is a fundamental type of matter that cannot be broken down into substances with other properties.
2. Elements are composed of atoms, the smallest component of an element that maintains the chemical properties of that element.
3. Sometimes there are two or more species of an element that have the same atomic number, but different mass numbers (differing numbers of neutrons); these are called isotopes.
4. Ions are electrically charged atoms or combinations of atoms.

C. Atoms bond to form molecules and compounds.

1. Atoms can bond together in chemical reactions to form molecules, combinations of two or more atoms.
2. If atoms in a molecule are composed of two or more different elements, the molecule is called a compound.
3. Atoms are held together in molecules by chemical bonds, ionic bonds, or covalent bonds.
4. Elements, molecules, and compounds can come together without chemical bonding in a substance called a mixture.

D. The chemical structure of the water molecule facilitates life.

1. The water molecule has unique chemical properties.
2. Water molecules can adhere to one another in a special type of interaction called a hydrogen bond.
3. Hydrogen bonding gives water the properties important in supporting life and stabilizing Earth's climate.

E. Hydrogen ions determine acidity, now an increasing environmental concern.

1. Water molecules occasionally dissociate, forming a hydrogen ion and a hydroxide ion.
2. The pH scale was devised to quantify the acidity or basicity of solutions, and runs from zero to 14.

F. Matter is composed of organic and inorganic compounds.

1. Organic compounds consist of carbon atoms and, generally, hydrogen atoms joined by covalent bonds and may include other elements.
2. Hydrocarbons contain atoms of carbon and hydrogen.
3. Bacteria used in bioremediation of petroleum spills degrade hydrocarbons by pulling carbon atoms from them.

G. Macromolecules are the building blocks of life.

1. Polymers—proteins, nucleic acids, and carbohydrates—play key roles as building blocks of life.
2. Proteins are made up of long chains of amino acids, which are each made up of a sugar group, an amine group, a central carbon, and a carbon side chain.

3. Nucleic acids are individual nucleotides linked together to form long chains.
4. Carbohydrates are organic compounds consisting of carbon atoms and water molecules.
5. Lipids are a fourth type of macromolecule, but are not polymers, and do not dissolve in water.

H. Organisms use cells to compartmentalize macromolecules.
  1. All living things are composed of cells, the most basic unit of organization in living organisms.
  2. Biologists classify organisms into two groups based on the structure of their cells.
     a. Eukaryotic organisms have cells with organelles, including a nucleus.
     b. Prokaryotic organisms are generally single celled and lack organelles and a nucleus.

III. Energy Fundamentals

A. Energy is that which can change the position, physical composition, or temperature of matter.

B. There are two types of energy: Potential energy is the energy of position and kinetic energy is the energy of motion.

C. The first law of thermodynamics states that energy can change from one form to another, but cannot be created or lost.

D. The second law of thermodynamics states that energy tends to change from a more-ordered state to a less-ordered state.
  1. In every transfer of energy, some usable energy is lost.
  2. The order of an object or system can be increased through the input of additional energy from outside the system.

E. Photosynthesis produces food for plants and animals.
  1. The sun supplies energy to those organisms that are able to use it to produce their own food (autotrophs).
  2. Photosynthesis occurs within cell organelles called chloroplasts, where chlorophyll uses solar energy to initiate a series of chemical reactions.
  3. In photosynthesis, water, carbon dioxide, and light energy are transformed into glucose and oxygen.

F. Cellular respiration releases chemical energy.
  1. Cells use the chemical reactivity of oxygen to pull at a glucose molecule, causing it to split into its constituent parts and release energy.
  2. This extraction of energy occurs in both autotrophs and heterotrophs.

G. Tidal and geothermal forces also provide energy to Earth's systems.
  1. The gravitational pull of the moon causes tides, providing low-quality energy.
  2. Radiation from radioactive elements deep in Earth heats the interior of the planet, producing geothermal energy.

- H. Hydrothermal vent communities utilize chemical energy instead of light energy.
  1. Hydrothermal vents are areas in the deep ocean from which jets of geothermally heated water emerge.
  2. Communities of living organisms at these locations fuel themselves by chemosynthesis.

IV. The Origin of Life on Earth

- A. Early Earth was a hostile place.
- B. The fossil record has revealed to us much about the history of life.
  1. The earliest evidence of life on Earth comes from 3.5-billion-year-old rocks.
  2. Fossils provide information about plants and animals in different time periods.
  3. The fossil record shows that the species living today are but a tiny fraction of all the species that have ever lived and that the overall number of species has increased through time.
- C. Present-day organisms and their genes can also help us decipher the history of life.
- D. The air was very different on early Earth.
- E. Several hypotheses have been proposed to explain life's origin.
  1. Primordial soup: The heterotrophic hypothesis
     - a. This is the idea that life evolved from a primordial soup of carbon dioxide, oxygen, and nitrogen gases dissolved in the ocean.
     - b. Lab experiments provided evidence that the proposed process could work.
  2. Seeds from space: The extraterrestrial hypothesis
     - a. This is the idea that bacteria from space crashed to Earth on meteorites and started life here.
     - b. In 1996, NASA scientists announced that a meteorite from Mars showed evidence of fossilized bacteria.
  3. Life from the depths: The chemoautotrophic hypothesis
     - a. This is the idea that early life was formed in deep-sea vents where sulfur was abundant.
     - b. Some of the most ancient ancestors of today's life forms likely lived in extremely hot and wet environments.
- F. Organic polymers had to develop the ability to self-replicate.
- G. Cell precursors were another crucial step.

V. The Theory of Evolution by Natural Selection

- A. Darwin and Wallace proposed the concept of natural selection.
- B. Natural selection shapes organisms and organismal diversity.
  1. Variation means that certain individuals within a species will be better suited to their environment than others and thus able to survive longer and/or reproduce more.

2. From one generation to another through time, species will evolve to possess characteristics that lead to better success in a given environment.
3. Fitness refers both to the likelihood that an individual will reproduce and to the number of offspring that an individual produces over its lifetime.

C. Adaptation is a moving target.

D. Evidence of natural selection is all around us.

E. Selection can operate in different ways.

1. Selection that acts to drive a feature in one direction rather than another is called directional selection.
2. Selection that acts to produce intermediate traits is stabilizing selection.
3. In disruptive selection, extreme traits are favored.

F. DNA is the source of heritability and variation.

1. Accidental changes in DNA are mutations.
2. DNA mutations occur naturally, but also arise upon exposure to certain chemicals and certain classes of radiation.

G. Selection is a positive, creative force.

VI. Conclusion

A. The process of evolution has produced the tremendous diversity of life on our planet.

B. Energy and chemistry are tied to nearly every significant process in environmental science.

C. Chemistry can be a tool for finding solutions to environmental problems.

## Key Terms

adaptation
adaptive trait
artificial selection
atoms
autotrophs
carbohydrates
cells
cellular respiration
chemical energy
chemosynthesis
compound
covalent bond
directional selection
disruptive selection
DNA
electrons
elements
energy
entropy
enzymes
eukaryotic
evolution
first law of thermodynamics
fitness
fossil
genes
geothermal energy
heritable
heterotrophs
hydrocarbons
hydrothermal vents
ionic bond
ions
isotopes
kinetic energy
lipids
macromolecules
mitochondria
molecules
mutations
natural selection
neutrons
nucleic acids
nucleus
organelles
organic compounds
photosynthesis
polymers
potential energy
prokaryotic
proteins
protons
pibosomes
RNA
second law of thermodynamics
stabilizing selection

## Teaching Tips

1. Ask students to generate a list of environmental problems and write them on the board. As a group, analyze each problem to determine how chemistry is involved in understanding it. For example, smog is the result of the chemical reaction of nitrogen oxides and hydrocarbons in the presence of sunlight. The major components of smog are ozone, peroxyacetyl nitrite, and other irritants. Allow students to use the textbook if they need more information.
2. Assign students to read a section of *The Origin of Species* or *Voyage of the Beagle* by Charles Darwin. Both books are available online at the Online Literature Library's website, www.literature.org/authors/darwin-charles/.
3. Ask students to conduct Internet research for updates on the recovery of Prince William Sound from the *Exxon Valdez* oil spill. A current and reliable Web page is NOAA's Office of Response and Restoration, "Prince William Sound: An Ecosystem in Transition," at http://response.restoration.noaa.gov/bat/about.html.
4. In this chapter, DNA and RNA are described. Recent scientific research on DNA has centered on genetic engineering and cloning. Lead a discussion about the pros and cons of these issues.

## Additional Resources

### Websites

1. "The *Exxon Valdez* Oil Spill," NOAA Office of Response and Restoration, http://response.restoration.noaa.gov/spotlight/spotlight.htm

   This Web page provides links to NOAA scientific reports on the *Exxon Valdez* oil spill.
2. "General Chemistry Online!," Frostburg State University, http://antoine.frostburg.edu/chem/senese/101/index.shtml

   This website is an interactive guide for students and teachers of introductory college chemistry.
3. "A History of Evolutionary Thought," University of California Museum of Paleontology, www.ucmp.berkeley.edu/history/evothought.html

   This Web page provides a list of scientists and thinkers who have contributed to the understanding of evolution. It is organized according to themes of evolutionary thought.
4. "Life on Mars?," Johnson Space Center, NASA, http://curator.jsc.nasa.gov/antmet/marsmets/life.htm

   This NASA Web page describes the ALH84001 meteorite that was found to contain organic molecules and mineral features indicative of primitive life on Mars.
5. "Vents Program," Pacific Marine Environmental Laboratory, NOAA, www.pmel.noaa.gov/vents

   The Vents Program Website provides information about submarine volcanoes and hydrothermal venting.

## Audiovisual Materials

1. *The Birth of Earth and Ancient Oceans,* Discovery Channel video (http://shopping.discovery.com).

   In this video, the primordial planet and the first life on Earth are explored.

2. *In the Wild: Galápagos Islands with Richard Dreyfuss,* PBS Home Video (www.shop.pbs.org).

   This video follows Richard Dreyfuss on his three-week trip through the Galápagos Islands. Viewers get a firsthand look at Darwin's theory in action.

3. *Life on Mars?,* Discovery Channel video (http://shopping.discovery.com).

   In this program, viewers meet the team of researchers who discovered meteorite ALH84001 and made the announcement that there was evidence of primitive life forms.

# *Weighing the Issues:* Suggested Answers

### Pros and Cons of Bioremediation

***Facts to consider:*** *Answers will vary but may include the following questions: What is the extent of the oil spill? What is the specific composition of the oil that spilled? What have been the effects of the oil spill so far? What plants and animals live in the affected water and its surrounding areas? Does the environment have naturally occurring bacteria that would be effective in bioremediation? What will happen if we just wait and let the natural processes do the recovery? What kinds of human resources and materials are available to participate in recovery efforts? Who will pay for recovery efforts?*

### Water's Properties for Life

***Facts to consider:*** *Water helps different organisms in different ways. It might help by transporting nutrients, transporting waste, providing oxygen, or providing protection against changes in temperature of the surrounding environment. On the other hand, these same qualities of water could, under some circumstances, lead to harm for organisms. Water could transport pollutants and other toxins; it could also maintain a temperature stressful to certain organisms.*

### Fossil Fuel Use and the Second Law of Thermodynamics

***Facts to consider:*** *The second law of thermodynamics states that the nature of energy will tend to change from a more ordered state to a less ordered state; any system moves toward increasing disorder. Fossil fuel is a very ordered, compact form of energy; when people use it, it is transformed to a less ordered state. This less ordered state could include the fossil fuel's energy dispersed into many more simple, forms, such as the movement of an engine and the resulting movement of an automobile, the combustion gases in the air, the heat of the exhaust, and the heat remaining in the engine.*

*These disperse, disorganized forms of energy will not be available again as fossil fuel; they will no longer be energy in a compact, easy-to-use form. In fact, humans have not developed ways to use most of that energy in those forms. No matter how great or small, how accessible or difficult to acquire, there is a finite amount of fossil fuels available. This suggests that conservation can help society have high-level fuels available long into the future for the purposes for which it is most appropriate*

## Energy Quality and Energy Policy

***Facts to consider:*** *Getting large amounts of energy from high-quality sources has been relatively easy because energy in such forms is concentrated. Getting useful energy from low-quality sources has been more difficult, because the energy is diffuse. Traditionally, harnessing high-quality sources has been more efficient and required less money than harnessing low-quality sources, and so society's energy-related decisions have tended to favor utilizing those sources. Most resource depletion, and most environmental degradation related to energy sources, has come from conversion and use of high-energy sources than from actions related to low-energy sources. For instance, fossil fuels contribute to air pollution; use of wood as fuel has depleted forests in many parts of the world. More recent technologies have allowed more efficient conversion of low-quality energy sources, so these may become more attractive. As obtaining low-quality energy more efficiently becomes easier, energy policy will probably evolve so that they are more frequently used as energy sources.*

## Microbes from Mars?

***Facts to consider:*** *Discovery of a meteorite from Mars containing fossilized or living microbial life would reinforce the idea that living material could survive travel through space and through the heat of falling through Earth's atmosphere. It would suggest that Earth was not necessarily the first (or only) place in the solar system where life has existed. Thus, it would increase the strength of the argument of those who propose the extraterrestrial hypothesis about how life on Earth began; this hypothesis states that life on Earth began when material containing living organisms fell to Earth from another planet.*

*Tests for whether life began first on Earth, or Mars, or both independently could vary significantly. They might include comparing the ability of the most simple molecules or amino acids in either system to survive extreme heat and extreme cold; comparing the likelihood that these most simple molecules could be formed from the amino acids synthesized in prebiotic experiments; or comparing their composition with the composition of the earliest Earth life forms (single-cell bacteria and their byproducts). The more that is learned about early conditions on each planet, the more specific experiments can be done to recreate those conditions and evaluate the potential of creating amino acids and other precursors of life under those conditions.*

## Natural Selection and "Survival of the Fittest"

***Facts to consider:*** *The evolved traits of domesticated animals make sense in terms of the kinds of characteristics that humans prefer. Dogs and cats are typically bred for the aesthetic traits preferred most in house pets—for example, a docile temperament or fur of a particular color. These traits often have nothing to do with particular environmental pressures that might, instead, favor a more aggressive personality or better camouflage. Cows, horses, and other livestock are typically bred to be* *larger, or faster, or provide more meat. Their wild counterparts might, instead, evolve to have less muscle mass or be smaller overall, depending on their environments could support.*

## Additional Questions

1. Crude oil, a hydrocarbon, is a fossil fuel available in limited quantities for our consumption. Describe other energy sources that can be used for transportation and electricity.

   *There are a variety of renewable energy sources that can be used to generate electricity, such as wind, hydropower, solar, and geothermal. Hybrid electric cars, such as the Toyota Prius and the Honda Insight, use both an electric motor and gasoline. Another promising alternative to gas-powered vehicles is the use of hydrogen fuel cells that combine hydrogen and oxygen to produce electricity, water, and waste heat.*

2. What is the main difference between today's atmosphere and Earth's early atmosphere? How do you think this difference affected the ability of living organisms to survive on land?

   *Today's atmosphere has 21% oxygen, whereas Earth's early atmosphere probably lacked oxygen. This greatly affected the movement of living organisms from the sea to land. Because there was no oxygen in the atmosphere, and therefore no ozone layer, the intensity of ultraviolet light was extremely high on Earth's surface, making it difficult for organisms to survive out of the water.*

3. Assign students to read the online case study, "Lake Acidification in the Adirondacks," and ask the following questions: What is the chemistry behind this environmental issue? How is chemistry used to address the problem?

   *Sulfur dioxide and nitrogen oxides combine with water in the atmosphere to form sulfuric acid and nitric acid, respectively. Although rainfall is naturally acidic because of carbonic acid, sulfuric and nitric acids cause rainfall to be more acidic than normal. Deposition of acid rain causes the acidification of lakes in the Adirondacks. One way to restore a highly acidic lake is to release lime, which has a high pH and therefore neutralizes the water.*

## Additional Questions

# 5 Ecology and evolution: Populations, communities, and biodiversity

## Chapter Objectives

**This chapter will help students understand:**

- How evolution generates biodiversity
- Concepts of speciation and extinction
- Outlines of the biodiversity "crisis"
- Fundamental ecological concepts and principles
- Units of ecological organization
- Fundamentals of population ecology, including carrying capacity and limiting factors
- Food webs, trophic levels, and ecological communities
- Species interactions, including predation, competition, parasitism, and mutualism
- Primary and secondary succession
- Challenges for biodiversity conservation

## Lecture Outline

I. Central Case: Striking Gold in a Costa Rican Cloud Forest

   A. Local residents in Costa Rica's mountainous Monteverde region told of an elusive golden toad that appeared only in spring.

   B. In 1964, Dr. Jay M. Savage and his colleagues encountered 200 golden toads during an expedition.

   C. The newly discovered species went extinct 25 years later when global climate change, caused drying of the forest.

II. Evolution as the Wellspring of Earth's Biodiversity
   A. Biological diversity is the product of evolution.
      1. Biological diversity is the sum total of all organisms in an area, taking into account the diversity of species, their genes, their populations, and their communities.
      2. A species is a population whose members share certain characteristics and can freely breed with one another and produce fertile offspring.
   B. Speciation is the process that produces new types of organisms.
      1. When populations of the same species are kept separate, their individuals no longer reproduce, so their genes no longer mix.
      2. When populations are separated, the mutations that occur in one cannot spread to the other.
   C. Populations can be separated in many ways.
      1. Allopatric speciation is the formation of species in separate locations.
      2. The Hawaiian Islands illustrate mechanisms of population isolation.
   D. The moment of truth for speciation is when isolated populations meet again.
   E. Not all speciation is allopatric—many species have arisen through sympatric speciation.
   F. Life's diversification results from numerous speciation events.
   G. Phylogenetic trees represent the history of divergence.
      1. Phylogenetic trees show scientists' hypotheses as to how divergence took place.
      2. Phylogenetic trees allow biologists to examine how certain traits likely evolved.
   H. Life has diversified in amazing ways.
   I. Extinction and speciation together determine Earth's biodiversity.
   J. Some species are more vulnerable to extinction than others.
      1. Generally, extinction occurs when environmental conditions change rapidly or severely enough that a species cannot genetically adapt to the change.
      2. The golden toad is an example of a vulnerable species because it was endemic to the Monteverde cloud forest.
   K. Earth has seen several episodes of mass extinction.
      1. There have been five mass extinction events at widely spaced intervals in Earth's history that have wiped out anywhere from 50–95% of Earth's species each time.
      2. The best known mass extinction occurred 65 million years ago and brought an end to the dinosaurs; it is called the K-T event.
      3. The largest mass extinction was at the end of the Permian period 250 million years ago, when between 75% and 95% of all living species perished.
   L. The sixth mass extinction is upon us.

III. Units of Ecological Organization
    A. The extinction and speciation of species, and other evolutionary mechanisms and patterns, have substantial impacts on ecology.
    B. Ecology is the study of interactions among organisms and between organisms and their environment.
    C. The science of ecology deals with the organismal, population, community, and ecosystem levels.

IV. Ecology on the Organismal Level
    A. Each organism relates to its abiotic environment in ways that in the long run tend to maximize its survival and reproduction.
    B. For example, organisms select habitats from among the range of options they encounter (habitat selection).
    C. Habitat selection is important to environmental science because the availability and quality of habitat is crucial to an organism's well-being.
    D. An organism also relates to its environment through its niche, its functional role in a community.

V. Population Ecology
    A. A population is a group of individuals of the same species, inhabiting a particular area.
    B. Populations exhibit characteristics that can help predict their future dynamics.
        1. Population size is the number of individual organisms present at a given time.
        2. Population density is the number of individuals in a population per unit area.
            a. High population density can make it easier for organisms to find mates and participate in other important social interactions, but can also increase competition.
            b. Low population density can provide organisms with more space and resources, but it may be harder for them to find mates and companions.
            c. The effects of overcrowding at high population densities are thought to have doomed the harlequin frog in the Monteverde cloud forest.
        3. Population distribution, or population dispersion, is the spatial arrangement of organisms within a particular area.
            a. In a random distribution, individuals are located haphazardly in space with no particular pattern.
            b. A uniform distribution is one in which individuals are evenly spaced out.
            c. In a clumped distribution, organisms arrange themselves according to the availability of resources.

4. Age structure describes the relative numbers of organisms of each age within a population.
    a. Age distribution, or age structure, is expressed as a ratio of age classes.
    b. Age structure diagrams, often called age pyramids, are visual tools that scientists use to show the age structure of a population.
5. A population's sex ratio is its proportion of males to females.

C. Populations may grow, shrink, or remain relatively stable.
    1. Population growth or decline is determined by births, deaths, immigration, and emigration.
    2. The growth rate equals the crude death rate plus the emigration rate subtracted from the crude birth rate plus the immigration rate.

D. Unregulated populations tend to increase by exponential growth.
    1. When a population increases by a fixed percentage each year, it is said to undergo exponential growth.
    2. Exponential growth usually occurs in nature when a population is small and environmental conditions are ideal for the organism.

E. Limiting factors restrain population growth.
    1. Every population is eventually contained by limiting factors, which are physical characteristics of the environment that restrain population growth.
    2. The interaction of the limiting factors, called environmental resistance, determines the carrying capacity.
    3. The logistic growth curve shows a population that increases sharply at first and then levels off as it is affected by limiting factors.
    4. Sometimes one limiting factor may outweigh all others and restrict population growth.

F. Carrying capacities can change.

G. The influence of some factors on population depends on population density.

H. Biotic potential and reproductive strategies vary from species to species.
    1. K-strategists are so named because their populations tend to stabilize over time at or near their carrying capacity.
    2. R-strategists are intrinsically capable of rapid population growth.

VI. Beyond Populations to Communities

A. A community is a group of populations of organisms that live in the same place at the same time.

B. How cohesive are communities?
    1. Frederick Clements promoted the view that communities are cohesive entities whose members remain associated over time as environmental conditions change.
    2. Henry Gleason maintained that each species responds independently to its own limiting factors, and that species can join or leave communities without greatly altering their composition.
    3. Today, ecologists side largely with Gleason.

C. A food web is a conceptual record of feeding relationships and energy flow.
   1. Producers are green plants that function at the first trophic level because they produce their own food.
   2. Consumers consume other organisms.
      a. Primary consumers consume producers.
      b. Secondary consumers prey on herbivorous animals.
      c. Tertiary consumers eat secondary consumers.
   3. Detritivores and decomposers consume nonliving organic matter.

D. Some organisms play bigger roles in communities than others.
   1. A keystone species is a species that has particularly far-reaching impacts.
   2. Secondary or tertiary consumers are often considered keystone species.
   3. Some species attain keystone species status not through what they eat, but by physically modifying the environment.

E. Species interact in several fundamental ways.
   1. The most common interactions are predation, competition, parasitism, and mutualism.
   2. Predation is the process in which one species, the predator, hunts and kills its prey.
      a. Predation can drive population dynamics, causing cycles in population sizes.
      b. Predation also has evolutionary ramifications.
      c. When animals eat plants, this is called herbivory.
   3. Competition occurs when multiple organisms seek the same limited resource.
      a. Competitive interactions can take place between members of two or more different species, interspecific competition, or between members of the same species, intraspecific competition.
      b. Competitive exclusion occurs when one species excludes the other from resource use and eventually excludes it from the community.
      c. Species that coexist and use the same resources tend to adjust to their competitors by displaying a realized niche or by resource partitioning.
   4. Parasitism is a relationship in which one organism depends on another for nourishment or some other benefit while simultaneously doing the host harm.
      a. Parasites that live in close contact with their hosts are either endoparasites or ectoparasites.
      b. Other types of parasites are free-living and come into contact with their hosts only infrequently.
      c. Host-parasite interactions have interesting evolutionary consequences when they become locked in a duel of escalating adaptations called the "evolutionary arms race."

        5. In mutualism, both organisms benefit from the interaction.
            a. Many of these interactions involve partners living closely together, such as the microbes living in your digestive tract.
            b. Free-living organisms such as pollinators and flowers also engage in mutualism.
        6. Commensalism and amensalism are two other types of interactions.
            a. Commensalism occurs when one organism benefits and the other is unaffected.
            b. Amensalism occurs when one organism is harmed and the other is unaffected.
    F. Succession occurs after a disturbance or after a new substrate emerges.
        1. Succession is the regular, predictable, and quantifiable sequence of changes that a community undergoes over time.
        2. Primary succession begins when a bare expanse of rock, sand, or sediment becomes newly exposed to the atmosphere.
            a. Pioneer species, such as lichens, are the first to arrive.
            b. Lichens secrete acid, starting the process of soil formation.
            c. New organisms arrive and eventually a climax community becomes established.
        3. Secondary succession begins when some event such as logging or a fire alters an existing community.
    G. Invasive species pose a new threat to community stability.
        1. Invasive species are those that spread rapidly and become a dominant species in the community, interfering with the community's normal functioning.
        2. Invasives can be native species or exotic species.
        3. The chestnut blight, an invasive species, was a fungus introduced from Asia.

VII. Humans and the Conservation of Biodiversity
    A. Human development, resource extraction, and population pressures are speeding the rate at which natural communities are changed.
    B. Social and economic factors affect species and communities.
    C. Costa Rica has taken steps to protect its environment.
        1. In the 1950s, Quakers moved to Monteverde, founding a village and conserving one-third of their land.
        2. In 1970, the Costa Rican government and international representatives created the country's first national parks and protected areas.
        3. Tourists now visit Costa Rica for ecotourism.
    D. Altered communities can be restored to their former condition using restoration ecology.

VIII. Conclusion

A. Speciation and extinction help determine Earth's biodiversity.

B. Many human activities are playing a role in biodiversity loss.

C. Alleviating the problems that threaten biodiversity requires science that untangles the complexities of ecological systems.

# Key Terms

age distribution
age pyramid
allopatric speciation
amensalism
anthropogenic
biodiversity
biological diversity
biotic potential
carnivores
carrying capacity
cloud forests
clumped distribution
commensalism
community
competition
competitive exclusion
decomposers
density dependent
density independent
detritivores
ecological restoration
ecotourism
ectoparasites
emigration
endemic
endoparasites
environmental resistance
equilibrium
evolutionary arms race
exponential growth
extinction
food chain
food web
fundamental niche
growth rate
habitat selection
habitats
herbivores
herbivory
host
immigration
interspecific competition
intraspecific competition
invasive species
keystone species
K-strategists
lichens
limiting factors
logistic growth
lower montane forests
mass extinction
mutualism
niche
omnivores
parasite
parasitism
phylogenetic trees
pioneer species
pollination
population density
population distribution
population growth curves
population size
predation
predator
prey
primary consumers
primary succession
pandom distribution
pealized niche
pesource partitioning
pestoration ecology
r-strategists
secondary consumers
secondary succession
sex ratio
speciation
species
species coexistence
succession
symbioses
sympatric speciation
tertiary consumers
trophic levels
uniform distribution
zero population growth

# Teaching Tips

1. It is very difficult to understand the vastness of geologic time. To gain a better appreciation for Earth's history, assign students to design a geologic time scale analogy. In this exercise, students compare the geologic history of Earth with

something measurable in time, length, weight, or distance. For example, Earth's history could be compared to a meter stick. Calculations are made to determine at what points along the meter stick major events in Earth's history took place:

$$\frac{\text{Known age of past event}}{\text{Known age of Earth}} = \frac{\text{Unknown equivalent}}{\text{Analogy maximum measurement (100 cm)}}$$

| Years Before Present | Major Event |
|---|---|
| 4,600,000,000 | Origin of Earth |
| 3,500,000,000 | Life evolves |
| 458,000,000 | First land plants |
| 375,000,000 | Amphibians evolve |
| 200,000,000 | First mammals |
| 160,000,000 | First birds |
| 65,000,000 | Dinosaurs go extinct |
| 100,000 | *Homo sapiens* appears in the fossil record |

In the meter stick analogy,

The origin of Earth took place at 0 cm

Life evolved at 24 cm

The first land plants evolved at 90 cm

Amphibians evolved at 92 cm

The first mammals occurred at 95.7 cm

The first birds occurred at 96.5 cm

Dinosaurs went extinct at 99.86 cm

*Homo sapiens* appeared at 99.98 cm

2. Ask students to think of examples of species interactions that are not discussed in the textbook. You may need to guide them through a classic example such as the commensalism between clownfish and anemones or the mutualism between oxpeckers and the black rhinoceros.

3. This chapter discusses the views of community ecology promoted by H. A. Gleason and Frederick Clements. Clements (1916) believed that communities are cohesive units, with the same species occurring together under a given set of environmental conditions. Gleason (1917) believed that communities are chance assemblages of species occurring together with similar environmental preferences.

   R. H. Whittaker (1975) studied patterns of vegetation in the Great Smoky Mountains and concluded that species are not distributed in terms of associations, but according to physiology and genetics. Does Whittaker side with Clements or with Gleason?

   Assign students to read some of Whittaker's work.

   Whittaker, R. H. 1975. *Communities and Ecosystems,* 2nd edition, New York: Macmillan.

4. Ask students to study information on the "Cloud Forest Alive" website about the Monteverde Cloud Forest at www.cloudforestalive.org. There is an online quiz that students can take to test their knowledge.

5. Species in danger of extinction are protected under the Endangered Species Act of 1973. The U.S. Fish and Wildlife Service is the agency that protects listed terrestrial and freshwater species. Information about endangered and threatened species can be found on the U.S.F.W.S. Endangered Species Program website at http://endangered.fws.gov. Using the website, students should be able to provide information about local species that are on the list.

# Additional Resources

## Websites

1. "Speciation and Biodiversity: Interview with Edward O. Wilson, Ph.D," Action Bioscience.org, www.actionbioscience.org/biodiversity/wilson.html

   An interview with Dr. Wilson, world-renowned expert on biodiversity, is provided on this Web page.
2. "Monteverde Cloud Forest Preserve," www.cct.or.cr/monte_in.htm

   This website offers information about the history of the preserve and species that live there.
3. "The Current Mass Extinction," PBS Evolution Library, www.pbs.org/wgbh/evolution/library/03/2/l_032_04.html

   This Web page gives background information about the current mass extinction of biodiversity.

## Audiovisual Materials

1. *Extinction!*, PBS Home Video (www.shop.pbs.org).

   This program discusses the five mass extinctions that have occurred in Earth's history and examines the possibility that humans are causing a sixth mass event.
2. *America's Endangered Species: Don't Say Goodbye,* National Geographic Video (http://shop.nationalgeographic.com).

   In this video, two photographers travel across the country learning about and photographing endangered species.
3. *David Attenborough's The Private Life of Plants: Living Together* (1995), Turner Entertainment Video.

   This video can be ordered from Amazon.com or Barnes and Noble. David Attenborough shows how plants form symbiotic partnerships with fungi, animals, and other plants in many different communities.

# *Weighing the Issues:* Suggested Answers

### Are We Causing a Mass Extinction?

***Facts to consider:*** *These questions require individual responses, but responses may mention some of the following points. Differences in opinion about whether humans* *may be causing a mass extinction event may correlate with differences in perspective or differences in interpretation of scientific data. Some believe that humans do not have a large influence on the ecosystem, or that the current rate of species loss is within the bounds of natural rises in such occurrences, or the ecosystem recovery from earlier mass extinctions indicates that mass extinctions are not cause for panic. Others believe that human actions are profoundly affecting certain environments and species, triggering population declines (and extinctions); they may see more species becoming extinct without new species developing, yielding a net loss in biodiversity; and they may look at extinction rates on a longer perspective than the human timescale.*

*Various ethical perspectives would support concern about biodiversity loss and mass extinction. Preservationists would want to keep species from becoming extinct, for their own sake as well as for the spiritual, aesthetic, and recreational benefit of human beings. Conservationists would stress that species should be kept from becoming extinct because human beings might learn to use them, or learn from them how to improve human health and well being. The Earth is a closed system. So, is species extinction reduces potential resources, there is no additional source that can be used to replace them; human economics, therefore, depends on species diversity.*

*If those who are not concerned about mass extinction believe that human beings will not be among the species that might become extinct, then their point of view may be termed anthropocentric. That is, if human beings would survive, then people do not have to be concerned about mass extinction.*

## Carrying Capacity and Human Population Growth

***Facts to consider:*** *Human beings are K-strategists, birthing few young and nurturing them for a long time. This species has a carrying capacity, influenced by limiting factors. Lists of limiting factors will vary, but many of the limiting factors are basically similar to those for other species. Physical limits might be food, water, prevalence of disease (including widespread killers such as AIDS and malaria), and suitable habitat. In the case of humans, who raise food (rather than hunt or forage, as other species do), food availability relates to soil quality, water sources, and climate. Chemical limits, such as pollutants, are more likely to affect survival rates in specific areas rather than globally. In more extreme scenarios, however, chemical limits could affect the worldwide carrying capacity for human beings. These might include reduced fertility caused by chemical exposure, global warming as a result of emissions, or nuclear accidents or warfare.*

*Human beings have significantly affected the carrying capacity for our species. One of the most basic ways we have done this is through the development of and improvements in agriculture, increasing the food supply. Similar advances in water supply, protective shelter, and health care also apply. We have learned how to survive and thrive in increasingly harsh environments by becoming more efficient and productive in terms of meeting our needs. At this point, some of the environments we have used in these efforts are becoming degraded; this may lead to a reduction, or at least a stabilization, of our carrying capacity. On the other hand, some additional improvements in developing sustainable practices in agriculture, water use, materials use, chemicals use, and health care may increase our ability to keep environments sustainable and, therefore, able to support a larger human population, a larger carrying capacity. If net sustainability is not increased, the limiting factors may actually increase, reducing carrying capacity. Carrying capacity could also decrease. This could happen if sustainability is not adopted on a wide-enough scale, or as a result of new diseases with effects as significant as AIDS, or some other disastrous development, such as nuclear explosion or weapons use.*

### Keystone Species and Conservation

***Facts to consider:*** *It would be good to develop a food web in order to make a decision. As a tertiary consumer, the bobcat is much more likely to be a keystone species than the pocket mouse or the lupine. What species does the bobcat eat—the pocket mouse, other herbivores? Are there other tertiary species in the community that also consume those species? If so, which tertiary consumer is more numerous or has a great effect? To achieve development with the least amount of environmental disturbance, it is important to preserve the keystone species, most likely in this case to be the bobcat. Option 3 would leave much of the ground exposed, and it would eliminate the food source for the pocket mouse (and presumably, all the other primary consumers). If there are other primary consumers in the environment, and if the bobcat also eats those, then the least environmental disturbance may be caused with Option 2.*

### How Best to Conserve Biodiversity?

***Facts to consider:*** *When Costa Rica's parks were first established they had little power or funding; improvements in these areas can help biodiversity conservation in many ways. Funding and political power increase the amount of study that can be done to learn about ecological communities; increase staffing for maintenance and restoration efforts; and increase protection from threats. The toads became extinct before scientists had realized what was happening; so, increasing the amount of funding for environmental study will increase the likelihood of being able to preserve species by understanding and supporting their environmental needs.*

*When scientists analyzed the causes of the golden toad's extinction, they determined that global climate change had probably played a significant role. This force did not result from actions inside the park boundaries; the human actions that influence biodiversity are diverse in number and geography. To preserve biodiversity will require not only careful respect for and management of the environments in which they live, and not only the efforts of the governments of those areas, but also increased understanding and adaptation of human behaviors in a much wider sphere.*

## Additional Questions

1. What is the difference between background extinction and mass extinction? What evidence supports the idea that the sixth mass extinction is upon us? What is different between the five mass extinctions of the past and today's mass extinction?

   *Background extinction is when species go extinct individually at a slow rate (2–3 per year). In contrast, mass extinction is defined by many species going extinct in a short period of time. Past mass extinctions have resulted in 75–95% of all living species going extinct. Today, it has been estimated that as many as 100 species may go extinct each day. Over the course of hundreds of years, this may result in the loss of a large percent of our species. The past five mass extinctions took place as a result of a catastrophic environmental event such as an asteroid impact or volcanic eruption. Today's extinctions are taking place because of the actions of one species—humans.*

2. The rate of natural increase in a population is the crude birth rate minus crude death rate divided by 10. Calculate the rate of natural increase for the human population in each of these countries:

   a. Uganda

      Births = 48

      Deaths = 18

   b. Costa Rica

      Births = 21

      Deaths = 4

   c. Japan

      Births = 9

      Deaths = 8

   d. United States

      Birth = 15

      Deaths = 9

   What might explain the differences in growth rate among these countries?

   In the United States in particular, immigration affects population growth. If the immigration rate is 5/1,000 and the emigration rate is 1/1,000, what is the true growth rate of the U.S. population? Use the equation given in the textbook.

   *The natural rates of increase are: Uganda 3%, Costa Rica 1.7%, Japan 0.1%, and the United States 0.6%. The variability in rates is due to many social and environmental factors such as medical advances, access to birth control, education, and social structure. In the United States, immigration and emigration rates affect population growth so that the true growth rate is 1%.*

3. Assign students to read the online case study, "Who's Afraid of the Big Bad Wolf: A Lesson in Extinction." How does interbreeding affect parent species? Why is it important to preserve the parent species such as the red wolf and the coyote?

   *Interbreeding results in hybrid offspring that have genetic information from both parents. If interbreeding continues for a long period of time, both parent species could be replaced by the hybrid. As a result, two species would be lost. It is important to preserve the parent species because they play a specific role in the ecosystem in which they evolved. The hybrid may or may not have "good" genes that will allow it to survive and reproduce successfully over the long term.*

# 6 Environmental systems: Connections, cycles, and feedback loops

## Chapter Objectives

**This chapter will help students understand:**

- The nature of systems and the fundamentals of systems thinking
- Ecosystem-level ecology
- Earth's biomes
- The rock and tectonic cycles
- The hydrologic cycle
- The nitrogen, carbon, phosphorous, and sulfur cycles
- The Gaia hypothesis

## Lecture Outline

I. Central Case: The Gulf of Mexico's "Dead Zone"

   A. In 2002, the dead zone grew to its largest size ever—8,500 square miles.

   B. The dead zone is a region in the Gulf of Mexico so depleted of oxygen that it cannot support marine organisms, a condition called hypoxia.

   C. The spread of the hypoxic zone threatens the Gulf's fishing industry, one of the most productive fisheries in the United States.

   D. Environmental advocates and fishermen across the country joined local shrimpers in expressing anxiety about the dead zone.

   E. Scientists studying the dead zone have determined that fertilizer runoff from Midwestern farms is the likely cause.

II. Earth's Environmental Systems

   A. Systems show several defining properties.

      1. A system is a network of relationships among a group of parts, elements, or components that interact with and influence one another through the exchange of energy, matter, and/or information.

2. Systems receive input, process it, and produce output.
3. Sometimes a system's output can serve as input to that same system in a circular process called a feedback loop.
    a. In negative feedback loops, output driving the system in one direction acts as input that moves the system in the other direction.
    b. In positive feedback loops, the output drives the system further toward one extreme or another.
4. The inputs and outputs of a complex natural system often occur simultaneously, keeping the system constantly active.
5. Often, it is difficult to fully understand systems by focusing on their individual components because systems can show emergent properties, characteristics that are not evident in the system's components.
6. Systems rarely have well-defined boundaries, so deciding where one system ends and another begins can be difficult.

B. The Mississippi River is an environmental system.

C. Understanding the hypoxia problem requires considering the river and the gulf together as a system.
1. The cause of hypoxia in the Gulf of Mexico stems from excess nitrogen from the Mississippi River watershed.
2. The process of nutrient enrichment is called eutrophication.

D. Environmental systems may be perceived in different ways.

E. Earth can be divided into several structural spheres: atmosphere, hydrosphere, lithosphere, and biosphere.
1. The atmosphere is comprised of the air surrounding our planet.
2. The hydrosphere encompasses all water in surface bodies, underground, and in the atmosphere.
3. The lithosphere is everything that is solid earth beneath our feet.
4. The biosphere consists of the sum total of all the planet's living organisms and the abiotic portions of the environment with which they interact.

F. Biomes are fundamental groupings of plant communities that cover large geographic areas.
1. A biome is a major regional complex of similar plant communities determined largely by climate.
2. Temperate deciduous forest is found in eastern North America and is characterized by broadleaf trees that lose their leaves in the fall.
3. West of the Mississippi River, we find temperate grasslands that were once widespread but now are mostly converted to farmland or rangeland.
4. Temperate rainforest is found in the Pacific Northwest and is a forest type known for its high biodiversity and its potential to produce large volumes of commercially important products.
5. Tropical rainforest is found in regions near the equator and is characterized by high rainfall and lush vegetation.

6. Tropical areas that are warm year round but where rainfall is lower overall and highly seasonal give rise to tropical dryforest or tropical deciduous forest.
7. Savannas, found in dry tropical areas across large stretches of Africa, South America, and Australia, are regions of grasslands interspersed with clusters of trees.
8. Desert is the driest biome on Earth and hosts sparse vegetation.
9. Tundra is nearly as dry as desert, but is located in cold regions, along the northern edges of Russia, Canada, and Scandinavia.
10. Taiga is the northern coniferous forest that develops in cooler, drier regions than temperate rainforests.
11. Chaparral is found in areas of Mediterranean climate and consists of densely thicketed evergreen shrubs.

G. Altitude creates patterns analogous to latitude.

H. Aquatic systems also show biome-like patterns of variation and similarity.

I. Ecosystems are key environmental systems.
1. An ecosystem describes all interacting organisms and abiotic factors that occur in a particular place at the same time.
2. A key component of ecosystems as opposed to communities is that they include abiotic elements and involve the flow of energy and nutrients.
3. Energy for most ecosystems comes from the sun and is converted to biomass by producers through photosynthesis.

J. Landscape ecology is the study of geographical areas that include multiple ecosystems.

III. How Environmental Systems Work

A. The rock cycle is a slow, but important, environmental system.
1. Rocks that form when magma cools are called igneous rocks.
   a. Intrusive igneous rocks form when magma cools slowly well below Earth's surface.
   b. Extrusive igneous rocks form when magma is spewed from a volcano and it cools relatively quickly.
2. Sedimentary rock is formed when dissolved minerals seep through sediment layers and crystallize and bind sediment particles together.
   a. Limestone and rock salt are chemical sedimentary rocks.
   b. Sandstone and shale are clastic sedimentary rocks.
3. When great heat or pressure is exerted on rock, it is transformed into metamorphic rock; marble and slate are examples.
4. The changes that occur as rocks are altered from one type to another are components of the rock cycle.

B. Plate tectonics shapes the geography of Earth.
1. Earth's surface consists of the crust, mantle, and core.
2. As the mantle moves, it drags along large plates of crust.
3. New crust is formed where two plates are pushed apart.
4. When two plates collide, uplift or subduction can result.

C. The hydrologic cycle influences all other cycles.
   1. Water moves into the atmosphere via evaporation and transpiration.
   2. Water returns to the surface as precipitation, most of which flows into water bodies as runoff.
   3. Some precipitation and surface water soaks down through the soil and rock to recharge underground water reservoirs known as aquifers.
   4. Human activity affects every aspect of the water cycle.
D. Biogeochemical cycles are essential to understanding ecosystems.
   1. Nutrients are elements and compounds that organisms consume and require for survival.
   2. Nutrients move through the environment in cycles called nutrient cycles or biogeochemical cycles.
   3. All organisms require 24 of the naturally occurring chemical elements to survive.
E. The nitrogen cycle has changed dramatically in recent decades.
   1. Nitrogen makes up 78% of the atmosphere and is the sixth most abundant element on Earth.
   2. There are two ways that inert nitrogen gas becomes "fixed" so that plants can use it: nitrogen fixation and nitrification.
   3. Consumers get the nitrogen they need by consuming plants or other animals; decomposers obtain nitrogen via dead and decaying organic matter.
   4. Denitrifying bacteria convert nitrates in the soil or water back to atmospheric nitrogen.
   5. Many human activities, such as burning fossil fuels and using fertilizers, alter the nitrogen cycle.
      a. By fixing nitrogen, we accelerate its movement into other reservoirs within the cycle.
      b. Activities increase the amounts of nitrogen available to aquatic plants, producing an effect much like that of intentionally fertilizing agricultural crops: a boom in aquatic plant growth.
F. The carbon cycle moves organic nutrients through the environment.
   1. Through photosynthesis, producers pull carbon dioxide out of the atmosphere to produce oxygen and carbohydrates.
   2. During respiration, consumers and decomposers break down carbohydrates to produce carbon dioxide and water.
   3. Remains of organisms may settle as sediments in water bodies to eventually be converted to fossil fuels.
   4. The world's oceans are the second largest reservoir in the carbon cycle.
   5. The burning of fossil fuels, forests, and fields has altered the relative rates at which steps in the carbon cycle occur.
G. The phosphorus cycle plays a key role in the conversion of energy via metabolism.
   1. The element phosphorus is a key component of DNA and RNA.
   2. Organisms also use elemental phosphorus to build ADP and ATP.

3. Phosphorus is most abundant in rocks, and weathering releases phosphates into water.
4. Primary consumers acquire phosphorus from water and plants, and pass it on to secondary and tertiary consumers.
5. Decomposers return phosphorus to the soil.
6. Concentrations of available phosphorus in the environment are very low.
7. Humans influence the phosphorous cycle by releasing sewage and using fertilizers.

H. The Gaia hypothesis portrays Earth as a self-regulating system.
1. In the 1970s, James Lovelock described Earth as a superorganism.
2. His Gaia hypothesis states that living things affect the environment in ways that stabilize the climate and make it possible for life to persist and flourish.
3. The Gaia hypothesis has attracted much harsh criticism from scientists, due in part to the mystical, almost religious, way some of its supporters have expressed its ideas.

III. Conclusion
A. Approaching questions holistically by taking a systems approach is helpful in environmental science.
B. The case of the Gulf of Mexico's hypoxic zone provides evidence that systems thinking can lead the way to solutions.
C. The ecosystems and other environmental systems that we see on Earth today are those that have survived the test of time; our industrialized civilization is young in comparison.

## Key Terms

anthropic principle
aquifers
atmosphere
basalt
biogeochemical cycles
biomass
biome
biosphere
calcium carbonate
carbon cycle
chaparral
chemical sedimentary rocks
clastic sedimentary rocks
climate diagrams
climatographs
closed system
conglomerate
core
crust
denitrifying bacteria
desert
dynamic equilibrium
ecosystem
ecotones
emergent properties
eutrophication
evaporation
extrusive igneous rock
feedback loop
Gaia hypothesis
granite
groundwater
homeostasis
hydrosphere
hypoxia
igneous rock
intrusive igneous rock
landscape ecology
lava
lithosphere
macronutrients
magma
mantle
marble
metamorphic rock
micronutrients

*continued*

## Key Terms, *continued*

negative feedback loop
net primary productivity
nitrification
nitrogen cycle
nitrogen fixation
nitrogen-fixing bacteria
nutrient cycles
nutrients
open systems
organic molecules
plate tectonics
positive feedback loop
precipitation
primary productivity
rainshadow
rock cycle
runoff
sandstone
savannas
sedimentary rock
sediments
shale
slate
system
taiga
temperate deciduous forest
temperate grasslands
temperate rainforest
transpiration
tropical dry forest
tropical rainforest
tundra
water table

## Teaching Tips

1. Illustrate the relative size of the lithosphere and the atmosphere by making a comparison with an apple. The skin of the apple represents the atmosphere, while the flesh and core of the apple represent the lithosphere.
2. Ask students to conduct Internet research on the Gulf of Mexico "dead zone." What is the current status of the dead zone? Has it increased or decreased in size since 2002? What is being done to address the problem?
3. Ask students to define the biome in which they live. What are the major characteristics of the region? Discuss climate and vegetation in particular. For more information about biomes, visit "Biomes of the World," a Web page published by the Missouri Botanical Garden, at http://mbgnet.mobot.org/sets.
4. Describe human activities that are negatively impacting each of the major biomes discussed in the chapter. For example, deforestation is causing a loss of habitat and topsoil in both temperate and tropical rainforests. Off-road vehicles cause soil damage in deserts. Overgrazing and desertification impact grasslands. Oil exploration and global warming are affecting tundra ecosystems.
5. Provide students with background information about James Lovelock, the author of the Gaia hypothesis. He was a British scientist and naturalist asked to participate as an experimenter in the first NASA lunar and planetary exploration. He became interested in the methods that NASA proposed to detect life on Mars, and this work led him to think about what constitutes life. In 1965, Lovelock published the first scientific paper proposing the Gaia hypothesis. The Gaia hypothesis is named after the Greek word meaning "earth mother," and states that life on the planet controls the temperature and composition of Earth's surface.

   Assign students to read Lovelock's work:

   a. *Gaia: A New Look at Life on Earth,* Oxford University Press, 1979
   b. *The Evolving Gaia Theory,* paper presented at the United Nations University on September 25, 1992, www.unu.edu/unupress/lecture1.html

# Additional Resources

### Websites

1. "Mississippi River Basin Gulf of Mexico," U.S. Environmental Protection Agency, www.epa.gov/msbasin/mexico.htm

   This Web page provides background information about the Gulf of Mexico and describes the Gulf of Mexico Program and its accomplishments.

2. "National Centers for Coastal Ocean Science Gulf of Mexico Hypoxia Assessment," NOAA's National Ocean Service, www.nos.noaa.gov/products/pubs_hypox.html

3. "The World's Biomes," University of California Museum of Paleontology, www.ucmp.berkeley.edu/glossary/gloss5/biome

   This Web page describes the major biomes: aquatic, deserts, grasslands, forests, and tundra.

4. "This Dynamic Earth: The Story of Plate Tectonics," USGS, http://pubs.usgs.gov/publications/text/dynamic.html

   This online publication describes plate tectonics with images and maps.

5. "USGS Rocks and Images," USGS Learning Web Explorer, http://interactive2.usgs.gov/learningweb/explorer/topicrocks.htm

   This Web page provides an introduction to geology and descriptions of the rock types.

### Audiovisual Materials

1. *Biomes,* video series from DiscoverySchool.com (http://shopping.discovery.com).

   This five-part series examines coasts, deserts, grasslands, freshwater systems, temperate forests, and islands.

2. *Gaia, the Living Planet,* video distributed by Bullfrog Films (www.bullfrogfilms.com).

   This video is a portrait of James Lovelock, who originated the theory that Earth is a superorganism.

3. *Plate Tectonics,* video from the EME Corporation (http://emescience.com).

   This is a comprehensive program on the development of the plate tectonics theory.

4. *Rocks,* video from DiscoverySchool.com (http://shopping.discovery.com).

   This video shows how rocks form and how erosion continually sculpts and carves the Arizona landscape.

# *Weighing the Issues:* Suggested Answers

### Emergent Properties and the Mississippi River

***Facts to consider:*** *Water, soil, organisms, chemical pollutants, dissolved oxygen, nutrients, etc. Such components give rise to streams, tributary rivers, and the main river itself; to processes of runoff; to communities and ecosystems; to hydrological forces that mold the geomorphology of the region; to flooding and the fertile* *farmland that results. We need to understand the components of a system to comprehend mechanistically how a system works; this is particularly useful when trying to diagnose the source of a problem. We need to think in terms of whole systems in order to understand the importance and ultimate functions of the components. A systems approach can reveal large-scale connections that also help in diagnosing problems.*

## Earth as a System

***Facts to consider:*** *In respect to energy, Earth is an open system, because our planet's life depends on energy from the sun, a constant external input. Earth also radiates heat into space. In respect to matter, Earth is in most respects a closed system, except that some material is added every year by meteorites, and occasionally by comets. The fact that Earth is a mostly closed system in terms of materials suggests we should be prudent in our use of limited natural resources if we want to have a sustainable society. The fact that Earth is open to input of energy from the sun suggests that if we want a sustainable society we should strive to shift our energy use toward solar energy and away from nonrenewable sources.*

## Human Impacts on Biomes

***Facts to consider:*** *Global climate change may affect air and water temperature, regional precipitation patterns, and potentially marine patterns of currents, waves (through storm frequency and strength), salinity, and depth. Various land use practices such as farming, grazing, and urbanization can increase soil erosion and runoff of artificial chemicals including nutrients, which may affect soil type on land, substrate condition underwater, and dissolved nutrient content of water.*

## Nitrogen Pollution and Its Financial Impacts

***Facts to consider:*** *This is a political question with no right or wrong answer. When the interests of different states or regions are at odds, the advantage of the states working out their differences themselves is that they know their own problems and needs best, and thus may be able to best reach an agreement that satisfies all sides. However, if they cannot come to an agreement, then federal intervention may be for the best, if it takes into account the problems and needs of all parties and attempts a fair compromise.*

## Gaia and the Anthropic Principle

***Facts to consider:*** *If Lovelock is right, then Earth is an amazing creation that should command our wonder and respect, and we should try to behave in ways that do not damage the system. However, using Lovelock's view one could also argue that even if humans cause a mass extinction, Earth's remaining life may eventually be able to rebuild a complex environment for itself and return Earth to a homeostatic state (albeit without us). If one holds to the anthropic principle to explain Earth's life, then it may mean that Earth's conditions are accidental, rare, or perhaps even unique in the universe. To many philosophers, this possibility provides an even stronger ethical reason for behaving in ways that minimize damage to our environment.*

# *The Science behind the Stories:* The Scientific Method

### Hypoxia and the Gulf of Mexico "Dead Zone"

**Observation:** Spots in the northern Gulf of Mexico appeared to "die" each summer because of low oxygen levels, or hypoxia.

**Hypothesis:** The hypoxia was not isolated or rare, and it represented a growing environmental problem.

**Experiments:** Long-term, widespread oxygen monitoring; water sampling for nitrogen and other substances; dives to observe sea life; measurements of current and historical levels and sources of nitrogen in the Mississippi River.

**Results:** The Gulf's dead zone covered thousands of square miles and reappeared each summer, fed by rivers polluted from farm runoff. The hypoxia stunned, drove away, or killed sea life. The U.S. government is instituting new policies to control river pollution and shrink the dead zone.

### Biosphere 2

**Observation:** In 1992, oxygen levels in Biosphere 2, an attempt to create a closed ecosystem in the Arizona desert, began dropping rapidly, leaving the eight biospherians inside gasping for breath.

**Hypothesis:** Microbes in Biosphere 2's unusually rich soils were consuming oxygen and emitting carbon dioxide, and the carbon dioxide, which should have been reconverted to oxygen by the project's abundant vegetation, was instead being deposited in the soil or elsewhere in Biosphere 2.

**Experiment:** The amount of organic matter, microbial life, and carbon dioxide in the soil was measured. Holes were drilled into Biosphere 2's exposed concrete to measure deposits of calcium carbonate, the product of a reaction between concrete and carbon dioxide.

**Results:** The soil was found to contain extraordinarily high levels of oxygen-consuming bacteria, and calcium carbonate deposits were found as deep as 6 inches into the concrete walls. The exposed concrete was covered with paint to prevent the formation of further deposits, and more than 23 tons of pure oxygen were injected into Biosphere 2 to compensate for what had been lost.

# Additional Questions

1. The discussion of biomes in this chapter focused exclusively on terrestrial systems. Aquatic systems are not characterized by air temperature and precipitation, but by other factors. What factors do you think determine different aquatic systems? Use those factors to describe major aquatic systems found on Earth.

   *Water salinity and temperature are major factors that influence species composition of aquatic systems.*

   - *Freshwater lakes are standing bodies of water formed in depressions in Earth's surface. Lakes are classified according to nutrient levels: eutrophic, mesotrophic, and oligotrophic.*

- *Freshwater streams and rivers are moving bodies of water that eventually meet the ocean. Streams and rivers vary greatly depending on elevation.*
- *Freshwater wetlands are areas of land that are flooded at some time of the year. There are many types of wetlands, including marshes, swamps, and peatlands.*
- *Coastal wetlands are areas along the coast that flood periodically. The Chesapeake Bay and the Everglades are examples.*
- *The continental shelf of the ocean is relatively shallow and supports ecosystems such as coral reefs, mangroves, and seagrass beds. Rivers and runoff provide nutrients to this area.*
- *The open ocean is generally a nutrient-poor and deep-water region.*

2. The chapter describes using the system approach to examine a water pollution problem (the Gulf of Mexico). Describe an air pollution problem that would require a system approach.

   *Some air pollutants remain in the atmosphere for weeks and travel hundreds of miles. Sulfur and nitrogen oxides are examples. These pollutants are released from the burning of fossil fuels. In the atmosphere, these compounds react with water to form sulfuric acid and nitric acid. These acids fall back to earth as acid deposition. The most serious problems with acid precipitation in the country are found in the Northeast. The pollution that forms these acids comes primarily from the Midwest. As a result, a system approach is required to address the problem.*

3. Assign students to read the online case study, "Hog Waste Woes in the Midwest." How do hog farms affect the nitrogen cycle?

   *Hog waste introduces nitrogen compounds to the land, atmosphere, and water in high amounts. First, waste-filled lagoons release two nitrogen compounds into the atmosphere—ammonia and methane. Methane is a greenhouse gas. Ammonia eventually falls out of the atmosphere, contaminating soil and water. Lagoons that leak or overflow contribute raw waste to rivers and streams. Hog waste contains high amounts of nitrates.*

# 7 Human population growth

## Chapter Objectives

**This chapter will help students understand:**

- The scope of human population growth
- The fundamentals of demography
- How human population, affluence, and technology affect the environment
- How wealth and poverty, the status of women, and other factors affect population growth
- Programs effective in controlling population growth
- The demographic transition theory
- Consumption and the ecological footprint concept
- Dimensions of the HIV/AIDS crisis

## Lecture Outline

I. Central Case: One-Child Policy

   A. The People's Republic of China is the world's most populous nation, home to over one-fifth of the 6.3 billion people living on Earth as of 2004.

   B. Under Mao Zedong's leadership, improved food production and distribution and better medical care allowed China's population to swell, causing environmental problems.

   C. The government instituted a population-control program in the 1970s.

      1. The program started with education and outreach efforts.

      2. In 1979, the government decided to enforce a one-child limit per family.

   D. China's growth rate is down to 0.7%; however, there have been unintended consequences of the program, including infanticide and an unbalanced sex ratio.

II. Human Population Growth: Baby 6 Billion and Beyond
   A. The human population is growing nearly as fast as ever.
      1. The human population has doubled since 1963.
      2. Human population growth has occurred at a greater-than-exponential rate.
   B. Is population growth really a "problem"?
      1. Our ongoing burst of population growth has resulted from technological innovations, improved sanitation, better medical care, and other factors that have led to a decline in death rates.
      2. There are many people today who deny that population growth is a problem.
      3. Under the Cornucopian view, resource depletion due to greater numbers of people is not a problem if new resources can be found to replace depleted resources.
      4. Environmental scientists argue that not all resources are replaceable by others once depleted, and that few resources are actually created by humans.
      5. Many governments have found it difficult to let go of the notion that population growth increases a nation's economic, political, and military strength.
   C. The human population is one of several major factors that affect the environment.
      1. The IPAT model represents how humans' total impact (I) results from the interaction among three factors, population (P), affluence (A), and technology (T): $I = P \times A \times T$.
      2. A sensitivity factor (S) can be added to the equation to denote how sensitive a given environment is to human pressures: $I = P \times A \times T \times S$.
      3. This IPAT equation was meant as a conceptual model, and not necessarily meant to receive exact numerical values.
      4. Modern-day China is an example of how all elements of the IPAT formula can combine to result in tremendous environmental impact in very little time.
   D. The principles of population ecology apply to humans.
      1. Like other organisms, humans have a carrying capacity set by environmental limitations on our population growth.
      2. Estimates of the human carrying capacity have ranged greatly—from 1–2 billion to 33 billion.

III. Demography is the science of human population.
   A. The application of population ecology to the study of statistical change in human populations is the focus of the social science of demography.
      1. Population size is the absolute number of individuals.
      2. People are very unevenly distributed over the globe.
         a. This uneven distribution means that certain areas bear far more environmental impact than others.

   b. At the same time, areas with low population density are often vulnerable to environmental impacts as well.
3. Age structure diagrams show the relative sizes of each age group in a population and are especially valuable to demographers in predicting future dynamics of a population.
4. The ratio of males to females, the sex ratio, can affect population dynamics.
   a. The naturally occurring sex ratio in human populations at birth features a slight preponderance of males.
   b. In China, selective abortion of female fetuses has skewed the natural sex ratio.

B. Population growth depends on the rates of birth, death, immigration, and emigration.
   1. In today's world, immigration and emigration play an increasingly large role because of refugees.
   2. Since 1970, growth rates in many countries have been declining and the global growth rate has declined.

C. A population's total fertility rate can shape its population growth rate.
   1. The total fertility rate is the average number of children born per female member of a population during her lifetime.
   2. The replacement fertility is the TFR that keeps the size of a population stable, and for humans the replacement fertility is 2.1.
   3. A lower infant mortality rate has alleviated people's tendency to conceive many children in order to ensure that at least some survive.

D. Women's empowerment and family planning greatly affect population growth.
   1. Drops in TFR have been most noticeable in countries where women have gained improved access to contraceptives and education, particularly family-planning education.
   2. Unfortunately, many women still lack the information and personal freedom of choice for childbearing.

E. Some nations have experienced a change called the demographic transition.
   1. Demographic transition is a theoretical model of economic and cultural change that explains the trend of declining death rates and birth rates that occurs when nations experience industrialization.
   2. The first stage, the pre-industrial stage, is characterized by conditions in which both death rates and birth rates are high.
   3. In the next stage, the transitional stage, death rates decline and birth rates remain high.
   4. The industrial stage creates employment opportunities for women in particular, causing the birth rate to fall.
   5. In the final stage, the post-industrial stage, both birth rates and death rates remain low and populations decline slightly.

F. Is the demographic transition a universal process?
   1. This transition has occurred in many European countries, the United States, Canada, and Japan over the past 200–300 years.
   2. It may or may not apply to all of the developing countries depending on their culture.

G. Population policies and family-planning programs are working around the globe.
   1. The government of Thailand has relied on an education-based approach to family planning.
   2. India has had long-standing policies, but some think they need to be strengthened.
   3. Brazil, Mexico, Iran, and Cuba have had active programs consisting of population reduction targets, incentives, education, contraception, and reproductive health care.
   4. In 1994, the United Nations hosted a conference in Cairo on population and development in which 179 nations endorsed a platform calling for all governments to offer universal access to reproductive health care within 20 years.

H. Women still need more empowerment.
   1. Improving the treatment of women, through health care and education, was one goal of the Cairo conference.
   2. Proponents of the view emerging from the Cairo conference maintain that gender equality promotes more efficient resource use.
   3. As more and more women come into positions of power, perhaps gender equality will become a more tangible reality.

I. Poverty is strongly correlated with population growth.

J. The consumption that comes with affluence creates a large environmental impact.

K. Individuals from affluent societies leave a larger "ecological footprint."

L. The wealth gap and population growth contribute to violent conflict—in 1999, the richest 20% of the world's people used 86% of the world's resources.

M. HIV/AIDS is a major factor affecting populations in some parts of the world.
   1. Of the 40 million people around the world infected with HIV/AIDS, 28.5 million live in sub-Saharan Africa.
   2. The AIDS epidemic illustrates the dramatic effect of a single cause of death on population dynamics and social cohesion.
   3. Premature deaths are reducing the average life expectancy in African nations.

N. Severe demographic changes have social, political, and economic repercussions.
   1. Everywhere in sub-Saharan Africa, AIDS is undermining the ability of developing countries to make the transition to modern technologies.
   2. Governments of AIDS-infected countries are experiencing "demographic fatigue."

IV. Conclusion

A. Today, the human population is more urban, more polarized between rich and poor, much younger, and much larger than at any time in the past.

B. Although global populations are still growing, the rate of growth has decreased nearly everywhere.

C. There has been progress in expanding rights for women worldwide.

D. True sustainability demands more than just leveling off population growth; humans must transition to ecologically sustainable economies.

## Key Terms

age pyramid
age structure
Cairo conference
crude birth rate
crude death rate
demographic fatigue
demographic transition
demography
doubling time
ecological footprint
emigration
family planning
greater-than-exponential growth
HIV/AIDS
immigration
industrial stage
IPAT model
life expectancy
natural rate of population change
population density
population distribution
population size
post-industrial stage
pre-industrial stage
replacement fertility
sex ratio
total fertility rate (TFR)
transitional stage
UN Population Fund (UNFPA)

## Teaching Tips

1. Ask each student to adopt a country and research the status of its population, including population size, crude birth rate, crude death rate, life expectancy, infant mortality, annual growth rate, and age structure. Current information can be found on the "People Facts and Figures" website at www.os-connect.com/pop.

   To make this an interactive activity, require each student to present the information to the class. Once presentations have been made, discuss the similarities and differences among the countries. This can lead to a discussion of the characteristics of "developed countries" versus "developing countries."

2. Death rates have dramatically declined in the United States over the past 100 years. To examine this change in greater detail, students can conduct a study on percent survival. First, students collect data from a local cemetery (preferably one in which people were buried before 1900) and compare that to data from current newspaper obituary pages. Ask students to record the age at death for 20 individuals from each source. Students will then organize the data according to 10-year age categories as shown below. There will be two tables, one for cemetery data and the other for obituary data. Percent survival is then calculated for each age category.

| Age Group | Number that Died | Percent Surviving |
|---|---|---|
| 0–10 | A | = (20 − A)/20 × 100 |
| 11–20 | B | = [20 −(A + B)] ÷ 20 × 100 |
| 21–30 | C | = [20 −(A + B + C)] ÷ 20 × 100 |
| 31–40 | D | |
| 41–50 | E | |
| 51–60 | F | |
| 61–70 | G | |
| 71–80 | H | |
| 81–90 | I | |
| 91–100 | J | |
| Over 100 | K | = [20 − (sum of A. . . . K)] ÷ 20 ×100 |

The resulting percent survival values can be graphed to show a survivorship curve with age classes on the *x* axis and the percent surviving values on the *y* axis. In general, there are three classes of survivorship curves: Type I, Type II, and Type III.

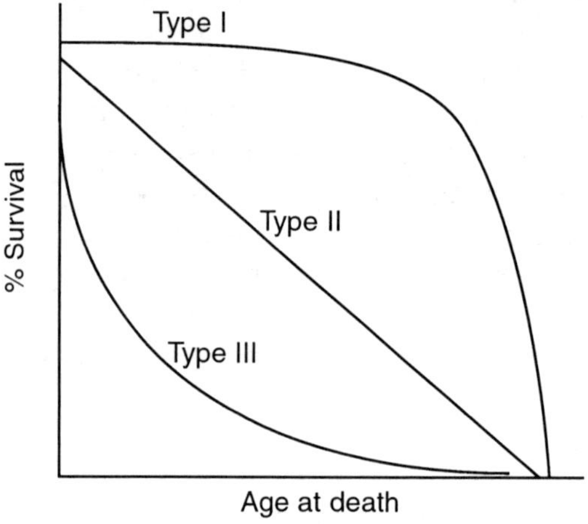


3. Use resources from the Population Resource Bureau (www.prb.org) for classroom presentations and activities.
   - The graphics bank contains over 100 graphics to be used in PowerPoint presentations. The graphics cover population trends, HIV/AIDS, and family planning.
   - The World Population Data Sheet contains the latest population estimates, projections, and other key indicators for 200 countries.

# Additional Resources

## Websites

1. "China," International Planned Parenthood Federation, http://ippfnet.ippf.org/pub/IPPFRegions/IPPFCountryProfile.asp?ISOCode=CN

   This Web page provides information about the sexual and reproductive health of the Chinese population and describes the China Family Planning Association.

2. "China's One-Child Policy OK for Kids' Health," Reuters Health, www.ucsfhealth.org/childrens/health_library/reuters/2003/06/20030613elin019.html

   This article describes a study that shows that children in China with no siblings are not at an increased risk for health problems.

3. "Population and Economic Household Topics," U.S. Census Bureau, www.census.gov/population/www

   This Web page provides populations clocks for the United States and the world, along with information about births, fertility, deaths, and migration in the United States.

4. "State of the World Population 2002: People, Poverty and Possibilities," United Nations Population Fund, www.unfpa.org/swp/swpmain.htm

   This is a report by the United Nations Population Fund, the world's largest international source of funding for population and reproductive health programs.

### Audiovisual Materials

1. *Decade of Decision,* video by Population Communication International and distributed by Bullfrog Films (www.bullfrogfilms.com).

   Narrated by Walter Cronkite, this program follows the history of population growth from the early 1900s to today.

2. *Jam Packed,* video by Population Communications International and distributed by The Video Project (http://videoproject.net).

   This program looks at the human population growth problem from a young person's point of view.

3. *Not the Numbers Game,* video distributed by Bullfrog Films (www.bullfrogfilms.com).

   This six-part series looks at how women are solving population and development problems in Bosnia, Cambodia, India, Indonesia, Peru, and Uganda.

4. *Sustainable Lives, Attainable Dreams,* video distributed by The Video Project (http://videoproject.net).

   This program shows the success of family-planning programs in three countries: Indonesia, Mexico, and Kenya.

## *Weighing the Issues:* Suggested Answers

### China's Reproductive Policy

***Facts to consider:*** *Some benefits of a reproductive policy such as China's might include: greater ability to provide food, health care, housing, and education, as well as reduced environmental pressure. Some problems include: social and legal punishment for people who do not follow the policy; reduction in personal choice about family decisions; elimination of unwanted fetuses and children; and pressure on government finances, industry, health care, families, and military forces because fewer working-age people are available to support these systems. People may disagree about whether a government should be able to enforce strict penalties for people who fail to abide by* *the policy. Alternative ways of dealing with resource demands of a quickly growing population include: finding new resources to replace depleted resources; using rewards but not punishments for smaller families; and using more efficient technologies to reduce resource-intensive processes and to reduce pollution.*

## Malaria and Africa's Dynamics

***Facts to consider:*** *Malaria may contribute to both lower life expectancy and lowered median age of the population. Because children are at relatively greater risk of dying from malaria, the child mortality rate remains high, increasing the likelihood that parents will feel the need to have more offspring in order to guarantee that a sufficient number of children survive to adulthood. When pregnant women die of malaria, not only do they add no more children to the population, but there are fewer children to grow to adulthood and reproduce. The frequency of such deaths may culturally influence surviving women to value childbirth even more highly and to have more offspring. Though malaria keeps the death rate in Africa high, the fact that it hits children and pregnant women hardest may also help keep birth rates high.*

*Much more often, people are affected by the illness but do not die. Because the debilitating effects of malaria reduce productivity, and its deaths reduce the population of present and future workers, poverty remains. Food, sanitation, and basic medical care are more likely to be lacking. These factors also keep the death rate high, so cultures continue to rely on high birth rates for survival. Societies focused on avoiding starvation and widespread disease are less likely to spend resources on education and other means of increasing health and well-being that might turn the cycle from malaria, poverty, and high birth and death rates, to increased well being, and decreases in poverty, death rates and, eventually, birth rates.*

## Economic Consequences of Low Fertility Rates

***Facts to consider:*** *A below-replacement fertility rate means that, overall, the population is aging. Changes in age composition of the population will alter patterns of consumption. Most notably, an increase in population age will trigger an increasing demand for health care services. Working-age people will need to supply the productivity and finances required to support the higher proportion of older, retired people as well.*

*(Further observations may also be noteworthy, based on a broader understanding of economics and social issues in Europe and elsewhere. These might include: increased immigration to provide a labor force; a reduction in the labor force, leading to wage increases and inflation, reducing the purchasing power of people who have already retired; greater savings rates as families spend less on dependents; or lower savings rates as older people, lacking income, spend their savings; increases in retirement age, in order to reduce demands on public welfare, as fewer younger workers are putting in funds while more older workers receive entitlements and services.)*

## Population Growth and Reproductive Freedom

*This question requires an individual response.*

## The Demographic Transition in Developed Nations

***Facts to consider:*** *Some developed countries might not continue in the post-industrial mode outlined by the demographic transition theory. For instance, their population* *growth rate might increase if they experience significant immigration, particularly immigration of people from transitional cultures still more likely to have large families. Developed countries may be particularly likely to allow or encourage significant immigration if their own populations age, so that they do not have a sufficiently large workforce to support their demands; then they would be more likely to increase legal immigration. Undocumented immigration might increase significantly, if the developed nations offer economic opportunity that was much higher than that in less developed countries.*

*The model also does not take into account what might happen if a developed society found itself pressured by reduced availability of environmental resources. If this happened, reduced resources might cause a reduction in economic well-being, coupled with an increase in death rates and emigration (and, therefore, reductions in population numbers). Though people may have different opinions about how complete and realistic this model may be, it does provide a structure for recognizing and analyzing patterns across cultures and around the world, patterns that, so far, seem to apply to most societies.*

### U.S. Involvement in International Family Planning

*This question requires an individual response.*

### HIV/AIDS and Population Growth

*This question requires an individual response.*

## *The Science behind the Stories:* The Scientific Method

### Causes of Fertility Decline in Bangladesh

**Observation:** In Bangladesh—one of the most densely populated countries on the planet—fertility declined dramatically from the late 1970s through the 1990s despite high rates of poverty, illiteracy, and gender inequality.

**Hypothesis:** The Bangladeshi government and international aid organizations began an aggressive campaign in the mid-1970s to provide women with access to and information about contraceptives. This may have compensated for the lack of significant improvement in other areas.

**Experiment:** Researchers measured the impact of outreach efforts on contraceptive use and fertility rates in Matlab, an isolated rural area in Bangladesh with a high-intensity family-planning outreach project. They also measured the same variables in a nearby area where contraceptives were available but services were limited.

**Results:** Ten years after the study was begun, contraceptive use in Matlab was higher and fertility was lower than in the comparison area. The results suggest that Bangladesh's success was due to a combination of widely available contraceptives and socially appropriate family planning services, both of which were present in an intensified form in Matlab.

## Additional Questions

1. At the beginning of the chapter, there are two quotes about population growth:

   "Population growth is analogous to a plague of locusts. What we have on this earth today is a plague of people."

   —*Ted Turner, media magnate and supporter of the UN Population Fund*

   "There is no population problem."

   —*Sheldon Richman, Senior Editor, Cato Institute*

   With which quote do you most agree? Support your answer with data and/or information from the textbook and other references.

   *Student responses will vary. Students who agree most with Ted Turner may refer to the world population size (>6.3 billion) and the environmental problems that have resulted from dense populations. Students who agree most with Sheldon Richmond may support the Cornucopian view that technology will sustain the human population.*

2. China's one-child policy consists of three main parts:
   - To advocate delayed marriage and delayed child bearing
   - To advocate fewer and healthier births
   - To advocate one child per couple

   Although is it hard to enforce, especially in rural areas, it has been successful in decreasing the total fertility rate and the annual growth rate. What have been the advantages and disadvantages of this program in China?

   *The one-child policy in China has had both favorable and unfavorable results:*
   - *The nation's growth rate is now 0.7%, down from 2.6%.*
   - *Selective abortion of female fetuses and infanticide of female infants*
   - *Unbalanced sex ratio: 117 boys to every 100 girls*
   - *Millions of Chinese have increased their material wealth and consumption of resources.*
   - *Change in age structure—children will be outnumbered by the elderly*
   - *Total fertility rate is 1.8, down from 5.8.*
   - *Population doubling time has increased from 27 years to 100 years.*
   - *Improved reproductive healthcare*
   - *Improved sex education in schools*

3. According to a study published in *Family Planning Perspectives* (www.agi-usa.org/pubs/journals/3201400.html), the United States and the Russian Federation lead the developed world in teenage pregnancy rates. What can be done to reduce the number of teenage pregnancies in the United States?

   *There are many factors that can contribute to lower rates of teenage pregnancy:*
   - *Easy access to contraception*
   - *Sex education in schools*
   - *Accessible health services for young women*
   - *Social acceptance of teenage sexual behavior*

   *For more information, see the study released by the Alan Guttmacher Institute: "Teenage Sexual and Reproductive Behavior in Developed Countries: Can More Progress be Made?" (www.guttmacher.org/media/moreprogress.html).*

# 8 Agriculture and soil formation, degradation, and conservation

## Chapter Objectives

**This chapter will help students understand:**

- The importance of soils to agriculture and the impact of agriculture on soils
- A brief history of agriculture
- The fundamentals of soil science, including soil formation and the properties of soil
- The causes and consequences of soil erosion and degradation
- The history and principles of soil conservation
- U.S. and international soil conservation policies and practices

## Lecture Outline

I. Central Case: No-Till Agriculture in Southern Brazil
   A. In Southernmost Brazil, decades of farming had used up the soil's fertility.
   B. In the 1990s, Brazil's farmers adopted no-tillage farming.
   C. With less soil eroding away and more organic material being added to it, the soil could hold water better and was better able to support crops.
   D. No-till farming reduced costs to farmers because less labor and fuels were used.

II. Soils: The Foundation for Feeding a Growing Human Population
   A. Increasing food production sustainably is necessary if we are to feed the world's rising human population.
      1. Agriculture is the practice of cultivating soil, producing crops, and raising livestock for human use and consumption.
      2. As the human population increases, so does the amount of land and other resources devoted to agriculture, which currently covers 38% of Earth's land surface.

3. Healthy soil is vital for agriculture and for the preservation of Earth's natural systems.

B. As population increases, soils are being degraded.

1. As our planet gains nearly 80 million people each year, we are losing 5–7 million hectares of productive cropland.

2. Soil degradation has direct and immediate impacts on agricultural production.

C. Human agriculture began to appear around 10,000 years ago.

1. During most of our species' 100,000-year existence, we were hunter-gatherers.

2. About 10,000 years ago, humans began to raise plants from seed.

3. The plants in the first gardens produced fruits that were larger and tastier than those in the wild.

4. Once our ancestors learned how to cultivate crops, they began to settle in more permanent camps and villages.

5. Archaeological and paleoecological evidence suggests that agriculture was invented multiple times by different cultures in different areas of the world.

6. For most of the thousands of years that humans have practiced agriculture, human and animal muscle power, along with hand tools and simple machines, performed the work of cultivating, harvesting, storing, and distributing crops.

D. Industrialized agriculture is newer still.

1. The industrial revolution introduced large-scale fossil-fuel combustion and mechanization to agriculture just as it did to industry.

2. Other advances facilitated irrigation, fertilizing, and the use of chemical pesticides.

3. Industrialized farming is widespread today because not everyone is a farmer.

E. The green revolution applied technology to boost crop yields.

1. Despite historical advances in agricultural production, some critics have argued that our growing population would overwhelm our best efforts to keep pace with food production.

2. The green revolution was an intensification of the industrialization of agriculture, a change in agricultural practices that dramatically increased the crops produced per acre of farmland between 1950 and the start of the 21st century.

   a. Large areas were devoted to identical crops bred for high yields and rapid growth.

   b. Farmers heavily used fertilizers, pesticides, and irrigation water.

   c. Farmers sowed and harvested on the same land more than one time per year or season.

3. The intensive cultivation of farmland is creating new problems and exacerbating old ones.

III. Soil as a System
   A. By weight, soil is about 50% mineral matter, 25% water, 5–10% organic matter, and 15–20% atmospheric gases.
   B. Soil formation is slow and complex.
      1. The formation of soil plays a key role in the ecological process of succession.
      2. The weathering of parent material is the first step in the formation of soil.
      3. Weathering is the term scientists use to describe the physical, chemical, and biological processes that break down rocks and minerals.
         a. Physical or mechanical weathering breaks rocks down into small particles without triggering a chemical change in the parent material.
         b. Chemical weathering results from the chemical interaction of water, atmospheric gases, and other substances with the parent material.
         c. Biological weathering is the breakdown of parent material into smaller particles through the activities of living things.
      4. Erosion, the process of moving soil from one area to another, may contribute to the formation of soil in one locality even as it depletes topsoil from another.
      5. Biological activity also contributes to soil formation through the deposition, decomposition, and accumulation of organic matter.
   C. Soil formation is influenced by five main factors: climate, organisms, relief, parent material, and time.
   D. A soil "profile" consists of distinct layers known as "horizons."
      1. Soils from different locations differ due to factors influencing their formation, but soil from any given location can nonetheless be divided into recognizable horizons.
      2. Many soil profiles contain an uppermost layer consisting mostly of organic matter; this layer is designated the O horizon (O for organic).
      3. Just below the O horizon in a typical soil profile is the A horizon (topsoil), which consists of mostly inorganic mineral components with some organic matter and humus.
      4. Beneath the A horizon lies the E horizon, also known as the zone of eluviation.
      5. The minerals that leach out of the E horizon are carried down into the layer beneath it, the B horizon (subsoil).
      6. The C horizon, beneath the B horizon, contains rock particles that are larger and less weathered than the layers above.
      7. The C horizon sits directly above the R horizon, which is also known as bedrock.
   E. Soil can be characterized by its color, texture, structure, and acidity.
      1. U.S. soil scientists have classified soils into 11 major groups, based largely on the processes thought to lead to their formation.
      2. Soil color is an indicator of soil composition and sometimes soil fertility.

3. Soil texture is determined by the size of particles and is the basis on which the USDA assigns soils to one of three general categories: clay, silt, and soil.
4. Soil structure is a measure of the arrangement of sand, silt, or clay particles into clumps or aggregates.
5. Soil pH is the degree of acidity or alkalinity and influences its ability to support plant growth.

F. Regional differences in soil traits can affect agriculture.

IV. Soil Degradation: Problems and Solutions

A. Erosion is the movement of soil from one place to another.
1. Erosion is the removal of material from one place and its transport toward another by the action of wind or water.
2. Deposition is the arrival of eroded material at another location.
3. Erosion becomes a problem when its rate exceeds the rate of soil formation.
4. Erosion is caused by overcultivation, overgrazing, and deforestation.

B. Soil may erode by various mechanisms.
1. Splash erosion occurs when rain striking the soil surface breaks aggregates into smaller sizes.
2. In sheet erosion, surface water flows downhill, washing topsoil away in uniform layers.
3. With rill erosion, surface water runs along small contours on the surface, gradually deepening and widening the contours into small channels.
4. Gully erosion occurs when small channels erode into gullies.

C. Soil erosion is a massive problem globally.
1. More than 19 billion hectares of the world's croplands suffer from erosion and other forms of soil degradation stemming from human activities.
2. Kazakhstan is one example.

D. Arid land may lose productivity in the process of desertification.
1. Desertification is a loss of more than 10% productivity due to soil erosion, soil compaction, forest removal, overgrazing, drought, salinization, climate change, depletion of water sources, or an array of other factors.
2. Arid and semi-arid lands are particularly prone to desertification because their precipitation is too meager to meet the demand for water to support the needs of growing human populations.
3. It has been estimated that fully one-third of the planet's land area suffers from desertification, affecting people in 110 countries.

E. The United States' Dust Bowl was a monumental event.
1. Prior to large-scale cultivation of the southern Great Plains of the United States, native prairie grasses of this temperate grassland region held erosion-prone soils in place.
2. During the 1930s a drought in the Great Plains exacerbated human impacts on the soil.

3. Large-scale wind erosion led to dust storms, destroying the land and affecting human health.

F. The U.S. Soil Conservation Service pioneered many measures to slow soil degradation.

1. As part of the effort to address the problem of soil degradation, the U.S. Congress passed the Soil Conservation Act of 1935, establishing the Soil Conservation Service (SCS).
2. The early teams that the SCS formed to combat erosion typically included soil scientists, forestry experts, engineers, economists, and biologists.
3. Under director Hugh Bennett's leadership, the agency promoted soil conservation practices through county-based entities known as conservation districts.
4. Hugh Bennett advocated a complex approach to reducing soil erosion that included contour farming, strip cropping, crop rotation, grazing management, reforestation, and wildlife management.

G. Farmers can protect soils against degradation in various ways.

1. Crop rotation is the practice of alternating the kind of crop grown in a particular field from one season or year to the next.
2. Contour farming consists of plowing furrows along the natural contours of the land.
3. The planting of alternating bands of different crops across a slope is called strip cropping.
4. Terraces, level platforms cut into hillsides, are used on extremely steep terrain.
5. Shelterbelts are rows of trees that are planted along the edges of fields to break the wind.
6. With conservation tillage, plowing is bypassed, as an approach to soil conservation.

H. Protecting and restoring plant cover is the theme of most erosion-control practices.

I. Irrigation has boosted productivity, but has also caused long-term soil problems.

1. Soils too saturated with water may become waterlogged.
2. An even more frequent problem is salinization, the buildup of salts in surface soil layers.

J. Salinization is easier to prevent than to correct.

K. Agricultural fertilizers boost crop yields, but can be overapplied.

1. Nutrient depletion creates a need for fertilizers.
   a. Organic fertilizers consist of natural materials.
   b. Inorganic fertilizers are mined or synthetically manufactured mineral supplements.
2. Excess nitrogen impacts the environment.
3. Organic fertilizers have benefits that synthetic ones do not.

L. Grazing practices and policies can contribute to soil degradation.
   1. Overgrazing has been shown to exacerbate damage to soils, natural communities, and the land's productivity for grazing.
   2. Overgrazing can compact soils and alter their structure.
   3. In the United States, ranchers have little incentive to conserve rangelands because most grazing has taken place on public lands leased from the government.

M. Forestry, too, has impacts on soils.

N. Recent U.S. laws have promoted soil conservation.
   1. The Conservation Reserve Program, enacted in 1985, pays farmers to stop cultivating highly erodible cropland and place it in conservation reserves planted with grasses and trees.
   2. The Federal Agricultural Improvement and Reform Act reduced subsidies and government influence over many farm products.

O. Several key international programs also promote soil conservation.

V. Conclusion

A. Many policies enacted and practices followed in the United States and worldwide have been quite successful in reducing erosion.

B. Many challenges remain; better technologies and wider adoption of soil conservation techniques are needed to avoid a food crisis.

# Key Terms

A horizon
agriculture
agroforestry
aquaculture sites
B horizon
bedrock
biological weathering
C horizon
chemical weathering
clay
compost
conservation districts
Conservation Reserve Program
contour farming
crop rotation
croplands
deposition
Dust Bowl
E horizon
erosion
erosion pin
Federal Agricultural Improvement and Reform Act (FAIR)
feedlots
fertilizer
Food and Agriculture Organization (FAO)
green manure
green revolution
gully erosion
hardpan
horizon
humification
humus
industrialized agriculture
inorganic fertilizers
intensive traditional agriculture
irrigation
leaching
litter layer
loam
macronutrients
mechanical weathering
micronutrients
mineralization
monoculture
Natural Resources Conservation Service
O horizon
organic fertilizers
overgrazing
parent material
R horizon
rangelands
regolith
rill erosion
salinization
sand
sheet erosion
shelterbelts

| | | |
|---|---|---|
| silt | soil porosity | topsoil |
| soil | soil profile | traditional agriculture |
| Soil Conservation Act of 1935 | splash erosion | waterlogging |
| Soil Conservation Service (SCS) | strip cropping | weathering |
| | subsistence agriculture | |
| | terracing | |

# Teaching Tips

1. Bring soil samples to class on which students can conduct a soil texture "feel test." In general, sandy soils feel gritty, silty soils feel like flour, and clay soils are sticky when moistened. Soils feel different because of the size of the most abundant particle type. The USDA categorizes particles as follows:

   Sand 2.0 mm–0.05 mm in diameter

   Silt 0.05 mm–0.002 mm in diameter

   Clay less than 0.002 mm in diameter

   To better visualize the differences in soil particle size, visualize a barrel to represent a sand particle, a plate to represent a silt particle, and a dime to represent a clay particle.

   Because most soils are a combination of sand, silt, and clay particles, soil scientists use a more complicated method to determine the percent composition of each type. These percentage values are used in the USDA textural triangle (which can be found at NASA's Goddard Space Flight Center [http://ltpwww.gsfc.nasa.gov/globe/tbf/txtriful.gif]) to determine the textural class of a soil.

2. Soil formation is a very slow process, and in some cases it can take 500 years for one inch of soil to develop. To emphasize the importance of soil conservation, use the timeline below to demonstrate the time required to form soil:

   2002 West Nile Virus infects humans in the United States.
   1996 The first animal, Dolly the sheep, is cloned from an adult cell.
   1989 The Berlin Wall is torn down.
   1970 The first Earth Day is celebrated.
   1962 British pop group The Beatles makes first recordings.
   1945 World War II ends.
   1934 Dust Bowl in the Great Plains occurs.
   1915 Albert Einstein formulated his general theory of relativity.
   1872 Congress establishes the first national park, Yellowstone.
   1854 Henry David Thoreau publishes *Walden.*
   1804 Lewis and Clark begin their expedition to the Northwest.
   1788 The U.S. Constitution is ratified.
   1681 The dodo, a large flightless bird, becomes extinct.
   1608 Native Americans teach colonists how to raise corn.
   1513 Juan Ponce de León discovers Florida.
   1500 The Incan Empire reaches its height.

3. Assign students to read the first chapter of *The Grapes of Wrath* by John Steinbeck. This chapter of the classic novel describes the conditions of Dust Bowl Oklahoma that ruined crops, causing massive numbers of foreclosures on farmland.

# Additional Resources

## Websites

1. "About the Dust Bowl," Modern American Poetry, www.english.uiuc.edu/maps/depression/dustbowl.htm

   This Web page provides a brief description of the Dust Bowl, plus a map, photos, and a timeline.

2. "Best Management Practices for Soil Erosion," U.S. Environmental Protection Agency, www.epa.gov/seahome/erosion.html

   This Web page has a downloadable file that provides information about soil erosion worldwide, in the United States, and in the Midwest in particular.

3. "Soil Science Basics," NASA's Goddard Space Flight Center, http://ltpwww.gsfc.nasa.gov/globe/basics.htm

   This Web page provides information about soil formation, chemistry, microbiology, and field characterization.

4. "SOILS," USDA Natural Resources Conservation Service, http://soils.usda.gov

   This Website is part of the National Cooperative Soil Survey, an effort by federal and state agencies to provide scientifically based soil information.

5. "What Is Overgrazing?," Yellowstone National Park, National Park Service, www.nps.gov/yell/nature/northernrange/natreg/overgrazing.html

   This Web page describes overgrazing in Yellowstone National Park.

# Audiovisual Materials

1. *Surviving the Dust Bowl,* WBGH American Experience video distributed by PBS (http://shop.pbs.org).

   This program looks at America's "worst ecological disaster" that brought financial and emotional ruin to thousands of people in the Great Plains.

2. *On American Soil,* video distributed by Bullfrog Films (http://bullfrogfilms.com).

   This video shows the nature and extent of erosion in America at present.

3. *My Father's Garden,* video distributed by Bullfrog Films (http://bullfrogfilms.com).

   This documentary examines the use and misuse of technology on American farms. Industrial farms and organic farms are shown and compared.

4. *Soil—A Medium for Plant Growth,* Visual Education Productions program, distributed by California Polytechnic University, San Luis Obispo, California (1-800-235-4146).

# *Weighing the Issues:* Suggested Answers

## Earth's Soil Resources

***Facts to consider:*** *At the rate of 500 to 1000 years to produce 1 inch of topsoil, soil can hardly be considered a renewable resource compared with human timescales. If soil resources renewed quickly and easily, we might have more latitude in agricultural, forestry, and development processes that influence soil survival. But because forming new soil requires such a long time, and because good soil is essential to our survival and wellbeing (as well as the wellbeing of the larger environment), we should take particular care to act in ways that preserve and enhance soil. Though some soil is forming, soil is presently being lost much more quickly than it is being gained. So, the best way to have the soil resources we need is to preserve the soil that exists today.*

*Fortunately, some human actions support soil formation. Preserving and allowing natural flooding deposits new sediment. No-till farming increases organic matter and soil biota to help build up soil. Compost can improve soil structure and provide nutritional benefit to it. Soil biodiversity increases the rate of soil formation, so reduced use of pesticides will help soil formation. Vegetation decomposition helps build up organic matter, and roots help break large particles into soil, so practices that encourage plant cover may also encourage soil formation.*

## How Would You Farm?

***Facts to consider:*** *To protect soil from wind erosion, techniques might include conservation tillage, including leaving crop residue on the fields; planting cover crops to protect the soil during fallow periods; and planting a shelterbelt of trees. In some strategic areas, natural plant communities might be preserved, to help retard erosion. Additional techniques that would maintain soil health might include crop rotation, intercropping, and terraced or contour farming depending on the degree of slope. To irrigate on a slope effectively without increasing erosion will probably involve drip irrigation or a similar method that applies water directly to plants.*

*Before undertaking such actions, it would be useful to know what kinds of conservation tillage methods would work best in this area, what crops would work best with that approach, which crops would fare best in this sunny exposure and climate, soil structure (sandy to claylike), nutrient levels are in the soil, patterns of water availability, and which crops require irrigation only within the limits of available water. It would be good to know more specifically how to decide whether to use contour or terraced farming.*

## Can We Measure Soil Quality?

***Facts to consider:*** *Researching and setting standards for soil pollutants could provide some measure for comparing various environments. If certain chemicals may harm humans or other organisms if they are present above particular levels, it would be good to determine these levels and test for them, at least in soils that may be used for producing food and when human activities may have affected such levels. Some potentially toxic chemicals occur naturally in some soils. So not all results above the standards would necessarily have been caused by human activity, but we might be more likely to pinpoint areas of human responsibility by having some standards.*

*The fact that some chemicals considered pollutants in other settings may occur naturally in soil might make setting soil-pollution standards more difficult. So would the fact that natural or healthy soil varies considerably in its chemical composition, unlike healthy water and air. Moreover, some chemicals that are considered pollutants in water and air are signs of health in soil, such as nitrogen and carbon compounds. Though chemical pollution causes problems for soil in some areas, poor soil quality is a much more widespread problem. Perhaps, then, more useful standards for soil quality would consider the qualities that help soil remain stable and support life. These might include texture, structure, acidity, soil biota, and organic content, as well as the thickness of the topsoil.*

## *The Science behind the Stories:* The Scientific Method

### Measuring Erosion

**Observation:** In Maryland, U.S. government researchers noted that rows of stiff grass seemed to help stop soil erosion on some slopes.

**Hypothesis:** The grass hedges could greatly reduce erosion problems at the Maryland site—and perhaps also elsewhere around the world.

**Experiment:** The researchers used both low-tech and high-tech erosion tracking around the hedges, including simple measurements with "erosion pin" markers and complicated analysis of the amounts of radioactive nuclear fallout in the soil.

**Results:** Researchers found that the hedges slowed erosion, but didn't eliminate it entirely.

### Overgrazing and Fire Suppression in the Malpai Borderlands

**Observation:** In the Malpai Borderlands between Arizona and New Mexico, decades of cattle ranching and fire suppression had damaged the land, causing native grasses to get crowded out by trees and shrubs.

**Hypothesis:** Returning natural fire cycles to the landscape, along with more careful control of cattle, would reduce shrubs and trees and allow grasses to grow back.

**Experiment:** On an experimental ranch, scientists set up separate research plots and allowed different combinations of fire and grazing on each. Long-term monitoring tracked which plants thrived under each set of conditions.

**Results:** Fire, found to be essential to keeping grasslands healthy, has been returned to the landscape through both natural wildfires and controlled burns. Ranchers also have access to special grazing areas so grasslands on their own property can recover.

## Additional Questions

1. As the chapter described, people often refer to soil as *dirt,* which connotes something "useless or undesirable." Make an argument that soil is just the opposite—useful and desirable. Why is soil important? What components of soil make it desirable for growing food?

   *Soil contains the materials that support plant life—minerals, nutrients, water, and oxygen. We need healthy soil to produce our food and to support ecosystems such as forests and grasslands. Soil also contains life. A tablespoon of soil can host many species of bacteria, fungi, algae, and protozoa. Earthworms, insects, arthropods, amphibians, reptiles, and burrowing mammals live in soil as well.*

2. What type of soil occurs in your area? Is it fertile? If not, what kinds of fertilizers are available to improve the nutrient content of the soil?

   *Student answers will vary. Students can find soil type maps on the Internet. There are two major types of fertilizers: chemical and natural. Chemical fertilizers are synthetic fossil-fuel products and supply high amounts of nitrogen, phosphorus, and potassium. Natural fertilizers like manure and compost provide lower amounts of macronutrients but do not overload the soil.*

3. Ask students to read the online case study "Hog Waste Woes in the Midwest." Why is this type of livestock farming considered *industrial*? How is it different from the traditional raising of livestock?

   *Industrial farming is, by definition, the intensive use of fossil fuels, irrigation, and mechanization to raise a single crop or kind of livestock. Factory farms use large amounts of water to manage the waste of thousands of animals. Animals are concentrated in a small area and are fed grains that may be genetically modified or may contain chemicals such as hormones and antibiotics. Traditionally, livestock animals were raised in pastures where they grazed or sought out food. Waste was not an issue because a relatively small number of animals were raised on large pieces of land.*

# 9 Agriculture, biotechnology, and the future of food

## Chapter Objectives

**This chapter will help students understand:**

- The challenge of feeding a rapidly growing human population
- The environmental impacts of food production
- Human nutritional needs and challenges
- The "green revolution"
- Pest management methods
- The importance of pollination
- The science behind genetically modified food
- Controversies and debate over genetically modified food
- Approaches for preserving crop diversity
- Feedlot agriculture for livestock and poultry
- Aquaculture
- Organic agriculture

## Lecture Outline

I. Central Case: Possible Transgenic Maize in Oaxaca, Mexico
   A. Corn is a staple grain of the world's food supply, and today Oaxaca, Mexico, is a world center of biodiversity for maize.
   B. In 2001, Mexican scientists found DNA in Oaxacan farmers' maize that seemed to match genes from genetically modified corn.
   C. Two researchers collected samples from wild maize and their lab analyses revealed traces of DNA from genetically engineered corn.
   D. Their findings were published in *Nature,* but the findings were disputed and *Nature* stated that the study should never have been published.
   E. No one yet knows for sure if transgenes have invaded wild Mexican maize.

II. The Race to Feed the World
   A. Agricultural production has, so far, outpaced population increase.
      1. Starting in the 1960s, a number of doomsayers predicted widespread starvation and catastrophic failure of agricultural systems.
      2. Instead, we have achieved dramatic increases in our carrying capacity, in part by increasing our ability to produce food.
   B. Undernourishment, overnutrition, and malnourishment are all common dietary problems.
      1. While some people do not have access to enough food to stay healthy, others are affluent enough to consume far more than is healthy.
         a. Those who are undernourished receive less than 90% of their daily caloric needs.
         b. Those who are overnourished receive too many calories each day.
      2. The quantity of food a person eats is important for health, but the quality of food is important as well.
      3. One-fifth of the world's people live on less than $1 per day, and almost half live on less than $2 per day, according to the World Bank.
   C. Malnutrition causes various diseases.
      1. Kwashiorkor results from a high-starch diet with little protein.
      2. Marasmus is caused by a combination of protein deficiency and lack of calories.
      3. Anemia is caused by an inability to absorb dietary iron.
      4. Hypothyroidism is caused by a lack of dietary iodine and can give rise to goiter, severe mental disability, and lethargy.
   D. The "green revolution" led to dramatic increases in agricultural production.
      1. Farmers in the United States had been dramatically increasing their yields using new methods and technology, and many people saw this as a way to end starvation in developing nations.
      2. The transfer of technology to the developing world began in 1940 when a specially bred wheat species was introduced to Mexico.
   E. The green revolution has caused the environment both benefit and harm.
      1. Developing countries imported the methods of industrialized agriculture such as the use of synthetic fertilizers, chemical pesticides, irrigation, and heavy equipment.
      2. This high-input agriculture was dramatically successful at allowing farmers to harvest more corn, wheat, rice, and soybeans from each hectare of land.
      3. However, the green revolution techniques have had negative consequences for biodiversity and mixed consequences for crop yields.
   F. Per capita grain production has begun to decline.
      1. World grain production per person peaked in the 1980s and has since slowly fallen.
      2. Most environmental scientists attribute these declining crop yields to the declining health of agricultural lands.

III. Pest Management
   A. A pest is any organism that damages crops that are valuable to us, and a weed is any plant that competes with our crops.
   B. Throughout the history of agriculture, pests have taken advantage of our clustering food plants into agricultural fields.
   C. Many thousands of chemical pesticides have been developed and applied.
   D. Pests evolve resistance to pesticides.
   E. Biological control pits one organism against another.
   F. Biological control agents themselves may become pests.
      1. One recent study examined the extent to which some biocontrol agents have missed their targets in Hawaii.
      2. Scientists argue over the relative benefits and risks of biocontrol measures.
   G. Integrated pest management combines biocontrol and chemical methods.

IV. Pollination: "Good" Insects, Unsung Heroes
   A. Pollination is the process by which one plant fertilizes another of its species.
   B. We depend on insects to pollinate many of our crops.
      1. While our staple grain crops are grasses that are wind-pollinated, many of our other crops depend on insects for pollination.
      2. Preserving the natural biodiversity of native pollinators is important.
      3. All insect pollinators are vulnerable to the vast arsenal of insecticides that are applied to crops in modern agriculture.
      4. There are ways that farmers can maintain populations of pollinating insects.

V. Genetic Modification of Food
   A. Genetic modification of organisms depends on recombinant DNA.
      1. Genetic engineering is any process whereby scientists directly manipulate an organism's genetic material in the lab by adding, deleting, or changing segments of DNA.
      2. Recombinant DNA technology was developed in the 1970s by scientists studying the *E. coli* bacterium.
      3. When scientists use recombinant DNA technology to develop new varieties of crops, they often can introduce the recombinant DNA directly into a plant cell and then regenerate an entire plant.
      4. An organism that contains DNA from another species is called a transgenic organism and the genes that have been moved between them are called transgenes.
   B. Genetic engineering is like and unlike traditional agricultural breeding.
      1. In a broad sense, the genetic modification of organisms by humans is an ancient exercise.
      2. However, the new techniques mix genes of different species in the lab, involving *in vitro* experiments with genetic material apart from the organism.

C. Biotechnology is transforming the food and products around us.

D. The debate over genetically modified (GM) foods involves more than science.

   1. Ethical issues have played a large role in the debate over GM foods because the idea of "tinkering" with the food supply seems dangerous or morally wrong.

   2. The perceived lack of control over one's own food has caused concern about the domination of the global food supply by a few large businesses.

   3. Public relations has played a role.

      a. In Canada, Monsanto has been engaged in a high-publicity battle with a third-generation Saskatchewan farmer.

      b. European consumers have expressed widespread unease about possible risks of GM technologies.

      c. Transnational spats between Europe and the United States will surely affect the future direction of agriculture.

VI. Preserving Crop Diversity

A. Preserving the integrity of native variants gives us a bulwark against commercial crop failure.

   1. Because accidental interbreeding can decrease the diversity of local variants, scientists argue that we need to protect areas like Oaxaca.

   2. One example of native cultivars potentially coming to the rescue of a major commercial crop involves potatoes.

   3. Data suggest that many fruit and vegetable crops in the United States have decreased in diversity by 90% in less than a century.

   4. A primary cause of this loss of biodiversity is that market forces have discouraged diversity in the appearance of fruits and vegetables.

B. Seed banks are living museums for seeds.

   1. In seed banks, institutions store seeds from crop varieties, keeping them in cold, dry conditions to encourage long-term viability.

   2. One seed bank, Native Seeds/SEARCH (NS/S) of Tucson, Arizona, shows the many types of biological and cultural efforts that such an organization can pursue.

      a. The NS/S keeps 2,000 seed collections of 99 species of plants used as traditional foods by Native Americans of the Desert Southwest region of Arizona, New Mexico, and northwestern Mexico.

      b. The organization sells food products to members and donates seeds to Native American farmers.

      c. The diet of people of the Desert Southwest shares similarities with that of natives of Oaxaca.

VII. Feedlot Agriculture: Livestock and Poultry

A. Consumption of animal products is growing.

   1. The world population of domesticated animals raised for food increased 180% between 1961 and 2000.

   2. Per capita meat consumption more than doubled between 1950 and 2000.

B. Heavy consumption of animal products has led to feedlot agriculture.
   1. Feedlots are concentrated animal feeding operations in which animals are housed in large buildings where energy-rich food is provided.
   2. Animals that are densely concentrated in feedlots will not contribute to overgrazing and soil degradation.
   3. Waste from feedlots can give off strong odors, and can pollute the air and water.
   4. Greeley, Colorado, is home to North America's largest meatpacking plant and two adjacent feedlots, all owned by ConAgra.
   5. Feedlot impacts can be minimized when properly managed, however.

C. Our food choices are also energy choices.
   1. The closer our food sources are to the sun as a direct source of energy, the more people the planet can support.
   2. People who rely heavily on meat as a source of food energy are far less energy efficient that those who rely primarily on a vegetarian diet.
   3. Today, there are more people eating more meat than ever before.
   4. Although much of the grain fed to animals is not of a quality suitable for human consumption, the resources required to grow it could have been used to grow food for people.

VIII. Aquaculture

A. Raising fish and shellfish on "fish farms" may be the only way to meet the demand for these foods because most fisheries are overharvested.

B. Aquaculture brings a number of benefits.
   1. Aquaculture provides a reliable source of protein for developing countries.
   2. At a large scale, aquaculture helps improve a nation's food security.
   3. Aquaculture reduces fishing pressures on wild stocks.
   4. Aquaculture relies far less on fossil fuels than do fishing vessels, and is very energy efficient.

C. Aquaculture has negative environmental impacts as well.
   1. The dense concentrations of farmed animals can increase the incidence of disease and necessitates the use of antibiotics.
   2. Aquaculture can also produce large amounts of waste.
   3. The escape of farmed animals into the environment can have negative consequences.

D. Shrimp farming illustrates some environmental impacts of aquaculture.
   1. In the wild, each female shrimp releases as many as 100,000 eggs that hatch within 24 hours to become planktonic larvae; the larvae migrate to coastal waters to mature.
   2. Shrimp aquaculture attempts to mimic this process by either using farm-raised larvae or capturing wild larvae with nets.
   3. In many areas, critical wetland and mangrove habitats have been destroyed to build shrimp ponds.

IX. Sustainable Agriculture

A. Sustainable agriculture is farming that does not deplete soils faster than they form and does not reduce the amount of healthy soil, clean water, and genetic diversity.

B. Low-input agriculture is farming that uses smaller amounts of pesticides, fertilizers, growth hormones, water, and fossil-fuel energy than is used in high-input farming.

C. Food growth practices that use no synthetic fertilizers or pesticides are often termed organic agriculture.

D. Organic agriculture is on the increase.

1. In 1990, the U.S. Congress signed the Organic Food Production Act that established national standards for organic products and facilitated the sale of organic food.
2. Long viewed as a small niche market, the market for organic foods is on the rise although it accounts for only 1% of food expenditures.
3. Production is increasing along with demand; although organic agriculture takes up less than 1% of cultivated land worldwide.
4. These trends have been fueled by the desire of many consumers to reduce health risks in their diets and to support improving environmental quality.
5. Government initiatives have also spurred the growth of organic farming.

E. Cuba has embraced organic agriculture.

1. Cuba suffered economic and agricultural upheaval upon the dissolution of the Soviet Union because it lost 75% of its imports.
2. With far less oil available, farmers began growing food closer to cities and even within them.
3. In addition, Cuban farmers are now using oxen and integrated pest management.

F. Organic and sustainable agriculture will likely need to play a large role in our future.

X. Conclusion

A. Many of the agricultural practices discussed have both positive and negative environmental impacts.

B. It is certain that if we are to support nine billion people we must make a shift to more sustainable agriculture.

# Key Terms

*autoconsumos*
anemia
aquaculture
*Bacillus thuringiensis*
biological control
biotechnology
*campesinos particulares*
*empresas estatales*
feedlots
food security
gene banks
genetic engineering

genetically modified (GM) organisms
green revolution
*huertos intensivos*
*huertos populares*
hypothyroidism
integrated pest management
kwashiorkor
low-input agriculture
malnutrition
marasmus
Native Seeds/SEARCH
Oaxaca, Mexico
organic agriculture
overnutrition
pest
pesticides
*Pfisteria*
pollination
precautionary principle
recombinant DNA
seed banks
sustainable agriculture
transgenic
undernourished
weed

# Teaching Tips

1. Show the video segment *The Desert's Perfect Foods* from the Scientific American Frontier online video archive (www.pbs.org/saf/1110/video/watchonline.htm).

   This program illustrates how the occurrence of obesity and diabetes in the Pima Indians of Arizona has greatly increased since the adoption of a contemporary Western diet. It also shows the people's attempts to go back to a traditional diet with foods from the desert.

   Ask students to describe some of the traditional foods that the Pima Indians collect, prepare, and eat from their environment.

2. This chapter describes the use of pesticides in agriculture. By their nature, pesticides may pose harm to humans, pets, and the environment because they are designed to adversely affect and/or kill certain organisms.

   What some people do not realize is that many household products are pesticides. Therefore, it is extremely important to read the label of those products for safe use and disposal. The Consumer Labeling Initiative (CLI) is an effort of the U.S. Environmental Protection Agency (EPA) that aims to "foster pollution prevention, empower consumer choice, and improve consumer understanding of safe use, environmental, and health information on household consumer product labels" using the Read the Label First program (www.epa.gov/opptintr/labeling/campaign.htm).

   To introduce students to pesticide labels, bring some pesticide products from home such as bug sprays, flea collars, and disinfecting cleaners. Ask students to examine the label of the product and identify the major sections required by the EPA.

3. In October 2002, the USDA published labeling standards for organic food that are based on the percentage of organic ingredients in a product:

   - Products labeled **"100 percent organic"** must contain only organically produced ingredients.
   - Products labeled **"organic"** must consist of at least 95 percent organically produced ingredients.

   *Products meeting the requirements for "100 percent organic" and "organic" may display the USDA Organic seal.*

   - Processed products that contain **at least 70 percent organic ingredients** can use the phrase "made with organic ingredients" and list up to three of the organic ingredients or food groups on the principal display panel. The USDA seal cannot be used anywhere on the package.

- Processed products that contain **less than 70 percent organic ingredients** cannot use the term "organic" other than to identify the specific ingredients that are organically produced in the ingredient statement.

*Source: The USDA National Organic Program*

# Additional Resources

## Websites

1. "Agriculture 21 Magazine," Food and Agricultural Organization of the United Nations, www.fao.org/ag

   This e-magazine has articles about agricultural topics from around the world such as biotechnology, new animal diseases, and conservation agriculture.

2. "National Agricultural Library," Agricultural Research Service of the USDA, www.nal.usda.gov

   This online library is a major international source for agriculture and related information.

3. "Animal Feeding Operations," National Pollution Discharge Elimination System, U.S. Environmental Protection Agency, http://cfpub.epa.gov/npdes/home.cfm?program_id=7

   This web page is an overview of animal feeding operations and the regulations of animal waste.

4. "Global Aquaculture Alliance: Feeding the World Through Responsible Aquaculture," www.gaalliance.org

   The Global Aquaculture Alliance is an international association dedicated to promoting best management practices for sustainable aquaculture.

5. "About Pesticides," U.S. Environmental Protection Agency, www.epa.gov pesticides/about/index.htm

   This EPA Web page introduces pesticides and how they are regulated.

## Audiovisual Materials

1. *Farmscaping: Advanced Tactics for Achieving Sustainability,* video produced by San Luis Video Publishing and distributed by The Video Project (www.videoproject.net).

   Farmers and entomological farm advisors are visited who use natural ways to enrich the soil, control insects, and control weeds.

2. *Genetic Time Bomb,* video produced by Oregon Public Broadcasting and distributed by The Video Project (www.videoproject.net).

   This program looks at the historic changes in farming, the importance of maintaining crop diversity, and the work of "seed savers."

3. *My Father's Garden,* video distributed by Bullfrog Films (http://bullfrogfilms.com).

   This documentary examines the use and misuse of technology on American farms. Industrial farms and organic farms are shown and compared.

# *Weighing the Issues:* Suggested Answers

## The Green Revolution and Population

***Facts to consider:*** *The green revolution has allowed us to increase the world food supply. Compared with one or two decades ago, fewer people lack a reliable and sufficient food supply. The fact that the net effect of the green revolution to date has been a reduction in rates of food insecurity, however, does not mean that it will necessarily continue. For instance, the green revolution entailed increased use of fossil fuels, irrigation, fertilizer, and pesticides; such practices may not be sustainable, because they can have negative environmental costs. The green revolution also promoted increases in land under cultivation, and this is certainly not sustainable, as the world's soils suitable for farming are now in decline, in terms of both quality and quantity.*

*The world's population has continued to grow during the green revolution, but its rate of growth has slowed. So, to some extent perhaps the green revolution and the demographic transition have worked together to reduce the likelihood of widespread starvation. Some countries have been working more actively than others to reduce population growth rates, and some countries have had economic, social, and educational developments that tend to reduce birth rates.*

## Early Hurdles for GM Foods

***Facts to consider:*** *The "glitches" in the introduction of GM foods may or may not have been unavoidable, but it might have been possible to reduce them significantly by more careful production development, testing, and communication with the public. For instance, if the "golden rice" was promoted as a solution to avoiding vitamin A deficiency, then perhaps in the societies in which it was promoted, it was reasonable to think that potential consumers would believe that this one product would eliminate risk of this vitamin deficiency. Because this is not the case, consumers might falsely believe that they have protected their families by using "golden rice" when this is not the case. So, perhaps the anti-GM activists have a point in criticizing this food for not being nutritious enough; on the other hand, the pro-GM food promoters could reasonably argue that some reduction in vitamin deficiency now would be preferable to not selling and promoting "golden rice" now, leaving today's children at greater risk until more genetic engineering can produce a more nutritious variety.*

*The "golden rice" problem demonstrates the importance of identifying the goal of product improvement in GM projects and the importance of thorough communication with consumers. The FlavrSavr tomato may provide a lesson in making sure that the product is ready before it is released to the public, and in planning a careful public-relations education campaign that acknowledges and fully responds to potential public concerns. GM developers can benefit from the ice-minus strawberries by doing careful testing of their public-relations material to gauge its effect before actual release. And the Bt corn that led to the death of march butterfly larvae is a lesson in the importance of putting any possible GM development in the context of its entire environmental setting. GM product development, testing, and evaluation should include time and money to look at possible effects on a broader range of other organisms and resources than has always been done in the past. Responses will vary on whether debates about GM foods will eventually subside, but since countries have widely varying laws about GM foods, and many of the GM foods released so far have encountered specific opposition, this issue will certainly remain for many years to come.*

### Are Feedlots Targets for Terrorism?

***Facts to consider:*** *Responses will vary about whether feedlots and related sites are realistic terrorist targets, and whether those threats warrant changes in agricultural practices, but certainly responses should acknowledge that there are many separate locations of this type, at which security varies considerably. Individual responses should include several steps that could increase the safety of animal and farm products. Such actions might include: more funding for inspections at such sites; more security procedures at such sites; more control and inspection of wholesale farm products crossing borders; more inspections for such products being carried by individual travelers at airports and other points of entry; more training of farm and ranch managers and workers about safety and security, and more control of potential pathogens.*

### Do You Want Your Food Labeled?

***Facts to consider:*** *This question requires an individual response. In many other cases, even the FlavrSavr tomatoes themselves, purchasing power has been an effective way for groups to make points that have, in fact, influenced food manufacturers, so GM foods may be another issue on which this proves to be the case.*

## *The Science behind the Stories:* The Scientific Method

### Transgenic Contamination of Native Maize

**Observation:** Mexico has banned the growing of transgenic corn since 1998, but it continues to be grown illegally. Southern Mexico is one of the world's capitals of genetic diversity for corn, and scientists have worried that the cross-pollination of transgenic corn and local varieties could threaten this diversity.

**Hypothesis:** Local corn grown in remote areas of Oaxaca, Mexico, would contain segments of DNA from transgenic corn.

**Experiment:** David Quist and Ignacio Chapela of the University of California, Berkeley, used polymerase chain reaction (PCR) to identify transgenes in local Mexican corn. They also used an experimental technique known as inverse PCR (i-PCR) to identify stretches of DNA adjacent to the transgenes.

**Results:** Based on their findings, Quist and Chapela published a paper in *Nature* arguing that transgenic corn was cross-pollinating with local corn, potentially threatening Mexico's genetic diversity. They also suggested that the transgenes were being randomly reshuffled into the genome, with unknown and potentially disastrous effects. However, other scientists who support genetically modified (GM) foods argued that their conclusions were based on faulty methods. Pro- and anti-GM organizations rallied around the two groups of scientists, and the debate received high-profile press coverage. In April 2002, *Nature* retracted its publication of Quist and Chapela's article, but the debate continues.

### Organic Farming

**Observation:** Organic farming may be better for the surrounding environment, but sometimes produces smaller amounts of crops than farms using synthetic fertilizers and other chemicals.

**Hypothesis:** The differences in yields between organic and conventional farms are noticeable but not significant enough to warrant the avoidance of organic farming, largely because organic farms are better able to sustain high soil quality that produces substantial amounts of food.

**Experiment:** Over more than two decades, Swiss researchers set up and monitored conventional and organic plots, tracking crop yields and soil quality on each.

**Results:** The organic plots produced, on average, about 80% of the yield seen on conventional plots. The organic fields also were found to have higher quality, self-sustaining soil.

## Additional Questions

1. What are the advantages and disadvantages of growing monocultures?

   *Monocultures, large areas grown in the same crop, have both positive and negative aspects. First, monocultures produce large quantities of food. They are easier to manage than a polyculture. However, as the book stated, it is like putting all of your eggs in one basket. It is a smorgasbord for insects, thereby promoting pest populations that can wipe out an entire field. Monocultures do not promote diversity because in most cases only one cultivar of a crop is grown at a time.*

2. This chapter discusses the importance of sustainable agriculture in providing food for future generations. Describe a sustainable farming operation that grows crops and raises livestock.

   *A sustainable farming operation would raise several species of crops at the same time (polyculture). Crop rotation and contour farming would be implemented. Shelterbelts would be planted along the croplands to help stop erosion. No chemical pesticides or fertilizers would be applied. Instead, biological methods of pest control and natural fertilizers such as compost would be used. Livestock would be raised in pastures with no antibiotics or growth hormones added to their feed.*

3. What kinds of pesticides do you use in your home and on your lawn? Do you use the specified amount? Why or why not?

   *Student answers will vary. Flea collars, bug sprays, insect repellents, antimicrobials, and lawn chemicals are all examples of household pesticides. It is unfortunate that most of us do not read and/or follow the directions given on the packaging of such products.*

# 10 Toxicology and environmental health

## Chapter Objectives

**This chapter will help students understand:**

- The study of toxic substances and their effects
- The types, abundances, distribution, and movement of synthetic and natural toxicants in the environment
- How concerns for wildlife translate into concerns for human health
- Epidemiology, case histories involving toxic agents, animal testing, and dose-response analysis
- Factors affecting toxicology
- Types of environmental health hazards
- Risk assessment and risk management
- Philosophical approaches to risk and environmental health
- Policy and regulation in the United States and internationally

## Lecture Outline

I. Central Case: Alligators and Endocrine Disruptors at Lake Apopka, Florida
   A. In 1985, Louis Guillette discovered bizarre reproductive problems in American alligators in Lake Apopka.
   B. He developed the hypothesis that certain chemical contaminants in Lake Apopka were disrupting the endocrine system of alligators during development in the egg.
   C. Guillette and his co-workers found that Lake Apopka alligators had abnormally low hatchling rates starting in the years after a pesticide spill.
   D. Guillette's results showed that atrazine and nitrates act as endocrine disruptors, causing smaller penises and lower testosterone levels in juvenile male alligators.

E. Many scientists suspect that chemical contaminants could be affecting people just as they have alligators.

II. The Growth of Environmental Toxicology

A. The science that examines the effects of poisonous chemicals and other agents on humans and wildlife is called toxicology.

B. Synthetic chemicals are now ubiquitous in our environment.

C. The science of toxicology has grown with concern for health and the environment.

1. Environmental toxicology deals specifically with those toxicants that come from or are discharged into the environment, and includes the study of health effects on humans, other animals, and ecosystems.

2. Among wildlife, Guillette's findings with alligators could be the tip of the iceberg.

3. Atrazine and many other compounds that kill insects and weeds that threaten crops were made possible by advances in chemistry during and following World War II.

D. *Silent Spring* began the public debate over pesticides.

1. Carson was a naturalist, author, and government scientist.

2. Carson's book was a bestseller and generated significant social change in view and actions toward the environment.

III. Toxic Agents in the Environment

A. Toxicants come in many different types.

1. Carcinogens are chemicals that cause cancer.

2. Mutagens are chemicals that cause mutations in the DNA of organisms.

3. Chemicals that cause harm to the unborn are called teratogens.

4. Allergens overactivate the immune system, causing an immune response when one is not necessary.

5. Neurotoxins assault the nervous system.

6. Endocrine disruptors are toxicants that interfere with the endocrine system.

B. The potential for endocrine disruption appears to be widespread.

1. The idea that synthetic chemicals might be altering the hormones of animals was presented in the 1996 book *Our Stolen Future.*

2. One common type of endocrine disruptor involves the feminization of male animals.

3. To date, endocrine effects have been most widely found in nonhuman animals, but scientists attribute the drop in sperm counts among men worldwide to endocrine disruptors.

4. Endocrine disruptors can affect more than just the reproductive system.

C. Endocrine disruption research is ongoing and contentious.

D. Toxicants may become concentrated in surface water or groundwater.

E. Airborne toxicants can move widely through the environment.
F. Some toxicants persist for a long time.
G. Toxicants may accumulate and move up the food chain.
    1. Fat-soluble toxicants like DDT and DDE are absorbed and stored in fatty tissues and may build up in animals in a process called bioaccumulation.
    2. Toxicants that bioaccumulate in the tissues of one organism may then be transferred to other organisms in the food chain in a process called biomagnification.
    3. A modern-day example is that of polar bears in arctic Norway that are suffering from PCB contamination.
H. Not all toxicants are synthetic.
    1. Chemical toxicants also exist naturally in the environment around us and in the foods we eat.
    2. Scientists have actively debated just how much risk is posed by natural toxicants.

IV. Studying Effects of Toxicants
A. Wildlife toxicology utilizes careful observations in the field and the lab.
B. Human toxicology relies on case histories and on epidemiology.
    1. Much knowledge has been gained by studying sickened individuals directly.
    2. Epidemiological studies involve large-scale comparisons among groups of people, usually contrasting a group known to have been exposed to some toxicant and a group that has not.
    3. The advantages of epidemiological studies are their realism and ability to enable relatively accurate predictions about risk.
    4. Manipulative experiments are needed to truly nail down causation.
C. Animals may serve as models for humans.
D. Dose-response analysis is a mainstay of toxicology.
    1. The standard method of testing lab animals in toxicology is called dose-response analysis.
    2. Scientists generally must give lab animals much higher relative doses than humans would ever expect to receive in the environment.
    3. Once a dose-response curve is plotted, scientists can calculate a convenient shorthand gauge of a substance's toxicity: the amount of toxicant it takes to kill half the population of study animals used ($LD_{50}$).
    4. Nonlethal health effects are determined by the level of toxicant at which 50% of the population is affected ($ED_{50}$).
    5. Common sense suggests that the greater the dose, the stronger the response will be; however, sometimes responses occur only above a certain dose.
    6. Sometimes responses decrease with dose.
E. Individuals vary considerably in their response to toxicants.

F. The type of exposure can affect toxicity.
    1. The toxicity of many substances varies according to whether the exposure is in high amounts for short periods of time—acute exposure—or in lower amounts over long periods of time—chronic exposure.
    2. Acute exposure is easier to recognize, but chronic exposure is more common.

G. Mixes may be more than the sum of their parts.
    1. Interactive impacts may arise when toxicants are mixed together, and when these impacts are more than or different from the simple sum of their constituent effects they are called synergistic effects.
    2. For example, with Florida's alligators, several lab experiments have indicated that DDE can either help cause or inhibit sex reversal, depending upon other chemicals with which it interacts.

V. Hazards to Environmental Health
  A. Environmental hazards can be chemical, physical, biological, or socioeconomic.
    1. Physical events such as natural catastrophes are environmental hazards.
    2. Biological hazards such as disease result from ecological interactions between organisms.
    3. Cultural or lifestyle hazards result from the place we live, our socioeconomic status, our occupation, and our behavioral choices.
  B. Some health threats are part of the natural environment.
    1. Electromagnetic radiation is one example.
    2. The Aborigines of the Kakadu area were affected by naturally radioactive uranium, thorium, and radon in their environment.
  C. Disease is a major focus of environmental health.
    1. Infectious disease involves a pathogen that attacks a host.
    2. In order to predict and prevent infectious disease, experts deal with the often-complicated interrelationships between technology, land use, and ecology.
    3. Environmental health workers also study nontransmissible diseases such as malnutrition and asthma.
  D. Environmental health is an issue indoors as well as outdoors.
    1. Environmental health threats indoors include home and occupational hazards such as radon and asbestos.
    2. Another indoor health hazard is lead poisoning.
    3. A recently recognized hazard is a group of chemicals known as polybrominated diphenyl ethers (PBDEs).

VI. Risk Assessment and Risk Management
  A. Risk is expressed in terms of probability.
  B. Our perception of risk may not match reality.
  C. Risk assessment analyzes risk subjectively and quantitatively.
  D. Risk management combines science and other social factors.

VII. Philosophical Approaches to Environmental Health

A. One approach is to assume that substances are harmless until shown to be harmful.

B. The other approach is to assume that substances are harmful until shown to be harmless.

VIII. Policy on Toxicants

A. In the United States, the tracking and regulation of synthetic chemicals is shared among several federal agencies.

B. Pesticides in the United States are registered through the EPA.

1. The registration process involves risk assessment and risk management.

2. Critics say the process allows hazardous chemicals to be approved if they offer great enough economic benefits.

C. The EPA also regulates diverse chemicals under the Toxic Substances Control Act (TSCA).

1. TSCA was the first law to require screening of substances before they entered the marketplace.

2. Many public health and environmental advocates view TSCA as being too weak.

3. Industry's critics say chemical manufacturers should be made to bear the burden of proof for the safety of their products before they market such products.

D. Toxicants are regulated internationally.

1. In 2003, the European Union commissioners proposed legislation that would require chemical manufacturers to test and register 30,000 chemicals already in use and would impose restrictions on 1,500 chemicals already considered hazardous.

2. An international treaty, the Stockholm Convention, aims first to end the use and release of 12 persistent organic pollutants (POPs) called the "dirty dozen."

IX. Conclusion

A. International agreements like the Stockholm Convention represent a hopeful sign that governments will act to protect the world's people, wildlife, and ecosystems from harm by chemical toxicants.

B. A society's philosophical approach to risk management will determine what policy decisions are made.

# Key Terms

acute exposure
allergens
asbestos
atrazine
bioaccumulation
biological hazards
biomagnification
breakdown products
carcinogens
Carson, Rachel
chronic exposure

*continued*

## Key Terms, *continued*

- communicable disease
- DDT
- dose-response analysis
- dose-response curve
- $ED_{50}$
- endocrine disruptors
- environmental hazard
- environmental health
- environmental toxicology
- epidemiological studies
- FIFRA
- global distillation
- hormone mimic
- infectious disease
- innocent-until-proven-guilty approach
- $LD_{50}$
- Lake Apopka
- lifestyle hazards
- mutagens
- natural experiment
- neurotoxins
- *Our Stolen Future*
- PCBs
- persistent organic pollutants
- pesticide drift
- precautionary principle
- risk
- risk assessment
- risk management
- *Silent Spring*
- Stockholm Convention
- synergistic
- thalidomide
- teratogens
- Toxic Substances Control Act (TSCA)
- toxicants
- toxicity
- toxicology
- vector

## Teaching Tips

1. Assign students to read selections from *Our Stolen Future* (Colburn, Dumanoski, and Myers, Dutton Publishing, 1996) and/or *Silent Spring* (Rachel Carson, 1962). There is a website that accompanies *Our Stolen Future* at www.ourstolenfuture.org, which provides links to current research on the effects of endocrine disruptors. The "Online Ethics Center" provides information about Rachel Carson with a summary of the book at http://onlineethics.org/moral/carson/SSsummary.html.
2. Ask students to conduct Internet research for updates on the Lake Apopka alligator issue presented as the central case study in this chapter. Is current research being done? If so, what are the results showing? There is a Frontline video and accompanying website that examined this issue in 1998 called "Frontline: Fooling with Nature" (www.pbs.org/wgbh/pages/frontline/shows/nature/).
3. Certain facilities in the United States are required to report their releases of toxic substances to the state and the EPA. These data are compiled and reported in the Toxic Releases Inventory (TRI) Public Data Release Report. The data are made available to the public via the Internet. Ask students to find information about toxic releases in their neighborhood by accessing the TRI Explorer at www.epa.gov/triexplorer. TRI Explorer is a searchable online database that lets users quickly get information about releases and transfers of toxic chemicals.

## Additional Resources

### Websites

1. "EXTOXNET," a cooperative effort of University of California—Davis, Oregon State University, Michigan State University, Cornell University, and the University of Idaho. http://ace.orst.edu/info/extoxnet/

This website provides information for the nonexpert about pesticides, including Pesticide Information Profiles (PIPs), Toxicology Information Briefs (TIBs), and Toxicology Issues of Concern (TICs).

2. "Indoor Air Quality," U.S. Environmental Protection Agency, www.epa.gov/iaq/

   This website is a source of information about indoor air pollutants, potential effects, and ways to minimize pollutant concentrations.

3. "Report on Carcinogens," 10th Edition, 2002, U.S. Department of Health and Human Services, Public Health Service, National Toxicology Program, http://ehp.niehs.nih.gov/roc/toc10.html

   This report is an informational scientific and public health document that identifies and discusses substances that may pose a carcinogenic hazard to human health.

4. "Toxicology Tutor," National Library of Medicine, National Institute of Health, www.sis.nlm.nih.gov/ToxTutor/Tox1/index.html

   This online tutorial introduces the basics of toxicology written at the introductory college level.

## Audiovisual Materials

1. *Cleaning Up Toxics at Home,* video produced by the League of Women Voters and distributed by The Video Project (www.videoproject.net).

   This video program gives practical advice on how to protect our families from toxic hazards found in our homes.

2. *NOW with Bill Moyers—Kids and Chemicals,* 2002, video distributed by PBS Home Video (www.shop.pbs.org).

   This special edition of NOW features medical experts and health officials researching links between childhood illness and environmental contamination.

3. *Drumbeat for Mother Earth,* 2002, video produced by the Indigenous Environmental Network and Greenpeace and distributed by Bullfrog Films (http://bullfrogfilms.com).

   This video program describes how toxic chemicals are the greatest threat to the survival of indigenous peoples.

# *Weighing the Issues:* Suggested Answers

### Circle of Poison

***Facts to consider:*** *This question requires an individual response but may include a variety of comments. For instance, to keep DDT residue out of foods in the United States, the United States could ban the import of foods that have been sprayed with DDT. The federal government could also increase funding for inspections of agricultural products being imported, to assure that they do not contain banned chemicals or excessive amounts of permitted chemicals. This would reduce the risk of not only DDT but also other harmful substances reaching U.S. consumers. On one hand, perhaps products should not be sold overseas if they are banned domestically; synthetic chemicals can travel great distances in the environment, far from their place* *of application, so exporting such chemicals to one country may mean harmful effects in other countries that did not agree to their use. On the other hand, other countries might have different priorities; they may deem the problem for which they will employ the chemical greater than the effect of the chemical on the human populations, or perhaps even the rest of the ecosystems that might be affected. In any event, if such sales are permitted, all information the United States has about the negative effects of such substances, and how to minimize them, should be disseminated publicly in the countries to which it is sold.*

## Natural and Synthetic Estrogen Mimics

***Facts to consider:*** *There may very well be distinctions between synthetic and natural estrogen-mimicking chemicals. If estrogen-mimicking chemicals are stored in the body longer than plant estrogens (which break down quickly), then they may simply have more time to harm the organism, bioaccumulate, and then biomagnify (if originally consumed by an organism lower on the food chain). Also, because higher rates of hormone disruption have been definitively correlated with higher levels of synthetic endocrine-disrupting hormones, at rates significantly above those that occur naturally, it is likely that synthetic chemicals are more likely to produce such aberrations than natural chemicals.*

*Some may also argue that, because humans evolved in a plant-dominated world, our bodies have "learned" to either ignore or break down these "natural" endocrine disrupters. Our bodies have not encountered synthetic chemicals, however, and these may have stronger or somewhat different interactions with the endocrine system.*

*Some may say that manufacturers could be held responsible for the health effects of their products research; others will say that responsibility extends only to the degree that those products have greater negative effects than comparable natural products. This may suggest that comparative research is needed. Finally, people can choose which plants to eat, and control their intake of phytoestrogens. They, and other organisms around them, cannot choose to avoid some of the encounters with these synthetic products, which may wind up in the water, air, soil, and food.*

## A Nationwide Health Tracking System

***Facts to consider:*** *Opinions may vary about whether the potential benefits of a nationwide health tracking system are worth the estimated cost. Overall, though this system would have a high price tag, it would also reduce some research costs and make research more effective. It could help identify situations appropriate for epidemiological study, reduce some of the data-gathering costs for such work, and make it easier to compare results among related studies. It could also aid in risk assessment, by speeding up the first step, identification of situations in which substance exposure and toxic effects seem related. With sufficient population data such as this registry would provide, risk assessment for a specific toxicant may be able to quantify more accurately and precisely a large population's frequency of contact, likely concentrations encountered, and length of time of likely encounters. The benefits of this system might also include quicker identification of outbreaks of disease and other negative health effects. It might accelerate identification of patterns in such events, leading to faster recognition of possible correlations with potential causes. By finding the cause of such events, public agencies and others could take action to halt exposure or otherwise reduce risk. Early detection of causes could give researchers valuable clues in the development not only of solutions for the negative* *health effects, such as ways to stop additional outbreaks, but even ways of preventing such problems in the future, by banning harmful agents and activities from the environment, removing such agents where they remain, and changing methods of handling agents that can be harmful if misused.*

### The Precautionary Principle

***Facts to consider:*** *Opinions may vary about whether proof of safety should be required and whether manufacturers should bear the burden of this proof. Many may argue that if substances are permitted to go to market without proof of safety, some dangerous chemicals may do great harm before their effects are discovered. Adopting the precautionary principle would certainly reduce the number of chemicals on the market. In the long run, manufacturers might develop new chemicals that have less toxic effects, or consumers may buy more of the chemicals that remain available, reducing or eliminating loss of revenue to manufacturers.*

---

## *The Science behind the Stories:* The Scientific Method

### Bisphenol-A

**Observation:** At a laboratory at Case Western Reserve University in 1998, a scientist who studies reproductive biology in mice noticed a sudden spike in the number of mice whose egg-producing cells showed severe genetic flaws.

**Hypothesis:** A common compound called bisphenol-A (BPA), used to make the plastic cages holding the mice, had leaked from the lab's mice cages and water bottles after the cages had been washed with the wrong soap. The BPA had caused the egg-producing cells to divide incorrectly.

**Experiment:** Another set of cages was washed with the same soap, and the egg-producing cells of mice in those cages were monitored. BPA was also added to the drinking water of a separate group of mice.

**Results:** The egg-producing cells of both groups of BPA-exposed mice showed genetic damage. The problems were severe enough to cause miscarriages and birth defects.

### Pesticides and Child Development in Yaqui

**Observation:** Pesticides appeared to cause long-term damage to the way people, especially small children, grow and develop.

**Hypothesis:** In Mexico's agricultural Yaqui Valley, children who lived in areas of heavy pesticide use would develop more slowly than children who lived in areas with low pesticide use.

**Experiment:** Fifty children—33 from the high-pesticide area and 17 from the low-pesticide area —were measured for coordination, memory, and other skills that measure development.

**Results:** The children from the high-pesticide area performed poorly on the tests compared to the children from the low-pesticide area.

## Additional Questions

1. Compare and contrast the six types of toxicants described in the text: carcinogens, mutagens, teratogens, allergens, neurotoxins, and endocrine disruptors. What is an example of each type?

   *All of these toxicants have been shown to affect human health, but in different ways. Carcinogens are chemicals that cause cancer, mutagens cause mutations in DNA, teratogens cause birth defects, allergens overactivate the immune system, neurotoxins affect the nervous system, and endocrine disruptors interfere with the endocrine system. Examples are shown below:*

   | | |
   |---|---|
   | *Carcinogen* | *Cigarette smoke, DDT* |
   | *Teratogen* | *Thalidomide* |
   | *Allergen* | *Pollen, mold* |
   | *Neurotoxin* | *Mercury* |
   | *Endocrine disruptor* | *Dicofol, atrazine* |

2. According to the text, "endocrine disruption research is ongoing and contentious." Why do you think the hypothesis that certain chemicals affect the endocrine system is controversial?

   *Endocrine disruption research is a new field of study. Some of the chemicals that are suspected as endocrine disruptors are widely used by the plastic industry to make products such as baby bottles and food containers. Allegations that widely used compounds affect human health could have disastrous impacts on society and the economy. Since the endocrine system functions with tiny amounts of chemicals, even small amounts of a contaminant can potentially impact the natural functioning of our endocrine systems.*

3. Assign students to read the online case study "Don't Eat the Fish: Hudson River's Toxic Legacy." This case study examines the impact of dumping PCBs in the Hudson River.

   Why are PCBs a threat to wildlife and human health?

   *PCBs are very stable compounds that are fat soluble. This means that PCBs are stored in animal tissue (bioaccumulation) and passed along the food chain. In the top predators of the food chain, PCB concentrations reach high levels because those consumers eat a large number of contaminated prey organisms. This process is called biomagnification. Humans become exposed to PCBs when they consume the top predators, usually large fish. PCBs are dangerous to both wildlife and humans because they are carcinogens.*

# 11 Atmospheric science and air pollution

## Chapter Objectives

**This chapter will help students understand:**

- The composition, structure, and function of Earth's atmosphere
- Outdoor air pollution
- Indoor air pollution
- Stratospheric ozone depletion
- Acid precipitation
- Solutions to air pollution problems

## Lecture Outline

I. Central Case: The 1952 "Killer Smog" of London
   A. Thick smog first settled over the city on December 5, 1952, when many residents stoked their coal stoves because of unusually cold temperatures.
   B. A wind finally relieved Londoners of the smog on Tuesday, the 9th, but by that time thousands of people had died from lung ailments.
   C. Many similar events have taken place in the United States, Mexico, and Malaysia.
   D. We have overcome much, as declines in air pollution represent some of the biggest successes of environmental policy.
   E. Much remains to be done because there are hundreds of people who die prematurely each year due to vehicle emissions.

II. Atmospheric Science
   A. The atmosphere is a thin layer of gases that surrounds Earth.
   B. The atmosphere's chemical composition has changed over Earth's history.

C. Important atmospheric properties include temperature, pressure, and humidity.
   1. Atmospheric pressure measures the weight per unit area produced by a column of air and decreases with altitude.
   2. Relative humidity is the amount of water vapor a given volume of air holds relative to the maximum amount it could contain, for a given temperature.
   3. The temperature of air varies with location and time and these temperature differences affect air circulation.

D. The atmosphere consists of several layers.
   1. The bottommost layer is the troposphere, where temperature decreases with altitude.
   2. The stratosphere extends from 11 km to 50 km above sea level, with its temperature rising gradually with altitude.
   3. Above the stratosphere lies the mesosphere, which extends from 50 to 90 km above sea level.
   4. From the outer mesosphere, the thermosphere extends upward to an altitude of 500 km, where solar rays produce temperatures over 1,700 degrees Celsius.

E. Solar energy heats the atmosphere, helps create seasons, and causes air to circulate.
   1. Radiation from the sun plays a major role in our atmosphere by driving most of its air movements.
   2. The spatial relationship between Earth and the sun determines the amount of solar radiation that strikes each point of Earth's surface.
   3. Because Earth is tilted on its axis by about 23.5 degrees, the northern and southern hemispheres each face the sun for one-half of the year.
   4. Land and surface waters absorb solar energy, reradiating some heat and causing some water to evaporate.

F. The atmosphere drives weather and climate.
   1. Weather consists of the local physical properties of the troposphere such as temperature, pressure, humidity, cloudiness, and wind.
   2. Climate describes the pattern of atmospheric conditions found across a relatively large geographic region over a long period.

G. Weather is produced by interacting air masses.
   1. The boundary between two air masses that differ in temperature and density is called a front.
   2. Opposing air masses may also differ in atmospheric pressure.
   3. One type of weather event has implications for environmental health.

H. Global climate patterns result from the differential heating of Earth's surface.
   1. Sunlight produces planetwide patterns of convection currents called Hadley cells.
   2. There are three pairs of Hadley cells that account for the major patterns of air circulation and latitudinal distribution of moisture across Earth's surface.

I. Global wind patterns are influenced by Earth's rotation.
   1. As cool air moves to replace rising warm air in a convection current, horizontal air currents are produced, which we know as wind.
   2. The interaction of the convection currents and Earth's rotation produces global wind patterns.
   3. The oceans and their interaction with the atmosphere also affect weather, climate, and the distribution of biomes.

III. Outdoor Air Pollution
   A. Air pollution is material added to the atmosphere that can affect climate and/or harm organisms, including ourselves.
   B. The majority of outdoor air pollution comes from natural sources.
      1. Outdoor air pollution consists of volatile chemicals or particulate matter that readily mix into the troposphere.
      2. Winds sweeping over arid terrain can send huge amounts of dust aloft.
      3. Volcanic eruptions also release large quantities of particulate matter, as well as sulfur dioxide, into the troposphere.
      4. The burning of vegetation pollutes the atmosphere with smoke and soot.
   C. Human activities create various types of outdoor air pollution.
      1. Outdoor air pollution from human activity can originate from stationary or mobile sources.
      2. Once in the air, a pollutant may do harm directly or may induce chemical reactions that produce harmful compounds.
   D. Six pollutants are closely tracked by the EPA.
      1. The EPA gives special attention to several pollutants judged to pose especially great threats to human health and welfare.
      2. Carbon monoxide is a colorless, odorless gas produced primarily by the incomplete combustion of fuels.
      3. Sulfur dioxide is a colorless gas released when coal is burned that contributes to acid rain.
      4. Nitrogen dioxide is a highly reactive, foul-smelling reddish gas that contributes to smog and acid rain.
      5. Tropospheric ozone results from the interaction of sunlight, heat, nitrogen oxides, and volatile organic compounds.
      6. Lead is a metal that enters the atmosphere as a particulate pollutant released by industrial processes and fuel combustion.
      7. Particulate matter is any solid or liquid particle small enough to be carried aloft and may cause damage to respiratory tissues when inhaled.
   E. Volatile organic compounds (VOCs) are ingredients in some other pollutants.
      1. Many governments regulate VOCs, a large group of potentially harmful organic chemicals used in industrial processes such as dry cleaning and manufacturing.
      2. Human activity accounts for about half of U.S. VOC emissions, but many tons of VOCs are released from natural sources each year.

3. VOCs are major contributors to urban smog, and once in the atmosphere can react to produce secondary pollutants like ozone.

F. Various other substances are considered toxic air pollutants.

1. The U.S. Clean Air Act of 1970 identified 188 different toxic air pollutants; most of them, such as benzene and methylene chloride, are VOCs.
2. Toxic air pollutants gain the most attention when large quantities are released accidentally and force people to be evacuated from an area.

G. Industrial smog is produced by burning fossil fuels.

1. This term describes unhealthy mixtures of air pollutants that often form over urban areas.
2. Industrial smog is far less common today than it was 50–100 years ago.
3. Although coal burning supplies the chemical ingredients for industrial smog, the weather also plays a role.

H. Photochemical smog is produced by a complex series of atmospheric reactions.

1. Photochemical smog is formed through light-driven reactions of primary pollutants and normal atmospheric compounds that produce a mix of over 100 different chemicals.
2. Photochemical smog afflicts many major cities, especially those with topography and weather conditions that promote it.

I. Stratospheric ozone depletion is caused by synthetic chemicals.

1. Ozone molecules are highly effective at absorbing incoming ultraviolet radiation from the sun, thus protecting life on Earth's surface.
2. Starting in the 1960s, atmospheric scientists began wondering why their measurements of ozone were lower than theoretical models predicted.
3. In 1974, Sherwood Rowland and Mario Molina broke the news that chlorofluorocarbons (CFCs) depleted stratospheric ozone by splitting ozone molecules and creating $O_2$ molecules from them.
4. In 1985, scientists from the British Antarctic Survey announced that stratospheric ozone levels over Antarctica had declined 40–60% in the previous decade, leaving behind a thinned ozone concentration that was soon dubbed the "ozone hole."

J. Ozone depletion was halted by the Montreal Protocol.

1. The world community came together in 1987 to design the Montreal Protocol, which has been signed by 180 nations.
2. Today, the production and use of ozone-depleting compounds has fallen 95% since the late 1980s.
3. Environmental scientists have attributed the success of the Montreal Protocol to two factors.
    a. Policymakers engaged industry in helping to solve the problem.
    b. The process after 1987 successfully followed an adaptive management approach, which allows for altering strategies midstream in response to new scientific data, technological advances, or economic figures.

K. Acid precipitation represents another transboundary pollution problem.
   1. Acid precipitation forms as a secondary pollutant in the atmosphere through the reactions of primary pollutants with water, oxygen, and oxidants.
   2. Although acid precipitation does not feel acidic to the touch, its low pH values have wide-ranging, cumulative, and detrimental effects on ecosystems and on our built environment.
   3. Because the pollutants leading to acid rain may travel long distances, their effects can be felt far from their point sources.

L. Acid precipitation has not been reduced as markedly as scientists had hoped.
   1. Reducing acid rain involves reducing amounts of the primary pollutants that contribute to it, and new technology has helped.
   2. A recent report by scientists working at New Hampshire's Hubbard Brook research forest has disputed the notion that the acid precipitation problem is being solved.

IV. Indoor Air Pollution

A. Indoor spaces generally have higher concentrations of pollutants than outdoor spaces.

B. If the scale of impact from indoor air pollution seems surprising, consider first that the average U.S. citizen spends at least 90% of his or her time indoors.

C. Some attempts to be environmentally prudent during the "energy crisis" of 1973–1974 resulted in worsening the environmental problem of indoor air pollution in developed countries.

D. Indoor air pollution in the developing world arises from fuelwood burning.
   1. A recent Australian report showed that nine out of ten of the 2.8 million annual deaths from indoor air pollution occur in the developing world.
   2. Many people who tend indoor fires are simply not aware of the health risks.

E. Recognizing indoor air pollution as a problem is still novel.
   1. The 1970 U.S. Clean Air Act did not even mention indoor air; rather, indoor spaces were assumed safe havens from outdoor pollution.
   2. Today we know far less about indoor air pollution than we do about outdoor air pollution.
   3. Scientists know enough, however, to have identified the most deadly indoor threats.

F. Tobacco smoke and radon are the most deadly indoor pollutants in the developed world.
   1. Secondhand smoke has been found to cause many of the same problems as directly inhaled cigarette smoke.
   2. Women living with a spouse who smokes have a 24% excess chance of developing lung cancer.
   3. After cigarette smoke, radon gas is the second-leading cause of lung cancer for Americans.

G. A great diversity of VOCs pollute indoor air.
    1. Carbon monoxide commonly occurs indoors.
    2. The most diverse and abundant indoor air pollutants are VOCs that exist in plastics, oils, perfumes, paints, adhesives, and pesticides.
    3. Products that emit VOCs surround us, but fortunately, VOCs are emitted in very small amounts.
    4. The implications for human health of chronic exposure to VOCs are far from clear.
    5. A 1990 EPA study showed that 90% of people's pesticide exposure came from indoor sources.

H. Living organisms can pollute indoor spaces.
    1. Dust mites, animal dander, fungi, mold, and bacteria can all cause health problems.
    2. Microbes that induce allergic responses are thought to be one frequent cause of "building-related illness."

I. We can reduce indoor air pollution.
    1. The use of low-toxicity materials and adequate ventilation are the key to alleviating indoor air pollution in almost any situation.
    2. Remedies for fuelwood pollution in the developing world include drying wood before burning, shifting to less-polluting fuels, and replacing inefficient fires with cleaner burning stoves.

V. Conclusion

A. Indoor air pollution is a potentially serious health threat, but one that we can do a great deal to minimize for ourselves and our families.

B. Outdoor air pollution has been addressed more effectively by government legislation and regulation.

C. Much room for improvement remains, particularly on the issues of acid precipitation and photochemical smog.

## Key Terms

acid precipitation
air pollution
atmospheric pressure
carbon monoxide
chlorofluorocarbons (CFCs)
Clean Air Act
climate
cold front
convection current
Coriolis effect
criteria pollutants
doldrums
Ferrel cells
front
Hadley cells
high-pressure system
indoor air pollution
industrial smog
lead
low-pressure system
mesosphere
Montreal Protocol
nitrogen dioxide
nonpoint source
ozone hole
ozone layer
particulate matter
peroxyacyl nitrates
photochemical smog
point source
polar cells
primary pollutants
radon
relative humidity
secondary pollutants
smog
stratosphere
stratospheric ozone

sulfur dioxide
thermal inversion
thermosphere
tobacco smoke
trade winds
tropopause
troposphere
tropospheric ozone
volatile organic compounds
warm front
weather
westerlies

# Teaching Tips

1. Use the AirData website made available by the U.S. Environmental Protection Agency at www.epa.gov/air/data/index.html. This website provides air pollution data for the entire United States and produces reports and maps using criteria that you specify. Air data are acquired from three EPA databases: Air Quality System (AQS), National Emission Trends (NET), and National Toxics Inventory (NTI).

   Present students with air data from your geographic area or ask them to retrieve it themselves. The table below was generated from the NTI database, and shows the top five facilities emitting acetylaldehyde in Tennessee.

   | Facility Name | Pollutant Emissions | % of Total Emissions |
   |---|---|---|
   | Tennessee-Eastman | 285,100 | 28.30 |
   | Dupont | 282,260 | 28.02 |
   | Tennessee Eastman Co. | 178,000 | 17.67 |
   | A. E. Staley Manufacturing Company | 110,030 | 10.92 |
   | Fleischmann's Yeast Inc. | 54,365 | 5.40 |

   Courtesy of U.S. EPA (www.epa.gov/air/data/ntiemis.html?st~TN~Tennessee)

2. Assign students to conduct an Internet search on the Union Carbide gas release in Bhopal, India. The University of Michigan has published an online case study about Bhopal at www.umich.edu/~snre492/lopatin.html.

   Ask students the following questions about the incident:

   - What lawsuits have been filed as a result of this accident? What were the outcomes?
   - What health effects have been documented among the people exposed to the gas release?
   - What do you think can be done to prevent similar catastrophes in the future?

3. Assign students to go to "Smog City" at www.smogcity.com, an interactive air pollution simulator developed by the Sacramento Metropolitan Air Quality Management District. The simulator is based on a simple model in which weather, population, and emissions affect the formation of ground-level ozone. Smog City allows the user to adjust these factors to see the effect on ozone formation.

   Ask students the following questions:

   - Does one factor seem to affect smog formation more than others?
   - How do weather variables affect smog formation?
   - How does population affect smog formation?
   - What can you do as an individual to reduce smog?

# Additional Resources

## Websites

1. "AIRNow," U.S. Environmental Protection Agency, www.epa.gov/airnow/index.html

   This EPA Web page provides air quality forecasts and reports to help people "protect themselves from ground-level ozone and its associated respiratory health effects during the warmer months of the year."

2. "Air Quality Where You Live," U.S. Environmental Protection Agency, www.epa.gov/air/urbanair/ginfo.html

   This Web page has general information about air quality and regulation, including criteria on air pollutants, air quality trends, and toxic air pollution.

3. "Encyclopedia of the Atmospheric Environment," ARIC, Manchester Metropolitan University, www.doc.mmu.ac.uk/aric/eae/index.html

   This website is published by the Atmosphere, Climate, and Environment Information Programme supported by the United Kingdom Department for Environment, Food, and Rural Affairs. It is a source of information on air quality, ozone depletion, acid rain, and global warming.

4. "The Great Smog of 1952," the Met Office Education Service, United Kingdom, www.met-office.gov.uk/education/historic/smog.html

   This Web page has a detailed summary of the Great Smog of 1952 in London.

5. The Hubbard Brook Ecosystem Study," Hubbard Brook Research Station, www.hubbardbrook.org

   The home page of the Hubbard Brook Ecosystem Study (HBES) provides access to its three websites: Research and Data, Hubbard Brook Research Foundation, and Educational Resources.

## Audiovisual Materials

1. *Ozone: Cancer of the Sky,* produced by Television New Zealand Natural History and distributed by The Video Project (www.videoproject.net).

   This video presents general information about the ozone layer and its current status. The program follows scientists as they convene in Antarctica to study the ozone hole that forms there each spring.

2. *Ozone: Double Trouble,* U.S. Environmental Protection Agency, Office of Air Quality and Planning Standards (www.epa.gov/oar/oaqps/ozvideo/).

   This downloadable 16-minute film discusses the two ozone problems: ground-level ozone in smog and ozone depletion in the stratosphere.

3. *What's Up with the Weather?,* a NOVA video distributed by WBGH (http://main.wbgh.org/wbgh/shop/index.html).

   This program examines today's extreme weather patterns such as flooding, hurricanes, and high temperatures, and addresses the question: Are these natural phenomena or global warming?

4. *The Air We Breathe,* 1997, produced by Hamm Productions and the National Film Board of Canada, distributed by Bullfrog Films (www.bullfrogfilms.com).

   This program shows the connection between suburban sprawl, air pollution, and increases in asthma and other respiratory diseases.

5. *What's In Our Air,* 1999, produced and distributed by Rainbow Video and Film Productions (www.rainbowvideoandfilm.com).

   This 25-minute video documents community members in Oregon, Washington, and California neighborhoods who use low-tech bucket monitors to sample the air for 43 hazardous air pollutants.

## *Weighing the Issues:* Suggested Answers

### Ozone as a Rural Pollutant?

***Facts to consider:*** *We have traditionally considered rural areas "safe havens" from urban pollution. The revelation of downwind effects such as this should perhaps spur not only a reconsidering of this perception but a growing realization that actions in one environment sometimes have negative environmental effects elsewhere. This suggests that better understanding and considering atmospheric conditions and the precursors of tropospheric ozone would help determine acceptable levels and find ways to maintain air quality within those boundaries. Additionally, air quality standards have been set in terms of human health; that this ozone also damages other organisms such as these trees suggests that future standards could also take such effects into account.*

*Opinions will vary about the possible implications of the reduced tree growth resulting from tropospheric ozone, but such ozone is known to damage living tissues; maybe it also retards the growth of other species, not only plants but also animals, even humans, though perhaps at rates too low to have been noticed or correlated. Perhaps other factors must also be present in order for these results to occur. Also, because growth is related to cell replication, perhaps other biotic processes involving cell replication are also more likely to be affected by tropospheric ozone.*

### Need for International Cooperation to Solve Global Problems

***Facts to consider:*** *If history is a guide, substantive action on issues such as organic pollutants, climate change, and biodiversity loss will require definitive proof of direct harm to human health. The human health consequences of the Antarctic ozone hole were so straightforward, governments and industry had no choice but to act accordingly. Negative environmental effects, and even more specifically negative human health effects, are not as straightforward in many other situations. As well, a relatively easy fix is more palatable to politicians than a complex set of lifestyle changes. CFCs were one culprit and alternative chemicals and processes could replace them. Organic pollutants are plentiful, and global climate change and biodiversity crises have multiple causes, so developing sufficient viable alternatives to the significant causal agents would pose enormously greater difficulty.*

*Fortunately, there have been some other large-scale environmental success stories. Most lead sources have been eliminated in the United States, such as lead-based paints and leaded gasoline. Urban air quality has improved significantly in the United States and Britain due to the results of clean-air legislation. Rates of exposure to indoor pollution from tobacco smoke have dropped greatly in the United States and some other nations. Growing awareness of the potential for homes to harbor naturally emitted radon has spurred solutions to that, so that over a million homes with radon-resistant features have been built since 1990. In the future, using low-toxicity building materials and good ventilation hold promise of reducing indoor air pollution. Indoor air pollution in developing countries can also be reduced in the near term, by drying wood before burning, and using less-polluting fuels and cleaner burning, more efficient stoves.*

### How Safe Is Your Indoor Environment?

***Facts to consider:*** *This question requires an individual response, but responses should consider a wide range of potential sources of air pollution, as designated by the EPA, including: asbestos; biological pollutants such as mold, mildew, or pollen; carbon monoxide from gas appliances or wood stoves; formaldehyde used in building materials; organic chemicals used in cleaning products, dry cleaning, or hobbies; lead from old paint; nitrogen dioxide from gas or kerosene heaters; pesticides to control indoor insects or microorganisms; naturally occurring radon gas; combustion products from fireplaces or wood stoves; and secondhand smoke.*

*Generally applicable ways to make indoor spaces safer from pollution include: limiting use of plastics and treated wood where possible, increasing ventilation, having the space tested for radon gas, and storing cleansers and other household products in a garage or shed.*

## *The Science behind the Stories:* The Scientific Method

### How Scientists Identified CFCs as the Main Cause of Ozone Depletion

**Observation:** By the 1970s, industrial chemicals known as chlorofluorocarbons (CFCs) were being produced in vast quantities. These chemicals had the potential to deplete the stratospheric ozone layer, which shields Earth from ultraviolet radiation.

**Hypothesis:** CFCs and other chemicals were causing significant decreases in global stratospheric ozone.

**Experiment:** Data from a number of different sources were analyzed. The sources included laboratory experiments on the rates of chemical reactions, long-term ozone measurements taken at ground stations, and short-term measurements of ozone, chlorine, and other chemicals collected by high-altitude balloons and aircraft.

**Results:** By the mid-1980s, scientists had conclusive evidence that global ozone levels were declining, particularly over Antarctica, and that those declines were due primarily to CFCs and other human-made chemicals.

## Additional Questions

1. Describe the troposphere and stratosphere. How does the concentration and function of ozone vary between the two layers? What is the status of the ozone layer? What is the status of ground-level ozone?

   *The troposphere is the layer of the atmosphere closest to Earth's surface where temperature declines with altitude. The stratosphere is the layer above the troposphere and here temperature increases with altitude. Ground-level ozone is formed close to the Earth's surface in a photochemical reaction. VOCs and nitrogen oxides released in vehicle exhaust react with sunlight and heat to form ozone and other compounds. Ground-level ozone is harmful to living organisms. Stratospheric ozone, on the other hand, is very beneficial in that it absorbs UV radiation from the sun. Here, ozone forms the "ozone layer" in which concentrations are about 12 parts per million. Because ozone-depleting compounds have been phased out in most parts of the world, the ozone layer is now recovering. Tropospheric ozone is still a major health issue despite data that show there has been a slight decline in recent years.*

2. Describe why the health effects from indoor air pollution outweigh those from outdoor air pollution. What can be done to reduce the concentration of indoor air pollution?

   *Indoor spaces generally have higher concentrations of pollutants than outdoor spaces. Because the average American spends at least 90% of his or her time indoors, then it is not surprising that indoor air pollution has a greater impact on our health. Although indoor air pollution is most serious in the developing world, there are threats to human health in the United States such as from cigarette smoke, radon, VOCs, and carbon monoxide. The use of low-toxicity building materials and adequate ventilation are two ways to reduce the concentration of indoor air pollution. Limiting the use of plastics, treated wood, pesticides, and cleaning fluids is also helpful.*

3. Assign students to read the online case study "Lake Acidification in the Adirondacks." Why are lakes in the Adirondacks especially sensitive to acid rain? What is the source of the pollution that forms acid rain in the Adirondacks? What can be done to reduce the acid rain that affects these lakes?

   *The lakes in the Adirondacks have little buffering capacity because of the thin soils that surround them. Nitrogen oxides and sulfur oxides that form acid rain are released primarily from coal-burning facilities in the Midwest. In order to address this acid rain issue, the sources of the pollution must be targeted. President Bush has introduced a plan called the "Clear Skies Initiative" that would implement a cap and trade program for coal-burning facilities, thereby reducing overall sulfur and nitrogen oxide emissions.*

# 12 Global climate change

## Chapter Objectives

**This chapter will help students understand:**

- Earth's climate
- The variety of factors influencing global climate
- Potential human influences on the atmosphere and global climate
- Effects of climate change
- Potential future impacts of climate change
- The general methods of modern climate researchers
- The scientific, political, and economic debates concerning global climate change
- Potential responses to global climate change

## Lecture Outline

I. Central Case: Rising Temperatures and Seas May Take the Maldives Under

A. A nation consisting of a chain of low-lying islands, or atolls, in the Indian Ocean, the Maldives is known for its spectacular equatorial setting, colorful coral reefs, and sun-drenched beaches.

B. Nearly 80% of the Maldives' land area of 300 $km^2$ lies less than 1 m above sea level.

C. The island's government has already evacuated residents from four of the lowest lying islands over the past five years.

D. Maldives islanders are not alone in their worries.

E. Despite the concerns of people from the Maldives to New Orleans, some people say that global warming is a good thing.

F. In this chapter, we will examine Earth's climate and the disagreements about its future.

II. Earth's Hospitable Climate

A. Weather describes an area's short-term atmospheric conditions (over hours and days), while climate is an area's long-term pattern of atmospheric conditions.

B. Although most scientists agree that human activities, including fossil-fuel combustion, farming, and deforestation, are altering Earth's atmosphere and climate, it would be inaccurate to think of global climate change as something new or as something caused entirely by people.

C. Three factors exert more influence on Earth's climate than all others combined: the sun, the atmosphere, and the oceans.

D. The sun and the atmosphere keep Earth warm.

E. "Greenhouse gases" warm the lower atmosphere.

1. The shape and composition of some molecules enable them to absorb radiation of specific wavelengths and make them transparent to radiation of other wavelengths.

2. After Earth's surface absorbs radiation, its temperature increases and it emits radiation in the infrared portion of the spectrum.

3. When these gases absorb heat, the atmosphere (specifically the troposphere) warms and then radiates heat back to Earth's surface.

4. The term *greenhouse effect* is used widely these days, but scientists recognize that it is actually a bit of a misnomer.

5. Global warming describes changes in Earth's climate, such as temperature, precipitation, and storm intensity.

6. Global warming potential is expressed in relation to carbon dioxide, which is assigned a relative global warming potential of 1.

F. Carbon dioxide is the primary greenhouse gas.

1. Carbon dioxide concentrations have increased 33% in the last 22 years, bringing it to its highest level in 400,000 years.

2. In the last 200 years, humans have been burning increasing amounts of fossil fuels in their homes, factories, and automobiles.

G. Other greenhouse gases add to warming.

a. We release methane into the atmosphere by tapping into fossil-fuel deposits, raising large herds of cattle, growing rice, and disposing of organic matter in landfills.

b. Nitrous oxide is a by-product of feedlots, chemical manufacturing plants, auto emissions, and modern agricultural practices.

c. Ozone concentrations in the troposphere have increased by 36% since 1750.

d. Chlorofluorocarbons add greatly to the heat-absorbing ability of the atmosphere.

e. Water vapor is the most abundant greenhouse gas, and its concentration increases as tropospheric temperatures rise.

H. Aerosols and other elements may exert a cooling effect on the lower atmosphere.

I. Feedback loops complicate climate systems.

J. The atmosphere is not the only factor that influences climate.
   1. Milankovitch cycles result in slight changes in the relative amount of solar radiation reaching Earth's surface at difference latitudes.
   2. Oceanic circulation, such as the North Atlantic Deep Water, also shapes climate.

III. Methods of Studying Climate Change
   A. Geologic records tell us about the past.
   B. Direct atmospheric sampling tells us about the present.
      1. Charles Keeling of the Scripps Institution of Oceanography has documented trends in atmospheric carbon dioxide concentrations since 1958.
      2. Keeling's data show that atmospheric carbon dioxide concentrations have increased from around 315 ppm to 373 ppm since 1958.
   C. Coupled general circulation models (CGMCs) help us understand climate change.
      1. CGCMs are computer programs that combine what is known about weather patterns, atmospheric circulation, atmosphere–ocean interactions, and feedback mechanisms to simulate climate change.
      2. As of 2001, there were 14 research labs around the world operating CGCMs.
      3. Tests suggest that today's computerized models provide a good approximation of the relative effects of natural and anthropogenic influences on global climate.

IV. Climate Change Estimates and Predictions
   A. The most thoroughly reviewed and widely accepted collection of scientific information concerning global climate change is a series of reports issued by the Intergovernmental Panel on Climate Change (IPCC).
   B. The IPCC reports summarize evidence of recent changes in global climate.
   C. In addition to the data on increases in atmospheric concentrations of greenhouse gases that we discussed earlier, the 2001 IPCC report presented a number of findings on how climate change has already influenced the weather, Earth's physical characteristics and processes, the habits of organisms, and our economies.
   D. Sea level rise is one of many impacts that climate change will likely bring about.
      1. In 1987, unusually high waves struck the Maldives and triggered a campaign to build a large seawall around Male, the nation's capital city.
      2. The Maldives is not the only nation that will suffer from sea level rise.
      3. Houston, Texas; New Orleans, Louisiana; and Charleston, South Carolina are among the major cities that are most likely to be affected by rising sea level.
   E. The IPCC and other groups project future impacts of climate change.
      1. In 2000, the U.S. Global Change Research Program issued a report entitled "Climate Change Impacts on the United States: The Potential Consequences of Climate Variability and Change."

2. Climate change will affect agriculture and forestry.
3. Freshwater ecosystems will also face challenges.
4. Marine ecosystems would also be affected.
5. Human health could suffer or, perhaps, benefit.

V. The Debate Concerning Global Climate Change

A. Nearly all environmental scientists agree that Earth's atmosphere and climate are changing, but disagree on some of the details.

B. Global climate change debates occur in the economic and political arenas as well.

VI. Technological and Political Methods of Emissions Reduction

A. Today most scientists are confident that anthropogenic greenhouse gas emissions are changing the composition of Earth's atmosphere.

B. Since 1990 the generation of electricity, largely through coal burning, has produced the largest portion (34%) of U.S. emissions.

C. Electricity conservation and efficiency is a possible solution.

1. The EPA promotes energy conservation through its Energy Star program.
2. You can also take a decidedly low-tech approach to energy conservation.

D. Renewable sources of electricity are another means of reducing greenhouse gas emissions.

E. Population reduction is a third way to reduce electricity consumption.

F. Transportation is the second largest source of greenhouse gases in the United States.

1. In 1970, cars in the United States traveled 1.6 trillion km and this number doubled in the 1990s.
2. There are substitutes for the inefficient automobile.
   a. Close to 86% of the fuel you use does something other than move your car down the road.
   b. Because of the high costs of automobile ownership, and concerns regarding traffic and environmental impacts, many people are making choices that reduce their reliance on cars.
   c. In an interesting intersection of transportation policy and economics, it is becoming increasingly common for entities such as universities to fund transit in exchange for unlimited free use by students.

G. Beyond technology and personal choice, international climate treaties play a role.

1. In 1992, the United Nations convened the United Nations Conference on Environment and Development Earth Summit in Rio de Janeiro.
2. The Kyoto Protocol was an outgrowth of the Framework Convention on Climate Change, and the United States has resisted it.
3. Some feel climate change demands the precautionary principle.

VII. Conclusion
   A. Many factors influence global climate, and human activities can shape atmospheric composition and global climate.
   B. Scientists and policymakers are beginning to understand anthropogenic climate change and its environmental impacts more fully.
   C. Global climate change and sea level rise will definitely affect places like the Maldives and the Florida coast.

## Key Terms

aerosols
atolls
biodiesel
chlorofluorocarbons
climate
compressed natural gas
convective loop
coupled global circulation models
Earth Summit
El Niño
Energy Star program
Framework Convention on Climate Change
Fourier, Jean-Baptiste-Joseph
Global Change Research Program
global climate change
global warming
global warming potential
greenhouse effect
greenhouse gases
halocarbon gases
heat index
hybrid gasoline-electric vehicles
ice cores
Intergovernmental Panel on Climate Change
Keeling, Charles
Kyoto Protocol
La Niña
Maldives
methane
Milankovitch cycles
Milankovitch, Milutin
nitrous oxide
North Atlantic Deep Water
ozone
parts per million (ppm)
proxy indicators
saltwater intrusion
storm surges
Tropical Atmosphere Ocean Project
water vapor
weather
working reference gas

## Teaching Tips

1. Assign students to conduct Internet research on the Maldives. Ask them to address the following questions: What is the climate and geography of the Maldives? How do atolls form? What types of terrestrial and aquatic ecosystems are present? What is the primary source of freshwater?
2. Provide students with detailed information about paleoclimate proxy data.
   a. The National Oceanic and Atmospheric Administration (NOAA) Paleoclimatology Program Website provides detailed information about paleoclimate proxy data. There are online slide sets with photographs of field research, important data sets, and descriptive diagrams appropriate for college-level courses. Go to www.ngdc.noaa.gov/paleo/slides.html to view the slides online. You can download digital slides free or order 35-mm copies. The available slide sets for this topic are the Ice Ages, Coral Paleoclimatology, Polar Ice Cores, Packrat Middens, Tree Rings, and Low Latitude Ice Cores.

b. In January 1998, a team of scientists from Russia, the United States, and France retrieved a deep ice core near the Russian Vostok station in east Antarctica. Preliminary data show that the ice core extends through four climate cycles, with the oldest ice more than 400,000 years old.

   Ask students to graph the carbon dioxide data from the ice core. The report was published in *Nature* (Petit et al., *Nature* v.399 (6735), pp. 429–436, 1999). The data can be downloaded from www.ngdc.noaa.gov/paleo/icecore/antarctica/vostok/vostok.html.

   Ask students the following questions:

   - Are climate cycles evident?
   - How did the temperature change with the carbon dioxide cycles?
   - Is the carbon dioxide concentration today higher or lower than those recorded in the ice core?

3. There are products in 35 categories eligible for the Energy Star designation. In general, these products use less energy, cost less money to operate, and protect the environment. Ask students to choose a product that they will likely buy over the next year. Assign them to search the Energy Star Website for the criteria required for that product, and ask them to share that information with the rest of the class (www.energystar.gov).
4. Compare the greenhouse effect of Earth to that of Mars and Venus. Venus has an intense greenhouse effect with an average surface temperature of 477°C, whereas Mars has a weak effect with an average surface temperature of −47°C. Earth is in the middle of the two with a moderate greenhouse effect and an average global temperature of 15°C.

# Additional Resources

## Websites

1. "EPA's Global Warming Site," http://yosemite.epa.gov/OAR/globalwarming.nsf

   This website has information about our climate, greenhouse emissions, potential impacts, actions, and links to other resources.
2. "Global Warming," Earth Observatory, NASA, http://earthobservatory.nasa.gov/Library/GlobalWarming/warming.html

   This NASA website gives basic information about global warming, summarizes the skeptics' point of view, and describes NASA's global climate change projects.
3. "Hybrid Electric Vehicle Program (HEV)," Department of Energy (DOE), www.ott.doe.gov/hev/what.html

   This DOE website provides a description of HEVs, discusses the advantages of using hybrid electric vehicles and the types of HEVs, and has links to HEV fact sheets.
4. "Intergovernmental Panel on Climate Change," The United Nations Environment Programme (UNEP) and World Metrological Organization (WMO), www.ipcc.ch

   The official IPCC web site has information about IPCC and its activities, publications, press releases, and official documents.

## Audiovisual Materials

1. *Greenhouse Crisis,* video produced by the Union of Concerned Scientists and distributed by The Video Project (www.videoproject.net).

   Based on research by the Union of Concerned Scientists, this video shows how energy consumption affects the greenhouse effect and may cause global warming.

2. *Rising Waters: Global Warming and the Fate of the Pacific Islands,* 2000, video produced by the Independent Television Service and Pacific Islanders in Communications, distributed by Bullfrog Films (www.bullfrogfilms.com).

   This video examines the problem of global climate change by showcasing the personal stories of Pacific Islanders.

3. *Turning Down the Heat,* 1999, video produced by Jim Hamm Productions and distributed by Bullfrog Films (www.bullfrogfilms.com).

   This program profiles innovative alternative energy projects such as solar energy in Holland and biogas in Denmark and Vietnam.

## *Weighing the Issues:* Suggested Answers

### Greenhouse Gases: Sources and Lifetimes

***Facts to consider:*** *Both methane and nitrous oxide are greenhouse gases, effective at trapping heat. In fact, methane has 23 times the heat-trapping potential of carbon dioxide, the most prevalent greenhouse gas, and nitrous oxide has 296 times more heat-trapping potential. So if emissions of these substances increase, warming trends could intensify.*

*Guesses will vary, but the source of nitrous oxide that has actually increased most in the past decade is fertilizers that contain nitrogen.*

### Agriculture in a Warmer World

***Facts to consider:*** *Analysts are divided about whether the shift in agricultural locations due to global climate change will, overall, raise or lower global agricultural output. To the extent that countries in higher latitudes tend to be more developed nations, and, therefore, more equipped to operate agriculture at higher rates of productivity, more food might be produced. On the other hand, in wealthier countries, much arable land may have already been developed for urban areas and so forth, so some potential may not be able to be realized.*

*If agriculture shifts northward, poorer nations may become even weaker economically; their impoverished governments, unable to provide even basic needs, may become overwhelmed, heightening the possibility of political unrest and war. More fighting may take place over essential resources such as freshwater and useful agricultural land. The gap between rich and poor nations may grow even wider. It is also possible that, at least to some extent, such nations could make positive adaptations, such as increasing use of water-conserving irrigation techniques and cultivating crops that need less water. If southern areas are less able to provide food, then northern areas so far preserved may become more likely to be converted to agricultural use. Lands now fairly wild may become farms. Such changes will affect all the organisms within such ecosystems. Land use conflicts may also rise in the north between development and agriculture.*

### Environmental Refugees

***Facts to consider:*** *For those who hold that climate change is uncertain, the refugee flow may not make any difference; they might respond that the sea rise is only temporary and that these people may soon be able to return to Tuvalu. They might also say that perhaps these "refugees" actually wanted to move to a more prosperous society, such as that in New Zealand. On the other hand, they might acknowledge that, even though 9 cm does not seem like much to most people, it appears that sea level changes have been moving in a consistently upward direction for a decade, somewhat increasing the likelihood that global climate change is a real phenomenon. A Tuvalu resident would tend to look at this issue in human, social, and cultural-survival terms; he or she might say that it is not fair that the actions of others are having such a devastating effect on island residents. A U.S. oil industry executive, though sympathetic, might argue that far fewer people have been disturbed than would be the case if fossil-fuel use were curtailed to the point required in order to reverse global warming. The economic and social dislocations caused by this shift could be much more massive than what has occurred in these island cultures.*

*To save their way of life, people in Tuvalu or the Maldives might try to build seawalls, buildings on stilts, and other structures to reduce the damage caused by storm surges; develop tourist-oriented markets and skills to help expose people from developed countries to the value of their island nation and to the threats it faces, so that those people might take action on behalf of these islands; take steps to encourage the coral reefs, in order to compensate for the damage being done by storm surges; ally together to gain political clout.*

### The Precautionary Principle

***Facts to consider:*** *Most of this question will require an individual response. On a practical level, economics will have to play a significant role in the discussion, because many of the most developed arguments against using the precautionary principle in these circumstances focus on the economic costs of retarding use of fossil fuels and on the social consequences these economics costs could bring. Of course, those arguing for the precautionary principle could also bring in economic factors that favor their approach, such as the economic benefits of maintaining established agriculture wherever it exists, especially agricultural productivity in developing countries, as well as the economic costs of land and coastline loss, health impacts, human relocations, and other effects of global climate change.*

## Additional Questions

1. In this chapter, Brennan emphasizes that "greenhouse effect," "global warming," and "global climate change" are frequently misused terms. Imagine that you are

explaining global climate change to the general public. How would you use these terms? Use diagrams, examples, and analogies where appropriate.

*Student responses will vary. Earth's climate is the result of many factors such as the greenhouse effect, the Milankovitch cycles, sun spots, aerosols, El Niño, and cloud cover. The greenhouse effect is a natural phenomenon in which certain gases in the atmosphere trap heat. Carbon dioxide, ozone, methane, water vapor, nitrous oxide, and CFCs are greenhouse gases. Without greenhouse gases, Earth would be a frozen ball of ice—we need these gases to maintain a livable climate.*

*Global climate change is the result of human activities and natural factors. The climate has always changed as Earth has gone through ice ages and interglacial periods over geologic history. Global warming is the idea that Earth's average global temperature is higher than normal. Most scientists believe that global warming is taking place as a result of human activities that increase the amount of greenhouse gases in the atmosphere.*

2. Describe El Niño. How do El Niño and La Niña affect climate?

   *El Niño and La Niña are extreme phases of the naturally occurring El Niño/Southern Oscillation in which sea-surface temperatures are relatively higher or cooler than normal in the eastern tropical Pacific. Under normal conditions, prevailing winds blow from east to west along the equator in the Pacific Ocean. During an El Niño period, prevailing winds weaken and the warm water that is "piled up" in the western Pacific flows eastward toward South America. The presence of warmer water weakens the upwelling along the coast of Peru and changes weather patterns around the world. Parts of Australia and Indonesia are prone to drought during El Niño, and cold-water fisheries of Peru are greatly impacted.*

   *During a La Niña phase, eastward-moving oceanic waves bring cold water to the surface, causing the presence of colder than normal temperatures in the equatorial Pacific Ocean. It brings the opposite effects of El Niño to the United States, with wetter than normal conditions across the Pacific Northwest and dryer and warmer conditions across the south.*

3. Assign students to read the online case study: "The L.A. of the South: Atlanta's Urban Sprawl." Compare and contrast the urban heat island effect and the greenhouse effect.

   *The urban heat island effect is localized to large cities, whereas the greenhouse effect occurs around the globe. Though both cause warming of the atmosphere, the mechanisms behind the warming are different. With the urban heat island effect, a city without the cooling effects of trees suffers from high temperatures when heat stored by asphalt and rooftops is slowly released. With the greenhouse effect, there are certain gases in the atmosphere that trap heat and slowly release it.*

# 13 The oceans: Natural systems, human use, and marine conservation

## Chapter Objectives

**This chapter will help students understand:**

- Physical, geological, chemical, and biological aspects of the marine environment
- Ocean currents
- Major types of marine ecosystems
- Historic and current human uses of marine resources
- Human impacts on marine environments
- The current state of ocean fisheries and reasons for their decline
- Marine protected areas and reserves as innovative solutions
- The scientific basis for claims that marine reserves increase fish populations

## Lecture Outline

I. Central Case: Seeding the Seas with Marine Reserves

A. Stretching southwest from the southern tip of Florida, the string of islands known as the Florida Keys hosts some of North America's richest marine ecosystems.

B. As human visitation increased, so did human impacts.

C. These impacts on water quality, seagrass, and coral reefs in turn depressed fish stocks.

D. Congress established the Florida Keys National Marine Sanctuary in 1989 to protect rare and endangered natural and cultural resources.

E. Although 24 reserves in the sanctuary amount to only 6% of the sanctuary's total area, they have been a magnet for controversy.

F. Sanctuaries and reserves are types of marine protected areas, a term used to describe any portion of the ocean that is protected from some human activities, but may be open to others.

II. Oceanography

   A. The study of the physics, chemistry, and geology of the oceans is called oceanography.

   B. The oceans cover most of Earth's surface.

   C. The oceans contain more than water.

      1. Ocean water is salty because the ocean basins are the final repository for water that runs off the land.

      2. The salinity of ocean water varies from place to place due to differences in evaporation, precipitation, and freshwater runoff from land and glaciers, but generally ranges from 3.3% to 3.7%.

      3. Another factor in ocean chemistry is dissolved gas content, particularly the dissolved oxygen upon which gill-breathing marine animals depend.

   D. Ocean water is vertically structured.

      1. Water density increases as salinity increases and as temperature decreases, giving rise to different layers of water.

      2. The waters of the surface zone are heated by sunlight each day and are stirred by wind.

      3. The pycnocline, or thermocline, is the region below the surface zone in which density increases and temperature decreases with depth.

      4. The deep zone of the ocean lies beneath the pycnocline and is not affected by wind and sunlight.

      5. The euphotic zone is the well-lit top layer of the ocean.

   E. Ocean water flows horizontally in currents.

   F. Vertical movement of water affects marine ecosystems.

      1. Upwellings are areas where deep water moves toward the surface, bringing nutrients.

      2. Downwelling transports warm water rich in oxygen downward.

   G. The topography of the seafloor can be rugged and complex.

      1. In the bathymetric profile, gently sloping continental shelves underlie the shallow waters bordering continents.

      2. The deep ocean basins consist of abyssal plains, volcanic peaks, and trenches.

      3. Pelagic organisms live between the ocean's surface and the ocean floor.

      4. Benthic organisms live on the ocean floor.

III. Marine Ecosystems

   A. Open-ocean ecosystems vary in their biological diversity.

      1. Most life is concentrated near the surface in areas of nutrient-rich upwelling.

      2. In the deep ocean, animals are adapted to deal with extreme water pressures.

      3. Some ecosystems cluster around hydrothermal vents.

   B. Kelp forests harbor many organisms in temperate waters.

C. Coral reefs are treasure troves of biodiversity in tropical and subtropical waters.
    1. A coral reef is a mass of calcium carbonate composed of the skeletons of tiny colonial marine organisms called corals.
    2. Corals are invertebrate animals that belong to the phylum Cnidaria and are relatives of sea anemones and jellyfish.
    3. The reefs of the Florida Keys National Marine Sanctuary host many types of coral.
    4. Coral populations and coral reefs are experiencing worldwide declines.
    5. A few coral species thrive in waters outside of the tropics, and build large reefs on the ocean floor at depths of 200–500 meters.

D. Intertidal zones are dynamic ecosystems that undergo constant change.
    1. The intertidal or littoral zone exists along shorelines between low tide and high tide.
    2. The intertidal zone is a tough place to make a living, but is home to a remarkable diversity of organisms.
    3. The rocky intertidal zone is so diverse because environmental conditions change dramatically from the low part of the intertidal zone to the high part.

E. Salt marshes cover large areas of coastline in temperate areas.

F. Mangrove forests line coastlines throughout the tropics and subtropics.
    1. Mangroves are trees with unique types of roots that curve upward like snorkels to obtain oxygen.
    2. In south Florida and elsewhere, many mangrove forests have been removed as people have converted coastal areas to residential, recreational, and commercial uses.

G. Freshwater meets saltwater in estuaries.
    1. Estuaries are areas where rivers flow into the ocean.
    2. Estuaries around the world have been affected by urban and coastal development.

IV. How Humans Use and Impact Oceans

A. The oceans provide transportation routes.

B. We extract energy and minerals from the oceans.
    1. By the 1980s, about 25% of our production of crude oil and natural gas was coming from exploitation of ocean deposits.
    2. The oceans hold potential for providing us with renewable energy sources.
    3. We extract minerals from the seafloor.

C. Marine pollution threatens resources.

D. Oil pollution comes not only from massive spills.
    1. The majority of oil pollution comes not from large spills, but from the accumulation of innumerable widely spread small sources.
    2. Minimizing the amount of oil we release is important because petroleum pollution is detrimental to the marine environment and the human economies that draw sustenance from the environment.

3. Over the past three decades, the amount of oil spilled in U.S. waters and worldwide has decreased, due in part to an increased emphasis on spill prevention and response.

E. Nets and plastic debris endanger marine life.

1. Because plastic is not biodegradable, it can drift for years and marine animals can mistake it for food.
2. Fishing nets lost or discarded frequently keep catching fish for decades.
3. We can minimize this type of harm by reducing our use of plastics, cutting the rings of plastic six-pack holders, and picking up trash from beaches.

F. Excess nutrients can cause algal blooms.

1. The release of excess nutrients into surface waters can spur unusually high growth rates of algae.
2. Several species of marine algae produce powerful toxins that attack the human nervous system.

V. Emptying the Oceans

A. Overfishing is nothing new.

1. Humans have been harvesting sea life for thousands of years.
2. A recent synthesis of historical evidence revealed that ancient overfishing likely affected ecosystems in astounding ways that we only partially understand today.
3. Florida Bay is suffering today from the overhunting of green sea turtles in past centuries.

B. Modern fishing fleets deplete marine life rapidly.

C. Many fisheries are collapsing today.

1. The percentage of oceanic fish stocks that are overfished increased tenfold from 1950 to 1994 and threefold from 1974 to 2001.
2. A prime example of fishery collapse took place in the 1990s with groundfish fisheries in the Atlantic off the Canadian and U.S. coasts.

D. Fishery declines are masked by several factors.

1. Despite the fact that fish stocks have been depleted in region after region as industrialized fishing intensified, the amount of overall global fish production has remained stable for 15 years.
2. Improved technology helps to explain high catches.

E. We are "fishing down the food chain."

F. Some fishing practices kill nontarget animals and damage ecosystems.

1. The removal of species at high trophic levels can have serious ramifications.
2. Many fishing practices catch more than target species.
   a. The removal of species at high trophic levels from marine environments, particularly those that act as keystone species, can have serious ramifications for marine ecosystems.
   b. Boats that drag drift nets through the water capture substantial numbers of large nontarget species.

c. Longline fishing involves dragging extremely long lines with baited hooks spaced along their lengths and results in a large by-catch.

d. Bottom trawling is the practice of dragging weighted nets over the floor of the continental shelf to catch benthic organisms and results in damaging entire benthic ecosystems.

VI. Marine Conservation Biology

A. Traditional fisheries management is based on maximum sustainable yield.

1. The goal of this strategy is to allow for maximal harvests of particular populations while keeping fish available for the future.

2. Despite such efforts, many fish stocks have plummeted.

B. We can protect areas in the ocean.

1. Large numbers of marine protected areas (MPAs) have been established, mostly along coastlines of developed countries.

2. Because of the lack of refuges from fishing pressure, many scientists have urged the establishment of areas where no fishing is allowed; these areas are called marine reserves.

C. Marine reserves have met forceful opposition.

1. Nearly every marine reserve proposed has met resistance from people and businesses that use the area for fishing or recreation.

2. In the Florida Keys, property rights advocates who had opposed the sanctuary protested the 1998 establishment of reserve zones.

D. Scientists insist that reserves work for both fish and fishermen.

1. Data indicate that marine reserves do work as scientists as hoped.

2. In all, the review of data from existing marine reserves as of 2001 revealed that the fish populations had increased in density, biomass, average size, and biodiversity.

E. The question is how best to design reserves.

VII. Conclusion

A. In the Florida Keys and hundreds of other protected areas around the country, scientists are gradually demonstrating that setting aside protected areas serves to maintain natural systems and enhances fisheries.

B. In some parts of the country, the public and politicians have supported such protection enthusiastically.

# Key Terms

algal blooms
bathymetry
benthic
bottom trawling
by-catch
continental shelves
coral reef
currents
deep zone
downwelling
drift nets
estuaries
euphotic zone
Florida Keys National Marine Sanctuary
heat capacity
intertidal
kelp
littoral
longline fishing
manganese nodules

*continued*

## Key Terms, *continued*

mangroves
marine protected areas
marine reserves
maximum sustainable yield
oceanography
overfishing
pelagic
pycnocline
red tides
salinity
salt marshes
seagrass
surface zone
tide pools
tides
topography
upwelling
zooxanthellae

## Teaching Tips

1. This chapter describes the Florida Keys National Marine Sanctuary. Provide students with information about another marine sanctuary found in or near your region. There are 13 sanctuaries in place today, with another one proposed for the Northwestern Hawaiian Islands. Information about the sanctuaries can be found at www.sanctuaries.nos.noaa.gov.
2. This chapter introduces mangrove forests and seagrass beds. It is important to emphasize that these ecosystems serve as nurseries for many juvenile fish and invertebrate species that live on coral reefs as adults. As a result, the health of mangroves and seagrass beds is directly related to the health of coral reef ecosystems.

   Seagrass beds, one of the world's most productive ecosystems, occur in Florida's estuaries and nearshore coastal waters, providing food and habitat for commercially important fish, shrimp, and lobster species. Unfortunately, seagrass meadows are declining worldwide due to human impacts. Declines in Tampa, Florida, have led to restoration efforts. For more information, read "Seagrass Restoration in Tampa, Florida," at http://soundwaves.usgs.gov/2002/11.
3. Use tide tables to teach the concept of tides. Tide tables that show predicted high and low tides at sites across the country can be accessed from NOAA at http://tidesandcurrents.noaa.gov.

   For a given month, the daily time and height for each tide is shown. Students will note that there is approximately a six-hour difference between each high tide and low tide, and tides are diurnal.

*Dyer Bay, Maine*

**December**

| Date | Day | Time | Height | Time | Height |
|---|---|---|---|---|---|
| 12/01 | Mon | 04:49 A.M. | 10.6 H | 10:57 A.M. | 1.4 L |
| 12/02 | Tue | 05:49 A.M. | 10.7 H | 12:02 P.M. | 1.4 L |
| 12/03 | Wed | 12:29 A.M. | 1.0 L | 06:44 A.M. | 10.8 H |
| 12/04 | Thu | 01:21 A.M. | 1.1 L | 07:34 A.M. | 11.0 H |
| 12/05 | Fri | 02:08 A.M. | 1.2 L | 08:19 A.M. | 11.2 H |
| 12/06 | Sat | 02:51 A.M. | 1.3 L | 08:59 A.M. | 11.4 H |
| 12/07 | Sun | 03:30 A.M. | 1.4 L | 09:36 A.M. | 11.5 H |

Note: This is only a partial table that shows the first two tidal cycles. Height is shown in meters.

The moon's gravity pulls the ocean toward it, creating a "bulge" on one side of the Earth (high tide). Centrifugal force creates another bulge on the other side of the Earth (high tide). These bulges move in relation to the position of the moon as Earth rotates on its axis, causing most places to have two high tides a day.

# Additional Resources

## Websites

1. "CoRIS," NOAA's Coral Reef Information System, www.coris.noaa.gov

   This website gives the user access to coral reef data and maps. There is also detailed information about coral reef biology.

2. "National Marine Sanctuaries," National Oceanic and Atmospheric Administration, www.sanctuaries.nos.noaa.gov

   This is the official website for the National Marine Sanctuaries Program with information about the history and current management of our nation's marine sanctuaries.

3. "Oceans Alive," The Museum of Science, www.mos.org/oceans

   This website has information about ocean formation, physical characteristics of oceans, the water cycle, tides, currents, ocean life, and marine scientists.

4. "Secrets of the Ocean Realm," PBS Online, www.pbs.org/oceanrealm

   This website provides information and classroom activities about unique and fascinating creatures that inhabit the ocean's depths.

5. "Wetlands, Oceans, and Watersheds," U.S. Environmental Protection Agency (EPA), www.epa.gov/OWOW

   This EPA website describes aquatic resources and approaches taken to protect them, such as the National Estuary Program and marine pollution control.

# Audiovisual Materials

1. *Canary of the Ocean: America's Troubled Reef,* 1997, video produced and distributed by Miranda Productions (www.mirandaproductions.com/canaryhome.html).

   This video, narrated by Andie MacDowell, is a documentary of the past and present condition of the coral reefs of the Florida Keys. It also describes the Florida Everglades and its connection to Florida Bay and the Keys.

2. *Coastal Fisheries: Case Study Series,* video set produced by Compass Light Documentary, Mainewatch Institute, and Island Institute and distributed by The Video Project (www.videoproject.net).

   This three-video set examines Maine fisheries that illustrate worldwide resource management issues. The set includes: *Underwater Out of Sight: An Ecosystem Case Study, A Tale of Two Fisheries,* and *Managing for the Future: Tragedy of the Commons Revisited.*

3. *Coral Reef Adventure,* video by MacGillivray Freeman Films (www.coralfilm.com).

   This IMAX film follows two divers as they explore reefs of the South Pacific and document problems with overfishing, sedimentation, and coral bleaching.

4. *Secrets of the Ocean Realm,* video set distributed by PBS Video (www.shop.pbs.org).

   This five-tape set explores the behavior of deep-sea creatures and includes: *Cathedral in the Sea, Survival in the Sea, Venom, Creatures of the Darkness, The Great Whales, Sharks, City in the Sea, Star Gardens, Mountain in the Sea,* and *Filming Secrets.*

# *Weighing the Issues:* Suggested Answers

## Why Understand Ocean Currents?

***Facts to consider:*** *Knowing where ocean currents flow helps scientists and other planners determine optimal locations and boundaries for marine reserves. The more appropriate the reserve location, the more likely it will receive significant numbers of species larvae, so significant numbers of important species young can settle and grow. The better the reserve supports increasing population density and diversity both within the reserve and in surrounding areas, the more benefits come not only to the ecosystems themselves but also to the fishing industry in that region. Ocean currents can carry not only larvae of marine organisms but also food supplies for these creatures, from marine plants to plankton. They also may carry undesirable material, such as spilled oil, other toxins, invasive species, and debris, including plastics. Thus, understanding ocean currents can help people control, treat, and prevent marine damage from such sources. It can also help fishing fleets locate fish populations, as well as helping not only these boats but other ocean-going vessels travel most efficiently on the ocean by working with the natural "routes" of surface currents. Knowledge of currents also helps people investigate marine ecosystems, plan and protect coastline areas, and enjoy ocean-based recreation.*

## The Coral Crisis

***Facts to consider:*** *New technologies may enhance coral growth and reef-inhabiting organisms. But the rate of coral destruction may be too fast for such methods to halt the decline of coral reefs overall, particularly because the damage is occurring now, whereas these methods are just being developed. Also, to the extent that coral reef problems have been enhanced by the warming of the oceans, such as through global climate change, new technologies cannot compensate adequately for such a huge factor.*

*Certain actions may be available now that could be effective much more quickly. For instance, avoiding trawling in coral areas would probably maintain coral reefs at a rate much greater than they could regrow, though such a restriction would face opposition from some fishing interests. Reducing artificial pollutants in ocean waters may reduce coral loss, but this connection has not yet been definitely proven, and perhaps some significant sources of such pollutants cannot be identified. Efforts that retard global climate change could help coral reefs, but such changes are large scale, controversial, and slow to affect the climate. Forbidding use of cyanide to catch fish would also help, though collectors, communities engaged in this enterprise, and representatives from developing countries might argue against the economic burden to be borne by those who currently use this method.*

### Preservation on Land and at Sea

***Facts to consider:*** *This question requires an individual response but may include that, as land animals, human beings have seen, tracked, and been generally more aware of the land's diversity than that of the ocean. It is more likely that humans notice changes in land ecosystems than changes in marine ecosystems, because more people actually see the land systems, while relatively few observe the oceans. For most of human existence, people's sense of marine ecosystem health has been gauged in terms of abundance of food resources; as long as human beings have found new ways to harvest from the sea, the general sense has probably been that such resources are boundless.*

## *The Science behind the Stories:* The Scientific Method

### China's Fisheries Data

**Observation:** China's marine fisheries catch increased dramatically in the 1990s, while fisheries catch in many other countries declined. Given the ecological conditions of its fishing waters, China's reported catch appeared suspiciously high.

**Hypothesis:** China was systematically overreporting its total catch to the United Nations Food and Agricultural Organization, thus contributing to an overly optimistic view of the health of the world's fisheries.

**Experiment:** Fisheries scientists at the University of British Columbia developed a statistical model to predict catches based on oceanographic factors, species distributions, and fishing access. They then compared the predicted catch to each country's reported catch.

**Results:** For most regions, the reported catch was similar to the predicted catch. In China, however, the reported catch (10.1 million metric tons in 1999) was almost twice as large as the predicted catch (5.5 million metric tons). The finding suggests that the total global catch, rather than remaining stable through the 1990s, actually began to decline in the 1980s.

## Additional Questions

1. The establishment of the Florida Keys National Marine Sanctuary protects the coastal waters from oil exploration, mining, and waste dumping. Unfortunately, this does not protect its watershed. What are potential sources of pollution from the watershed? What can be done to address these pollution sources?

*The land area that drains into the Florida Keys coastal waters is highly developed. Because the quality of the drainage basin is directly related to the quality of the water, the use of the drainage basin is key to the quality of the Florida Keys ecosystems and fisheries. Industry, residential areas, and roadways all pollute the coastal waters through runoff. Sediment, sewage, and petroleum products are just a few of the pollutants that drain into the ocean. A* systems approach *is needed to address water quality issues in the Florida Keys. As with the Mississippi River drainage basin, community leaders need to work with policymakers and the public to reduce runoff and/or reduce the pollutants.*

2. Describe deep-ocean communities. How are the organisms adapted to live in their unique environment?

   *Deep-ocean organisms are adapted to live under intense water pressures and in complete darkness. Some creatures have the ability to emit light in a process called bioluminescence. Some have enlarged eyes for gathering as much light as possible and others are black in color to blend in with their environment. Many obtain food by consuming detritus that falls from above or having symbiotic bacteria that provide food. Entire communities live only around hydrothermal vents where heated water is released from the seafloor. Chemosynthetic bacteria are the base of the food chain and convert chemical energy into food.*

3. Assign students to read the online case study "The Restoration of an Ecosystem—The Everglades." Do you think the restoration of the Everglades will affect the Florida Keys? Why or why not?

   *The water flow of the Everglades system starts with Lake Okeechobee, flows like a river through Everglades National Park, and ends in Florida Bay. With more water to be restored to its natural flow, there will be an increase in the freshwater input in Florida Bay, making it cooler and less salty. This change will improve conditions for the native plant and animal species such as the manatee, seagrasses, and mangroves. Because seagrass beds and mangroves are nurseries for juvenile coral reef fish, there may be an increase in coral reef fish species to help repopulate coral reefs of the Florida Keys.*

# 14 Freshwater resources

## Chapter Objectives

**This chapter will help students understand:**

- The importance of water to ecosystems, human health, and economic pursuits
- The hydrologic cycle and human interactions with it
- Freshwater distribution on Earth
- Freshwater ecosystems
- How we use water and alter freshwater systems
- Water quantity problems: freshwater depletion
- Water quality problems: water pollution
- Solutions to problems of depletion and pollution

## Lecture Outline

I. Central Case: Plumbing the Colorado River

A. In January 2003, the U.S. government cut off 15% of California's water supply from the Colorado River.

B. The Colorado River begins in the high peaks of the Rocky Mountains, charges through the Grand Canyon, crosses the border into Mexico, and dumps into the Sea of Cortez, draining 637,000 $km^2$ of southwestern North America.

C. The waters of the Colorado River irrigate 7% of U.S. cropland, provide drinking water to over 20 million people, keep hundreds of golf courses green in the desert, and fill the swimming pools and fountains of Las Vegas casinos.

D. For 80 years, the seven states through which the Colorado passes have attempted to divide the river's water among them, guided by the Colorado River Compact signed in 1922.
   1. California has long exceeded its allotment because the other states were unable to fully use their shares.
   2. In 2000, the federal government pressured California to lower its usage to 4.4 million acre-feet gradually over 15 years.

E. California worked hard to get agricultural districts that controlled most of the water in the state to sell part of their shares, but at the last minute, the Imperial Irrigation District backed out.

II. Freshwater's Movement and Distribution on Earth

A. Of all water on Earth, only 2.5% is considered freshwater.

B. Water moves in the hydrologic cycle.
   1. From rain, snow, and glacial ice deposited on the western slope of the Rockies, thousands of rivulets and creeks flow downhill into small rivers, which eventually flow into the Colorado River.
   2. In the past, the Colorado River's copious supply of water surged into the Sea of Cortez, but today the withdrawals have turned it into a small stream that barely reaches the sea.
   3. Because the Colorado River is located in a region of naturally low precipitation, the movement of the Colorado River's water has particularly strong influence on the ecology and human communities of its watershed.

C. Groundwater plays a key role in the hydrologic cycle.
   1. Groundwater makes up one-fifth of Earth's freshwater supply.
   2. Groundwater is contained in aquifers—porous, spongelike layers of rock, sand, or gravel that hold water.
   3. There are two broad categories of aquifers—confined or artesian aquifers and unconfined aquifers.
   4. Groundwater is not stationary, but flows downhill and from areas of high pressure to areas of low pressure.
   5. The world's largest known aquifer is the Ogallala Aquifer, which underlies the Great Plains of the United States.

D. Water is unequally distributed across Earth's surface.
   1. People are not distributed across the globe in accordance with water availability, and areas that are dense with people are often water poor.
   2. One challenge for human societies has always been to transport freshwater from where it occurs to where it is needed.
   3. The natural distribution of freshwater is uneven across time as well as space; rain does not always fall when people need it.

III. Freshwater Ecosystems

A. Rivers and streams wind through the landscape.
   1. Bodies of actively flowing water comprise one major class of freshwater ecosystems.

2. As streams flow downhill, they join one another and eventually form larger water channels, or rivers.
3. Due to their size and power, rivers often exert significant forces to shape the local landscape.

B. Lakes and ponds change with time.
1. Small bodies of water that do not actively flow are often called ponds, and large bodies of still water are termed lakes.
2. Both ponds and lakes are potentially subject to the process of eutrophication.

C. Inland seas are the largest freshwater bodies.

D. Wetlands include marshes, swamps, and bogs.
1. Just as ecosystems that straddle the line between ocean and land are some of the most productive and species rich, those that combine elements of freshwater and dry land are enormously rich and productive.
2. All of these types of wetlands are extremely valuable to wildlife, and all have been extensively drained and filled, largely for agriculture.

IV. How We Use Water

A. Water supplies our households, agriculture, and industry.
1. Most uses of water are consumptive, in which water is removed from a particular source and is not returned to it.
2. Nonconsumptive use of water does not remove, or only temporarily removes, water from an aquifer or surface water body.
3. Agriculture accounts for 87% of the world's consumptive use of freshwater.
4. When water becomes scarce and more valuable, economic considerations favor its use in industry, where a given amount of water can produce 70 times the dollar value of output.

B. We extract water from aquifers.
1. One-third of the human population relies directly on groundwater for its water needs.
2. Today, extraction of water from aquifers is on the rise.

C. We divert surface water to suit our needs.
1. In areas near surface water, people have found it far easier to make use of rivers, streams, lakes, and ponds, moving water from these sources to farm fields and houses.
2. The Colorado River's water is diverted and utilized every bit as much today.
3. Today, more large-scale diversion projects are under development.

D. We control floods with dikes and levees.
1. Flood prevention ranks high among reasons we control the movement of freshwater.
2. Floods can do tremendous damage to the farms, homes, and property of people who choose to live in floodplains.

E. We have erected thousands of dams.
   1. A dam is any obstruction placed in a river or stream to block the flow of water so that water can be stored in a reservoir.
   2. Two large dams of the Colorado River are the Hoover Dam and the Glen Canyon Dam.
F. China's Three Gorges Dam is the world's largest and most expensive.
   1. The dam was completed in 2003 and the reservoir should be filled by 2009.
   2. It will generate hydroelectric power, enable boats and barges to travel farther upstream, and provide flood control.
   3. One of the costs of the Three Gorges Dam is that it will flood 22 cities and the homes of 1.13 million people.
   4. It will also inundate archaeological sites, farmland, and wildlife habitat.
G. More and more dams are now being removed.
   1. Some people believe that by removing dams and letting rivers flow freely, we can restore riparian ecosystems, reestablish economically valuable fisheries, and reintroduce river recreation.
   2. The drive to remove dams gathered steam in 1999 with the dismantling of Edwards Dam on the Kennebec River in Maine, which resulted from the first Federal Energy Regulatory Commission (FERC) decision that environmental benefits of removal outweighed economic benefits of relicensing it.
   3. More small dams will come down in years ahead, as over 500 FERC licenses are set to come up for renewal in the next decade.

V. Freshwater Depletion: The Challenge of Quantity
   A. Ensuring adequate quantities of freshwater for our basic needs is an endeavor as old as our species, and despite all our technological advances, this challenge is not going to disappear.
   B. The hydrologic cycle makes freshwater a renewable resource.
   C. We are depleting surface water.
      1. Nowhere are the effects of surface water depletion so evident than at the Aral Sea.
      2. Once the fourth largest lake on Earth, it has lost four-fifths of its volume in 40 years as it has fallen victim to poor farming and irrigation practices.
   D. We are depleting groundwater.
      1. Groundwater is at even greater risk of depletion than surface water because most aquifers recharge either very slowly or not at all.
      2. As aquifers are depleted, water tables drop, and groundwater becomes more difficult to extract; it eventually can run out.
      3. Overpumping of groundwater in coastal areas can cause saltwater to intrude into aquifers, making water undrinkable.
      4. As aquifers lose water, their substrate can become weaker and less capable of supporting overlying strata and any human structures built upon them.
      5. While falling water tables cause problems for farmers and others who depend on wells for their water, they also do vast ecological harm.

E. Inefficient irrigation wastes water.
   1. Worldwide, the amount of land under irrigation has been increasing.
   2. Governments of several Middle Eastern nations have greatly subsidized irrigation in order to promote agricultural self-sufficiency.

F. Will we see water wars?
   1. Freshwater depletion leads to shortages, and the scarcity of any vital resource can lead to social conflict.
   2. Many predict that water's role in regional conflicts will only increase as human population continues to grow in water-poor areas.
   3. On the positive side, a great many nations have found ways to cooperate with their neighbors over water issues.

VI. Solutions to Depletion of Freshwater

A. To address the problem of freshwater depletion, we can try either to increase the supply of water or to reduce the demand for water.

B. Strategies that aim to reduce demand include conservation and efficiency measures.

C. We can "make" more water by desalination.
   1. As of 2000, 7,500 desalination plants were in operation around the world.
   2. Desalination works, but is expensive.

D. Demand by agriculture can be reduced.
   1. Farmers can improve efficiency of water use in many ways, including lining irrigation canals to prevent leaks and leveling fields to minimize runoff.
   2. In addition, choosing crops to match the land and climate in which they are being farmed can save huge amounts of water.

E. We can lessen residential, municipal, and industrial use in many ways.
   1. We can reduce our household water use by installing low-flow faucets, shower heads, washing machines, and toilets.
   2. Industry and municipalities can take water-saving steps as well.
   3. Some governments are capturing excess surface runoff during the rainy season and pumping it into underground aquifers.

F. Various economic solutions to water conservation are being debated.
   1. Many economists have suggested market-based strategies for achieving sustainability in our water use, ending government subsidies of inefficient practices, and letting water become a commodity whose price reflects the true costs of its extraction.
   2. Similar concerns surround another potential solution, the privatization of water supplies.
   3. Regardless of how demand is addressed, the ongoing shift from supply-side to demand-side solutions is beginning to pay dividends.

VII. Pollution of Freshwater: The Challenge of Quality

A. Scientists use several indicators of water quality.
   1. Biological properties, such as the presence of disease-causing organisms, can indicate how safe water is for human consumption.

   2. There are three important chemical properties: pH, hardness, and dissolved oxygen content.
   3. Scientists also classify water according to three physical characteristics: turbidity, color, and temperature.

B. Water pollution comes from point sources and from larger areas.
   1. The term *pollution* describes any matter or energy released into the environment that causes undesirable impacts on the health and well-being of humans or other organisms.
   2. Regardless of its source, water pollution is in many forms and can cause diverse impacts on aquatic ecosystems and human health.

C. Pathogens and waterborne diseases are a biological form of water pollution.
   1. Many disease-causing organisms survive in surface water and some enter inadequately treated drinking water supplies via human and animal waste.
   2. As our understanding of these pathogens found in water has advanced, we have developed several strategies for reducing risks they pose.

D. Nutrient pollution can cause eutrophication.
   1. The process of eutrophication, or overnourishment, of surface water and its plants by nutrient pollution occurs readily in freshwater bodies.
   2. The growth of microscopic aquatic algae and larger aquatic plants that grow from the bottoms of lakes and ponds is limited when certain nutrients are in short supply.
   3. When excess levels of nitrogen and phosphorus enter surface waters, they fertilize aquatic plants.
   4. Both phosphorus and nitrogen are common in runoff from farms, golf courses, lawns, and sewage.

E. Toxic synthetic chemicals pollute our waterways.

F. Sediment can be a pollutant.

G. Even heat and cold can pollute.

H. Groundwater pollution is a serious dilemma.
   1. Increasingly, groundwater sources once assumed to be ancient and pristine have been found to be contaminated by pollution, much of which is from industrial and agricultural practices.
   2. Groundwater pollution is more serious than surface water pollution because it is longer lasting.

I. There are many sources of groundwater pollution.
   1. Some groundwater contamination is natural.
   2. Anthropogenic groundwater pollution is widespread, and includes a variety of industrial, agricultural, and urban wastes.
      a. Leakage from underground storage tanks is a major contributor.
      b. Nitrates, pathogens, and fertilizers are pollutants from agriculture.

   c. Manufacturing industries have been heavy polluters for years.
   d. Military sites have added to groundwater contamination with nitroaromatic compounds and radioactive waste.

VIII. Solutions to Pollution of Freshwater
   A. As numerous as our freshwater pollution problems seem, many of them were worse a few decades ago.
   B. The Clean Water Act made it illegal to discharge pollution from a point source without a permit, set standards for industrial wastewater, set standards for contaminant levels in surface waters, and funded construction of sewage treatment plants.
   C. Nonpoint source pollution continues to be a major challenge for developed countries.
   D. The Great Lakes of Canada and the United States represent a success story in fighting water pollution.
   E. In some cases, solutions will likely need to be preventive ones, not simply treatment and cleanup.
      1. We can filter groundwater before distributing it.
      2. We can pump water out of an aquifer, treat it, and inject it back in, repeatedly.
      3. We can restrict usage of pollutants on lands above selected aquifers.
   F. There are many things that ordinary people can do to help minimize freshwater pollution.
      1. Exercise consumer choice in the marketplace.
      2. Get to know your local waterways and become involved in protecting them.

IX. Conclusion
   A. Citizen action, government legislation and regulation, new technologies, economic incentives, and public awareness are all beginning to confront the problems with quantity and quality of water.
   B. We have grown to take freshwater for granted.
   C. There is reason to hope that we may yet attain sustainability in our water usage.

# Key Terms

aquifer recharge zone
arsenic
artesian well
bog
Central Arizona Project
China's Three Gorges Dam
Colorado River Aqueduct
confined aquifer
consumptive uses
desalination
dissolved oxygen
*E. coli*
eutrophication
Federal Energy Regulatory Commission
floodplain
freshwater
groundwater
hardness
inland seas
lakes
marsh

*continued*

## Key Terms, *continued*

nonconsumptive uses
nonpoint source
nutrient pollution
Ogallala Aquifer
point source
pond
rainshadow
river
saltwater intrusion
sediment
sinkholes
stream
swamp
turbidity
unconfined aquifer
water mining
water table
wetland

## Teaching Tips

1. Use the EPA website "Surf Your Watershed" (www.epa.gov/surf/watershed.html) to retrieve information about water quality in your area. From your watershed's home page, you can visit the Envirofacts Warehouse to access EPA databases on community water sources, water dischargers, and toxic releases.
2. In 2001, the Colorado River Task Force of the Sierra Club published a study about the Colorado River called "The Colorado River Report." The Background section of the report contains information about the natural history of the river, the political boundaries, and the basic agreements that dictate the use of the river's water. The Conclusions section characterizes problems in the river basin, and the Recommendations section suggests policies, actions, and alliances that could help restore the Colorado River. Assign students to read all or part of the report at www.sierraclub.org/rcc/southwest/coreport/index.asp.

   Questions for the students:

   - Explain what is meant by "an inhospitable desert has become a playground, and the Colorado River has become a plumbing system." *The answer is found in the Executive Summary of the report.*
   - Describe the flow of the Colorado River. Where does it begin? What are its main tributaries? Through what states does it flow? Where does it empty? *The answer to this can be found in the Background section of the report. There is a wonderful map by the Colorado Water Conservation District at www.crwcd.gov/map2.html.*
   - Describe the Central Utah Project and the Central Arizona Project. *The answer is found in the Background section.*
   - What are some of the problems identified by the Colorado River Task Force? How would the California 4.4 Plan help alleviate these problems? *The answer is found in the Conclusions section and the Recommendations section.*
3. Use activities from "Water on the Web" (http://wow.nrri.umn.edu/wow) to teach the ecology of lakes. The site contains online lessons designed for entry-level college students that use actual lake data to explore basic science concepts. Topics covered include:
   - Conductivity
   - Effect of pH
   - Fish Stocking Decisions
   - Heat Budgets

- Oxygen Solubility
- Temperature Variation
- Water Quality Modeling
- Turbidity

# Additional Resources

## Websites

1. "Freshwater Ecosystems," Missouri Botanical Garden, http://mbgnet.mobot.org/fresh

   This website provides information about rivers and streams, ponds and lakes, and wetlands. For each ecosystem type, there are photographs and diagrams illustrating the basic concepts.
2. "Water on the Web," University of Minnesota and National Science Foundation, http://wow.nrri.umn.edu/wow

   Water on the Web provides real water quality data in real-time and archived formats through Remote Underwater Sampling Stations (RUSS) in Minnesota's lakes. There are also teacher and student lessons for high school and first-year college students to learn science through hands-on activities.
3. "Water Quality Information Center," National Agricultural Library, Agricultural Research Service, U.S. Department of Agriculture, www.nal.usda.gov/wqic

   This website has a searchable database of online documents about water and agriculture.
4. "Water Quality Report," U.S. Environmental Protection Agency, www.epa.gov/305b

   This Web page has links to the National Water Quality Inventory Report to Congress for the years 1992 to the present. This report informed Congress and the public about water quality conditions of water bodies in the United States.

## Audiovisual Materials

1. *American Experience: Hoover Dam,* PBS Home Video (www.shop.pbs.org).

   This PBS program shows the story of the Hoover Dam, one of the world's greatest engineering projects.
2. *America's First River: Bill Moyers on the Hudson,* PBS Home Video (www.shop.pbs.org).

   This two-video set follows Bill Moyers as he surveys the Hudson River, its historical role, and the fight to conserve it.
3. *Great Wall across the Yangtze,* PBS Home Video (www.shop.pbs.org).

   This PBS documentary examines the controversial Three Gorges Dam. The Chinese government's case for the dam is presented, as are the many environmental and social consequences.
4. *The Water Rules,* 2000, Emmy and Emma Production, KLVX Communications Group, distributed by Amazon.com (www.amazon.com).

   This video is divided into three programs that look at the history of Las Vegas and its increasing need for water: *A Day's Journey Without Water, Cheapest Water in the West,* and *The Law of the River.*

# *Weighing the Issues:* Suggested Answers

## The Klamath Crisis

***Facts to consider:*** *Because water ran out during a dry year, it is clear that water supply and demand are not balanced. Supply-side solutions might include obtaining water from some other sources, such as capturing more of the surface runoff that occurs during the rainy months of the year or trying to find other water-rich areas that would sell water to the Klamath region. Demand-side solutions might include: paying farmers incentives to use less water or to install more efficient irrigation systems, as well as charging higher prices for water usage above certain levels. Changes in crops may also ease demands; different crops may need less water or at least less water during the times of the year most critical for this water supply. To help sustain fish populations, other habitat restoration efforts may be undertaken, so that some reduction in water levels may be balanced with other habitat improvements, resulting in no net loss of fish. In order to be effective, solutions must involve representatives of each involved group—farmers, fishers, wildlife advocates, and others.*

## How Far Can You Reach for Water?

***Facts to consider:*** *In the abstract, it might be possible to think that these desert cities might get water from areas with more precipitation, that is, states and countries either significantly above or below the 30th parallel. Or they might get water from areas with deeper aquifers, such as the Ogallala Aquifer. In reality, these areas may not have water resources that are not already in demand or needed to preserve environmental integrity. Even if desert cities could contract for such water, piping it in would face significant obstacles, such as: high cost of the water contract itself, high cost of the distribution system to get the water into the area, the limited availability of water in dry years or under other circumstances, and competition with other water-poor areas for these resources. People living in those more water-rich areas, and agencies responsible for their environment, would likely also raise objections to the extent that such possible water transfers would harm the environment from which it was proposed to be exported.*

*Alternatives to obtaining new water sources include: water conservation, increased use of water-efficient devices and procedures, desalinization, municipal water recycling, and economic incentives that promote demand-side reduction of water.*

## Sedimentation Can Impact Water Resources and Habitat

***Facts to consider:*** *These impacts that harm salmon-spawning habitat would likely reduce salmon survival rates. This would reduce both recreational and commercial fishing, which would, in turn, harm the economies of coastal and river communities. Salmon, in more limited supply, would become more expensive in markets, reducing the amount of salmon available for consumption (and raising its price). With fewer salmon eggs, small salmon, and full-grown salmon in the food chain, animals that prey on the salmon at these stages would all be affected. Some predators may decline in numbers because of decreased food supply; other predators might eat more of other food sources, thus reducing the populations of those species.*

*Sediment may impact many aspects of water quality. Sediment may contain a variety of compounds that can chemically damage water quality, such as phosphates and nitrates (perhaps from agricultural runoff), bacteria, chemical toxins, or chemicals that affect taste and odor. Sediments that contain calcium or magnesium ions could affect the hardness of the water, and sediment of certain origins may affect the water's pH. Suspended sediment increases water turbidity; when water is less clear, it may also absorb sunlight at a different rate, thus affecting the temperature of the water. The change in temperature may, in turn, affect the level of dissolved oxygen in the water.*

## Additional Questions

1. Diagram and label the hydrologic cycle using the following terms: evaporation, transpiration, infiltration, condensation, precipitation, and runoff.
2. There are many strategies used by governments and water companies to increase the amount of usable freshwater. Describe the advantages and disadvantages of strategies described in the textbook and make an argument for the "best" way to increase the freshwater availability in a region.

   *Student responses will vary. The textbook describes dams and reservoirs, groundwater extraction, canals and aqueducts, and desalination. For governments to use dams and reservoirs, location is critical. Dams can provide millions of gallons of water for municipal use, irrigation, hydropower, and recreation. Unfortunately, dams change the ecology of a river system and the reservoirs flood farmland and homes. Groundwater extraction is an important source of freshwater for one-third of the U.S. population. In the past, groundwater has been a clean, reliable source of water; however, groundwater supplies have become polluted by industry and agriculture. In addition, the overpumping of groundwater leads to depletion of aquifers as recharge is a slow process. Canals and aqueducts can transport water from areas that are "water rich" to those that are "water poor." Although this is very effective in moving water, large amounts of water are lost to evaporation. Desalination is a great tool for increasing amounts of freshwater as salts are removed from seawater. At this time, desalination is expensive and only coastal cities can take advantage of it.*
3. Assign students to read the online case study "Why is Lake Erie Dying Again?" How does phosphorus pollution affect Lake Erie? How do zebra mussels come into the picture?

   *Excessive amounts of phosphorus cause a dramatic increase in the growth of aquatic plants and algae. As the plants and algae die, bacteria decompose them, consuming oxygen in the process. Oxygen levels decline and cause aquatic animals to die. It is thought that zebra mussels may increase phosphorus levels in the lake because they expel phosphorus as a waste product as they consume organic material.*

# 15 Biodiversity and conservation biology

## Chapter Objectives

**This chapter will help students understand:**

- The scope of biodiversity on Earth
- Measurements of biodiversity
- Background extinction rates and periods of mass extinction
- Primary causes of biodiversity loss
- Benefits of biodiversity
- Conservation biology and its practice
- The island biogeography theory
- Traditional and more innovative biodiversity conservation efforts

## Lecture Outline

I. Central Case: Saving the Siberian Tiger
   A. Up until the past 200 years, tigers roamed widely across the Asian continent from Turkey to northeast Russia to Indonesia.
   B. Of the tigers that still survive in small pockets of their former range, those of the subspecies known as the Siberian tiger are the largest cats in the world.
   C. For thousands of years, the Siberian tiger coexisted with the Tungus, the native people of what is today the Russian Far East, who equated the tiger with royalty and viewed it as a guardian.
   D. The Russians who moved into and exerted control over the region in the early to mid-20th century had no cultural traditions that expressed respect for the animal, leading to the decline of the species.

E. International conservation groups began to get involved, working with Russian biologists to try to save the dwindling tiger population.

F. Today, the Siberian tiger population is up to roughly 150–450, and 500 more survive in zoos around the world.

II. Our Planet of Life

A. What is biodiversity?

1. Many people who study our planet's life have been inspired by the work of Edward O. Wilson, a professor and curator in entomology at Harvard University.

2. In Wilson's book *The Diversity of Life,* he defines biodiversity as "the variety of organisms considered at all levels, from genetic variants belonging to the same species through arrays of species to arrays of genetic, families, and still higher taxonomic levels; [it] includes the variety of ecosystems, which comprise both the communities of organisms within particular habitats and the physical conditions under which they live."

3. Definitions of biodiversity are plentiful, some more technical than Wilson's and some much simpler.

B. Biodiversity encompasses several levels of life's organization.

1. Species diversity is expressed in terms of the number or variety of species in the world or in a particular region.

a. Taxonomists, the scientists who classify species, use an organism's physical appearance and genetic makeup to determine to which species it belongs.

b. Speciation, the generation of new species, adds to species diversity, while extinction decreases species diversity.

c. Biodiversity exists below the species level in the form of subspecies.

2. Genetic diversity encompasses the differences in DNA composition among individuals within a given species.

a. Whether genetic diversity is extremely minor or great enough to warrant subspecies status, such diversity has repercussions for the well-being of a species in at least two major ways.

b. First, as a species becomes adapted to local environmental conditions, its genetic diversity may decrease.

c. In the long term, species with more genetic diversity have better chances of persisting, because their built-in variation better enables them to cope with environmental change.

3. Ecosystem diversity, community diversity, habitat diversity, and landscape diversity are all ways to view biodiversity.

C. Measuring biodiversity is not easy.

1. As of 2002, scientists had identified approximately 1.75 million species of plants, animals, and microorganisms.

2. Species are not evenly distributed among taxonomic groups.

3. Our estimates of species numbers are incomplete for several reasons.
    a. There are some areas of Earth that remain little explored.
    b. Many species are tiny and easily overlooked.
    c. Many organisms are so difficult to identify that species thought to be identified often turn out to be two or more different species.
4. Smithsonian Institution entomologist Terry Erwin carried out one famous attempt to inventory the number of arthropod species in the world.
5. In 2000, Kevin Kelley started the All Species Foundation in an attempt to identify all living organisms on Earth in one human generation.

D. You may be able to help measure biodiversity where you live.
    1. The All Taxa Biodiversity Inventory involves Great Smoky Mountain National Park, for instance.
    2. However, biodiversity is not just something that exists in national parks and tropical rainforests—it is everywhere.

E. Global biodiversity is not distributed evenly.
    1. Not all groups of organisms contain equal numbers of species diversity.
    2. Species diversity also varies according to the biome.
        a. Tropical dryforests and rainforests tend to support more species than tundra and deserts, for instance.
        b. Species richness generally increases as one approaches the equator.

III. Biodiversity Loss and Species Extinction

A. Extinction occurs when the last member of a species dies and the species ceases to exist; in contrast, the extinction of a certain population from a given area, but not the entire species globally, is called extirpation.

B. Extinction is "natural."
    1. Most extinctions preceding the appearance of humans have occurred one by one, at a rate that paleontologists refer to as the background rate of extinction.
    2. Extinction rates have risen far above this background rate during several mass extinction events of Earth's history.

C. The Earth has experienced five previous mass extinction episodes.

D. Humans set the sixth mass extinction in motion years ago.

E. Current extinction rates are much higher than normal.
    1. In 1995, 1,500 of the world's leading scientists reported to the United Nations that the current global extinction rate was more than 1,000 times greater than it would have been without human destruction of habitat.
    2. To keep track of the current status of endangered species, the World Conservation Union (IUCN) maintains the Red List.
    3. Among the 1,130 mammals facing possible extinction in the IUCN's Red List is the tiger, which is one of the most endangered large animals on the planet.

F. The major causes of species loss spell "HIPPO."
   1. Habitat alteration
      a. Changes in habitat significantly affect the organisms that depend on them.
      b. Habitat alteration is by far the greatest cause of species extinction today, biologists agree.
   2. Invasive species
      a. The introduction of invasive species to new environments has also pushed native species toward extinction.
      b. Most organisms introduced to new areas perish, but the few types that survive may do very well, especially if they find themselves without the predators and parasites that attacked them back home or without the competitors that had limited their access to resources.
      c. Modern-day Hawaii showcases the devastation that invasive species can cause.
   3. Pollution can negatively affect organisms in many ways.
   4. The increasing human population has touched just about every environmental issue.
   5. Overexploitation refers to both overexploitation and overconsumption.
      a. For most species, a high intensity of hunting by humans will not in itself pose a threat of extinction, but for some species it can.
      b. The Siberian tiger, the saiga, and whales have all seen steep decreases in numbers due to hunting.

G. Sometimes, causes of biodiversity loss are difficult to determine.

IV. Benefits of Biodiversity

A. Biodiversity provides valuable ecosystem services free of charge.

B. Top predators play key roles in their ecosystems.
   1. Often, top predators such as tigers are considered keystone species.
   2. Although top predators may be relatively few in number, they are often among the species most vulnerable to human impact.
   3. Top predators are not the only species that exert far-reaching influence over their ecosystems: the influence of other species can be equally significant.

C. Biodiversity gives us natural classrooms.

D. Biodiversity enhances food security.
   1. Genetic diversity within crop species and their ancestors is an enormously valued agricultural and economic factor.
   2. Other potentially important food crops await utilization.

E. Biodiversity provides traditional medicines and high-tech pharmaceutical products.
   1. Wild species yield new products, including pharmaceuticals, fibers, crops, and petroleum substitutes.
   2. In 1997, 10 of the 25 best selling pharmaceuticals owed their origins to wild species.

3. In Australia, where the government has made research into the products of rare and endangered species a high priority, a rare species of cork now provides medical researchers with hyoscine, a compound used to treat cancer, stomach disorders, and motion sickness.

F. Biodiversity provides economic benefits through tourism and recreation.
   1. Ecotourism has become a vital source of income for nations such as Costa Rica with its rainforests; Australia, with its Great Barrier Reef; Belize, with its reefs, caves, and rainforests; and Kenya and Tanzania, with their savanna wildlife.
   2. As ecotourism increases in popularity, however, a number of critics have warned that too many visitors to natural areas can degrade the outdoor experience and disturb wildlife.

G. People value and seek out connections with nature.

H. Do we have an ethical responsibility to prevent species extinction?
   1. If Wilson and others are right, then biophilia not only may be the root of such phenomena as ecotourism and real estate prices, but also may influence our ethics.
   2. As our society's sphere of ethical consideration has widened over time, and as more of us take up biocentric or ecocentric worldviews, more people have come to feel that other organisms have an inherent right to exist.
   3. Despite our ethical convictions, however, and despite biodiversity's many benefits, the future of biodiversity is far from secure.

V. Conservation Biology: The Search for Solutions

A. Conservation biology arose in response to increasing extinction rates.
   1. Conservation biology is a scientific discipline devoted to understanding the factors, forces, and processes that influence the loss, protection, and restoration of biological diversity within and among ecosystems.
   2. Conservation biologists choose their questions and pursue their research with the aim of developing solutions to problems like habitat degradation and species loss.
   3. Conservation biology suffered disdain in its early years from many scientists who considered it lacking in objectivity.
   4. Conservation biology began to take shape as a discipline in 1959 when Raymond Dasmann's book *Environmental Conservation* was published.

B. Island biogeography theory is a key component of conservation biology.
   1. Much of modern conservation biology is based on the equilibrium theory of island biogeography.
   2. Since its development, researchers have increasingly applied the theory's tenets to other types of islands, including islands of habitat—patches of one type of habitat isolated within vast "seas" of others.
   3. Island biogeography theory predicts the number of species on an island based on the island's size and its distance from the nearest mainland.

4. Several patterns are apparent from the theory of biogeography.
    a. Immigration rates are higher for large islands than for small islands; extinction rates are lower for large islands than for small islands.
    b. The distance between an island and the nearest continent also affects the number of species on the island.

C. Some species act as "umbrellas."

D. Should endangered species be the focus of conservation efforts?
1. Currently, the primary legislation for protecting biodiversity in the United States is the Endangered Species Act (ESA).
2. The ESA has had a number of notable successes.
3. Although most Americans support endangered species protection, some have vocally opposed provisions of the ESA.
4. Most popular resentment toward the ESA, however, has stemmed from worries of landowners that federal officials will restrict the use of private land if threatened or endangered species are found on it.
5. A number of provisions of the Act and its amendments attempt to soften this potential blow to landowners.
6. Because of the controversies the U.S. law has engendered, when Canada enacted its long-awaited endangered species act in 2002, the Canadian government was careful to stress the approach of cooperation with landowners and provincial governments.

E. Can captive breeding, reintroduction efforts, or cloning help save endangered species?
1. Zoos and botanical gardens have become centers for the captive breeding of endangered species, so that large numbers of individuals can be raised and then reintroduced into the wild.
2. The newest idea for a technological fix for species extinction is to clone endangered animals.

F. International conservation efforts include widely signed treaties.
1. CITES protects endangered species by banning the international transport of their body parts.
2. In 1992, the leaders of many nations agreed to the Convention on Biological Diversity, a treaty outlining the importance of conserving biodiversity and committing signatory nations to conserving this diversity.

G. Nongovernmental organizations also play a role.
1. A number of U.S.-based conservation organizations have taken leadership roles in biodiversity conservation within U.S. borders and abroad.
2. Various countries have taken steps to protect biodiversity within their borders.
3. Several current efforts in biodiversity conservation are now moving beyond the single-species approach.

H. Biodiversity hotspots pinpoint areas of high diversity.
   1. A hotspot is an area that supports an especially great diversity of species, particularly species that are endemic to the area.
   2. The nonprofit group Conservation International maintains a list of 25 biodiversity hotspots.

I. Community-based conservation is a popular approach today.
   1. Many conservation biologists actively engage local people in efforts to protect the land and wildlife in their own backyards, in an approach called community-based conservation.
   2. In the small Central American country of Belize, conservation biologist Robert Horwich and his Wisconsin-based group Community Conservation, Inc. have helped start a number of community-based conservation projects.

J. Further innovative strategies are being employed.
   1. Debt-for-nature swaps occur when an NGO raises money and then offers to pay off a portion of a developing country's international debt in exchange for a promise by the recipient country to set aside reserves, fund environmental education, and better manage protected areas.
   2. A newer strategy that Conservation International has pioneered is the conservation concession, where nations sell concessions for conservation rather than for resource extraction.

VI. Conclusion
   A. The erosion of biological diversity threatens to result in a mass extinction event equivalent to the major ones of the geological past.
   B. The primary causes of biodiversity loss spell HIPPO.
   C. Many conservation biologists are rising to the challenge with traditional and innovative strategies to save endangered species and their habitats.

# Key Terms

adaptive radiation
area effect
background rate of extinction
biocentric
biodiversity hotspots
biophilia
bioprospecting
CITES
community diversity
community-based conservation
conservation biology
conservation concession
Convention on Biological Diversity
corridors
Costa Rica
debt-for-nature swap
distance effect
ecocentric
ecosystem diversity
ecosystem services
Endangered Species Act (ESA)
endemic
extinction
extirpation
fragmentation
genera
genetic diversity
habitat alterations
habitat conservation plans
habitat diversity
HIPPO
inbreeding
invasive species
island biogeography theory

*continued*

## Key Terms, *continued*

landscape diversity
latitudinal gradient
mass extinction
overexploitation
Red List
relative abundance
safe harbor agreements
Siberian tiger
SLOSS
speciation
Species at Risk Act (SARA)
species diversity
species richness
subspecies
taxonomists
umbrella species
Wilson, E. O.

## Teaching Tips

1. Download the NatureServe 2002 report: "States of the Union: Ranking America's Biodiversity" from www.natureserve.org/publications/statesUnion.jsp. NatureServe ranks the 50 states and the District of Columbia based on diversity of species, levels of rarity and risk, endemism, and number of extinct species.

   Provide students with information about your state. How does it rank? Is your state high or low in biodiversity? High or low in endemism? High or low in extinction rates? How does it compare to surrounding states?

2. Assign students to research a species that is listed with the current IUCN Red List of Threatened Species (www.redlist.org). Information is accessible via the Red List database through a search by category, region, and/or country. Where does the species live? What threatens the species? What is the status of the species? What is being done to protect the species?

   Species on the Red List are placed in a category based on their status, and the categories include: Extinct, Extinct in the Wild, Critically Endangered, Endangered, Vulnerable, Lower Risk, Near Threatened, and Data Deficient. A description of each category can be found on www.redlist.org/info/categories. Ask the students what they think the categories mean, and then provide them with the official definition.

3. Download an overview of the Endangered Species Act published in the November/December 1999 issue of the *Endangered Species Bulletin* of the U.S. Fish and Wildlife Service (http://endangered.fws.gov/esb/99/11-12/toc.html). This issue of the Bulletin gives basic information about the ESA, including how species become listed, a timeline of major events, how the law is enforced, and how habitat conservation plans are implemented. Ask students to compare the Endangered Species Act with the Red List.

4. Assign students to conduct Internet research for updates on the Siberian tiger population. They can check with the Hornocker Wildlife Institute (www.hwi.org) or search for recent news items. For example, in February 2003, a photograph was taken of a wild Siberian tiger in northeastern China, suggesting that the population is returning to areas it formerly populated (www.savechinastigers.org).

# Additional Resources

## Websites

1. "Conservation International," www.conservation.org/xp/CIWEB/home

   Conservation International's (CI's) goals are to conserve Earth's natural heritage and global biodiversity. CI's website describes its conservation regions, conservation strategies, and conservation programs.

2. "Convention on Biological Diversity," United Nations Environment Programme, www.biodiv.org

   This UN website provides information about the Convention on Biological Diversity, an international treaty to conserve the world's biodiversity. The full text of the treaty can be accessed along with case studies from around the world.

3. "Invasivespecies.gov," National Agricultural Library for the National Invasive Species Council, www.invasivespecies.gov

   This website gives information about federal efforts concerning invasive species. The website also describes the impacts of invasive species and provides species profiles.

4. "National Biological Information Infrastructure (NBII)," U.S. Geological Survey, www.nbii.gov

   NBII is a collaborative program to provide increased access to data and information about the nation's biodiversity.

5. "Species," Newsletter of the Species Survival Commission, IUCN—The World Conservation Union, www.iucn.org/themes/ssc/species/spec-int.htm

   This newsletter is published twice a year and provides information about the efforts of the SSC to protect species worldwide.

6. "The Nature Conservancy," http://nature.org

   The mission of The Nature Conservancy (TNC) is "to preserve the plants, animals and natural communities that represent the diversity of life on Earth by protecting the lands and waters they need to survive." The website provides information about TNC's programs and success stories around the world.

## Audiovisual Materials

1. *Before It's Too Late,* Storyteller Productions video, distributed by The Video Project (www.videoproject.net).

   This video investigates the efforts of scientists worldwide to save endangered species and preserve global biodiversity.

2. *Natural Connections,* 2000, Howard Rosen Productions video, distributed by Bullfrog Films (www.bullfrogfilms.com).

   This video is divided into five programs: *Introduction to Biodiversity, The Significance of Salmon, Keystone Species, Forests, Biodiversity and You,* and *Biodiversity vs. Extinction.*

3. *Wild Places,* Scientific American Frontiers, PBS Home Video (www.shop.pbs.org).

   This episode of Scientific American Frontiers looks at the current extinction crisis and innovative conservation strategies implemented around the world.

## CD-ROM

1. *Conserving Earth's Biodiversity*, E. O. Wilson and Dan Perlman, distributed by Island Press (www.islandpress.org/wilsoncd/).

   This CD-ROM program features video clips of E. O. Wilson, interactive exercises, and maps to introduce the topic of biodiversity and its current crisis.

# *Weighing the Issues:* Suggested Answers

### Bioprospecting in Costa Rica

***Facts to consider:*** *Much of this question requires an individual response. Some responses may indicate that this agreement is at least a starting point, a partial model, showing that there are constructive alternatives to bioprospecting benefiting companies in developed nations but not the countries of origin. Though both sides did get some benefit in this agreement, many might argue that it would be more equitable if greater benefits to the contracting company also led to greater benefits to the developing country.*

### Biophilia

***Facts to consider:*** *Most of this question requires an individual response. A survey might help determine whether most people in a community do have an affinity for other living things, asking questions about recreation, values, and charitable preferences. So, too, might a tally of how many households have pets, how well pet-supply businesses are doing, activity levels in local parks, or participation in outdoor recreational activities. Using a more interactive, applied approach, a day in front of a local grocery store promoting animal adoptions with a local animal shelter might yield interesting, even quantifiable, results.*

### Fragmentation and Biodiversity

***Facts to consider:*** *Answers will vary but may include: Some species require large habitats in order to survive, so simply the fragmentation of large habitat will reduce survival of such species. Many species require specific types of habitat; substitution of one habitat for another does not in any way mean that the new habitat is providing support for less valued species. In fact, because habitat changes due to human development have been correlated with rises in the rate of extirpation and extinction, it is reasonable to extrapolate that the types of habitats that are gained through development are less likely to preserve biodiversity than the types that are lost.*

## *The Science behind the Stories:* The Scientific Method

### Tasting and Applying Island Biogeography Theory

**Observation:** Looking at historical data, scientists Robert MacArthur and Edward O. Wilson noticed that island ecosystems seemed to maintain a natural balance, with new species arriving as older species died off. Larger islands seemed to support a larger number of species.

**Hypothesis:** Island ecosystems maintain an equilibrium of species, with rates of gains and losses canceling each other out. An island's size and isolation influence how many species could live there and how easily that equilibrium could be maintained.

**Experiment:** Wilson, together with another scientist, Daniel Simberloff, counted arthropods on small islands off the coast of Florida. They then fumigated the islands to kill off the creatures and then monitored the islands to watch for species recovery.

**Results:** Most of the islands recovered within a year. Although the types of species changed in some cases, the total number of species and creatures on each island remained roughly the same as new arthropods migrated to the depopulated islands. Larger islands had more species before and after the fumigation. More isolated islands recovered more slowly. The research is now a cornerstone of scientific thought on ecosystems and conservation.

## Additional Questions

1. How does genetic diversity affect the success of a species? How does high genetic diversity give a species a better chance of surviving? How does little genetic diversity make species vulnerable to environmental change?

   *Species with more genetic diversity have a better chance of survival because their "built-in variation" gives them the ability to cope with the environment. Species with little genetic variability are more vulnerable to disease and predation and may suffer the effects of inbreeding. Inbreeding results when parents that are too genetically similar mate and produce offspring that are not viable.*

2. Support the statement "not all groups of organisms show equal amounts of species diversity."

   *Organisms are categorized in a hierarchical system of taxonomy that consists of Kingdom, Phylum, Class, Order, Family, Genus, and Species. At any given level, the number of species greatly varies. If we look at the kingdoms, for example, there are far more animal species than species in all other kingdoms (approximate numbers shown):*

   *Plants 248,000*

   *Protists 57,000*

   *Fungi 47,000*

   *Bacteria 5,000*

   *Animals 1.1 million (750,000 insect species)*

   *In the Kingdom Animalia, insects make up over half of all species. Among insects, beetles make up 25% of the species.*

3. Assign students to read the online case study, "An Invasive Species out of Control: Leafy Spurge in the Great Plains." What characteristics of the leafy spurge make it a successful invasive species?

   *Leafy spurge is a successful invader for many reasons. Because it was introduced from Europe, the plant has no natural predators in the Great Plains, allowing it to grow and spread unchecked. It is the first plant to emerge in the spring, enabling it to shade out competing plants. It has extremely deep roots that dominate the water and nutrients in the soil. Leafy spurge also has a successful seed dispersal mechanism. The seeds explode from the seed capsule, traveling up to 15 feet from the plant. In addition, the plant is not eaten by grazing animals (other than sheep and goats), allowing it to spread even more.*

# 16 Land use, forest management, and creating livable cities

## Chapter Objectives

**This chapter will help students understand:**

- Land use decisions
- Urbanization and urban sprawl
- Forestry and forest management
- Agricultural land use
- Parks and reserves
- Planning for livable cities

## Lecture Outline

I. Central Case: The Chicago-Area Forest Preserve System
   A. A network of forest preserves surrounds the city of Chicago in a great crescent, meandering through its suburbs.
   B. Chicago-area residents have places nearby to hike, fish, birdwatch, and study nature.
   C. Chicago owes its forest preserve system to two men, landscape architects Dwight Perkins and Jens Jensen.
   D. The blueprint that was drawn up by Perkins and Jensen was incorporated into a landmark city-planning document produced by architect Daniel Burnham, the 1909 *Plan of Chicago.*
   E. Despite many challenges over the years from periods of neglect, invasive species, fire suppression, and deer overpopulation, the forest preserves are being revitalized.

II. Our Urbanizing World

A. Urban environments need natural land.

1. Large stretches of undeveloped land outside of cities provide natural resources needed to support urban populations.
2. Areas of natural land provide ecosystem services, including purification of water and air, nutrient cycling, and waste treatment.
3. Natural lands provide escape from the stresses of urban life.
4. Many people feel an ethical obligation to preserve wild landscapes and biodiversity for the sake of nonhuman organisms and/or the integrity of ecological systems.

B. Land use and resource management are intertwined.

C. Cities are not new, but the scale and speed of our urbanization is new.

1. Though cities themselves are not new, what is novel is the current scale of urbanization and the speed at which change is occurring.
2. In addition, the world's cities are interconnected to an unprecedented degree.
3. The world's most populous city, Tokyo, Japan, grew from a paltry 690,000 people in 1800 to 1.5 million a century later and today stands at 28 million.

D. Today's urban areas sprawl.

1. Urban areas have grown spatially as well, and in many cases this geographic growth has been more dramatic than the growth in numbers.
2. Chicago's metropolitan area now consists of more than 9 million people spread over 23,000 $km^2$, an area 40 times the size of the city proper.
3. Economists, politicians, and city boosters have almost universally encouraged this unbridled growth of cities and suburbs.
4. Suburban expansion has put more distance between urban and suburban dwellers and the natural lands outside metropolitan areas.

III. Forestry, Land Use, and Resource Management

A. Forests are ecologically valuable, but timber is economically valued.

1. Most of the world's forests occur as taiga and tropical rainforest.
2. Because of their structural complexity and ability to provide many niches for forest organisms, forests comprise some of the richest ecosystems for biodiversity.
3. Deforestation has occurred on all continents, and in some cases has helped to bring entire civilizations to ruin.

B. The growth of the United States was fed by the deforestation of its land.

1. Timber harvesting propelled the growth of the United States throughout its phenomenal expansion across the continent in the 19th century, and into the 20th century.
2. The fortunes of timber companies have risen and fallen with the availability of big trees.

C. Timber harvesting takes place on public lands.

   1. Most timber harvesting in the United States takes place on private land, including that owned by timber companies, but some takes place on public lands, notably the national forests.
   2. The depletion of eastern forests and the fear of a "timber famine" spurred the formation of the Forest Service in 1905 under the leadership of Gifford Pinchot.
   3. When timber companies harvest trees, any of several methods may be used.
   4. In 1996, the most recent year for which good data are available, timber companies extracted 23.5 million $m^3$ of live timber from national forests.
   5. Many environmental advocates and scientists debate whether the Forest Service has in fact managed the forests sustainably.

D. National forests are beginning to be managed for public recreation and ecosystem health.

   1. The Forest Service has developed new programs to manage wildlife and endangered species, including nongame species.
   2. For over a century, the Forest Service and other land management agencies have suppressed fire whenever and wherever it has broken out.
   3. Fire suppression increases the likelihood of catastrophic fires that damage forests, destroy human property, and threaten human lives.
   4. To reduce fuel load and improve the health and safety of forests, the Forest Service and other agencies have in recent years been burning areas of forest under carefully controlled conditions.
   5. In the wake of the 2003 California fires, the U.S. Congress passed the Healthy Forests Restoration Act.

E. Deforestation is proceeding rapidly in many countries.

   1. Many current U.S. trends are being paralleled internationally.
   2. In Sarawak, the Malaysian portion of the island of Borneo, foreign corporations with logging concessions have deforested several million hectares of tropical forest since 1963.
   3. For Sarawak and other places in the world, conflicts over resources, land, and lifestyle can be minimized by the introduction of sustainable forestry practices.

IV. Agricultural Land Use

A. Agriculture now covers more of the planet's surface than does forest.

B. Intensive farming on degraded land should in theory be discouraged by the marketplace if such practices are not profitable.

C. Vast areas of wetlands have been drained to accommodate farming.

   1. Few farmers have had the good fortune to plow the kind of rich and fertile prairie soil that settlers found west of Chicago in the 19th century.
   2. Today, less than half the original wetlands in the lower 48 states and southern Canada remain.

D. Livestock graze one-fourth of the Earth's land surface.
    1. As severe as its ecological impacts have proven to be, cropland agriculture uses less than half the land taken up by livestock grazing.
    2. Human use of rangeland does not exclude its use by wildlife or its continued functioning as a grassland ecosystem.
    3. Most U.S. rangelands are federally owned and managed by the Bureau of Land Management (BLM).

E. Land use in the American West might have been better managed.
    1. Land uses like grazing, farming, and timber harvesting need not have strongly adverse impacts on the landscape.
    2. Most land to the west of the 100th meridian receives less than 50 cm of rain per year, making it too arid for nonirrigated agriculture.
    3. The ideas of John Wesley Powell were too revolutionary for the entrenched political interests and the prevailing misconception that the West was a utopia for frontier settlement.
    4. For agriculture and forestry, debates continue today over how to best utilize land and manage resources.

V. Parks, Reserves, and Wildlands

A. Why have we created parks and reserves?
    1. Many people believe that enormous, beautiful, or unusual features should be protected.
    2. Parks have been created as a way to make use of sites lacking economically valuable material resources.
    3. Protected areas offer utilitarian benefits.
    4. Protected areas offer recreational value to tourists, hikers, fishermen, hunters, and others.
    5. A park or reserve is widely viewed as a kind of Noah's Ark, an island or habitat that can maintain species that might otherwise disappear.

B. Federal parks and reserves began in the United States.
    1. The striking scenery of the American west impelled the U.S. government to create the world's first national parks, largely for reasons of monumentalism and recreation.
    2. The National Park Service (NPS) was created in 1916 to administer the growing system of parks and monuments, which today comprises 388 sites totaling 32 million hectares.
    3. The National Wildlife Refuge is another type of protected area and is managed by the U.S. Fish and Wildlife Service.

C. Wilderness areas have been established on various federal lands.

D. Not everyone supports land set-asides.
    1. The restriction of activities in wilderness areas has helped generate opposition to the land protection policies of the U.S. government.
    2. The drive to extract more resources, obtain greater local control of lands, and to obtain greater recreational access is epitomized by the "wise use" movement.

E. Land is also protected by various nonfederal entities.
   1. Efforts to set aside land and the debates over such decisions at the federal level are paralleled at the state and local levels.
   2. Each U.S. state has agencies that manage land and resources on state lands, as do many counties and municipalities.
   3. Some land conservation is also accomplished by private nonprofit groups such as land trusts.

F. Parks and reserves are increasing internationally.
   1. Many nations have established national park systems, and are benefiting from ecotourism as a result.
   2. Many of the world's protected areas are so-called "paper parks," protected on paper but not in reality.
   3. Some types of protected areas fall under national sovereignty, but are designated or protected by the United Nations.
   4. Many nations have cooperated to establish parks and reserves along the boundaries between them.

G. The design of parks and reserves has important consequences for biodiversity.
   1. Often, it is not the outright destruction of habitat that threatens species, but the fragmentation of habitat.
   2. Because habitat fragmentation is an important issue for biodiversity conservation, conservation biologists debate the SLOSS (single large or several small) dilemma.
   3. A related issue is whether corridors of protected land are important for allowing animals to travel between islands of habitat.
   4. William Newmark's research suggests that North America's national parks are too isolated from each other to sustain populations of large mammals.

VI. Creating Livable Cities

A. City parks were widely established at the turn of the last century.
   1. In the late 1800s, public parks and gardens began to be established in eastern U.S. cities.
   2. Two sometimes conflicting goals motivated the establishment and design of early city parks.
   3. In Chicago in 1893, civic boosters striving to overcome negative aspects of the city's reputation staged the World's Columbian Exposition.
   4. Burnham's 1909 *Plan of Chicago* represented the first thorough city planning program for an American city.

B. City and regional planning are tools for creating livable urban areas.
   1. The Burnham plan and the forest preserves in Chicago set early standards for city planning, the professional pursuit that attempts to design cities in such as way as to maximize their efficiency, functionality, and beauty.

2. Zoning boards and planners face many constraints, and one of the biggest is the road-based transportation system that encourages individuals to drive their own automobiles.
3. Large city parks are a key component of a healthy urban environment.

C. Several success stories stand out.
1. One shining model for creating livable cities is Curitiba, Brazil.
2. In the United States Portland, Oregon, stands out for the success of its planning.
3. While some cities are creating new types of urban spaces, others are working hard to increase the "naturalness" of their park environments.

VII. Conclusion

A. As half the human population has shifted from rural to urban lifestyles, the nature of our impact on the environment has changed.
B. The management of resources must be made sustainable.
C. If we are to remain an urbanized society, cities must be made increasingly livable.

# Key Terms

biosphere reserves
buffer zone
Bureau of Land Management
Burnham, Daniel
city planning
clear-cutting
core area
corridors
deforestation
ecosystem management
geographic information systems
greenway
land use
monumentalism
national forests
national parks
national wilderness areas
national wildlife refuges
Newmark, William
Olmsted, Frederick
*Plan of Chicago*
reconciliation ecology
regional planning
resource management
second-growth trees
seed-tree cutting
selective logging
shelterwood cutting
SLOSS
sprawl
transitional area
U.S. Fish and Wildlife Service
Wetland Reserve Program
wetlands
wilderness
Wilderness Act of 1964
Wildlands Project
wise use movement
world heritage sites
zoning

# Teaching Tips

1. Provide students with information about the three categories of public lands:
   - *Multiple Use Lands* These public lands are the National Forests, managed by the U.S. Forest Service, and National Resource Lands, managed by the Bureau of Land Management. Consumptive activities are allowed such as mining, logging, and grazing.
   - *Moderately Restricted Use Lands* National Wildlife Refuges, managed by the U.S. Fish and Wildlife Service, are in this category. Consumptive activities are allowed, but on a case-by-case basis.
   - *Restricted Use Lands* These lands are the National Parks, managed by the National Park Service, and wilderness areas. No consumptive activities are allowed in these areas. No motor vehicles are allowed in wilderness areas (roadless areas).
2. Ask students to conduct Internet research on the Chicago Wilderness described in this chapter. What ecosystems are preserved? Information can be found on the website "Chicago Wilderness" (www.chicagowilderness.org). This website contains information about the regional nature reserve in the Chicago area. There are descriptions of the prairies, woodlands, wetlands, and water that are protected as well as highlights of things to do and see.
3. Ask students to investigate land use patterns in your state. There is a National Land Cover Data Set available online at http://landcover.usgs.gov/natllandcover.html. This data set is based on a 21-class land cover classification scheme that details the coverage of water, forests, scrublands, barren areas, wetlands, grasslands, cultivated areas, and developed areas in each state. The land use statistics can be accessed free of charge. The data was retrieved from Landsat remote-sensed images of Earth's land surface.

   *Vogelmann, J. E., S. M. Howard, L. Yang, C. R. Larson, B. K. Wylie, and N. Van Driel, 2001. Completion of the 1990s National Land Cover Data Set for the Conterminous United States from Landsat Thematic Mapper Data and Ancillary Data Sources, Photogrammetric Engineering and Remote Sensing, 67:650–652.*

   Ask students to compute percent cover for each land cover class. What are the dominant land cover classes? Does residential and commercial development cover a large percent of land in your state?

# Additional Resources

## Websites

1. "Healthy Forests Initiative," USDA Forest Service, www.fs.fed.us/projects/HFI-general.shtml

   This Web page provides general information about President George W. Bush's Healthy Forests Initiative, which aims to reduce the threat and damage sustained by forest fires by thinning forests.

2. "ParkNet," the National Park Service, www.nps.gov

   This website has a wealth of information about the national parks managed by the NPS including the nature, culture, history, and science of each park. There is also a Web page for educators.

3. "Smart Growth Online," Smart Growth Network, www.smartgrowth.org

   In 1996, the EPA joined with several nonprofit environmental groups and government agencies to form the Smart Growth Network. Their website provides basic information about smart growth and current projects undertaken across the country.

4. "Sprawl Guide," Planning Commissioners Journal, www.plannersweb.com/sprawl/home.html

   This website consists of information that defines sprawl, describes the roots of sprawl (zoning policies, regional planning), examines the problems, and poses solutions to urban sprawl.

## Audiovisual Materials

1. *In Good Hands: Culture and Agriculture in the Lacandon Rainforest,* distributed by The Video Project (www.videoproject.net).

   This video follows Dr. James Nations as he works with the Lacandon Maya of Chiapas in southern Mexico, who have been practicing a sustainable form of rainforest farming for centuries.

2. *Journey into Amazonia,* PBS Home Video (www.shop.pbs.org).

   This two-tape series shows the world's largest tropical wilderness—the Amazon rainforest—featuring rivers, flooded forests, and the dense canopy.

3. *Living Edens: Yellowstone, America's Sacred Wilderness,* PBS Home Video (www.shop.pbs.org).

   A naturalist shows viewers the natural events of each season in Yellowstone National Park.

4. *Reinventing the World: Cities,* 2000, produced by Asterisk Productions, distributed by Bullfrog Films (www.bullfrogfilms.com).

   This program shows cities that have taken measures to become more sustainable: East L.A., São Paolo and Curitiba, Brazil, Vancouver, and Portland.

5. *Subdivide and Conquer: A Modern Western,* 1999, distributed by Bullfrog Films (www.bullfrogfilms.com).

   This 27-minute video, narrated by Dennis Weaver, describes how sprawl affects people and the environment and shows ways of building more livable cities.

# *Weighing the Issues:* Suggested Answers

### Sprawl and Transportation

***Facts to consider:*** *Many strategies can contribute to alleviating urban sprawl. Cities can take this into account in doing proactive city and regional planning; providing greenbelts; supporting rural-urban alliances to preserve land being used for* *less developed uses such as ranching and farming; and funding public improvements such as parks and redevelopment to make existing developed areas more appealing. In long-term planning, new housing can be permitted along mass-transit corridors, and new potential commercial development can be carefully evaluated to make sure that it is truly economic development instead of economic displacement. City dwellers' transportation needs can be helped by providing well-planned public transportation systems that connect residential and business districts. People are more likely to use bicycles if bike lanes and paths are widespread and well maintained. They are more likely to use walking as a form of transportation if sidewalks are maintained, landscaped, and designed with safe street crossings. Though some roads will certainly be necessary, some significant transportation needs can be met while minimizing sprawl by basing urban and suburban land use planning on creating well-designed and popular mass transit, bicycle, and pedestrian alternatives.*

## Subsidies, Soil, and Wetlands

***Facts to consider:*** *Even after agreeing voluntarily to participate in the Conservation Reserve Program, some farmers, accustomed to making independent decisions about their farms, may resent loss of control over their land. The program may also affect farmers in many positive ways, by giving them financial support so they are less likely to have to sell their land, allowing them to spend more time and energy on the land that they do still farm, letting them see firsthand what their land is like when it is not being eroded by traditional agricultural practices, motivating them to increase the practice of sustainable agriculture, giving them a direct experience in which the government clearly values environmental factors, and perhaps causing them to place increased economic and ethical value on wildlife conservation.*

*Some of these benefits will also accrue to the affected rural communities. They may experience more social and economic stability because fewer farmers sell their farms. Communities may value and take pride in their re-emerging wetlands and wildlife. Farm-related businesses may suffer at some level, because farmers would be spending less on equipment, supplies, and farm-related services. On the other hand, some other types of business may flourish, such as recreation and even tourism.*

*Wildlife and ecosystems in the area would start to increase in number, health, and diversity. Plants could take root and survive without being washed away or tilled up as weeds. With less soil disturbance, ground-dwelling animals might come back. With less silt in waterways, fish could flourish more, leading to increases in certain bird populations. Each small improvement in habitat and ecosystem could support the likelihood of improvement in other parts of the ecosystem.*

## Managing Wilderness?

***Facts to consider:*** *Many aspects of this question require an individual response. They might take into account that humans can enjoy recreational activities such as fishing in many locations, even many lakes in beautiful surroundings, but where those activities are not harming the wilderness itself. To try to make the two seemingly opposing goals more compatible in this case, perhaps fish stocking could take place more in areas that are not wilderness, rather than in wilderness areas, coupled with educating the public about why these changes are important. Also, studies may reveal that some lake ecosystems are not having problems with the nonnative species, and fish stocking could be maintained in those lakes. Moreover, already only* *some human uses are permitted in wilderness areas. Our society has learned a lot about wilderness management since the Wilderness Act was passed in 1864, and we have a much higher population density, with more people visiting wilderness areas. Now that we understand more about how certain human uses can harm wilderness, perhaps it is necessary to adjust our policies about which human uses can take place in wilderness areas, or at least under more limited circumstances.*

*If human beings did not intrude on wilderness areas, it might seem fine to have no management of such areas. But when humans are permitted access to wilderness areas, some management is needed at least to minimize or compensate for the effects of humans. This might be as straightforward as planning, building, and maintaining trails, so that people can travel in the wilderness with minimal impact. Opinions will vary on other possible management activities.*

## *The Science behind the Stories:* The Scientific Method

### Using Geographic Information Systems to Survey Earth's Forests

**Observation:** In the late 1990s, the United Nations wanted better protection for Earth's last intact forests, but realized there was little reliable information on where such forests are and what pressures they face.

**Hypothesis:** Advanced technologies based on satellite imagery and a computerized mapping system called a GIS could show the location and status of such forests.

**Experiment:** Using four sets of data—satellite pictures of forests around the world, global population centers, political boundaries, and forest protection laws within those boundaries—scientists tried to build a comprehensive forest GIS map.

**Results:** The map, released in 2001, showed that more than 80% of the world's intact forests were concentrated in just 15 countries, offering a clear focus for conservation efforts. The map also showed that 88% of such forest habitat was sparsely populated by people—meaning it still has some chance at survival if protections are put in place now.

## Additional Questions

1. Describe why urban environments need natural land. How much natural land is required to sustain a town or city?

   *Urban environments need natural land for food, energy resources, solid waste disposal, and timber. We need natural land for recreation. Natural land provides many ecological services that keep our air and water clean. It is estimated that a city needs natural land that is 60 times its size to sustain its human population (based on information provided on London, England).*

2. This chapter describes how deforestation has altered the landscape of our planet. Are there resources that can be used in place of trees? Describe.

   *Student answers will vary based on their background. Timber is used primarily for buildings, furniture, and paper products. Because paper is a disposable product that makes up a large percent of our waste, it makes sense to find alternatives for making paper. Crops like hemp and kenaf are productive fiber crops that can be made into paper. Hemp is illegal to grow in the United States because it is closely related to marijuana. Kenaf, however, can be grown in the United States and is an annual plant that can be farmed. Kenaf is naturally resistant to many pests and requires few nutrients and little water, so it has a small impact on the environment. Residues of crops (corn, soybeans) and recycled clothing have also been used to make paper.*

3. Assign students to read the online case study, "The L.A. of the South: Atlanta's Urban Sprawl." Some measures have been taken in Atlanta to slow urban sprawl as described in the case study. What are other actions that can be taken at a personal level to curb urban sprawl or lessen its impact?

   *Student answers will vary. As an individual, one could live downtown to help slow urban sprawl. Using mass transportation and carpooling help air quality. Telecommuting is a relatively new strategy where individuals work at home and communicate with colleagues/customers by email and teleconferencing, resulting in fewer people on the road. Using alternative modes of transportation that do not pollute, such as bicycling and walking, would also lessen the impact of urban sprawl.*

# 17 Nonrenewable energy sources and their environmental impacts

## Chapter Objectives

**This chapter will help students understand:**

- The nonrenewable energy sources that fuel modern life
- The history of human energy use
- Patterns of energy production and consumption today
- Crude oil, its origins, and the consequences of its use
- Coal, its origins, and the consequences of its use
- Natural gas, its origins, and the consequences of its use
- Environmental impacts of fossil-fuel use
- Political, social, and economic impacts of fossil-fuel use
- Nuclear energy, its origin, and its history

## Lecture Outline

I. Central Case: Oil or Wilderness on Alaska's North Slope?
   A. For some U.S. citizens, Alaska's North Slope is the last great expanse of wilderness in their sprawling industrialized country.
   B. For millions of others, this land represents a source of petroleum, the natural resource that fuels our society and shapes our way of life.
   C. Ever since oil was found in this area a century ago, these two visions for Alaska's North Slope have competed and now exist side by side across three regions of this vast swath of land.
      1. The westernmost portion was set aside in 1923 by the U.S. government as an emergency reserve for petroleum.
      2. In the central portion of the North Slope is an already developed oil industry infrastructure on state lands.

3. The Arctic National Wildlife Refuge (ANWR) lies in the east region on federal lands set aside in 1960 and 1980 to protect wildlife and preserve pristine tundra ecosystems.

D. The ANWR has been the focus of debate for decades as advocates of oil drilling have tried to open its lands for development while advocates of wildlife preservation fought for its protection.

E. In a compromise in 1980, the U.S. Congress passed legislation that put most of the refuge off-limits to oil-drilling but reserved for future decision making a 600,000-hectare area of coastal plain.

F. Behind the noisy policy debate over the ANWR, scientists have attempted to inform the dialogue through research.

II. Sources of Energy

A. Humans have long exploited energy sources.

1. Ever since our ancestors first discovered fire, humans have extracted energy from natural resources to cook food and to light and heat dwellings.

2. In the 20th century, fossil fuels—highly combustible substances formed from the remains of animals and plants from past geological ages—became the dominant source of power in industrialized countries, and then in developing nations.

B. A variety of renewable and nonrenewable energy sources are available today.

1. Energy on Earth comes from a number of sources.

2. Energy sources like solar, geothermal, and tidal energy are considered renewable because their supplies will not be depleted by our use of them.

3. In contrast, energy sources like oil, coal, and natural gas are considered nonrenewable, because at our current rates of consumption, we will use up Earth's accessible store of them in a matter of decades to centuries.

C. Developed nations consume more energy than developing nations.

III. Fossil Fuels

A. Fossil fuels are indeed fuels created from "fossils."

1. The fuels we burn today in our cars and electrical power plants were formed from the tissues of organisms that lived 100–500 million years ago.

2. Fossil fuels are produced only when organic material is broken down in an environment that has little or no oxygen.

a. Coal forms when little decomposition takes place because the material cannot be digested or the appropriate decomposers are not present.

b. Natural gas, primarily methane, is produced as a by-product when bacteria decompose organic material under anaerobic conditions.

c. The sludgelike liquid we know as crude oil, or petroleum, tends to form within a window of temperature and pressure conditions often found 1.5–3 km below the surface.

3. The crude oil of Alaska's North Slope was formed when dead plant and animal material drifted down through coastal marine waters millions of years ago and was buried in sediments in the ocean floor.

B. Petroleum geologists infer the location and size of fossil-fuel deposits.

1. Geologists use a number of techniques to map underground rock formations, understand geologic history, and predict where fossil-fuel deposits might lie.

2. Seismic surveying involves sending sound waves into the ground and measuring their return to the surface at receiving stations.

3. By using such techniques, geologists from the U.S. Geological Survey (USGS) in 1998 estimated the total amount of oil underneath the ANWR's 1002 Area to be between 11.6 and 31.5 billion barrels.

4. Some portion of this amount of oil, whatever it may be, will be impossible to extract using current technology and may have to wait for future technological advances.

5. Oil companies will likely not be willing to extract this entire amount, because some oil will be difficult enough to extract that it is not economically feasible.

6. Thus, technology sets a limit on the maximum that can be extracted, whereas economics determines how much will be extracted.

C. Fossil-fuel reserves are unequally distributed.

IV. Oil

A. The age of oil began in the mid-19th century.

1. Historical evidence suggests that people used solid forms of oil as long ago as 4000 B.C., taking them from deposits that were easily accessible at Earth's surface.

2. The modern use of petroleum began in the 1850s.

B. We drill to extract oil from rocks.

1. Most oil deposits consist of small droplets adhering to the surfaces of holes in porous rocks, just like a sponge whose pores are full of oil.

2. The oil in rocks is typically under pressure from one of several sources.

3. Once pressure is relieved, oil becomes more difficult to extract, and may need to be pumped out.

4. As much as two-thirds of the total deposit may remain after primary extraction.

5. Secondary extraction is more expensive than primary extraction.

C. Offshore drilling produces much of our oil.

D. Oil and petroleum products have many uses.

1. Raw crude oil is put through a refining process before it is used.

2. Because crude oil is a complex mix of hydrocarbons of varying sizes, it has been possible to create many types of oil products by separating its different components.

E. Oil supply and prices affect the economies of nations.
   1. The "energy crisis" of 1973–1974 in the United States demonstrated how the price of oil could affect U.S. government policies and the energy-using habits of the nation.
   2. In response to the embargo, the U.S. government enacted a series of policies designed to reduce reliance on foreign oil.

F. Conservation in the United States has been a function of economic need.
   1. The policies enacted in response to events in 1973 also included conservation measures.
   2. Thirty years later, many of the conservation policies developed after the 1973 oil crisis have been abandoned.
   3. Many critics of oil drilling in the ANWR point out the vast amounts of oil wasted by fuel-inefficient automobiles, and argue that a small amount of conservation would save the nation far more oil than it would obtain there.
   4. The United States consumes over 25% of the world's oil.

G. We may have already depleted half our oil resources.

V. Coal

A. Coal use has a long history.
   1. Coal has been used longer than any other fossil fuel.
   2. The first commercial coal mines in the United States were established in Virginia in the 1740s, and soon found an expanded market after the invention of the steam engine.
   3. Beginning in the 1880s, people began to put coal to use in generating electricity.

B. Coal varies in its qualities.
   1. Scientists classify coal into four types, from the least to most energy rich: lignite, sub-bituminous, bituminous, and anthracite.
   2. Peat is the precursor to coal.
   3. In each of these coal types, sulfur content varies depending on whether the coal was formed in an area of freshwater or saltwater sediments.

C. Coal is mined from the surface and from below ground.
   1. To reach subsurface deposits of coal, shafts are dug deep into the ground and networks of tunnels are built to follow coal seams.
   2. In strip mining, huge amounts of earth are removed by heavy machinery to expose the coal, which is dug out directly.

VI. Natural Gas

A. Natural gas is the fastest growing fossil fuel in use today.

B. Natural gas was discovered long ago, but only recently has become widely used in homes.
   1. The Greek essayist Plutarch wrote the earliest known description of natural gas around 100 A.D., describing its "eternal fires."
   2. During much of the 19th century, its use was localized because the technology did not exist to pipe gas safely over long distances.

3. Heating and cooking were two major new uses for gas at the end of the 19th century.
4. During the 1950s and 1960s, thousands of miles of underground pipelines were laid throughout the United States.

C. Natural gas is formed in two ways.
   1. Biogenic gas is created at shallow depths by the anaerobic decomposition of organic matter by bacteria.
   2. Thermogenic gas is formed at deep depths as geothermal heating separates hydrocarbons from organic materials.

D. Natural gas extraction becomes more challenging with time.
   1. In order to access some natural gas deposits, prospectors need only drill an opening to allow gas to flow to the surface, because pressure drives the gas upward naturally.
   2. Most fields remaining today require that gas be pumped to Earth's surface.
   3. Until the 1970s, much of the gas that rose to the surface during oil drilling was simply burned off.
   4. Biogenic natural gas is also produced as part of the decay process in landfills, and certain landfill owners are now capturing this methane to sell as fuel.

VII. Environmental Impacts of Fossil-Fuel Use

A. Fossil-fuel emissions cause air pollution, drive climate change, and affect the carbon cycle.
   1. Carbon dioxide released from the burning of fossil fuels has been inferred to affect global climate.
   2. Fossil fuels release more than carbon dioxide when they burn, and air pollution from the combustion of fossil fuels can have serious consequences for human health as well as the natural environment.

B. Water pollution results from fossil-fuel use.
   1. Oil enters bodies of freshwater and the ocean in a number of ways.
   2. Little oil is from large headline-grabbing oil spills like that of the *Exxon Valdez,* but rather from small spills and nonpoint source pollution.
   3. Catastrophic oil spills can, however, have significant impacts in the marine environment.

C. Coal mining affects the environment.

D. Coal and oil both can pose threats to human health.
   1. Underground coal mining is one of the world's most dangerous occupations.
   2. Human health can be affected by the chemistry of some oil components.

E. Oil extraction can harm the environment.
   1. Drilling activities themselves have a fairly minimal impact.
   2. Road networks must be constructed, fragmenting habitats.

3. The extensive infrastructure to support a full-scale drilling operation includes housing for workers, access roads, pipelines, and waste piles.
4. Ecosystems in arctic, desert, and semi-arid regions are sensitive to minor changes.
5. Whether Prudhoe Bay's oil operations have had a negative impact on the region's caribou is widely debated.

F. Many scientists anticipate negative environmental impacts of drilling in the ANWR.
1. Scientists have examined the effects of development on arctic vegetation, air quality, water quality, and wildlife.
2. Based on these studies, if drilling takes place in the ANWR, many scientists anticipate damage to vegetation and wildlife.

VIII. Political and Economic Impacts of Fossil-Fuel Use

A. Nations can become overly dependent on foreign oil.
1. Economies tied to the use of fossil fuels are vulnerable if oil supplies become suddenly unavailable or extremely costly.
2. In the United States, concern over reliance on foreign oil sources has repeatedly driven the proposal to open the ANWR to drilling.
3. To counter foreign oil dependence, the United States has diversified its sources of oil, and now receives much of its oil from non-Middle Eastern nations.

B. People in regions with oil reserves may or may not benefit from them.
1. Oil production can be extremely lucrative; many of the world's wealthiest corporations deal in oil or oil-related industries.
2. Alaska's distribution of oil revenue among its citizenry is a rare example of local residents seeing the benefits.
3. In Nigeria, oil was discovered in 1958 in the territory of the Ogoni, one of Nigeria's native people, and the Shell Oil company moved in to develop oil fields.

C. Conversion to renewable energy lies in the future.

IX. Nuclear Power

A. Nuclear power contributes significantly to the energy we consume and the electricity we produce.

B. Nuclear power comes from uranium via a long process.

C. Fission releases energy we can harness.
1. Nuclear energy is the energy that holds together protons and neutrons within the nuclei of atoms.
2. In fission, the nuclei of large, heavy atoms such as uranium and plutonium are bombarded with neutrons.
3. In order for fission to begin, neutrons must be slowed down.
4. All this takes place within the reactor core, and is the first step in the electricity-generating process of a nuclear reactor.

D. Nuclear power grew fast, but ran into problems.
1. As nuclear power was developed in the second half of the 20th century, it showed great promise as a clean power source.

2. Since then, the industry's growth has stalled primarily because of cost overruns.
3. In 1979, the partial meltdown at the Three Mile Island nuclear plant in Pennsylvania released radiation into the environment, necessitating evacuation of area residents and causing public alarm.
4. Growth in nuclear generating capacity slowed to a crawl during the 1990s and today, more than 100 of the world's nuclear plants have been decommissioned, leaving nearly 450 operational.

X. Conclusion
   A. Harnessing energy sources has played a large role in the development of human cultures around the world.
   B. The ongoing debate about the future of the Arctic National Wildlife Refuge is a microcosm of the debate about our energy future.

# Key Terms

1002 area
aerobic
Alaska's North Slope
anaerobic
anthracite
Arctic National Wildlife Refuge
biogenic natural gas
Bissell, George
bituminous
Bunsen, Robert
coal
crude oil
Drake, Edwin
economically recoverable
*Exxon Valdez*
fission
fossil fuels
fracturing technique
fusion
horse head pump
Hubbert's Peak
hydrocarbons
lignite
natural gas
Natural Petroleum Reserve—Alaska
nonrenewable energy sources
nuclear power
nuclear reactor
offshore drilling
Organization of Petroleum Exporting Countries
peat
petroleum
plutonium
Porcupine Caribou Herd
primary extraction
proven reserve
Prudhoe Bay
Saro-Wiwa, Ken
secondary extraction
seismic surveying
Strategic Petroleum Reserve
strip mining
sub-bituminous
sulfur
technically recoverable
thermogenic natural gas
Three Mile Island
underground mining
uranium

# Teaching Tips

1. Discuss the Arctic National Wildlife Refuge issue in class using the case study information in the textbook and the following resources:
   a. Provide students with a visual reference by showing the video program *Arctic Quest: Our Search for Truth.* This program, distributed by The Video Project (www.videoproject.net), follows a group of high school students as they

travel to Alaska to talk to the people and see the habitat and wildlife of the ANWR for themselves.

As your students are viewing the program, ask them to write down the pros and cons of oil exploration and drilling in the ANWR.

b. Search for policy updates on the issue by searching the U.S. House of Representatives website at www.house.gov.

c. The views of the native people fall on both sides of the ANWR debate. Ask students to search for information about the native people of the area, the Gwich'in Nation and Inupiat Eskimos. What are their views on the issue of oil exploration and drilling in the ANWR? How do they depend on the environment for their livelihoods? How do they think oil drilling would affect or improve their lives?

2. Discuss with the students how electricity is produced in your area. Provide them with information about area power plants. Are they fueled by renewable or nonrenewable resources? Are there any documented environmental impacts of the power plants?
3. Ask a few students to lead a panel discussion on power generation. Each student will be an "expert" on one power source (coal, nuclear, natural gas, solar, hydropower, etc.). The students should know the basics of the power source along with the major advantages and disadvantages of its use. The rest of the class interacts with the panel experts by asking questions and debating which source is the best for the environment.

# Additional Resources

## Websites

1. "Arctic National Wildlife Refuge," U.S. Fish and Wildlife Service, http://alaska.fws.gov/nwr/arctic/refinfo.html

   This comprehensive Web page provides basic information about the refuge along with descriptions of its wildlife, habitats, and people.
2. "Coalbed Methane Outreach Program," U.S. Environmental Protection Agency (EPA), www.epa.gov/cmop/index.htm

   This EPA website serves as a resource portal to the development and use of coalbed methane (CBM) and coal mine methane (CMM).
3. "Fossil Fuels," Office of Fossil Energy, U.S. Department of Energy, http://fossil.energy.gov/education

   This is a student Web page that is a primer on fossil-fuel energy. The topics covered are introduction to energy, cleaning up coal, looking down an oil well, and fueling the blue flame.
4. "Radioactive Waste Quick Links," U.S. Nuclear Regulatory Commission (NRC), www.nrc.gov/waste/ql-waste.html

   This NRC Web page provides links to basic information on its website regarding nuclear waste. Here you can find information about waste facilities, including the proposed high-level waste repository, Yucca Mountain.

5. "What Coal Miners Do," United Mine Workers of America, www.umwa.org/mining/colminrs.shtml

   The types of coal mines and mining processes are described here along with images of coal miners at work.

## Audiovisual Materials

1. *Energy on Earth,* 2001, distributed by Hawkhill Video (www.hawkhill.com).

   This programs covers the basic laws of energy flow, the energy sources used today, and the options for the future.
2. *King Coal,* August 2, 2002, NOW with Bill Moyers, PBS Home Video (http://shop.pbs.org).

   In this episode, Bill Moyers reports on the rescue of nine Pennsylvania miners, and goes on to discuss our reliance on coal and its environmental impacts.
3. *Nuclear Power,* 1998, distributed by Hawkhill Video (www.hawkhill.com).

   This is a two-part program that first describes the history of nuclear power and then delves into the basic scientific principles involved in nuclear reactions and the advantages and disadvantages of nuclear power plants.
4. *Radioactive Waste Disposal: The 10,000-Year Test,* distributed by Films for the Humanities and Sciences (www.films.com).

   This program examines the proposed high-level nuclear waste repository in Nevada. It follows scientists who are studying the rocks, weather, groundwater, and human activities to create computer simulations for the waste site.
5. *Fueling the Future,* video series produced by KBKI-TV Denver and distributed by The Video Project (www.videoproject.net).

   This four-part series, produced for a PBS broadcast, covers the use of energy in transportation, farming, housing, and manufacturing. In each segment, the history, current use, and future options are described.

# *Weighing the Issues:* Suggested Answers

### More Miles, Less Gas

***Facts to consider:*** *The first questions require an individual response. If all U.S. vehicles increased fuel efficiency by 10 mpg, Americans would conserve about 1.72 billion barrels of oil annually. (U.S. total annual oil consumption is 7.7 billion barrels, of which 67 percent is used for transportation. The current average fuel efficiency is 20.8 mpg, so increasing that by 10 mpg would reduce consumption by about one-third. So 7.7 billion multiplied by 0.67, divided by 3 is 1.72 billion barrels. This calculation does not take into account that the 67 percent is for transportation, which presumably includes planes and railroads. It also does not account for the fact that 20.8 mpg is the average fuel efficiency for new vehicles, not all vehicles, and not commercial vehicles, such as large trucks. But it is the most accurate figure that can be derived from the figures provided in the chapter.)*

*Other ways to conserve fossil fuels include: improve efficiency of fossil-fueled power plants, improve renewable resource technologies so that they can substitute in trans-*

*portation and energy production; improve efficiency of other forms of fossil-fuel use for transportation (such as trains and planes); and improve energy efficiency of household and industrial appliances and buildings and improve their designs in ways that use renewable forms of energy.*

*Such options would help, but, because transportation is responsible for over two-thirds of U.S. fossil-fuel consumption, probably none of these improvements would have as much effect as a significant improvement in fossil-fuel efficiency. Of course, if the improvement in vehicle efficiency was quite small, other improvements might have a relatively greater effect.*

## The Science of Oil's Arctic Impacts

***Facts to consider:*** *Proposed studies will vary. Given the studies that have already been performed, additional useful studies might include the following. In other areas already being drilled, measure fumes from similar equipment and drilling operations, natural gas burning associated with oil extraction, sludge ponds, waste pits, and oil spills; then either compare these values with known levels at which those chemicals harm organisms, or use them to design a controlled experiment exposing various local species to those levels, to study the effects. Other research might study animal movement patterns in the areas of concern, then build a sample ice road, and then study, even in winter when the road is solid, whether and in what ways it affects animal movement patterns and other behaviors (such as ability to find food and mates). Install samples of the new proposed technologies in some of the existing Prudhoe Bay settings, and then study the extent to which the improvements in technology reduce or eliminate negative environmental effects that were observed in earlier studies.*

## Will Capitalism Drive a Shift to Renewables?

***Facts to consider:*** *Answers will vary. Arguments in favor of the outlook provided might be: It is much easier to change behavior of manufacturers and consumers when there is financial incentive to do so, and the shift to renewable energy sources will involve some very significant barriers, which may otherwise seem too great to overcome. Also, then these changes are voluntary, rather than imposed by a government already viewed by many as too intrusive. Arguments against that outlook might be: By the time the supplies of fossil fuel decline enough to raise fuel prices to a point that manufacturers and consumers are motivated to change, there may not be enough fossil fuel available to avoid great economic disruption from shortages and extremely high prices, while manufacturers and researchers would face tremendous pressure to develop practical alternatives as quickly as possible.*

*Government involvement in development of renewable energy sources might help speed up that process, thus spurring U.S. economic stability and prosperity in the long run. It might also provide unbiased assessment and support of alternatives most likely to succeed, with less bias than manufacturers already invested in particular technologies. On the other hand, government may be less efficient than private enterprise, so this might be a poor use of government resources. Also, government may be more likely to support organizations that are already well established, even though many innovative ideas come from small companies.*

## *The Science behind the Stories:* The Scientific Method

### How Electricity Is Generated

**Observation:** At a coal-fired power plant in Niles, Ohio, burning high-sulfur coal mined in the United States was resulting in emissions with high amounts of pollutants such as sulfur dioxide and nitrogen oxides (NOX).

**Hypothesis:** Treating the plant's emission gases with chemical processes could remove sulfur dioxide and NOX before the emissions were released into the air.

**Experiment:** Emissions were cleaned with more efficient filter bags to remove more ash, and then reheated. Ammonia was added to the reheated gas to turn NOX into harmless nitrogen and water vapor. Further chemical reactions converted sulfur dioxide into sulfuric acid.

**Results:** The cleaning process removed about 95% of sulfur dioxide and 90% of NOX from flue gas. The power plant bottled and sold the sulfuric acid, turning a waste product into a source of revenue. The plant continues to use the anti-pollution process developed there.

## Additional Questions

1. What factors should be considered in the Arctic National Wildlife Refuge debate? The environment? The wants and needs of the native people? The wants and needs of Americans in general? The Porcupine Caribou Herd?

   *Student answers will vary. Ideally, students will realize that decisions about oil exploration and drilling can be complicated, with many factors to consider. There are social, economic, political, environmental, and scientific views that are all important.*

2. Ask students to read the online case study, "The Cost of Coal." Describe the Surface Mining Control and Reclamation Act. How does it aim to reduce acid mine drainage?

   *The Surface Mining Control and Reclamation Act (SMCRA) established federal regulations for active mines and provides funds to reclaim old abandoned mines. By reclaiming abandoned coal mines, this reduces or eliminates exposed pyrite that would otherwise react with water to form sulfuric acid.*

3. Ask students to read the online case study, "Nuclear Waste Disposal: Is Yucca Mountain the Answer?" Describe the current status of high-level nuclear waste. Where is it stored? Is this storage safe? Also, describe the proposed underground repository in Nevada. Why are some people against this site?

   *Today, all high-level nuclear waste is either housed on-site or trucked to a hazardous waste landfill. There are 131 sites across the country that store high-level waste. Since this waste will be radioactive for thousands of years and can pose environmental and health threats, scientists have determined that it must be stored underground in a geologically stable area. The Yucca Mountain site in Nevada was officially endorsed by President Bush in 2002. Although it is in a remote, dry area, some scientists believe it is unsafe because of nearby seismic activity and earthquake faults.*

# 18 Renewable energy sources

## Chapter Objectives

**This chapter will help students understand:**

- The sources of renewable energy
- Biomass energy
- Hydroelectric energy
- Solar energy
- Wind energy
- Geothermal energy
- Ocean energy sources
- Hydrogen fuel cells and new transportation options
- Principles of energy conservation

## Lecture Outline

I. Central Case: Iceland Moves toward a Hydrogen Economy

A. Iceland is a hunk of lava the size of Kentucky that has risen out of the North Atlantic from the rift between tectonic plates known as the mid-Atlantic ridge.

B. The magma that gave birth to the island heats its groundwater, giving Iceland some of the world's best sources of geothermal energy.

C. Iceland also depends on fossil fuels and has one of the highest per capita rates of greenhouse gas emissions in the world.

D. In the 1970s, Bragi Arnason, a University of Iceland professor, began arguing that Iceland could achieve independence from fossil fuel imports, boost its economy, and serve as a model to the world by converting to a renewable energy economy based on hydrogen.

E. In the late 1990s, the interest of international energy companies in his ideas and the nation's "Kyoto dilemma" finally forced Arnason's countrymen to pay attention.

F. Those planning the shift to a hydrogen economy sketched a stepwise transition, with fossil fuels phased out over 30–50 years.

G. To make this happen, Icelanders in 1999 teamed up with corporate partners who were looking to develop technology for the future.

H. Iceland may already be serving as a model for the world.

II. Renewable Energy Sources

A. Renewable energy sources.

1. Renewable energy currently provides only a small portion of our power.

a. Today's economies are powered by fossil fuels, with 80% of all primary energy coming from coal, oil, and natural gas.

b. Developing countries account for most use of combustible renewables, while developed countries account for most use of renewable energy sources that require higher technology.

c. Renewable energy is used for heating buildings and for generating electricity, with very little going to transportation.

B. Renewable energy has multiple benefits and its uses are growing.

1. Renewable sources are inexhaustible on time scales relevant to human societies, and will help alleviate air pollution and greenhouse gas emissions that are driving global warming.

2. Rapid growth in renewable energy sectors seems likely to continue, as population and consumption grow, global energy demand expands, fossil-fuel supplies decline, and citizens demand cleaner environments.

C. The transition cannot be immediate, but it must be soon.

1. Many renewables are expensive, lack adequate technological development, or lack infrastructure to transfer energy on the required scale.

2. The best hope may be for a gradual transition from fossil fuels to renewable energy sources.

III. Biomass Energy

A. Biomass consists of those organic substances produced by recent photosynthesis.

B. Biomass can be used for energy in diverse ways.

C. Biomass energy brings a mix of benefits and drawbacks.

1. Biomass energy can be efficient in terms of both energy use and cost; biomass tends to be the least expensive type of fuel for combustion in power plants, and improved energy efficiency can lead to lower prices for consumers.

2. In terms of environmental impacts, biomass energy has a mixed record.

a. Unsustainable wood harvesting can lead to deforestation, soil erosion, and desertification.

b. A larger issue is that the combustion of biomass does not reduce emissions to the extent that other renewable energy sources do.

c. Growing crops for energy establishes monoculture agriculture, with all its impacts.

IV. Hydroelectric Power
   A. Hydroelectric power is widely used.
   B. Hydropower brings benefits, but has negative environmental impacts.
      1. Hydropower is renewable as long as rain still falls and fills rivers and reservoirs.
      2. Hydropower is cleaner than fossil fuels.
      3. Hydropower causes thermal pollution, and dams disrupt the local ecology and economy of riverside areas.
   C. Hydropower may not expand much more.
      1. The majority of the world's rivers that offer excellent opportunities for hydropower have been dammed.
      2. Moreover, in developed nations, awareness of the environmental impacts of dams is causing people to propose removing many of the dams that exist.
      3. In the United States, 98% of rivers appropriate for dam construction are already dammed, and many of the remaining 2% are protected from dam building.

V. Solar Energy
   A. The sun provides energy for almost all biological activity on Earth by converting hydrogen to helium in nuclear fusion.
   B. Passive solar heating is simple and effective.
      1. In passive solar heating, buildings are designed and building materials are chosen to maximize their direct absorption of sunlight in winter.
      2. Passive solar design techniques include using heat-absorbing construction materials, and installing low, south-facing windows to maximize sunlight capture in the northern-hemisphere summer.
   C. Active solar energy collection can be used to heat air and water in buildings.
      1. Solar panels or flat-plate solar collectors generally consist of dark-colored heat-absorbing metal plates mounted in large flat boxes covered with glass panes.
      2. Active solar energy is being used for heating, cooling, and water purification in Gaviotas, a small remote town in the high plains of Colombia.
   D. Concentrating solar rays can magnify the energy received.
      1. The strength of solar energy can be magnified by gathering sunlight from a wide area and focusing it on a single point.
      2. The principle of concentrating the sun's rays has also been put to work by utilities in large-scale high-tech approaches to producing electricity from solar energy.
   E. Photovoltaic cells produce electricity directly from sunlight.
      1. Photovoltaic (PV) cells collect sunlight and convert it to electrical energy directly by making use of the photoelectric effect.
      2. The plates of a PV cell are made primarily of silicon, enriched on one side with phosphorus and on the other with boron.

3. Multiple PV cells are arranged in modules, which can comprise panels, which can be gathered together in flat arrays.
4. One drawback of PV systems is that they rely on batteries and once they are fully charged, no additional energy can be stored.

F. Solar power is little used but fast growing.
1. Although solar technology dates from the 19th century, solar power was pushed to the sidelines as fossil fuels gained a stronger foothold in our energy economy.
2. Largely because of the lack of investment, solar power presently contributes only a minuscule portion of our energy production.
3. Sales of PV cells are growing fast—by 25% per year in the United States.

G. Solar power offers many benefits.
1. The fact that the sun will continue burning for another 4–5 billion years makes it practically inexhaustible as an energy source for human civilization.
2. PV cells and other solar technologies use no fuel, are quiet and safe, contain no moving parts, require little maintenance, and do not even require a turbine or generator.
3. Another advantage of solar systems is that they enable local, decentralized control over power.
4. A major benefit of solar power over fossil fuels is that it does not pollute the air with emissions, and thus greatly reduces levels of greenhouse gases and pollutants released into the atmosphere relative to fossil fuels.

H. Location and cost can be disadvantages of solar power.
1. Not all regions are sunny enough to provide adequate power with current technology.
2. The up-front cost of investing in the equipment is prohibitive.
3. Decreases in price and improvements in energy efficiency of solar technologies so far are encouraging.

VI. Wind Energy

A. Wind has long been used for energy.
1. Today's wind turbines have their historical roots in Europe, where wooden windmills have been used for 800 years.
2. The first wind turbine or windmill built for the generation of electricity was constructed in the late 1800s by inventor Charles Brush.

B. Modern wind turbines convert kinetic energy to electrical energy.
1. Wind turbines use the motion of wind passing through their blades to create electricity.
2. Turbines can be erected singly, but are most often erected in groups called wind parks or wind farms.
3. Engineers have designed turbines to begin turning at specific wind speeds in order to harvest wind power as efficiently as possible.

C. Wind power is the fastest growing energy sector.

D. Wind power has many benefits.

1. Like solar power, wind produces no emissions once wind power is manufactured and installed.
2. Wind power appears considerably more energy efficient than conventional power sources and uses less water than traditional power sources.
3. Wind turbine technology can be used on many scales, from a single tower for local use to fields of thousands for utilities to supply large regions.
4. Another societal benefit of wind power is that landowners can lease their land for wind development.
5. Wind energy involves up-front costs for the erection of turbines and the expansion of the infrastructure, but over the lifetime of the project requires only maintenance costs.

E. Wind energy has some downsides.

1. Humans have no control over the wind.
2. Good wind resources are not always near population centers that need the energy, so the transmission networks will need to be greatly expanded.
3. Wind turbines are known to pose a threat to flying birds, which can be killed by the rotating blades.
4. Offshore sites can be promising.
   a. Wind speeds over water are often greater than those over land.
   b. The first offshore wind farm was erected by Denmark in 1991.

VII. Geothermal Energy

A. Geothermal energy is one form of renewable energy that does not originate from the sun, but from deep within Earth.

1. The radioactive decay of elements amid the extremely high pressures and temperatures deep in Earth generates heat that rises to the surface through magma, and then through fissures and cracks.
2. Geothermal power plants use the heat energy of natural hot springs to generate power.

B. Geothermal energy is harnessed for heating and electricity.

1. Tapping the energy of geothermal sources requires that wells be drilled down hundreds or thousands of meters toward the heated ground water.
2. Hot groundwater can also be used directly for heating homes, offices, and greenhouses.
3. Thermal energy from either water or solid earth can also be used to drive a heat pump to provide energy.

C. The use of geothermal power is growing.

D. Geothermal power has benefits and limitations.

1. Geothermal power greatly reduces emissions relative to fossil-fuel combustion.

2. The water of many hot springs is laced with salts and other minerals that corrode equipment and pollute the air.
3. Geothermal is limited to being used in the particular areas in which it occurs.

VIII. Ocean Energy Sources

A. We can harness energy from tides.
B. We can harness energy from waves.
C. We can use thermal energy from the ocean.

IX. Hydrogen

A. The development of fuel cells and hydrogen fuel shows promise as a way to store electricity conveniently and in considerable quantities, and to produce it at least as cleanly and efficiently as renewable energy sources.
B. In this system, electricity generated from wind or solar can be used to produce hydrogen and store it in fuel cells.
C. Hydrogen fuel may be produced from water or from other matter.
   1. Hydrogen atoms tend to bind to other molecules, becoming incorporated in everything from water to organic molecules.
   2. Electrolysis produces pure hydrogen without emitting carbon- or nitrogen-based pollutants.
D. Fuel cells produce electricity by joining hydrogen and oxygen.
   1. Once hydrogen gas has been isolated, it can be used as a fuel to produce electricity within fuel cells.
   2. Hydrogen gas is allowed into one side of the cell, whose middle consists of two electrodes that sandwich a membrane that only protons can move across.
E. Hydrogen and fuel cells have many benefits.
   1. As it is the most abundant element in the universe, we will never run out of hydrogen.
   2. It is clean and nontoxic to use, and may produce few greenhouse gases and other pollutants.
   3. Fuel cells are silent, nonpolluting, and allow energy to be stored in the form of hydrogen.
   4. Hydrogen and its use in fuel cells is energy efficient.

X. Energy Conservation

A. Energy conservation is the practice of reducing energy use as a way of extending the lifetime of our fossil-fuel supplies, of being less wasteful, and of reducing our environmental impact.
B. Personal choice and increased efficiency are two routes to effective energy conservation.
   1. As individuals, we can make conscious choices to adjust our behavior by taking steps to reduce energy consumption.
   2. Cogeneration can almost double the efficiency of a power plant.
   3. Consumers can "vote with their wallets" by purchasing energy-efficient appliances.
C. Both conservation and renewable energy are needed.

XI. Conclusion

A. The coming decline of fossil-fuel supplies and the increasing concern over air pollution and global climate change have convinced many people that we will need to shift our energy use to renewable energy sources.

B. Biomass and hydropower have been playing major roles so far and solar, wind, and geothermal are promising for the future.

C. Electricity from hydrogen fuel can help convert our transportation sector to a nonpolluting renewable basis.

D. Most renewable energy sources have been held back for a variety of reasons, including a lower level of funding for research and development relative to nonrenewable resources, and artificially cheap market prices for nonrenewable resources that do not include external costs.

# Key Terms

active solar energy collection
biodiesel
biomass energy
closed cycle approach
cogeneration
dams
electrolysis
energy conservation
fossil fuels
fuel cells
gasohol
geothermal energy
global climate change
hybrid vehicle
hydrogen economy
hydrogen fuel
hydroelectric power
Iceland
nacelle
not in my back yard (NIMBY)
ocean energy sources
ocean thermal energy conversion (OTEC)
open cycle approach
passive solar energy collection
photoelectric effect
photovoltaic (PV) cells
power tower
solar cookers
solar energy
solar panel
thermogram
tidal energy
turbine
wave energy
wind energy
wind farms
wind turbines
windmill

# Teaching Tips

1. In a recent study, the National Environmental Education and Training Foundation (www.neetf.org) found that only 12% of American adults could pass a test about the sources and consumption of energy in the United States. Ask your students to take the 10-question quiz to see how they measure up in energy knowledge as compared with the general public. The quiz questions are found in the Tenth Annual National Report Card: Energy Knowledge, Attitudes, and Behavior (August 2002), "Americans' Low 'Energy IQ': A Risk to Our Energy Future" at www.bigfishpond.com/clients/neetf/Roper2002.pdf.
2. Ask students to visit www.fueleconomy.gov to find the gas mileage, greenhouse gas emissions, and air pollution ratings for their car (or a family member's car). This government website also has information about gas mileage, hybrid electric

vehicles, and hydrogen fuel cell vehicles. How do your students' cars compare to hybrid electric cars? What kind of vehicle emits the most greenhouse gas emissions?

3. Discuss how electricity is generated in your region. The EPA has a "Power Profiler" program at www.epa.gov/cleanenergy/powerprofiler.htm. The program allows users to input a zip code to generate two charts related to energy production in their region.
4. Discuss some actions that students can take at home, work, and school to reduce their daily energy consumption. The Department of Energy has a Web page called "Energy Savers: Tips on Saving Energy and Money at Home." (www.eere.energy.gov/consumerinfo/energysavers/index.html). Here are some basic tips for saving energy:
   - Turn off the lights when leaving a room.
   - Replace incandescent light bulbs with energy-efficient compact fluorescent bulbs.
   - Use only cold or warm, not hot, water in the washing machine. It takes a lot of energy to heat water.
   - Activate the "sleep" mode on computers and copiers.
   - Replace old appliances and computers with Energy Star products that are more energy efficient.
   - Turn up your thermostat in the summer (78 degrees) and down in the winter (68 degrees).
   - Install ceiling fans.
   - Regularly change the filter on the air conditioner.

# Additional Resources

## Websites

1. "Energy Information Administration," U.S. Department of Energy (DOE), www.eia.doe.gov

   This DOE website provides official energy statistics on coal, electricity, natural gas, nuclear energy, and petroleum.
2. "Electricity from Non-Hydroelectric Renewable Energy Sources," U.S. Environmental Protection Agency, www.epa.gov/cleanenergy/renew.htm#solar

   This Web page features a summary of wind power, solar power, biomass, geothermal, and landfill gases in the United States.
3. "Energy Efficiency and Renewable Energy," U.S. Department of Energy, www.eere.energy.gov

   An energy information portal, this Web page has links to many other websites and online documents about renewable energy.

## Audiovisual Materials

1. *American Experience: The Hoover Dam,* PBS Home Video (www.shop.pbs.org).

   This PBS program shows the history of the Hoover Dam and its role in transforming the West by providing water and electricity.

2. *Hydrogen Generators, Fuel Cells, and Energy,* 1999, a CD-ROM produced by the American Hydrogen Association and distributed by Knowledge Publications (http://knowledgepublications.com).

   This 7-hour video program on CD-ROM takes students through basic electrochemistry, a modern hydrogen lab, and hydrogen engines.

3. *Renewable Power: Earth's Clean Energy Destiny,* video produced by William Hoagland and distributed by The Video Project (www.videoproject.net).

   The focus of this program is the hydrogen fuel cell. Along with a description of fuel cells, the program discusses the promise of zero-emissions vehicles for the future.

4. *Science in Action: Solar Energy,* (1996) TMW Media Group, distributed by Amazon (www.amazon.com).

   This program shows how we capture, store, and use solar energy to heat our homes, provide transportation, and generate electricity.

# *Weighing the Issues:* Suggested Answers

### Ethanol

***Facts to consider:*** *Producing ethanol from corn and other crops is much less efficient than burning those crops as biomass. Certain uses of biomass can help minimize environmental impacts. Some are available now: Use of biomass as an energy source can help minimize environmental impact if the material would otherwise be even more damaging to the environment. For instance, some farmers burn agricultural waste in the field; burning it as useful biomass would reduce use of some fossil fuel (and avoid its consequences). Similarly, methane from landfills would be released as a greenhouse gas if it were not captured and used as an energy source. Some biomass sources are less environmentally problematic than others: If firewood is traditionally used as a biomass energy source, then substituting an agricultural crop as the energy source, though still releasing carbon into the atmosphere and perhaps depleting the soil, would at least slow the rate of forest destruction. Perhaps in the future more biomass can be deliberately brought together in order to create piles from which methane could be extracted for biomass conversion to energy. Increased use of combined heat-and-power systems would increase the efficiency of biomass operations, thereby reducing the environmental impact per unit of energy produced.*

### Your Island's Energy

***Facts to consider:*** *Because the island knows it has sun, wind, and wave energy options, these would be the paths to investigate, at least in the long run. Of these, wave energy would be least likely to be developed, because it has not been commercialized yet, and because it has negative environmental effects on coastlines, boating,* *and aesthetics. In the short run, Congress should support energy efficiency and energy conservation by using incentives and standards, as successfully keeping such energy use low will allow the nation to minimize dependence on foreign sources of fossil fuel, not only helping preserve the natural environment but reducing debt and trade imbalances. Other ways Congress can minimize energy expenditure while maintaining quality of life are to support mass transit and careful land use planning. Because wind power is a technology that is already producing commercial power at significant levels, this technology is mature enough that Congress should fund its implementation in the near term. Meanwhile, Congress should offer support to research in these technologies, particularly wind and solar. The research should emphasize development of efficient energy storage capacity, as neither wind nor solar power yet has economically viable storage capacity. In terms of trade, the island nation will certainly need to make deals to import some fossil fuel. It will also need to import wind and solar technologies, but perhaps can reduce costs by working out agreements to serve as the model for some of the advances in these technologies. Economic advisors might be able to project future fossil-fuel prices. Then they could analyze how quickly each possible renewable energy technology must pay for itself in order to be economically feasible at current and projected fossil-fuel prices. They may also know which kinds of industries the nation could encourage that would generate maximum revenue and national independence while minimizing energy demand. Scientists could focus on creation of storage capacities for wind and solar systems, as well as increasing the efficiency of such systems. Offshore wind systems might also be investigated, as a more efficient option.*

## Precaution over Hydrogen?

***Facts to consider:*** *Answers will vary. Some may argue that, at this point in time, the warnings about possible global warming effects seem based on a hypothesis rather than on hard evidence. In any event, both hydrogen fuel and fuel cells are really just in the early stages of application. A few model buses and some experimental vehicles will not significantly impact the planet. Because developing alternatives to nonrenewable energy resources is so important, society should continue to vigorously support, investigate, and try hydrogen technology. These early versions can help us learn more about how to make these technologies more efficient; meanwhile, we can carefully study their possible environmental complications. No matter how fast we move, even Iceland is still a long way from having a hydrogen-based economy.*

*Others might say that global warming is already a significant and growing problem; society would not be responsible if it were to commit to a technology that may make this critical situation worse. Also, once manufacturers invest in a new field, such as these technologies represent, they want to know that their efforts will pay off. The more forward progress is made, the more difficult it will be to turn manufacturers from this path, no matter what negative environmental consequences of these approaches may be discovered later on. Also, if manufacturers and governments invest in this renewable energy source, and proves it not to have a good payback, they might be resistant to exploring and supporting other renewable energy sources in the future. So, even if no potential problems with global warming are confirmed, following the precautionary principle still makes sense.*

## *The Science behind the Stories:* The Scientific Method

### Hydrogen V2

**Observation:** Researchers had noted that certain green algae produced little hydrogen when cut off from sunlight, which stopped normal photosynthesis.

**Hypothesis:** By hampering the plants' photosynthetic process, more hydrogen could be produced more consistently.

**Experiment:** Scientists in California and Colorado put the algae on a diet without sulfur, which is necessary for normal photosynthesis in this plant. Without sulfur, the plants' metabolic processes shifted, and they began producing hydrogen.

**Results:** The algae produced large amounts of hydrogen over a sustained period of time, with low amounts of greenhouse gases as a by-product.

### Wind Farms

**Observation:** The state of Idaho has regions with strong winds, but no one knew if the areas could support large-scale commercial wind farms.

**Hypothesis:** Many parts of the state experienced winds strong enough to create successful wind farms, and those areas could be detected by a broad, publicly conducted research effort.

**Experiment:** Under a program started in 2001, Idaho has loaned out anemometers, or devices that measure wind speed, to more than 80 landowners. Participants in the program take long-term wind measurements and share their findings with the state.

**Results:** Several sites have already shown promise as wind farms, with one site near Idaho Falls receiving a $500,000 grant to start construction.

## Additional Questions

1. What are some ways that you could conserve energy at home, work, or school? Would it be economically feasible to invest in an energy efficient technology such as a hybrid-electric car or an Energy Star appliance? Explain.

   *Student responses will vary. Simple actions to reduce energy consumption include things like turning off lights when not in use, adjusting the thermostat, carpooling, using mass transit, insulating windows and doors, and replacing incandescent light bulbs with fluorescent bulbs. More costly measures include things like replacing appliances with Energy Star products, buying a hybrid-electric car like the Honda Civic or Toyota Prius, or installing roof-top solar panels. These measures are typically more expensive investments than traditional options, but pay off in the life of the product.*

2. Hydroelectric power accounts for over 90% of the electricity produced by renewable sources. Describe the advantages and disadvantages of hydropower. Is it really an environmentally friendly option? Why or why not.

   *Hydropower is generated when water stored in a reservoir flows through turbines in a dam. The process itself does not produce air pollution—a definite benefit. However, the construction of the dam, the flooding of land to fill the reservoir, and the alteration of the natural flow of the river are all negative consequences. The quality of the river changes as water temperature increases, dissolved oxygen decreases, and sedimentation causes the river bottom to change. These alterations cause a change in the river's biotic community to one that can survive such conditions. As a result, most scientists believe that hydropower is not an environmentally friendly option as compared to solar, wind, or geothermal.*

3. Assign students to read the online case study "San Francisco: A New Leader in Solar Power." Ask students to elaborate on this statement from the case study: "The trick is to bundle solar power projects with other projects with shorter payback periods."

   *Since solar technology is more expensive than other options, it is more economically feasible to propose a project that uses a variety of energy efficient technologies. In the case of San Francisco, wind turbines and energy efficient upgrades provide a faster pay-back than solar panels, allowing the revenue bond to be paid in a timely manner*

# 19 Waste management

## Chapter Objectives

**This chapter will help students understand:**

- The types of waste we generate
- The scale of the waste problem
- Municipal solid waste, industrial waste, and hazardous waste
- Wastewater and sewage treatment
- Conventional waste disposal methods: landfilling and incineration
- Waste reduction solutions
- Composting approaches
- Recycling approaches

## Lecture Outline

I. Central Case: Dump Dwellers and Manila's Garbage Crisis

  A. On July 10, 2000, a week of typhoon rains triggered an avalanche of wet garbage to collapse from the 50-foot slopes of the Payatas dump and smash into a shantytown of squatters, smothering at least 200 people.

  B. Located in Quezon City, the gigantic trash heap at Payatas was home to roughly 80,000 to 90,000 people.

  C. After the deadly avalanche, the government closed the dump, depriving the scavengers of their livelihood.

  D. The fact that so many people live at such a site is a testament to the seriousness of the problems of poverty in the Philippines, not to mention other nations in the world.

  E. As material consumption has risen among Filipino citizens, and as the population has continued to grow, so has the generation of waste.

- F. When the government shut down Payatas in the wake of the garbage avalanche, it turned metro Manila's garbage problem into a full-blown crisis.
- G. Landfill closures and deterioration of garbage collection services has meant that only 70% of municipal solid waste is successfully collected and disposed of in Philippine cities.
- H. Incineration of waste is prohibited by air pollution laws, but there is promise that recycling and composting will reduce waste.
- I. Today, Filipinos are doing their best to meet the ambitious goals of the waste-control legislation passed in 2000 and signed into law in 2001.

II. Types of Waste

- A. Waste refers to any unwanted material that results from a human activity or process.
- B. Wastewater refers to any water that is used in our households, businesses, industries, or public facilities and is drained or flushed down our pipes, as well as to the polluted runoff from our streets and storm drains.
- C. There are several reasons for managing waste.
- D. There are several ways of managing waste.
    1. The goals of waste management are to dispose of waste safely and effectively and to reduce the amount of waste generated, and the single most effective approach is to reduce the amount of waste generated.
    2. Recycling is widely viewed as the next best approach to managing waste.
    3. Regardless of how effectively we can encourage reduction, reuse, composting, and recycling, there will always be some amount of waste that we will need to dispose of.

III. Municipal Solid Waste

- A. Municipal solid waste is the waste produced by consumers, public facilities, and small businesses.
- B. Patterns in the municipal solid waste stream vary from place to place.
    1. In North America, paper, yard debris, food scraps, and plastics are the principal components of municipal solid waste, together accounting for over 70% of the waste stream.
    2. The majority of municipal solid waste comes from packaging and from nondurable goods.
    3. The average American produces over 2.0 kg (4.5 lb) of trash per day.
    4. Following the United States in per capita solid waste production are Canada with 1.7 kg (3.75 lb) per day and the Netherlands with roughly 1.4 kg (3 lb) per day.
    5. Consumption and waste patterns are somewhat different in developing countries.
    6. In both developed and developing nations, consumption and the generation of waste has been rising.
    7. Although waste has been increasing for decades and is presently rapidly increasing in developing countries, it has slowed and in some cases decreased in many developed nations in recent years.

C. Open dumping of the past has given way to improved disposal methods.
   1. Historically, people have dumped their garbage wherever it suited them to do so.
   2. As population and consumption have risen, however, amounts of waste have increased, making dumps larger.
   3. In the 1980s in the United States, waste generation increased while incineration was restricted, and recycling was economically infeasible and widely unpopular.

D. Sanitary landfills follow health and environmental guidelines.
   1. In modern sanitary landfills, waste is buried in the ground or piled up in large mounds and every effort is made to prevent waste from contaminating the environment.
   2. Guidelines specify how waste is added to the landfill; it cannot simply be heaped on.
   3. Following regulations to ensure public health and safety is not cheap, and in developing countries, landfill operators often lack the technology or funds to safely dispose of waste.
   4. Whereas the Philippines and many other nations are in need of more sanitary landfills, the United States has greatly reduced its number as landfill sites are becoming consolidated.

E. Landfills have drawbacks.
   1. Despite improvements in liner technology and landfill siting, many experts believe that leachate will very likely escape from even well-lined landfills.
   2. Another problem is that finding areas to locate new landfills has become increasingly difficult, resulting in waste being shipped long distances from where it is generated.
   3. One famed case of long-distance waste transport involved a barge full of garbage that left New York and traveled 9,700 km (6,000 mi) before eventually returning to New York because it was contaminated with medical waste.

F. Incinerating trash reduces pressure on landfills.
   1. Incineration is a controlled process of burning in which mixed garbage is combusted at very high temperatures.
   2. Simply reducing the volume and weight does not get rid of those elements in trash that are toxic.
   3. As a result of real and perceived health threats from incinerator emissions and community oppositions to these plants, a number of technologies have been developed to mitigate emissions.

G. Many incinerators burn waste to create energy.
   1. Most North American incinerators today use the heat generated by waste combustion to create energy.
   2. In 2000, there were 102 operational waste-to-energy (WTE) facilities across the United States with a total capacity to process 96,000 tons of waste per day.

3. Although burning waste is an effective means of reducing its volume, the considerable financial cost of incineration is not offset by power generation, and it may take many years for a WTE facility to become profitable.

H. Landfills can also produce energy when gas is collected.
   1. Landfill gas can be collected, processed, and used as natural gas, one of our prime sources of fossil-fuel energy.
   2. Today, more than 330 operational projects collect landfill gas in the United States.

I. Reducing waste is a better option than disposal.
   1. Source reduction means preventing the generation of waste.
   2. A number of strategies for source reduction exist, some of which involve the operating procedures of manufacturers and businesses, and some of which involve the behavior of consumers.

J. Reuse is one main strategy for source reduction.
   1. Using already-used goods is one major way to reduce waste.
   2. Although reuse and source reduction comprise the most preferred options for addressing the solid waste problem, it can be difficult for those of us in developed nations to battle our own consumerist tendencies.

K. Financial incentives can tackle overconsumption in a throwaway society.
   1. Some states in the United States have developed ways of being efficient with beverage containers.
   2. It is a testament to the lobbying power of the beverage industries, which have traditionally opposed the passage of bottle bills, that more states do not have such legislation.
   3. Another approach that uses financial incentive to influence consumer behavior is the "pay-as-you-throw" approach to garbage collection.

L. Composting is a strategy for reducing and recycling organic waste.
   1. Organic waste, such as yard trimmings and food scraps, can be reduced and recycled by composting.
   2. At the municipal level, many communities are trying to reduce waste through community composting programs; there were 3,800 such programs across the United States at last count.

M. Recycling consists of three steps.
   1. Recycling consists of collecting materials that can be broken down and reprocessed in order to manufacture new items.
   2. There are three basic steps in the recycling loop, and the first step is collection of recyclable goods and materials after they have been used.
   3. Items collected are taken to material recovery facilities (MRFs) to be sorted and processed.
   4. Once readied, these materials are used in manufacturing new goods.
   5. If the recycling loop is to work and become economically sustainable, consumers and businesses must then purchase the products made from recycled materials.

N. Recycling has grown rapidly.
   1. Today's thousands of curbside recycling programs have sprung up only in the last 20 years.
   2. Recycling rates vary greatly from one product to another and from one location to another.
   3. Between 1998 and 2000 alone, total waste recovery in metro Manila rose from 69,400 tons to 101,850 tons.

O. The economics of recycling is in transition.
   1. The growth of recycling has been propelled in part by economic reasons, as established businesses see opportunities to save money and as entrepreneurs see opportunities to start new businesses.
   2. As more and more manufacturers use recycled products and as more technologies and methods are developed to use recycled materials in new ways, the market will likely continue to expand, demand will rise with supply, and new business opportunities will arise.

P. One Canadian city showcases the shift from disposal to reduction and recycling.
   1. By developing a 30-year plan and sinking $850 million into it, Edmonton, Alberta, has created one of the world's most advanced programs for waste management.
   2. When Edmonton's residents put out their trash, city trucks take it to the city's new co-composting plant.
   3. Besides the co-composting facility and a sanitary landfill, Edmonton's waste program also includes a state-of-the-art MRF.

IV. Industrial Solid Waste

A. Industrial solid waste is solid waste that is considered neither municipal solid waste nor hazardous waste under the federal Resource Conservation and Recovery Act (RCRA).
   1. Waste managers in the United States differentiate between municipal solid waste and industrial solid waste largely because these categories are regulated differently.
   2. Many of the methods and strategies of disposal, reduction, and recycling of waste by industry are similar or identical to those used for municipal solid waste.

B. Industrial ecology seeks to reduce waste and make industry more sustainable.
   1. Industrial ecology involves modifying processing and manufacturing techniques and finding new uses for materials previously considered waste.
   2. Industrial ecologists examine the entire lifetime of a given product and look for ways to make the process more ecologically efficient (life-cycle analysis).
   3. Industrial ecologists also examine industries broadly and try to identify points at which waste products from one manufacturing process could be used as raw materials for a different process.

4. These approaches signal a radical departure from our previous attitudes toward waste production.
5. For example, American Airlines has enacted a number of reforms that have both saved money and reduced environmental impact.

V. Hazardous Waste

A. Hazardous waste is waste that poses a danger or potential danger to human health.

B. Heavy metals and organic compounds are primary types of hazardous waste.

1. Heavy metals such as lead, chromium, mercury, arsenic, cadmium, tin, and copper are used widely in industry.
2. In our day-to-day lives, we rely on the capacity of synthetic organic compounds and petroleum-derived compounds to resist bacterial, fungal, and insect activity.
3. These and other types of toxic substances have a number of negative impacts on human health and environmental quality.

C. Hazardous wastes have diverse sources.

D. Several steps precede the disposal of hazardous waste.

1. For many years, we produced hazardous waste and discarded it carelessly into the environment.
2. Today, a number of disposal methods for hazardous waste have been developed.
3. U.S. law mandates that hazardous materials be tracked "from cradle to grave."
4. Because current U.S. laws make disposing of hazardous waste quite costly, irresponsible companies have sometimes been guilty of illegally and anonymously dumping waste on abandoned property.

E. There are three main disposal methods for hazardous waste.

1. Hazardous waste landfills have several impervious liners, leachate removal systems, and are located far from aquifers.
2. Surface impoundments are a method of storing liquid hazardous waste.
3. In deep-well injection, a well is drilled deep beneath an area's water table.

F. Radioactive waste is a special type of hazardous waste.

1. Because NIMBY opposition prevents the location of nuclear waste disposal sites just about everywhere in wealthy and educated nations, the U.S. government has been trying for years to establish a single large site for radioactive waste disposal.
2. Currently, a site in the Chihuahuan Desert in southeastern New Mexico serves as a permanent disposal site for radioactive waste.
3. During the Cold War, radioactive material was disposed of unsafely in both the United States and the Soviet Union.
4. One example from the former Soviet Union involves the Mayak Nuclear Complex in Chelyabinsk, Russia, where radioactive wastes were long dumped into local rivers and lakes used as drinking water supplies by 24 villages.

G. Contaminated sites are being cleaned up, slowly.
    1. Many thousands of former military and industrial sites lie contaminated today with hazardous waste in Russia, in eastern Europe, in the Philippines, and in the United States.
    2. In the 1970s, the U.S. Congress passed a series of laws regulating waste in general and hazardous waste in particular.
    3. The Superfund program, administered by the EPA, employs experts to identify sites polluted with hazardous chemicals, protect groundwater near these sites, and clean up the pollution.
    4. Identified sites are called Superfund sites, and include abandoned factories, old landfills, and abandoned utilities.
    5. Once a Superfund site has been identified, the EPA determines whether it is a threat to human health.

VI. Sewage Treatment and Wastewater Management
  A. Until recent decades, wastewater was not treated before being disposed of, even in wealthy countries like the United States.
  B. Wastewater treatment involves several steps.
    1. Upon its arrival at a municipal wastewater treatment plant, wastewater first passes through bar screens that block the passage of large pieces of debris.
    2. The wastewater then undergoes primary treatment, which involves physical removal of contaminants.
    3. Wastewater from the primary treatment process then proceeds to secondary treatment, which involves using biological means to further remove pollutants.
    4. Finally, the clarified water from secondary treatment is treated with chlorine and sometimes ultraviolet light in order to kill bacteria.
  C. Artificial wetlands can aid the treatment process.

VII. Conclusion
  A. Our societies have made great strides in addressing many of our waste problems.
  B. In many countries, recycling and composting efforts are making rapid strides.
  C. Our waste management efforts are still marked by a number of difficult dilemmas.
  D. The best hope lies in adopting new ways of producing and using goods, changing our linear economic model into a circular one.

## Key Terms

artificial wetlands
biosolids
Chernobyl nuclear accident
composting
corrosivity
deep-well injection
hazardous waste
heavy metals
ignitability
incineration
industrial ecology
industrial solid waste
landfill gas
landfills
leachate
life-cycle analysis
municipal solid waste
open dumping
organic compounds
Payatas dump
primary wastewater treatment
radioactive waste
reactivity
recycling
recycling loop
reduce
Resource Conservation and Recovery Act (RCRA)
reuse
sanitary landfills
secondary wastewater treatment
source reduction
Superfund
surface impoundments
toxicity
waste
wastewater
waste-to-energy (WTE) facility
Yucca Mountain

## Teaching Tips

1. Ask students to collect household garbage for one week to be analyzed in class (except food waste). During class time, have students separate their waste into paper, plastics, glass, metal, and other. What type of waste is the most abundant? What type of waste takes up the most space (has the largest volume)?
2. According to the text, Manila is suffering from a garbage crisis. Metro Manila produces 8,000 tons of garbage a day. Ask students to find updated information on the Internet about Manila's solid waste problem. How is the garbage being collected? How is it being managed? What is the plan for the future?
3. Present the class with information about solid waste in your state. See the EPA's state data Web page at www.epa.gov/epaoswer/non-hw/muncpl/states.htm. How much is produced per person? How is the majority of waste managed?
4. Show landfill video clips from the PBS *American Field Guide.* There is a unit on landfills that has information about garbage, landfills, recycling, and solid waste management programs. See http://pbs.org/americanfieldguide/teachers/landfills/landfills.

## Additional Resources

### Websites

1. "Municipal Solid Waste," U.S. Environmental Protection Agency, www.epa.gov/epaoswer/non-hw/muncpl

   This website provides the basic facts about MSW along with answers to frequently asked questions and information about MSW disposal, programs, and state data.

2. "Payatas Conversion and Closure," National Solid Waste Management Commission Secretariat, www.emb.gov.ph/nswmc

   This website has a set of news articles and press releases regarding the Payatas dump in Manila.

3. "Reduce, Reuse, Recycle," U.S. Environmental Protection Agency (EPA), www.epa.gov/epaoswer/non-hw/muncpl/reduce.htm

   This EPA Web page describes source reduction, ways to reuse, and recycling.

4. "Solid Waste and Recycling Magazine," www.solidwastemag.com

   This Canadian bimonthly magazine, available online, provides articles about collection, hauling, processing, and disposal of solid waste.

5. "Why Yucca Mountain?," Office of Civilian Radioactive Waste Management, www.ocrwm.doe.gov/ymp/about/why.shmtl

   This website describes the Yucca Mountain project for radioactive waste disposal; it has two downloadable fact sheets.

### Audiovisuals

1. *Garbage into Gold,* 1995, produced by Beth Pike and Stephen Hudnell and distributed by The Video Project (www.videoproject.net).

   This video profiles new recycling enterprises that take waste products and turn them into usable items.

2. *Global Dumping Ground,* produced by Lowell Bergman and distributed by The Video Project (http://videoproject.net).

   This documentary, a PBS Frontline special report, reveals how toxic waste exports have become big business in the United States, posing serious health threats to individuals in foreign countries that receive the waste.

3. *Here's My Question: Where Does My Garbage Go?,* 2000, produced by Middlemarch Productions and distributed by Bullfrog Films (www.bullfrogfilms.com).

   This film describes municipal solid waste issues and takes the viewer to a landfill.

4. *Protectors and Polluters,* produced by Margeurite Arnold and distributed by The Video Project (http://videoproject.net).

   From the *America's Defense Monitor* TV series, this program shows the toxic wastes dumped on military bases across the country.

## *Weighing the Issues:* Suggested Answers

### Recycling Pays

***Facts to consider:*** *Extracting, transporting, and processing new raw materials requires significant energy input. Reducing or nearly eliminating the need for these processes achieves huge savings in energy.*

*Avoiding such energy consumption also avoids the negative environmental effects of that energy use, from the environmental damage involved in the extraction of the energy source (such as water pollution from surface mining) to the consequences of the conversion of that source to energy (such as atmospheric emissions from fossil-fuel combustion). Using virgin paper and minerals means increased expand forestry and mining operations; using recycled materials conserves those limited natural resources and protects from harm the ecosystems of which they are a part. Finally, paper and related products require the harvesting of trees; living trees help control levels of greenhouse gases. So, use of recycled paper products helps keep our atmosphere healthier by reducing the number of trees that would otherwise be cut.*

## Toxic Computers

***Facts to consider:*** *As the number of cathode-ray devices grows, the number of these devices needing disposal will also grow. If allowed into the regular waste stream, they will leach heavy metals, which may escape from landfills; these long-lasting metals may wind up in groundwater and other environmentally unsound places. If simply banned from the waste stream, they will likely appear in larger numbers in even less desirable locations, such as open dumping in closed landfills and empty lots. A more specific, organized disposal system would help minimize such problems. This system would require both a designated means for consumers to get rid of these devices and safe ways to treat these devices after disposal. If recyclers could figure out how to generate income from dismantling devices containing such tubes, then recycling pathways would also include acceptance of cathode-ray devices. Finding ways to re-use the heavy metals (such as in new cathode-ray devices) would be particularly advantageous, because then those materials would remain within the manufacturing cycle, rather than in a waste stream that requires physical space and may cause environmental damage. A related approach might be to use the same procedures now used for household hazardous waste, such as designated places or dates for such disposal, with special treatment after collection.*

*Opinions will vary about who should be responsible, mentioning manufacturers, consumers, and government. Perhaps a large-scale "tube bill" like the "bottle bills" could mandate that manufacturers pay consumers a small amount to return cathode-ray devices to particular locations. This would at least concentrate this type of waste. This might also motivate manufacturers to develop alternatives to using such heavy metals, or at least to make it easier to re-use them.*

## Land Application of Biosolids

***Facts to consider:*** *The land application of sewage sludge is certainly an efficient use of resources, but answers will vary about whether it is an unnecessary risk. Some may argue that alternatives to such uses should be emphasized, at least until more study either confirms or denies the concerns mentioned. They may point out that toxic metals tend to be long lasting and build up in trophic levels, so that the negative environmental and health effects of biosolid applications may not show up at first. Others may say that perhaps these problems occur in a small percentage of biosolid applications, and perhaps those incidents can be identified and eliminated or reduced. They may also say that care in choosing sites for biosolid application may avoid or minimize such problems, at least in terms of their effects on humans. Making good decisions in this area would involve knowing more about: the prevalence, types, and concentrations of toxic metals and pathogens in sewage sludge; the types of safety standards required for sewage sludge to be used for land application; and other treatment and disposal methods for sewage sludge, including the effects of toxics, pathogens, and odors in those environments.*

## *The Science behind the Stories:* The Scientific Method

### Digging Garbage: The Archaelogy of Solid Waste

**Observation:** By the 1980s, plastic packaging had become a focus of the debate over U.S. landfill space, with critics saying plastics were taking up too much space in trash dumps.

**Hypothesis:** As part of his Garbage Project research, scientist William Rathje thought landfill excavations could show how much of a problem plastic packaging really represented.

**Experiment:** Rathje's teams bored into 15 landfills with heavy drilling equipment. Landfill contents were sorted, identified, weighed, and analyzed.

**Results:** Rathje surprised some other scientists by saying that plastic packaging represents only a small part of landfill content. In findings published in 1997, he said plastic packaging makes up about 4.5% of landfill content, and that figure has not increased substantially since the 1970s.

### Using Nature to Treat Our Waste Water

**Observation:** In the California town of Arcata, scientists trying to find a sewage treatment solution took note of decades of research showing how natural wetlands filtered and cleansed dirty water.

**Hypothesis:** A human-engineered wetland, created to follow the biological processes of a natural one, could be used to help filter Arcata's wastewater.

**Experiment:** Researchers set up 10 small experimental marshes, lining them with different aquatic plants, to see if the plants and the microbial life they host could filter contaminants out of the wastewater.

**Results:** The marshes, planted with a mix of aquatic vegetation including native bulrushes, gave rise to rich colonies of single-celled bacteria and algae that removed pollution from the wastewater. Arcata later built a full-scale treatment system based on such marshes to clean up its sewage problems.

## Additional Questions

1. What are the advantages and disadvantages of using landfills and incinerators to manage solid waste? Which management option is better for the environment? Which option is better for human health and safety?

   *Landfills are a relatively inexpensive way to deal with garbage. The immediate environmental impacts of landfills have been substantially reduced with the use of modern sanitary landfills that collect leachate and methane. However, the fact still remains that tons of recyclable and compostable materials are deposited into landfills where little decomposition takes place. On the bright side, methane that is collected can be used to generate electricity. Incineration is more expensive than using landfills because of the equipment required. The volume of garbage is greatly reduced through incineration; however, the ash that is left over can be toxic in na-*

*ture. Incineration releases air pollution, but electricity can be generated in the process. Both management options pose risks to the environment and human health. The best alternative is to reduce, reuse, and recycle.*

2. Explain how, although the volume of garbage produced per year in the United States has grown since the 1980s, the number of landfills has greatly decreased.

   *As new landfill regulations have been implemented, small landfills have been closed and the garbage stream has gone to new, larger landfills. Many municipalities now combine efforts and money to build and maintain large regional landfills.*

3. Assign students to read the online case study, "Nuclear Waste Disposal: Is Yucca Mountain the Answer?" What is high-level radioactive waste? Why does Yucca Mountain seem to be a good site for the disposal of high-level radioactive waste?

   *Used nuclear fuel is high-level radioactive waste. It has the potential to stay highly radioactive for hundreds to thousands of years. Yucca Mountain was chosen as the first permanent repository for high-level waste because of its remote location, dry climate, and deep water table.*

# 20 Sustainable solutions

## Chapter Objectives

**This chapter will help students understand:**

- The concept of sustainable development
- How humans are part of the environment
- How promoting economic welfare and protecting the environment are compatible
- How growth is not equivalent to progress
- The roles that consumption, population, and technology play in human impact on the environment
- Several key approaches to designing sustainable solutions
- That time is limited but the human potential to solve problems is tremendous

## Lecture Outline

I. Central Case: The World Summit in Johannesburg
   A. In 2002, the World Summit on Sustainable Development was held in Johannesburg, South Africa, drawing more than 10,000 delegates from nearly 200 countries.
   B. The attendees gathered to hammer out agreements for moving their nations and our global society toward sustainable development.
   C. The United Nations defines sustainable development as "development that meets the needs of the present without compromising the ability of future generations to meet their own needs."
   D. Johannesburg, a city of 3.2 million people, seemed an appropriate location for the summit.
   E. South Africa is in many ways a microcosm of the world and illustrates the world's need for sustainable development.

F. The Johannesburg meeting was the third historic international conference on human interactions with the environment.

G. The UN Conference on Environment and Development was held in Rio de Janeiro, Brazil, in 1992, where Agenda 21 was agreed upon that drew a road map for nations to improve people's lives and improve environmental conditions.

H. Few of the goals of Agenda 21 have been fulfilled by the world's nations, and as participants ventured to Johannesburg, they knew that more had to be accomplished.

I. Many critics said the meeting featured too much talk and not enough action.

II. Sustainable Development

A. What precisely do we want to sustain?

1. One goal is to sustain human civilization in a healthy state.
2. Another goal is to sustain the natural environment, its species, and its systems in a healthy and functional state.

B. Humans are not separate from the environment.

1. In developed nations and in the large cities of the developing world, it is easy to feel completely disconnected from the natural environment.
2. Consider one of the most un-"natural" inventions of the human species: the banana split.

C. Win-win situations are possible.

1. The only way for our species to "win"—to survive and thrive—is to conduct our activities in ways that sustain the processes and resources of our environment.
2. Furthermore, in a lose-lose scenario, it may be only humans who lose in the very long term.
3. If we succeed in sustaining the environmental conditions that have supported our species to this day, however, then we preserve the chance to sustain our species and our phenomenal society.

D. What accounts for the perceived economy-versus-environment divide?

1. Although command-and-control regulation may have been the best way to slow human impacts at the outset of the environmental movement, the regulatory approach has today become so ingrained that people often feel it infringes on their liberties.
2. One common perception is that environmental protection measures hurt the economy by costing people jobs.

E. Environmental protection measures can enhance economic opportunity.

1. Even as some industries decline, new ones spring up to take their place.
2. In addition, people desire to live in areas that have clean air and water, intact forests, and parks and open spaces.
3. Thus, it is clear that environmental protection need not lead to economic stagnation and, to the contrary, is often likely to enhance economic opportunities.

III. Growth versus Progress

   A. Correlating economic expansion with environmental protection measures is one way of addressing whether there is or is not a trade-off between environmental protection and economic development.
   B. It is conventional among economists and the policymakers who heed their advice to speak of economic growth as a goal for a nation, or the world.
   C. Can consumption continue growing?
      1. Some analysts estimate that there are not nearly enough resources for the rest of the world's people ever to attain the level of consumption already reached by the average U.S. citizen.
      2. Cornucopian critics often scoff at the notion that resources are limited, but we must remember that our perspective in time is limited as well.
   D. Consuming less can be more satisfying.
      1. Consuming goods and services is certainly an important element in making our lives comfortable and happy; however, consumption alone does not reflect a person's quality of life.
      2. Consumption can be greatly reduced even while one's happiness or quality of life increases.
         a. Improvements in the technology of materials and in the efficiency of manufacturing processes are one way.
         b. Another way is by developing a sustainable manufacturing system.
         c. A third way is to halt runaway consumption involving consumers rather than industry.
      3. By changing the way we measure prosperity and progress, and by adopting sustainable practices in industry, government, and our daily lives, it may be possible to continue increasing our quality of life while reducing, or keeping constant, our level of consumption.
   E. Population cannot keep growing.
      1. No population of organisms can continue growing forever.
      2. The demographic transition provides reason to expect that population sizes will stabilize and even begin to fall.
   F. Technology can help us toward sustainability.
      1. It is largely technology that spurred our population growth.
      2. Technology can exert either a positive or a negative impact on the environment.
      3. In developed nations, much technology has begun reducing our environmental impact.
      4. Producing responsible and constructive technology that can lead us toward sustainable solutions requires scientific research.
   G. Growth does not equal progress.
      1. Progress toward sustainability, then, can come from wisely harnessing technology, halting population growth, and reducing consumption.
      2. Having too many people on Earth can crowd societies and make life miserable for all.

IV. Sustainable Solutions

A. We can redefine our priorities regarding economic growth and quality of life.

1. Of foremost importance is to incorporate external costs into the market price of goods and services.
2. If we can make our accounting practices reflect indirect negative consequences and give a clearer view of the full costs and benefits of any particular action or product, then the free market itself can become a force for improvement.
3. The political obstacles to this are great, however, because environmentally and economically destructive taxes and subsidies remain strikingly widespread.

B. We can mimic natural systems and make human industrial systems circular and recycle oriented.

1. Human processes of manufacturing have run on a linear model.
2. We could in theory make all our industrial processes sustainable if we could transform linear processes into circular ones.
3. The Swiss Zero Emissions Research and Initiatives (ZERI) Foundation sponsors dozens of innovative projects worldwide that attempt to create goods and services without generating wastes.

C. We can base our decisions on long-term thinking.

1. Businesses may act according either to long-term or short-term interests.
2. In 2002, the UN Environment Programme conducted analyses to predict the likely effects of a large-scale shift to sustainable development strategies over the next 30 years.

D. We can promote local self-sufficiency and be aware of the effects of globalization.

1. Modern enthusiasm for locally grown and organic foods in North America first blossomed on the West Coast.
2. The urge among some people to base their economies locally is complemented by the desire of others to combat globalization.
3. The prominent ecological economist Herman Daly has untangled two distinct sets of ideas that people have often lumped together under the term globalization.
4. People who view the phenomenon called globalization in a negative light generally accentuate certain aspects that Daly reserves for his use of the term globalization.
5. Internationalization will likely foster the pursuit of sustainability, and globalization in itself does not necessarily threaten it.
6. American democracy still serves as a model for many countries with more repressive governments.
7. Though people may disagree over whether global homogenization of cultures in itself is desirable, it can definitively be said that putting all your eggs in one basket is always a risky strategy.

E. We can vote with our wallets.

    1. Consumers can exercise a great deal of power through their choices of what to buy.
    2. Products produced with sustainable forestry methods are labeled as such so that consumers can make choices and exert power in the marketplace to reward these efforts.

F. We can vote with ballots.

    1. Although economic decisions can make large differences, many of the changes that will be needed to attain sustainable solutions are political, requiring policymakers to see them through.
    2. Today's major environmental laws came about because of the activity of citizens pressuring their representatives in government to do something about perceived environmental problems.

G. We can promote research and education.

V. Precious Time

A. We need to reach again for the moon.

    1. John F. Kennedy's directive in 1961 had powerful motivation behind it.
    2. The rapid and historic accomplishments of both the United States and the Soviet Union during the space race show what societies can accomplish when they provide focused support for a chosen goal.

B. We must pass through the environmental bottleneck.

C. We must think of Earth as an island.

    1. As Easter Island's trees disappeared, the people must have known at some level that their resources were vanishing.
    2. It would be tragic folly to let such a fate occur to our planet as a whole.

VI. Conclusion

A. Today we have thousands of scientists who study Earth's processes and resources closely.

B. We have access to an accumulated knowledge and ever-developing understanding of our dynamic Earth.

C. The challenge to our global society today is to support that science and to listen to those scientists who can accurately judge false alarms from real problems.

D. This science is what offers us hope for our future.

## Key Terms

affluenza
Agenda 21
command-and-control regulation
*consilience*
cornucopians
demographic transition
ecological economics
environmental bottleneck
globalization
green labeling
green taxes
I = PAT equation
internationalization
Johannesburg, South Africa
sustainability
sustainable development
World Summit on Sustainable Development
Zero Emissions Research and Initiatives

## Teaching Tips

1. The Global Leaders for Tomorrow Environment Task Force publishes a ranking of 142 countries according to their "Environmental Sustainability Index" (ESI). The ESI is a measure of a country's progress toward environmental sustainability based on a set of 20 core indicators.

   Ask students to visit www.ciesin.org/indicators/ESI/index.html and view the 2002 ESI report and spreadsheet. Where is the United States in the ranking? On what indicators was the United States given high scores? low scores?

   *World Economic Forum, Yale Center for Environmental Law and Policy, and CIESIN, 2002 Environmental Sustainability Index, www.ciesin.columbia.edu/indicators/ESI, February 2002.*

2. Discuss with the class the United Nations Conference on Environment and Development of 1992, held in Rio de Janeiro, Brazil. Also called the Earth Summit, 172 governments and 2,400 nongovernmental organizations participated in what's called the largest international meeting on the environment. The UN "sought to help Governments rethink economic development and find ways to halt the destruction of irreplaceable natural resources and pollution of the planet" (www.un.org/geninfo/bp/enviro.html). There were five resulting documents of the conference:

   - Agenda 21—a program of action for global sustainable development
   - The Rio Declaration on Environment and Development—principles outlining the rights and responsibilities of states
   - The Statement of Forest Principles—principles for sustainable management of forests around the world
   - The United Nations Framework Convention on Climate Change—a legally binding treaty for reduction of greenhouse gas emissions
   - The United Nations Convention on Biological Diversity—a legally binding treaty for the conservation of biodiversity

   In 1997, governments met in New York for the UN General Assembly's review of progress since 1992 (Earth Summit + 5). Success stories and reports were given by each participating government. The report given by the United States can be accessed at www.un.org/esa/earthsummit/usa-cp.htm.

3. Start a Global Action Plan EcoTeam with your students. The EcoTeam program, sponsored by the Empowerment Institute, helps individuals lessen their environmental impact through the adoption of sustainable lifestyle practices. EcoTeams meet every two weeks to discuss one of the chapters in the EcoTeam workbook and each individual pledges to take environmentally friendly actions at home, work, and school. Garbage, water, energy, transportation, and consumption are the topics covered in the workbook. For more information, visit http://globalactionplan.org.

# Additional Resources

## Magazine Article

Pugh, Thomas and Erik Assadourian. 2003. "What is Sustainability, Anyway?," *World Watch* 16(5): 10–21.

## Websites

1. "Center for Sustainability," U.S. Environmental Protection Agency (EPA), www.epa.gov/r3chespk/center.htm

   EPA Region III's Center for Sustainability is managed by the Chesapeake Bay Program Office. The mission of the Center is to connect its environmental protection efforts with "larger economic and social goals." Sustainable development documents are available on the website.
2. "Disposable Planet?," BBC News Online, http://news.bbc.co.ut/hi/english/static/indepth/world/2002

   This website features a six-part series on sustainable development that addresses population, food, cities, waste, tourism, and energy.
3. "Eco-Portal—The Environmental Sustainability Info Source," Ecological Internet, www.eco-portal.com

   This website provides news on environmental sustainability and is a database of reviewed environmental sustainability websites.
4. "Johannesburg Summit 2002," United Nations Department of Economic Development and Social Affairs, Division for Sustainable Development, www.johannesburgsummit.org

   This is a comprehensive website for the world summit on sustainable development and includes basic information, documents, major groups involved, and highlights from the meeting.
5. "Resources at the Sustainability Institute," Sustainability Institute, www.sustainer.org/resources.html

   This institute is a "think-do tank dedicated to sustainable resource use, sustainable economics, and sustainable community." This Web page provides links to papers, columns, and websites about sustainability.

## Audiovisual Materials

1. *Building Sustainability,* produced by University of Texas and Northcutt Productions, distributed by The Video Project (www.videoproject.net).

   This video follows the designing of an environmentally friendly building at the University of Houston Health Science Center.

2. *Hawaii in Transition,* 1996, produced by Sheila Laffey and ECO Productions, distributed by The Video Project (www.videoproject.net).

   This video shows how Hawaiians are making strides with sustainable projects in aquaculture, renewable energy, and sustainable agriculture.

3. *The Earth Debate,* 2002, NOW with Bill Moyers and the BBC, distributed by PBS (http://shop.pbs.org).

   First aired on PBS in August 2002, this 90-minute program was taped at the World Summit on Sustainable Development in Johannesburg, South Africa. The program features panelists who discuss the issues on the table at the summit.

4. *Sustainable Futures,* produced by Ian Murray and distributed by The Video Project (www.videoproject.net).

   This program takes the viewer to seven communities in Canada, the United States and Mexico where sustainability efforts are making a difference.

# *Weighing the Issues:* Suggested Answers

### Unavoidable Impacts

***Factors to consider:*** *Responses will vary. Human beings have probably been responsible for species extinction from the very earliest times, long before technology increased the rate at which we seem to be triggering such extinctions. So far, our species does not have a very good record in terms of preserving other species. There are, however, a few good notes, as we have taken action that has helped bring some species back from near-extinction. Yet the pace of extinction continues to be rapid. Only by embracing and accelerating sustainability can we slow, and perhaps eventually halt, our harm to other species. In an ideal world, societal development might not demand harm to other species or the environment. As Wilson's "environmental bottleneck" metaphor suggests, however, by now our actions are harming the environment in so many ways that it is perhaps impossible to envision that we, as an intelligent but imperfect species, as a dominant species, as a culturally and politically disparate species, could ever reach that goal.*

*Some impacts might be unavoidable, such as reduction of water in freshwater systems as we continue to use it for drinking, irrigation, and other basic needs; habitat degradation in places of agriculture, settlement, and transportation routes; and some disturbance in areas used for extraction of even renewable resources (such as forests and wind farms). Others might be avoidable, such as global climate change (by minimizing use of fossil fuels and other sources), oceanic species depletion (by managing fishery resources carefully), and species extirpation.*

## Renewable Energy and Sustainability

***Facts to consider:*** *Responses will vary. Some may argue that, even though renewable energy may one day provide abundant and cheap energy, that will be quite a long time in the future. By then, humans may have enough environmental knowledge, and tough lessons about the costs of environmental impacts, that even an abundant supply of cheap energy would be unlikely to lead to unsustainable development. On the other hand, in an earlier century, fossil fuel created a shift in energy usage. It was easier to burn, store and use than earlier energy sources; the consequent expansion of electricity production made energy even more accessible. These new energy sources had revolutionary effects, including massive levels of development with negative environmental consequences. The availability of abundant and cheap renewable energy sources might have revolutionary effects that we cannot yet imagine, ones that would somehow result in humans engaging in development that damages the environment. (For instance, perhaps such resources would tempt us to develop space exploration, underwater colonization, or personal flying craft.)*

*Renewable energy sources may make important contributions to our ability to achieve sustainable development. By using renewable energy, developing nations without fossil fuels may be more able to engage in self-sufficient industrial activity without massive debt or habitat destruction, and this activity could bring higher income to inhabitants, which could eventually lead not only to improvements in health care and education but also to population stability.*

## Globalization and Internationalization

***Facts to consider:*** *Answers will vary, requiring at least some individual response. Globalization and internationalization have both advantages and disadvantages. On one hand, people learn about each other's cultures and are more likely to respect and appreciate this diversity. More people in other countries speak English, so it is easier for Americans to travel in those places. Other travel barriers are also eased by such shifts as the reduction of visa requirements and the widespread available of automated teller machines worldwide. Innovative, even environmentally advantageous, products can more easily be marketed and put to good use in other countries. Not all aspects of globalization and internationalization are positive, however. American culture, delivered via television, advertising, and multinational corporations, seems to result in the devaluing and decline of other cultures. Traveling to other countries reveals less about human diversity than earlier. And multinational corporations may control large areas of land in other countries, for resource extraction, for tourism, and for factories. Globalization may reduce domestic employment, as companies find it easier than ever to locate jobs overseas, where wages and other expenses are lower.*

*Local self-sufficiency can be a powerful strategy for moving toward global sustainability. When people depend on the surrounding region for food, energy, and other necessities, they care more about the environment in that area, and they value its continued health and strength. It is possible, however, that the more people identify with their own region, the fewer ties they have to other areas, and the less they are willing to invest in improving or maintaining the environment in those areas. Also, self-sufficiency may reduce connection and communication between communities, thereby slowing down the rate at which more sustainable innovations may spread.*

*As for whether eating at a Vietnamese restaurant in the United States is the same as accepting the presence of McDonald's in Vietnam, the two circumstances have significant differences. The first difference is ownership. The Vietnamese restaurant is likely owned by a single person or a family; restaurant profits go back into the local community where the owners live. McDonald's is owned by a multinational corporation, whose profits leave Vietnam, for later use by the corporation or distribution to stockholders. The second difference is relative cultural influence. The United States faces little danger of being culturally overwhelmed by Vietnam or any other nation. As for McDonald's, however, America, is the most dominant culture in the world, and its dominance over traditions in other countries continues to grow. Many people believe that American fast food chains, particularly McDonald's, erode the cultural integrity of Vietnam and other developing countries. The third difference is culinary and health-related. The food in the Vietnamese restaurant is probably made from fresh ingredients, which might even be locally grown. A sizeable percentage of choices may involve vegetables and other healthy options. At McDonald's, many of the food choices are previously frozen; this involves not only a standardization of taste, even a reduction in taste, but also additional energy costs for freezing and transportation; finally, relatively few menu selections are likely to be healthy choices.*

## *The Science behind the Stories:* The Scientific Method

### Assessing Coss and Benefits of Environmental Regulations

**Observation:** Scientists and analysts at the EPA believed air pollution from diesel fuel to be a costly environmental health hazard.

**Hypothesis:** Making diesel fuel cleaner, they surmised, would bring enough environmental and public health benefits to make the costs of improving diesel fuel worthwhile.

**Experiment:** Using industry, environmental, and public health data, EPA analysts estimated costs and benefits from improving diesel fuel. They included everything from the cost of overhauling a single engine to how many cases of asthma might be prevented.

**Results:** Making diesel cleaner was determined to be cost effective, with total annualized costs of about $4.2 billion by 2030 and benefits reaching $70 billion by 2030.

## Additional Questions

1. Ask students to read the online case study, "San Francisco: A New Leader in Solar Power." Why is the Moscone Convention Center project a more sustainable alternative to using coal-fired power plants?

   *Solar roof and energy efficiency upgrades will not only reduce the city's power bill by over $600,000 per year, but will reduce the amount of power produced by the area's coal-fired power plants. Coal-fired power plants emit tons of air pollution, including carbon dioxide, sulfur dioxide, and small amounts of radioactive material.*

*Carbon dioxide is a greenhouse gas and sulfur dioxide mixes with moisture in the atmosphere to form acid rain. As a result, there will be less pollution emitted into the atmosphere in and around San Francisco.*

2. What are some actions you can take at home, work, and school to lessen your environmental impact? In particular, address your impact on energy use, transportation, water, and solid waste.

   *Student answers will vary. Students may list things such as turning off lights, regulating the thermostat, carpooling, biking, using mass transportation, using less water, recycling, purchasing products made of recycled materials, and composting. It is important for them to realize that individual efforts do make a difference.*

3. What does "sustainability" mean to you? Do you think the U.S. government is doing its part to make the United States become a more environmentally sustainable place? Why or why not?

   *Student responses will vary. Sustainability can mean different things and there are many published definitions of the word and concept. In short, it can be summarized as "economy, equity, and environment." Sustainable development is the idea that economic development takes place with the environment in mind so that the natural world can function indefinitely in the midst of human development. Sustainability can take place at many different levels—in individual actions, manufacturing processes, business procedures, and government policies.*

   *The United States, according to the ESI, ranks 45th among 142 countries in its environmental sustainability (www.ciesin.org/indicators/ESI/rank.html). Certainly, there are successful sustainability projects taking place at the local, regional, and state levels, such as the San Francisco renewable energy project. However, the United States has not significantly progressed toward the goals set forth during the 1992 Earth Summit. For example, the United States government has not signed the Kyoto Protocol of the Convention on Climate Change. This treaty requires developed countries to reduce greenhouse gas emissions to curb the threat of global warming, to which the United States is a major contributor.*

# TEST BANK

# *Chapter 1* An Introduction to Environmental Science

## Matching Questions

*Match the following.*

1) A scientific field of study
2) Information expressed with numbers
3) The variable that is manipulated
4) Expectations of experimental outcome
5) Numerical expression of the likelihood that a conclusion is true

A) qualitative data
B) independent variable
C) hypothesis
D) toxicology
E) environmentalism
F) dependent variable
G) quantitative data
H) probability
I) prediction

1) D 2) G 3) B 4) I 5) H

## Short Answer Questions

1) Differentiate between renewable and nonrenewable natural resources. Give examples of each.

Answer: Renewable resources are virtually unlimited (sunlight) or are replenished over short periods of time (plants). Nonrenewable natural resources are in limited supply and are not replenished or are formed much more slowly than we use them.

2) What was the lesson of Easter Island?

Answer: Civilizations can crumble when population pressure overwhelms resource availability.

3) Why is environmental science an interdisciplinary field?

Answer: Environmental science is an interdisciplinary field because it involves techniques from numerous, more traditional fields of study.

4) What is the relationship between correlation and causation in scientific experimentation?

Answer: A correlation is a relationship between two variables, and causation is when there is demonstration that one variable causes another to change. Causation is stronger evidence to support a hypothesis.

5) Define the term tragedy of the commons.

Answer: Unfettered exercise of individual self-interest will result in destruction of land that is held in common.

6) Discuss the difference between a manipulative experiment and a natural experiment.

Answer: The manipulative experiment is one in which the researcher chooses and manipulates the independent variable, and a natural experiment is one in which the researcher records data from variables that have not been manipulated, such as weights of all organisms currently on an island.

## Fill-in-the-Blank Questions

1) A __________ is a widely accepted, well-tested explanation of one or more cause-and-effect relationship that has been rigorously tested.

Answer: theory

2) The field of __________ studies the impact of pollutants and chemicals on human bodies.

Answer: toxicology

3) The process of science, called the __________, is used to develop new information in scientific fields.

Answer: scientific method

4) The total sum of our surroundings, the __________ is impacted by living and nonliving things.

Answer: environment

5) The systematic process for learning about the world and testing our understanding of it is called __________.

Answer: science

6) A(n) __________ is an activity designed to test the validity of a hypothesis; it involves manipulating __________ or conditions that can change.

Answer: experiment; variables

## Multiple-Choice Questions

1) A paradigm

A) is a group of several hypotheses that can be tested together

B) is a dominant view in science

C) can be discredited with new research

D) is synonymous with the scientific method

E) B and C

Answer: E

2) Advances in agriculture

A) include pesticide use

B) include chemical fertilizers

C) are viewed as one of humanity's greatest achievements

D) have resulted in destruction of natural systems

E) all of the above

Answer: E

3) Technology is

A) the process by which science is done

B) a product of science

C) a tool by which science can be done

D) B and C

E) all of the above

Answer: D

4) The scientific process is based on

A) observation

B) testing hypotheses built on observation

C) revising hypotheses based on results

D) only B and C

E) all of the above

Answer: E

5) Scientific inquiry is based on

A) an incremental approach to the truth

B) facts that can only be proven by testing hypotheses

C) the production of technological advances

D) designing experiments that have never been done before

E) all of the above

Answer: A

6) A hypothesis is

A) a prediction

B) an educated guess that explains a phenomenon or answers a question

C) an instrument that is used to examine environmental conditions

D) the design of an experiment that can be used for the process of science

E) A and D

Answer: B

7) An experiment

A) is an activity designed to test the validity of a hypothesis

B) often involves manipulating variables

C) should be repeated

D) can involve collection of qualitative data

E) all of the above

Answer: E

8) Ecology is

A) concerned only with solving environmental problems

B) the study of organisms and their interactions with each other and the environment

C) a subfield of environmentalism

D) B and C

E) all of the above

Answer: B

9) E. O. Wilson's great concern is

A) the impact of pollution on fishing

B) depletion of biodiversity

C) elimination of fossil fuel use

D) the population explosion

E) none of the above

Answer: B

10) In general, natural resources

A) should not be used

B) should be conserved

C) belong only to those whose property they exist on

D) are evenly divided among all countries

E) will be depleted in the near future

Answer: B

11) Solutions to environmental problems

A) can only be implemented by scientists

B) must be sustainable

C) must be on a local scale

D) must be short term

E) all of the above

Answer: B

12) The process by which several researchers review another researcher's manuscript prior to publication to ensure research quality is referred to as

A) scientific community

B) investigative inquiry

C) peer review

D) quality control

E) This is not done as it would cause introduction of bias.

Answer: C

13) Which of the following is not an abiotic factor?

A) rock

B) wood

C) wind

D) water

E) All of the above are abiotic factors.

Answer: B

14) Why was human population growth initially regarded as a good thing?

A) more children to support folks in old age

B) greater pool of factory workers

C) A and B

D) spread Christianity

E) It was never viewed as a good thing.

Answer: C

15) Malthus was responsible for

A) the book The Population Bomb that described the disastrous effects of human population growth

B) the idea that the increase in the human population would lead to famine and war without social strictures

C) the concept that human population growth would lead to greater industry and prosperity through education

D) instituting fertilizer use for agriculture

E) all of the above

Answer: B

16) Ehrlich's predictions have not come true on the scale he imagined because

A) Malthus was right

B) agricultural advances have been made in recent decades

C) pollution has reduced the birth rate in all countries

D) all of the above

E) none of the above

Answer: B

17) The cumulative total and kind of living things on earth is

A) called taxonomy

B) its biodiversity

C) increasing

D) B and C

E) none of the above

Answer: B

18) The oceans face pressure from

A) increasing whale populations

B) pollution

C) overfishing

D) too many preserves

E) B and C

Answer: E

19) The types of pollution that are responsible for damaging human health include

A) $O_2$ production by trees

B) indoor pollution

C) outdoor pollution

D) B and C

E) all of the above

Answer: D

20) Pesticide use
   A) may be a necessary part of modern agriculture
   B) can be eliminated by changing crops planted
   C) will be eliminated as pests are decreasing as a consequence of years of pesticide use
   D) is not a problem in this country
   E) B and C

   Answer: A

21) In a controlled experiment
   A) the researcher has several hypotheses
   B) the researcher knows the outcome
   C) the scientist controls for the effects of all variables but one
   D) the experimental organisms evaluated have been chosen carefully
   E) B and C

   Answer: C

22) The use of qualitative data is problematic because
   A) they may not have been recorded properly by the researcher
   B) statistics may not be readily available for data of this type
   C) variables may not have been properly manipulated
   D) they can't be used to support hypotheses
   E) predictions cannot be made about the outcome

   Answer: B

## True/False Questions

1) The goal of science is to prove hypotheses.

   Answer: FALSE

2) Environmentalism is a scientific approach to understanding environmental problems.

   Answer: FALSE

3) Scientists believe that fossil fuel use is contributing to warming of the lower atmosphere.

   Answer: TRUE

4) Globalization will impact the development of environmental law as the global community is interconnected by trade, politics, and movement of people and species.

   Answer: TRUE

5) Over half of the earth's surface is used for some kind of agriculture.

   Answer: TRUE

6) Genetically modified crops will never be sold as food products in grocery stores in the United States.

Answer: FALSE

## Essay Questions

1) Why is it important to understand our interactions with the environment? What will studying environmental science enable you to do?

Answer: We depend on the environment for air, water, food, shelter, and everything else. We are capable of modifying the environment whether we intend to or not. Understanding our interactions with the environment is the essential first step towards devising solutions. Studying environmental science will give students the tools that can help them evaluate information on environmental change and think critically and creatively about possible actions to take in response.

2) Define the term environmental problem. Give an example of an environmental problem. Why does the perception of what is an environmental problem differ from time to time and country to country? Give an example of how the perception of an environmental problem may have changed.

Answer: An environmental problem is an undesirable change in the environment. An example would be decreased air quality caused by pollution in Los Angeles. Perception changes due to the definition of the word undesirable and the awareness of the consequences of certain actions. The environmental problems resulting from DDT use are undesirable in this country and are the lesser of two evils in a country with severe malaria problems.

3) Differentiate between environmental science and environmentalism. Define each term and explain how they are similar and how they differ.

Answer: Environmental science is the pursuit of knowledge about the workings of the environment and our interactions with it, while environmentalism is a social movement dedicated to protecting the natural environment and, by extension, humans, from undesirable changes brought about by certain human choices. Environmental scientists and environmentalists study the same issues, but environmental scientists use an objective scientific approach to understanding environmental problems, whereas environmentalists use dramatic and often emotional approaches to alter the political and social understanding of environmental problems.

4) List the steps of the scientific method and describe each briefly. Which steps are important to repeat? Why is this process important?

Answer:
Observation
Ask a question
Develop hypothesis
Make predictions
Test predictions
Analyze and interpret results
Students should offer a one-sentence descriptions of these tasks.
All steps are important to repeat.
The process is the only way that we can learn about and test our understanding of the world.

5) What two events caused human population size to increase? Describe each, briefly explaining the contributions that each made to human population growth including pros and cons of each.

Answer: Neolithic revolution — transition from hunter gatherer lifestyle to agricultural lifestyle.
Industrial revolution — shifts from rural life, animal-powered agriculture, and manufacture by craftsmen to an urban society powered by fossil fuels like coal and oil.
Students should describe the benefits and problems associated with each revolution.

# *Chapter 2* Environmental Ethics and Economics: Values and Choices

## Matching Questions

*Match the following.*

1) A human-centered view of our relationship with the environment
2) The study of how we decide to use resources to provide goods and services in the face of demand for them
3) The oldest type of survival economy
4) A social system that converts resources into goods
5) An economy that does not grow or shrink

A) steady-state economy
B) economy
C) centrally planned economics
D) anthropocentrism
E) biocentrism
F) environmental ethics
G) capital market economy
H) economics
I) worldview
J) subsistence economy

1) D 2) H 3) J 4) B 5) A

## Short Answer Questions

1) What was the principal lesson to be learned from the struggle of the Mirrar Clan?

Answer: Values, beliefs, and traditions interact with economic interests to influence the choices we make about how we want to live within our environment.

2) Describe the contribution of Aldo Leopold to our understanding of humankind's link to the environment.

Answer: Leopold enlarged the idea of community to include "the land," encompassing soils, waters, plants, and animals.

3) What is meant by the term Natural Resource? Give examples.

Answer: Natural resources are substances and forces we need in order to survive — for example, the sun's energy, fresh water.

4) How are the fields of ecology and economics related in their origin?

Answer: Ecology and economics come from the same Greek root oikos, meaning household and in its broadest context, the human household, Earth itself. Economists study the household of human society, and ecologists study the broader household of all life.

5) What are externalities? Give an example of a positive and negative externality.

Answer: Externalities are the cost or benefit of a transaction that involves people other than the buyer or seller. Negative externalities may include human health problems, and positive externalities may include improved transportation systems.

6) Does environmental protection positively or negatively affect economics? How is the economist's view of the environment changing?

Answer: Environmental protection is good for economics. Environment and economy are intricately linked through the resources that the environment provides. The old school made the environment a subset of human economy. The new school solidifies the link by making human economy a subset of the environment.

## Fill-in-the-Blank Questions

1) __________ can be defined as the overall ensemble of knowledge, beliefs values, and learned ways of life shared by a group of people.

Answer: Culture

2) The field of __________ involves the study of good and bad, of right and wrong.

Answer: ethics

3) The U.S. Environmental Protection Agency defines __________ as the fair treatment and meaningful involvement of all people with respect to the development, implementation, and enforcement of environmental laws, regulations, and policies.

Answer: environmental justice

4) __________ serves to tell consumers which brands use processes believed to be environmentally beneficial and which brands do not.

Answer: Ecolabeling

5) Economists assess the economic health of a nation by calculating its __________.

Answer: Gross Domestic Product

## Multiple-Choice Questions

1) A bicentric view of the world would emphasize
   A) the role of corporations in environmental law
   B) the importance of impacts on living things
   C) a human-centered view of natural resources
   D) the dual-natured view of humans and animals as environmental controls
   E) the importance of economics in environmental decisions

   Answer: B

2) Transcendentalism
   A) is an environmental movement created in conjunction with modern scientific approaches
   B) was an early 18th century philosophical movement that linked the environment with God
   C) forced protection of biodiversity
   D) is a combination of ethics and economics
   E) was a late 19th century philosophical movement linked with the creation of Earth Day.

   Answer: B

3) The categorical imperative
   A) is roughly Christianity's Golden Rule
   B) is an ethical standard
   C) is a tool for decision making
   D) can be used to differentiate between right and wrong
   E) all of the above

   Answer: E

4) The principle of utility
   A) holds that any natural resource should be available for use in manufacturing
   B) holds that something is right when it produces the greatest benefit for the greatest number of people
   C) is not an ethical standard
   D) cannot be estimated by understanding the value of natural resources
   E) none of the above

   Answer: B

5) The preservation ethic holds that we should

A) be responsible for wise management while using natural resources

B) protect areas against development while allowing public access

C) harvest natural resources

D) protect the environment in a pristine, unaltered state

E) B and C

Answer: D

6) The conservation ethic holds that we should

A) be responsible for wise management while using natural resources

B) protect areas against development while allowing public access

C) harvest natural resources

D) protect the environment in a pristine, unaltered state

E) B and C

Answer: A

7) The essay "The Land Ethic"

A) was largely ignored as environmental rhetoric

B) was the best-known work of Aldo Leopold

C) expanded the boundaries of the community to include "the land"

D) B and C

E) none of the above

Answer: D

8) An outgrowth of environmental ethics that goes beyond Leopold's ecocentrism and rests on the principles of "self realization" and bicentric equality is called

A) environmentalism

B) deep ecology

C) ecocentrism

D) evolution

E) none of the above

Answer: B

9) The school of thought that links the patriarchal structure of society with environmental and social problems is called

A) ecocentrism

B) ecofeminism

C) ecology

D) ecopatriotism

E) economics

Answer: B

10) A worldview is developed as a result of

A) education

B) religion

C) culture

D) B and C

E) all of the above

Answer: E

11) The environmental justice movement began with

A) transcendentalism

B) a protest in North Carolina against a toxic dump

C) the election of Ronald Reagan as president

D) the development of the Environmental Protection Agency

E) B and C

Answer: B

12) Environmental ethics have only now become important because of

A) the increase in economic prosperity in western cultures

B) people's increased leisure time

C) the expansion of science, especially the field of ecology

D) the evolutionary understanding that we are only one of many species

E) all of the above

Answer: E

13) A centrally planned economy is

A) a survival economy

B) a state socialist economy

C) one in which buyers and sellers control the market

D) the hybrid system of most European countries

E) B and C

Answer: B

14) Externalities include

A) elimination of local sport fish

B) aesthetic harm such as destruction of a local park

C) worry and anxiety of those downstream from pollution sources

D) all of the above

E) none of the above

Answer: D

15) Ecosystem services include

A) the physical and intellectual abilities of people

B) functions that the environment performs that support economies

C) essential services including items such as water purification and carbon dioxide production

D) items produced from natural resources through the application of human and financial resources

E) B and C

Answer: C

16) The idea that long-term effects are discounted in economics means that

A) an event in the far future counts much less than one in the present

B) the value of a natural resource decreases every year that it is not harvested for use

C) short-term costs and benefits are granted more importance than long-term costs and benefits

D) B and C

E) all of the above

Answer: E

17) Health problems incurred by the Navajo children from uranium mining is a

A) positive externality

B) negative externality

C) consequence of poor parenting

D) negative internality

E) problem not addressed by environmental law

Answer: B

18) Ecological economists argue that

A) Malthus was wrong and population growth will produce more workers able to produce more goods

B) if nothing is done to rein in population growth and increased resource consumption, human economies will plunge into ruin

C) technological solutions will always be found to overcome resource depletion

D) increased human resources can replace natural resources

E) the economy must be driven exclusively by market growth

Answer: B

19) Mill believed that a steady-state economy would be achieved because

A) natural resources depletion would cause growth to slow and eventually stabilize

B) population growth would stabilize

C) technological advances would allow for a high standard of living in all countries

D) supply and demand economics demand it

E) most countries would go to the socialist model of government

Answer: A

20) Contingent valuation

A) uses surveys to determine how much people would be willing to pay to protect or restore a resource

B) is used for calculating nonmarket values

C) describes the valuation of ecosystem services

D) B and C

E) all of the above

Answer: E

21) Improperly assessing and assigning the effects of production on the environment can lead to

A) poor product manufacture

B) human resource depletion

C) poor product marketing

D) market failure

E) B and C

Answer: D

22) The role of green taxes is to

A) create national parks

B) educate children about recycling

C) penalize environmentally harmful activities

D) pave roads in national forests

E) create greenbelts for movement of organisms between preserves

Answer: C

23) Permit trading for air pollution

A) will never be allowed in this country

B) was established with the Clean Air Act in the seventies

C) gives corporations the right to pollute without regulation

D) is a new creation resulting from the current effort to curb global warming

E) B and C

Answer: B

## True / False Questions

1) An ecocentrist would view economics as the most important determinant in making environmental legislation.

   Answer: FALSE

2) For Americans, religion influences personal views of environmental protection.

   Answer: TRUE

3) Originally economists believed the marketplace would behave as if guided by an invisible hand that ensured their actions would benefit society as a whole.

   Answer: TRUE

4) Contingent valuation often results in inflated prices for services that people would not be willing to pay.

   Answer: TRUE

5) Permits that allow companies the right to conduct environmentally harmful manufacturing can be bought and sold among polluters.

   Answer: TRUE

6) Environmental hazards are distributed inequitably.

   Answer: TRUE

## Essay Questions

1) Discuss the history and basis for the field of environmental ethics.

   Answer: A new branch of philosophy arose once people began to identify the environmental changes brought about by modern industrialism. As ethical consideration expanded, past slavery and treatment of women and other entities (species) were included in legislation. Expansion of science, especially the field of ecology, played a role.

2) Differentiate between the approaches of Pinchot and Muir to protection of the environment. Which is more practical with the population growth of the last century?

   Answer: Pinchot was instrumental in the development of the conservation ethic. This ethic suggested that natural resources be put to use but it must be done wisely. The best use of resources would provide the greatest good to the greatest number of people for the longest time. In contrast, Muir espoused the "preservation ethic" that required preservation of natural environment in a pristine, unaltered state. The preservation ethic is not reasonable, especially in the face of globalization.

3) Explain how environmental injustice can be caused by processes such as uranium mining. Give an example of a case where mining resulted in environmental injustice and how it was dealt with legally. How does ignorance of what constitutes an environmental hazard make such situations worse?

Answer: In the case of the Navajo tribe, an environmental problem was caused by the mining of uranium on their land. The injustice was dealt with by the Radiation Exposure Compensation Act of 1990. Failure of Federal authorities and the mining company to tell workers the dangers of uranium made this problem worse because people could not protect themselves, and they used waste products in their homes for food preparation that ultimately damaged their health.

4) Describe four ways that neoclassical economics contributes to environmental problems.

Answer: There are four ways that neoclassical economics contributes to environmental problems. First, the idea that resources are infinite is a problem. There is a belief that if we deplete a resource, it can be replenished by something else. This is not always the case. Second, long-term effects are discounted. Only short-term effects are estimated in costs, and long-term damage is less important, so the immediate harvest and use of resources often looks more profitable. Third, the idea that costs and benefits are internal to business transactions is not correct. There are externalities that affect the environment and ultimately human health. Lastly, neoclassical economies contribute to environmental problems by promoting growth as good. The traditional belief that growth is necessary for high employment and is key to maintaining social order is not good for the environment but more importantly may not be good for economics either.

5) What are ecosystem goods and ecosystem services? Give several examples of each. What are nonmarket values? Discuss how economists go about calculating these values.

Answer: Ecosystem goods are goods produced by ecosystems and harvested by human populations including items such as wood and fur. Services are functions such as $CO_2$ production and water purification performed by the environment that keep humans alive. Nonmarket values are values that are not usually included in the price of a good or service. They are an assessment of the true costs and benefits of natural systems and reflect the ecosystem goods and services that are not included in the price of an item. The nonmarket values are calculated by contingent valuation which includes surveys of people who use the items. The surveys request the price that consumers would pay for goods or services. They often overestimate the value to human populations, as the prices given are often not what the specific individuals would be willing to pay.

# *Chapter 3* Environmental Policy: Decision-Making and Problem-Solving

## Matching Questions

*Match the following.*

1) Rule or guideline that directs individual, organizational, or societal behavior
2) Agreements with foreign countries
3) Specific rules based on more broadly written statutory law passed by Congress
4) Specific legal instructions for government agencies drafted by the president
5) Early environmental laws that gave federal government the right to manage Western lands
6) Law addressing harm to another person

A) congressional act
B) regulations
C) executive order
D) treaties
E) environmental clause
F) statutory law
G) general land ordinances
H) National Environmental Policy Act
I) tort law
J) Western Merit Law
K) policy

1) K 2) D 3) B 4) C 5) G 6) I

## Short Answer Questions

1) Political boundaries do not always match environmental boundaries. What does this mean for environmental protection in each country?

   Answer: Countries are often dependent on each other for solving environmental problems, as the source of pollution that is a cause of concern may be from another country. In such cases, international cooperation is required to correct the problem.

2) Why is the takings clause cited in arguments against environmental regulations that restrict the use of private property?

   Answer: Environmental laws often deprive citizens of economic use of their property without compensation. This is not allowed under the takings clause.

3) What is the role of an environmental impact statement, who is required to prepare it, and what agency is in charge of these documents?

Answer: An environmental impact statement is required for any major federal action. It is a report of results from detailed studies that assess potential effects on the environment that would likely result from a development project or other action undertaken by the government. The Council on Environmental Quality is in charge of these documents.

4) Why did the *Boomer v. Atlantic Cement Co.* end the tort era?

Answer: The decision set a legal precedent that if pollution control was more expensive than the damage pollution causes, the pollution can continue.

5) Differentiate between a green tax and marketable emission permits. Which is superior for U.S. markets?

Answer: A green tax is a tax on activities and products that cause undesirable environmental change. Marketable emission permits are issued to polluters and allow holders to emit a fraction of the industry-set limit. Releasing amounts of pollution that are less than the permit total means that the holder can sell the remaining units of pollution to other polluters. This is superior as it gives an incentive to industry participants to reduce pollution per unit product made or item sold.

6) What is a subsidy? Describe the role of subsidies in natural resource management.

Answer: A subsidy is a government giveaway of publicly owned resources, or cash or tax break, intended to encourage certain activities while discouraging others. Subsidies can be used to promote sustainable activities, although more often they are not used that way.

## Fill-in-the-Blank Questions

1) All of the land from which water drains into the river is called a __________.

Answer: watershed

2) A decision made on one case on a certain question serves as a __________ or legal guide.

Answer: case law

3) __________ have been nicknamed the fourth branch of the government.

Answer: Administrative agencies

4) One of the landmark environmental events of the 1960s was the publication of __________ by Rachel Carson.

Answer: Silent Spring

5) Previous court rulings serve as __________ or legal guides for later cases.

Answer: precedents

6) Citizens that are involved with trying to change an elected official's mind are engaged in __________.

Answer: lobbying

## Multiple–Choice Questions

1) Environmental policy aims to
   A) protect the natural resources people use
   B) protect the values people hold
   C) promote fairness among people in the use of resources
   D) all of the above
   E) none of the above

   Answer: D

2) The role of the U.N is
   A) to maintain international peace and security
   B) to develop friendly relations among nations
   C) to cooperate in solving international economic , social , cultural, and humanitarian problems
   D) in promoting respect for human rights and fundamental freedoms
   E) all of the above

   Answer: E

3) Decisions rendered by the courts make up a body of law known as
   A) statutory law
   B) case law
   C) mandatory law
   D) environmental law
   E) executive decisions

   Answer: B

4) Enforcement and elaboration of statutory law is given to
   A) watchdog groups
   B) the legislative branch
   C) the judicial branch
   D) an administrative agency
   E) none of the above

   Answer: D

5) Statutory laws are passed by

A) federal preemption

B) the legislative branch

C) CEOs

D) the President of the United States

E) all of the above

Answer: B

6) The judicial system is important for environmental policy because

A) grassroots and other non-governmental organizations have brought lawsuits to correct environmental damage

B) it regulates administrative agencies

C) it mandates that environmental law preempt all other federal laws

D) it allows corporations in the United States to disregard environmental laws of other countries

E) none of the above

Answer: A

7) The takings clause means that

A) the government can cause environmental damage without compensation

B) private property shall not be taken for public use without just compensation

C) natural resources cannot be taken without payment

D) state entities can take private property for less than market value

E) none of the above

Answer: B

8) A regulatory taking

A) means that the government can cause environmental damage without being subject to regulations

B) means that the government does not take possession of the property but deprives the owner of most economic value

C) takes property without allowing for compensation for natural resources

D) removes environmental regulations from individual owners

E) all of the above

Answer: B

9) The environmental justice movement is

A) currently ignored by most legislative bodies

B) based on the notion of fairness toward people of all races, cultures, and economic backgrounds

C) provided for by the 14th amendment

D) B and C

E) all of the above

Answer: D

10) The first laws in U.S. environmental policy

A) were passed as early as 1780

B) dealt primarily with management of public land

C) were intended to promote settlement of the West

D) B and C

E) all of the above

Answer: E

11) The Mineral Lands Act of 1866

A) has been subjected to major overhauls in the last century

B) provided no governmental oversight to mining

C) provided free land to promote mining and settlement

D) B and C

E) all of the above

Answer: D

12) The first national park in the world was

A) Yosemite

B) Yellowstone

C) Grand Canyon

D) Glacier National Park

E) Acadia

Answer: B

13) Rachel Carson's book Silent Spring, published in the 1960s,

A) awakened the American public to negative effects of pesticides

B) was the beginning of the second wave of U.S. environmental policy

C) focused on chemical pollutants including industrial chemicals

D) warned of bird losses through pesticide use

E) all of the above

Answer: E

14) The National Environmental Policy Act

A) was signed into law by Bill Clinton

B) required environmental impact statements

C) altered the amount of chemicals allowed in water

D) put all federal land under stringent environmental protection

E) all of the above

Answer: B

15) Water law in the United States

A) was initially left to local and state governments

B) was altered in the late 1960s and early 1970s by the Clean Water Act

C) changed in response to the burning of the Cuyahoga River

D) was intended to protect water quality

E) all of the above

Answer: E

16) To achieve control on pollution, industry has been given limits and threatened with punishment if these limits are violated. This approach is called

A) end of alley

B) bad behavior legislation

C) command and control

D) limit and manage

E) eliminate and prosecute

Answer: C

17) The Green Scissors report

A) compiles data on environmentally harmful subsidies

B) reported $54 billion was spent on environmentally harmful subsidies in 2002

C) is a publication of Friends of the Earth, Taxpayers for Common Sense, and the U.S. Public Interest Research Group

D) is a project of a nongovernmental organization

E) all of the above

Answer: E

18) The problems of sewage in the Tijuana river watershed was

A) caused primarily by maquiladoras

B) a transboundary problem

C) caused by the pressure on American companies to hire low-wage workers

D) difficult to legislate

E) all of the above

Answer: E

19) The revolving door

A) allows lobbyists to work for many political entities at the same time

B) is the movement of powerful officials between the private sector and government agencies

C) is illegal

D) pairs environmental causes with lobbyists already working on other causes

E) none of the above

Answer: B

20) International environmental law arises from

A) due diligence

B) law based on conventions or treaties

C) customary law based on long-standing practices

D) good neighborliness

E) all of the above

Answer: E

21) The UNEP

A) is the environmental arm of the United nations

B) has a mission of sustainability

C) has three subsections that govern international cooperation, oversight, and research

D) is based in Nairobi, Kenya

E) all of the above

Answer: E

## True/False Questions

1) Environmental problems were first discussed in the first century.

Answer: TRUE

2) Historically, the United States has been a pioneer in creating and enforcing environmental laws.

Answer: TRUE

3) Environmental legislation is only created at the federal level.

Answer: FALSE

4) Earth Day is a worldwide celebration of environmental protection.

Answer: TRUE

5) Marketable emissions permits can be bought, sold, and traded among polluters allowing industry to manage who is allowed to pollute.

Answer: TRUE

## Essay Questions

1) What is the main goal of environmental policy? Describe the tragedy of the commons and externalities and explain why environmental policy would focus on these problems.

   Answer: The role of environmental policy is to protect the natural resources that people use while considering values people place on resources and promoting equity in peoples use of resources
   Tragedy of the commons is the idea that unless the land held in common is regulated, there will be overuse and degradation to the detriment of individuals and society. Environmental policy it designed to limit degradation and overuse of all lands. Externalities are inputs caused by market transactions but borne by people not involved. These can be negative or positive. The role of environmental policy is to promote fairness by dealing with negative externalities

2) What is the significance of the National Environmental Policy Act?

   Answer: NEPA created an agency called the Council on Environmental Quality and required that an environmental impact statement be prepared for any major federal action. The EIS process forces government agencies and any businesses that contract with them to slow down and evaluate impacts on the environment before proceeding with a new dam or highway or building project. It serves as a powerful disincentive for environmentally damaging work.

3) Discuss the three major eras of environmental law in the United States. What key events sparked or resulted from each one?

   Answer: The first major era addressed public land management and encouraged western expansion. The end of this era saw the development of the national park system aimed at earmarking pieces of land for public use.The second major era sought to address the impacts of the first major era of environmental law and lasted through the beginning of the twentieth century.
   The third era was a response to address environmental pollution. Pollution policy was driven by new evidence such as Carson's *Silent Spring* and the burning of the Cuyahoga River that focused attention on poor environmental standards in this country.

4) List the economic-based approaches to environmental policy. How are these superior to the use of tort law for controlling pollution?

   Answer: The economic-based approaches include green taxes and marketable emission permits. The superior ones involve financial incentives for "good" behavior rather than punishment for bad behavior. These are superior to the use of tort law because tort law set a legal precedent that if pollution control was more expensive than the damage pollution causes, the pollution can continue.These changes have a real chance of reducing pollution that tort law did not.

5) Discuss the steps of environmental policy and give examples of how each is achieved.

Answer: a. Identify problem — curiosity, observation, record keeping, and awareness of our relationship with environment
b. Identify cause — find source of problem
c. Envision solution — what changes might be required to eliminate problem
d. Get organized — organizations are better able to achieve law
e. Gain access to political process — lobbying, campaign contributions and revolving door all offer opportunities
f. Make law — bill preparation: get it introduced, then passed

6) The Tijuana watershed demonstrated a transboundary problem. Explain what this means, and then discuss the organizations that oversee international environmental law. Conventional and customary law are the basis of international law. How do they differ?

Answer: Environmental problems, by their nature, often are not limited to the bounds of particular countries. International law is an important part of solving such transboundary problems. Creative agreements hammered out after a lot of hard work and diplomacy will work better for solving environmental problems. The United Nations, the World Bank, and a wide variety of nongovernmental organizations are key to international law. Conventional law arises from conventions or treaties that nations agree to enter into. Customary law arises from long-standing practices or customs.

# *Chapter 4* From Chemistry and Energy to Life

## Matching Questions

*Match the following.*

1) Smallest components of an element that maintain the chemical properties of that element
2) A postively charged particle
3) Atoms that gain or lose electrons
4) All multicellular organisms are __________.
5) All photosynthetic organisms are __________.

A) autotrophs
B) atoms
C) ions
D) electrons
E) eukaryotes
F) heterotrophs
G) cations
H) organelles
I) nuetrons
J) protons

1) B 2) J 3) C 4) E 5) A

## Short Answer Questions

1) What was the role of fertilization in bioremediation of the Exxon Valdez spill?

Answer: The bacteria used to clean up the hydrocarbons needed essential nutrients such as N and P to be able to use the oil as a source of energy. Organisms need more than just C for growth and development as macromolecules that are the structural components of organisms contain more than C and H.

2) What are isotopes? Give an example of how they can be used in science.

Answer: They are atoms with differing numbers of neutrons. Researchers can track the movement of isotopes to determine the age of matter, flow of water or nutrients within ecosystems, and the movement of organisms from one location to another.

3) Define and give examples of potential energy and kinetic energy.

Answer: Potential energy is the energy of position, and kinetic energy is the energy of motion. Water behind a dam is potential energy that becomes kinetic energy when the dam breaks or water is released.

4) What is the origin of energy for living organisms, and what is the process by which organisms get it?

Answer: The origin of energy for living organisms is the sun, and plants get their energy through photosynthesis from the sun.

5) Differentiate between heterotroph and autotroph. Give an example of each.

Answer: Autotrophs are primary producers that can produce their own source of energy (food). Heterotrophs are organisms that consume other organisms to obtain their energy. Autotrophs include plants and cyanobacteria. Heterotrophs include fungi and animals.

6) Define an adaptive trait in terms of the fitness of an organism.

Answer: An adaptive trait is one that confers greater fitness for an organism or increases the likelihood that an organism will reproduce.

## Fill-in-the-Blank Questions

1) A(n) __________ is a fundamental type of matter, a chemical substance with a given set of properties, which cannot be broken down into substances with other properties.

Answer: element

2) Stretches of DNA that perform functions such as producing particular proteins are called __________.

Answer: genes

3) Oppositely charged atoms often form __________ where electrical attractions between ions hold them together.

Answer: ionic bonds

4) Proteins can serve as __________, molecules that catalyze or promote certain chemical reactions.

Answer: enzymes

5) The basic unit of organization in living organisms is the __________.

Answer: cell

6) Photosynthesis occurs within cell organelles called __________, where light-absorbing pigments occur.

Answer: chloroplast

## Multiple-Choice Questions

1) Atoms can bond to form
   A) elements
   B) mixes
   C) protons
   D) molecules
   E) cells

   Answer: D

2) Uncharged atoms in molecules are held together by
   A) hydrogen bonds
   B) ionic bonds
   C) covalent bonds
   D) neutron bonds
   E) none of the above

   Answer: C

3) Hydrogen bonds allow water to
   A) stick together
   B) resist temperature change
   C) dissolve other molecules
   D) all of the above
   E) Water has covalent bonds not hydrogen bonds.

   Answer: D

4) The pH scale was devised to quantify the __________ of a solution.
   A) salinity B) acidity C) plasticity D) hardness E) toxicity

   Answer: B

5) Molecules that consist of carbon atoms joined by covalent bonds and with or without other elements are
   A) salts
   B) a consequence of abiotic processes
   C) inorganic
   D) organic
   E) phosphates

   Answer: D

6) A nucleotide consists of

A) hydrocarbon chains

B) a nitrogen containing base, a sugar, and a phosphate group

C) a sugar group, a nitrogen–containing amine group, a central carbon, and a side chain

D) a water–repelling side and a water–attracting side

E) all of the above

Answer: B

7) Which macromolecule encodes the genetic messages that are transmitted between generations?

A) protein

B) DNA

C) polymers

D) hydrocarbons

E) phospholipids

Answer: B

8) The roles of carbohydrates include

A) genetic material

B) energy storage form

C) catalyst

D) membranes

E) all of the above

Answer: B

9) All organisms with organelles in their fluid–filled inner chambers are

A) prokaryotes

B) unikaryotes

C) eukaryotes

D) karyotic organisms

E) semikaryotes

Answer: C

10) Chemical energy is

A) kinetic energy

B) potential energy

C) the energy held in the bonds between atoms

D) B and C

E) all of the above

Answer: D

11) Which of the following equations represents cellular respiration?

A) $12H_2O + 6CO_2$ + energy → $C_6H_{12}O_6 + 6O_2 + 6H_2O$

B) $C_6H_{12}O_6 + 6O_2 + 6H_2O$ → $12H_2O + 6CO_2$ + energy

C) $12H_2O + 6CO_2$ → $C_6H_{12}O_6 + 6O_2 + 6H_2O$ + energy

D) $12NO_2 + CO_2$ + energy → $C_6N_{12}O_6 + 6O_2 + 6N_2O$

E) none of the above

Answer: B

12) The degree of disorder in a substance, system, or process is called

A) allegory B) entropy C) energy D) gas E) electricity

Answer: B

13) Geothermal energy is

A) not available to provide energy for human use

B) comes from the center of the Earth

C) powered by radioactivity

D) B and C

E) all of the above

Answer: D

14) The primary component of cell membranes are

A) carbohydrates

B) lipids

C) nucleotides

D) amino acids

E) depends on the membrane

Answer: B

15) Radioactive compounds

A) continue to decay and will never be stable

B) release high-energy rays as their nuclei decay

C) are a natural phenomenon that have existed since the beginning of time

D) B and C

E) all of the above

Answer: D

16) Fitness is a term used to describe the

A) likelihood that an individual will carry the most fitting trait for a specific environment

B) likelihood that an individual will reproduce

C) overall strength of an individual

D) best trait for a given environment

E) none of the above

Answer: B

17) Autotrophs that do not get their energy from the sun are

A) heterotrophs

B) chemoautotrophs

C) cyanobacteria

D) B and C

E) none of the above

Answer: B

18) Jets of heated water that emerge into the cold depths of the ocean are called

A) solar spas

B) geothermal hot tubs

C) hydrothermal vents

D) ocean swirls

E) heat sink expulsions

Answer: C

19) The overall number of species has __________ over time.

A) increased

B) decreased

C) remained stable

D) There is no way to determine the number of overall species.

E) none of the above

Answer: A

20) The traditionally favored theory to explain life's origin on Earth

A) involved space travel

B) involved primordial soup

C) involved meteorites

D) involved the chemoautotrophic hypothesis

E) has not been explored

Answer: B

21) Artificial selection has been

A) used successfully by humans

B) used to demonstrate natural selection

C) used to improve agricultural crops

D) all of the above

E) proved to be a hoax by evolutionary scientists

Answer: D

22) The key to variation in populations is

A) the environment

B) mutations

C) extreme traits

D) partial extinction

E) loss of DNA

Answer: B

## True / False Questions

1) There are 92 naturally occurring elements.

Answer: TRUE

2) Scientists think life originated and stayed in water for the last 3 million years.

Answer: FALSE

3) The origination of animals on Earth occurred only after the planet's atmosphere had been supplied with oxygen by photosynthesizers.

Answer: TRUE

4) Fossil fuels actually represent fossil organisms.

Answer: TRUE

5) The fossil record clearly shows that the species living today are but a tiny fraction of all the species that have ever lived.

Answer: TRUE

## Essay Questions

1) What is bioremediation, and how can it help with environmental problems? Give an example. Why might this process be used?

Answer: Bioremediation is the process by which organisms are used to metabolize toxins to remove them from the environment. It is a process in which the natural processes of biodegradation are speeded up. The example that was given in the text was of the oil spill of the Exxon Valdez. Microbes were used to break down the hydrocarbons that were lost in the ocean. This process might be used as a low-cost alternative to very expensive, large-scale cleanup operations.

2) List the four types of macromolecules essential to life. Briefly describe the structures of each and give two roles.

Answer: Carbohydrates are made of carbon and water molecules. They are used as energy molecules and in cell walls.
Proteins are made of chains of amino acids (amino groups, sugar groups, a central carbon, and a side chain). They are enzymes and structural molecules.
Nucleic acids are made of chains of nucleotides (phosphate groups, sugars, and a nitrogenous base). They are the genetic material that passes traits from generation to generation and the energy molecules.
Lipids are not polymers but are long chains of hydrocarbons or have hydrophobic and hydrophilic region. They are used in membranes and hormones.

3) Differentiate between the first and second laws of thermodynamics. What does the second law mean for living organisms?

Answer: The first law of thermodynamics states that energy can change from one form to another; it cannot be created or lost. The total energy in the universe remains constant. The second law of thermodynamics states that the nature of energy will change from a more ordered state to a less ordered state. This means that organisms must consume energy to maintain structure and keep entropy at bay.

4) Briefly describe the processes of photosynthesis and cellular respiration. Which of these processes is performed by autotrophs and which by heterotrophs?

Answer: Light energy is converted into chemical energy, or glucose, through the process called photosynthesis. In cellular respiration, chemical energy is broken down into kinetic energy to fuel organisms. Autotrophs do both cellular respiration and photosynthesis, and heterotrophs do only cellular respiration.

5) Differentiate between the heterotrophic hypothesis, the heterotrophic extraterrestrial hypothesis, and the chemoautotrophic hypothesis for the development of life on Earth?

Answer: The primordial soup hypothesis or heterotrophic hypothesis advances the idea that life evolved from a primordial soup of simple inorganic chemicals — carbon dioxide, oxygen, and nitrogen — dissolved in the surface waters of the oceans or tidal shallows around oceanic margins. Simple amino acids may have formed under these conditions and more complex organic compounds may have followed, including nucleic acids that could replicate and give rise to basic forms of life. It is called the heterotrophic hypothesis because it advances that heterotrophs evolved first. The heterotrophic extraterrestrial hypothesis is similar but suggests that early chemical reactions on Earth may have received help from outer space. Bacteria from space may have been deposited on meteorites that crashed to earth, seeding our planet. This idea was rejected in favor of the simpler heterotrophic hypothesis. The chemoautotrophic hypothesis suggests that early life was formed at the scalding hot, deep-sea vent systems where sulfur was abundant.

6) Define evolution and discuss the role of natural selection in evolution of life on Earth. Give an example of how directional and stabilizing selection would differ in their impact on an organism.

Answer: Evolution is the genetically based change in appearance, functioning and/or behavior of organisms across generations, often by the process of natural selection. Natural selection is the idea that organisms best suited to their environment will have the ability to produce more offspring and increase the likelihood that those traits that confer competitive advantage in a given environment will exist in the next generation. Directional selection will favor the movement of a trait in one direction, such as to greater height or longer tails. Stabilizing selection will confer an advantage to organisms with the mean trait and increase the number of organisms with an average trait. If height ranges from 5–10 and the mean is 8, then stabilizing selection will decrease the range, for example, from 6–9, and the number of organisms with height of 8 will increase.

# Chapter 5 Ecology and Evolution: Populations, Communities, and Biodiversity

## Matching Questions

*Match the following.*

1) Multiple interacting species that live in the same area

2) Communities and the abiotic material with which their members interact

3) Specific environment in which an organism lives.

4) Number of individuais within a population per unit area

5) Stabilizes a population at its carrying capacity

6) Ranks in a feeding hierarchy is

A) population

B) population size

C) environmental resistance

D) ecosystems

E) trophic levels

F) population density

G) habitat

H) community

I) endemics

J) ecotones

K) biomes

L) niche

1) H 2) D 3) G 4) F 5) C 6) E

## Short Answer Questions

1) What is the lesson learned from the Monteverde rain forest?

Answer: Extinction is common as a consequence of human disturbance to natural ecosystems. Equally important is that species are disappearing at rates higher than we are discovering them.

2) What is biological diversity, and what specific categories of diversity are included in the definition?

Answer: It is the sum total of all organisms in an area, taking into account the diversity of species, their genes, their populations, and their communities.

3) What is habitat selection, and how does it differ for different organisms?

Answer: Habitat selection is when an organism selects a habitat to live in from among the range of options they encounter. Criteria differ among organisms. For soil organisms, for example, chemistry may be important, for a squirrel, tree density might be important.

4) Write the equation used to determine growth rate.

Answer: Growth rate = (crude birth rate + immigration rate) – (crude death rate + emigration rate).

5) Differentiate between fundamental and realized niche.

Answer: The fundamental niche is the full ecological role that a species is capable of playing. The realized niche is the portion of the fundamental niche that the species actually uses as a result of competition with or interference by other species.

6) Define succession.

Answer: Succession is the regular, predictable, and quantifiable changes in community composition over time.

## Fill-in-the-Blank Questions

1) The process by which new species are generated is ___________.

Answer: speciation

2) A branching diagram or ___________ can be used to illustrate a scientists' hypothesis as to how divergence took place among species.

Answer: phylogenetic tree or cladogram

3) The departure of individuals from a population is called ___________.

Answer: emigration

4) The innate reproductive capacity of a species is its ___________.

Answer: biotic potential

5) Relationships between organisms that live in close physical contract with one another are called ___________.

Answer: symbioses

## Multiple-Choice Questions

1) Extinction is
   A) a natural process
   B) caused by human disturbance
   C) the loss of species from the planet
   D) B and C
   E) all of the above

   Answer: E

2) Most extinction is
   A) the result of catastrophe
   B) gradual
   C) the result of slow climate change
   D) problematic for generalists
   E) not often a problem for endemics

   Answer: B

3) The two processes that determine the world's current biodiversity are
   A) allopatric and sympatric speciation
   B) mutation and cleavage
   C) endemism and climate change
   D) extinction and speciation
   E) breeding and ecotourism

   Answer: D

4) A population is a
   A) group of individuals of interacting species that live in one area
   B) group of individuals of interacting species that interact in multiple ecosystems
   C) group of individuals of a single species that live in one area
   D) subset of bacteria that grow on a petri dish
   E) group of cells that have similar function

   Answer: C

5) Endemic species
   A) are generalist organisms
   B) cause disease
   C) are invasive species that cause extinction
   D) have high rates of mutations that lead to large numbers of offspring species
   E) are only found in one place on the planet

   Answer: E

6) The functional role of a species in its community is its
   A) habitat
   B) place in the food chain
   C) selection
   D) niche
   E) evolution

Answer: D

7) High population density can
   A) allow organisms to find mates
   B) lead to extinction
   C) result in high levels of disease transmission
   D) B and C
   E) all of the above

Answer: E

8) Population distribution describes
   A) placement of species around the globe
   B) placement of species within a country
   C) spatial arrangement of individuals of a single species within a particular area
   D) spatial arrangement of multiple species within a particular area
   E) all of the above

Answer: C

9) Tools used to show the age structure of a population
   A) have no inherent value for predicting growth
   B) are called age pyramids
   C) have bars that represent size of an age class
   D) B and C
   E) all of the above

Answer: D

10) Unregulated populations tend to increase by
   A) linear growth
   B) exponential growth
   C) pyramidal growth
   D) emigration
   E) immigration

Answer: B

11) The carrying capacity is the

A) maximum population size that a given environment can sustain.

B) greatest number of niches possible in a given area

C) potential number of species in a given area

D) limitation on species number for an ecosystem

E) average number of offspring carried to term by a species

Answer: A

12) Density-dependent factors

A) include temperature extremes

B) act at the community level

C) cause decreases in species number in an ecosystem as a result of disease

D) have greater impact at higher population densities

E) cannot be identified for populations but only for ecosystems

Answer: E

13) Groups of organisms with low biotic potential such as elephants are grouped as

A) r-strategists

B) K-strategists

C) density-independent organisms

D) cannot be determined from information given

E) Elephants have high biotic potential.

Answer: B

14) Henry Gleason's ideas of communities suggested

A) ideas similar in nature to Clements'

B) that species can move into and out of communities without greatly altering community composition

C) that movement of species into and out of communities greatly alters their composition

D) that population dynamics determine ecosystem structure

E) None of the above as Gleason focused on individuals.

Answer: B

15) Energy flow in an ecosystem is diagrammed as

A) exponential curves

B) trophic levels

C) food chains

D) B and C

E) all of the above

Answer: D

16) Detritivores can include

A) decomposers

B) bacteria

C) fungi

D) consumers of dead bodies

E) all of the above

Answer: E

17) An organism that has particularly far-reaching impacts on community structure is

A) relatively rare

B) always a top consumer

C) a keystone species

D) responsible for population-independent dynamics

E) a regulator of its own population dynamics first

Answer: C

18) Interspecific competition

A) refers to competition between individuals of the same species

B) refers to competition between individuals of different species

C) refers to competition between mutualistic organisms

D) refers to a population of elephants at a watering hole, for example

E) does not occur in communities without human intervention

Answer: B

19) The possible consequences of resource use interference through interspecific competition is

A) competitive exclusion

B) extinction

C) evolution

D) B and C

E) all of the above

Answer: E

20) Evolution in response to competition through altered resource use

A) is called evolutionary endemism

B) is called resource partitioning

C) is development of social partitioning in organisms

D) can occur in the tropics only as reproductive rates are higher

E) does not occur

Answer: B

21) Primary succession

A) precedes secondary succession

B) is community development after catastrophic events such as volcanic activity

C) is community development on bare rock following removal of previous community including growth substrates such as soil

D) B and C

E) all of the above

Answer: D

22) The term invasive species

A) is equivalent to endemic species

B) refers only to non-native species

C) includes any species that spreads widely and rapidly becomes dominant

D) B and C

E) all of the above

Answer: C

23) The destruction of ecosystems is not a problem

A) because restoration ecology can restore ecosystems

B) because humans can find and make their own resources

C) because zoos contain most important species and breeding technologies are improving

D) all of the above

E) Destruction of ecosystems is always a problem.

Answer: E

## True/False Questions

1) Paleontologists calculate that the average time a species spends on earth is 10 million years.

Answer: TRUE

2) A population that is limited by a resource is expected to have an exponential growth curve.

Answer: FALSE

3) Ants are K-strategists.

Answer: FALSE

4) A primary consumer is most likely an herbivore.

Answer: TRUE

5) The phenomenon called ecotourism was short-lived and doomed to failure as tourists do not consider vacations to countries like Costa Rica to see wildlife.

Answer: FALSE

## Essay Questions

1) Briefly describe speciation. Differentiate between allopatric and sympatric speciation.

Answer: When mutations occur in one population that are not passed to another population, speciation can occur if gene flow becomes restricted permanently between the two populations (i.e., they can no longer mate and produce fertile offspring). If a physical boundary such as a stream divides the two populations, restricting gene flow between them, and a speciation event occurs, this is termed allopatric speciation. If it occurs in one location without a physical barrier, this is sympatric speciation.

2) Describe the sixth mass extinction event, when it occurred and the specific causes.

Answer: Currently, Earth is in the throes of its sixth mass extinction event, most biologists believe, and we are the cause. The changes to Earth's environment by human population growth, resource use, and development have greatly altered conditions for many species, have driven many to extinction already, and are threatening countless more. The alteration and outright destruction of natural habitats, the hunting and harvesting of species, and the introduction of invasive species from one place to another have contributed to the threat to Earth's biodiversity.

3) Differentiate between exponential and logistic growth curves. Give examples of the conditions under which each would occur.

Answer: Exponential growth (a J-shaped curve) is growth when there are no constraints. This occurs when a population is small and environmental conditions are ideal for the organism in question. Mold on a piece of bread or bacteria colonizing a dead animal are examples. Logistic growth (S-shaped growth curve) rises sharply at first, and then begins to level off as the effects of limiting factors become stronger. A population introduced into a new environment where there are other organisms will reach limitations quickly, and these limitations will limit the population growth.

4) Is a carrying capacity a fixed entity? Discuss the role of humans in regulating carrying capacity for the human species and in altering the carrying capacity for other species.

Answer: While all organisms are subject to environmental resistance, they may be capable of altering their environment to reduce environmental resistance. Humans can alter the carrying capacity for humans by finding resources and through technology, but other species have less flexibility in altering their carrying capacity. Humans often alter the carrying capacity for other species by altering climate. An example are the golden toads, which lacked enough moisture. Humans can encroach on an area and reduce breeding areas, food resources, or alter trophic structure within an ecosystem through hunting.

5) List the three major trophic levels in a food web. What types of organisms are found in each level? Where are the autotrophs and heterotrophs found? List the three levels in terms of importance in an ecosystem and why.

Answer: The three major trophic levels are producer, consumer, and decomposer. Producers include green plants and chemo- and photosynthetic bacteria. All organisms are autotrophs in this level. The next level, consumers, includes herbivores as primary consumers and carnivores as secondary and tertiary consumers. All organisms at this level are heterotrophs. The final level are the decomposers, which include all detritivores, bacteria, and fungi. These are all heterotrophs. Producers are the most important as they provide the basis for consumption of all other levels; the decomposers are next as they recycle nutrients to the producers. The consumers are the least important but do play an important role in speeding recycling to the producers.

# Chapter 6 Environmental Systems: Connections, Cycles, and Feedback Loops

## Matching Questions

*Match the following.*

1) A large ecological unit defined by its dominant plant community
2) Matter contained in living organisms
3) The solid earth beneath our feet
4) Rocks that form when they melt and then cool
5) The process by which waters moves from lakes or ponds to the atmosphere
6) Water returns to Earth's surface as

A) evaporation
B) biome
C) metamorphic
D) precipitation
E) igneous
F) hydrosphere
G) atmosphere
H) biosphere
I) lithosphere
J) ecosystem
K) biomass

1) B 2) K 3) I 4) E 5) A 6) D

## Short Answer Questions

1) What three factors contribute to the "dead zone" in the waters off the Gulf of Mexico?

Answer: Invention of synthetic ammonia; Midwestern farm practices; Global nitrogen cycle thrown out of balance

2) Describe the term emergent properties and give an example from a natural system.

Answer: Characteristics that are not evident in the system's components (the whole is greater than the sum of its parts). The component parts of a tree (leaves, branches, roots, bole) do not lead to the whole tree's emergent properties as a source of shade for understory vegetation and home for birds, insects, etc.

3) What determines which biome covers any particular portion of the planet?

Answer: A variety of abiotic factors including temperature, precipitation, atmospheric circulation, and soil characteristics, of which temperature and precipitation exert the greatest influence on biomes.

4) What factors result in the biome-like patterns of specific aquatic systems?

Answer: Water temperature, dissolved nutrients, wave action, currents, depth, and type of substrate (sandy, muddy, rocky bottom, etc.).

5) Briefly, what are plate tectonics, and why are they important for the study of geography?

Answer: Plate tectonics are the processes that underlie earthquakes and volcanoes and determine the geography of Earth's surface.

6) What are the anthropogenic sources of phosphorus, and why are they a problem?

Answer: Effluents from sewage treatments tend to be phosphate rich. Introduction of phosphates cause algal growth, leading to murkier waters and changes in structure and function of ecosystems.

## Fill-in-the-Blank Questions

1) The extremely low dissolved oxygen concentrations in the "dead zone" represent a condition called __________.

Answer: hypoxia

2) The process of nutrient enrichment, increased production of organic matter, and subsequent ecosystem degradation is known as __________.

Answer: eutrophication

3) The term __________ describes all the interacting organisms and abiotic factors that occur in a particular place at the same time.

Answer: ecosystem

4) Earth's surface consists of a lightweight thin __________ of rock floating atop a malleable __________.

Answer: crust; mantle

5) Substances move though the environment in cycles called nutrient cycles or __________ cycles.

Answer: biogeochemical

6) James Lovelock's description of Earth as a superorganism that is alive is called the __________.

Answer: Gaia hypothesis

## Multiple-Choice Questions

1) A network of relationships among a group of parts, elements, or components, that interact with and influence one another through exchange of matter and/or information is referred to as

A) an interchange

B) a system

C) an ecosystem

D) an environmental collaboration

E) an intersystem

Answer: B

2) A system actively receiving inputs and producing outputs without undergoing a change in size or function due to its own activity is said to be in

A) static control

B) environmental balance

C) dynamic equilibrium

D) normal balance

E) none of the above

Answer: C

3) Which list includes biomes in the correct order of highest to lowest rainfall?

A) tropical rainforest, temperate deciduous forest, grassland, desert

B) grassland, desert, tropical rainforest, temperate deciduous forest

C) grassland, tropical rainforest, deser, temperate deciduous forest

D) tropical rainforest, grassland, temperate deciduous forest, desert

E) tropical rainforest, desert, temperate deciduous forest, grassland

Answer: A

4) Which animals would one expect to find in a typical savanna?

A) polar bears

B) moose and bears

C) zebras and giraffes

D) penguins and seals

E) monkeys and frogs

Answer: C

5) Which animals would one expect to find in a typical taiga?

A) polar bears

B) moose and bears

C) zebras and giraffes

D) penguins and seals

E) monkeys and frogs

Answer: B

6) Which biome is likely to have mild wet winters, warm dry summers with oceanic influences, and is often termed "Mediterranean"?

A) taiga

B) tundra

C) rain forest

D) chaparral

E) tropical dry forest

Answer: D

7) The rate at which biomass becomes available to consumers is termed

A) biomass

B) ecosystem productivity

C) net primary productivity

D) density

E) net density production

Answer: C

8) The biosphere consists of the

A) water, saltwater, and freshwater in surface bodies and the atmosphere

B) solid earth beneath our feet

C) sum of all the planet's living organisms and the abiotic portions of the environment

D) air surrounding our planet

E) none of the above

Answer: C

9) Ecotones are the

A) sounds that animal communities make in ecosystems

B) transitional zones between ecosystems

C) areas between territories of organisms

D) studies of specific biomes by ecologists

E) animals that fulfill essential niches

Answer: B

10) Examining areas from the landscape scale is useful because
A) humans have not yet caused alterations to landscapes
B) the dynamics of animals result in localized problems
C) the role of ecosystems is often overstated
D) multiple ecosystems may exist in a single area with many transitional zones
E) transitional zones cannot be separated from specific biomes

Answer: D

11) Rock that has undergone heat or pressure that causes it to change form is called
A) conglomerate
B) igneous
C) sedimentary
D) intrusive igneous
E) metamorphic

Answer: E

12) The process of subduction
A) causes the formation of mountains
B) occurs when denser ocean crusts slide beneath lighter continental crusts
C) can result in volcanoes
D) B and C
E) all of the above

Answer: D

13) The freshwater we depend on for our survival accounts for
A) two-thirds of all water on Earth
B) one-third of all water on Earth
C) 10% of all water on Earth
D) 3% of all water on Earth
E) There is no way to estimate this.

Answer: D

14) Plants release water to the atmosphere through
A) evaporation
B) transpiration
C) exchange processes for oxygen for photosynthesis
D) B and C
E) none of the above

Answer: B

15) Aquifers are

A) ponds

B) recharge lakes at water quality facilities

C) underground water reservoirs

D) the result of transpiration

E) none of the above

Answer: C

16) Macronutrients

A) are large molecules necessary for making macromolecules

B) are required in large doses for organisms to survive

C) are the only nutrients that can be tracked in nutrient cycles

D) can only be taken up by plants from rock cycles

E) all of the above

Answer: B

17) Nitrogen fixation is

A) the source of all nitrogen taken up by biological organisms

B) a process that makes nitrogen available to plants by mutualistic and free-living bacteria

C) a process that makes nitrogen available to plants by human industrial applications

D) a process that makes nitrogen available to plants by lightning

E) all of the above

Answer: E

18) The origin of all nitrogen in biological tissues is

A) earthquake activities

B) atmospheric N2 gas

C) nitrogen weathered from rock

D) B and C

E) all of the above

Answer: B

19) Nitrogen is released to the atmosphere as a gas by

A) nitrogen-fixing bacteria

B) organisms that convert ammonia to nitrate

C) denitrifying bacteria

D) nitrifying bacteria

E) all of the above

Answer: C

20) The largest pools of carbon in the carbon cycle are
   A) freshwater systems and oceans
   B) plants and animals
   C) sedimentary rock and fossil fuels
   D) atmosphere
   E) all of the above

   Answer: C

21) The origin of all phosphorus in biological tissues is
   A) volcanic activities
   B) atmospheric phosphorus gas
   C) phosphorus weathered from rock
   D) B and C
   E) all of the above

   Answer: C

22) Climatographs depict
   A) Weather patterns
   B) Graphic patterns of average monthly temperature and precipitation
   C) monthly change in net primary productivity
   D) B and C
   E) all of the above

   Answer: B

## True/False Questions

1) Climbing up in elevation causes a much more rapid change in climate than moving towards the poles the same distance.

   Answer: TRUE

2) Ecosystems that convert solar energy to biomass rapidly are said to have low primary productivity.

   Answer: FALSE

3) All landmasses were once joined together in a supercontinent called Pangaea.

   Answer: TRUE

4) Deserts are not always hot; temperatures can vary widely across days and across seasons of the year.

   Answer: TRUE

5) Most ecosystems are limited by nitrogen as phosphorus is weathered from rock at relatively high rates.

Answer: FALSE

## Essay Questions

1) Compare and contrast feedback loops. Give an example of each and how common each is in natural systems.

Answer: A system's output can serve as input to that same system, a circular process described as a feedback loop. In a negative feedback loop, output pushing the system in one direction acts as input that moves the system in another direction. The output and input essentially neutralize one another, stabilizing the system. An example would be the regulation of our body temperature, and negative feedback loops are relatively common in nature. In a positive feedback loop, inputs don't stabilize a system but drive them further toward one extreme or another. An example of this process in natural systems is erosion. These are relatively rare in nature but are common in natural systems altered by human actions.

2) Differentiate between an open and closed system. If possible, give a specific and somewhat detailed example of each. Do both exist in nature? Why or why not?

Answer: A closed system is one that is isolated and self-contained. It is hypothetical and allows scientists to grapple with complex systems. An open system is one that exchanges energy matter and information with another system. The Mississippi River is an open system that interacts with all aquatic systems, terrestrial systems, and atmospheric systems from its origin to the Gulf of Mexico. It is impacted by all sources of pollution, fertilizer, temperature change, and other human impacts that can access its waters. Closed systems do not exist. Even a system as closed as a desktop computer becomes an open system when plugged into the wall socket that is in contact with the electricity that runs through an entire local community.

3) Human activity has affected every aspect of the water cycle. List four ways that humans have altered the water cycle. What are the concerns currently for the future? Why?

Answer: Humans have dammed rivers to create reservoirs, increased evaporation and infiltration of surface water into aquifers, decreased vegetation available for transpiration and return of water to the atmosphere, and emitted pollutants into the atmosphere that come down in our rainwater. The greatest concerns for the future will be shortages of potable water. Shortages in other countries are already evident. Groundwater is being removed at high rates due to agriculture in this country. Water tables in previously plentiful aquifers are dropping at high rates and may limit agricultural production and clean, fresh water supplies for Americans.

4) Human activity has affected every aspect of the nitrogen cycle. List the ways that humans have altered N content starting with where the new nitrogen comes from, where it goes, and what it impacts. What are the concerns currently for the future? Why?

Answer: Humans have spent a great deal of money on producing and distributing nitrogen, doubled the amount of nitrogen available for use by plants, and increased the amount of nitrogen that makes its way into waterways, resulting in alterations to terrestrial community composition and causing eutrophication in water systems. We have also increased the distribution of N into systems through pollution in the atmosphere that comes down as rain. Concerns for the future include climate change through increased concentrations of nitrous oxides, depleted nutrients from soils, and acidified surface water and soils.

5) Give a brief overview of the carbon cycle. Include the source of carbon that enters ecosystems, how it moves through ecosystems, and where it is ultimately deposited. What part of this cycle is believed to contribute to global warming?

Answer: Plants take up $CO_2$ from the atmosphere and then incorporate the carbon into their tissue. Animals then eat plants and gain carbon. When animals and plants die, the tissues are eaten by decomposers and are then deposited into soils. At each stage along the way, carbon is released back to the atmosphere as carbon dioxide. The use of fossil fuels (previously undecomposed organic materials) causes stored $CO_2$ to be released to the atmosphere. This is occurring at very high rates and is believed to contribute to global warming.

# *Chapter 7* Human Population Growth

## Matching Questions

*Match the following.*

1) Population's potential for growth
2) Population's potential for growth that keeps its size stable
3) Average number of years that individuals live
4) Maximum population size that a given environment can sustain
5) Declining death rates due to high food production and medical care
6) Movement of individuals into a population

A) immigration
B) mortality rate
C) transitional stage
D) demographic transition
E) life expectancy
F) adjusted mortality rates
G) stabililzing fertility
H) maximum population density
I) replacement fertility
J) carrying capacity
K) total fertility rate
L) emigration

1) K 2) I 3) E 4) J 5) C 6) A

## Short Answer Questions

1) What is the model used for representing the total impact on environment results from the interaction of three factors

Answer: I=P+A+T I= total impact on the environment, P= population, A= Affluence, and T= technology

2) How do carrying capacity estimates differ based on standard of living?

Answer: The most rigorous human carrying capacity estimates range from 1–2 billion people living prosperously in a healthy environment to 33 billion living in poverty in an environment fully in intensive cultivation without natural areas.

3) What specific population characteristics do demographers study?

Answer: They study population size, density, distribution, age structure, sex ratio, and rates of birth, death, immigration, and emigration of humans.

4) What was the cause of the change in the sex ratio in China?

Answer: Many pregnant women were selectively aborting female fetuses because of the value placed on male children.

5) What factors determine whether a population of humans grows, shrinks, or remains stable?

Answer: Rates of birth, death, immigration, and emigration.

6) Briefly, what is the consequence of unequal distribution of human populations?

Answer: Certain areas bear far more environmental impact than others.

## Short Answer Questions

1) The application of population ecology principles to the study of statistical change in human populations is the focus of the social science of __________.

Answer: demography

2) Population impact on an environment depends on __________, __________, and __________.

Answer: density, distribution, and composition

3) TFR drops have been most noticeable in countries where women have gained access to __________ and __________.

Answer: contraceptives, education

4) The environmental impact of an individual or of a population can be expressed in terms of a(n) __________.

Answer: ecological footprint

5) __________, or people who flee their home country or region, usually do it for economic or political reasons.

Answer: Refugees

## Multiple-Choice Questions

1) The cries of a newborn baby in Sarajevo, Bosnia-Herzegovina on October 12th, 1999 marked the milestone of the arrival of the

A) 12-millionth human being on our planet

B) 6-billionth human being on our planet

C) 8-billionth human being on our planet

D) 6-millionth human being on our planet

E) 12-billionth human being on our planet

Answer: B

2) Exponential growth

A) levels off after a period of time

B) increases by a fixed percentage per unit time

C) was predicted by Malthus

D) B and C

E) all of the above

Answer: D

3) The Cornucopian view held by many economists suggests that

A) resource depletion due to greater numbers of people is not a problem if new resources can be found to replace depleted ones

B) resource depletion due to greater numbers of people is not a problem because disease will limit population size

C) resource depletion due to greater numbers of people is not a problem because humans are too intelligent to allow it to be

D) resource depletion due to greater numbers of people is a problem

E) none of the above

Answer: A

4) The sensitivity factor of the model used to represent human impact on the environment is used to denote

A) human sensitivity to what needs to be done to protect the environment

B) the sensitivity of an environment to human pressures

C) the sensitivity of endangered species in an extended area

D) the sensitivity of governments to carrying capacity demands

E) economic sensitivity to resource use

Answer: B

5) Why have neo–Malthusian followers not yet seen their direst predictions come true?

A) Carrying capacity does not exist for human populations.

B) Humans have developed technology to relieve strain on resources.

C) Malthus was incorrect in assuming exponential growth of human populations.

D) A number of countries, like China, have adopted populations control.

E) Their predictions were based on calculations that included large numbers of animal populations that humans have reduced in natural ecosystems.

Answer: B

6) What do the population characteristics studied by demographers allow them to predict?

A) human population impacts on the environment

B) rate of growth of animal populations in the wild

C) passage rates of disease among indigenous populations

D) density–dependent and density–independent factors

E) rate of resource depletion of natural elements from ecosystems

Answer: A

7) Areas with low population density

A) are not sensitive to environmental impact

B) have a high S value in the environmental impact model

C) are often vulnerable because they cannot support large numbers

D) B and C

E) There are no areas with low population density left.

Answer: D

8) The age structure of a population

A) includes relative sizes of age group in a population

B) can be used to predict future dynamics of a population

C) allows development of appropriate social programs

D) can be sued to calculate population growth rate

E) all of the above

Answer: E

9) Refugees have become more numerous in recent decades because of

A) environmental degradation

B) civil strife

C) war

D) B and C

E) all of the above

Answer: E

10) A decrease in the infant mortality rate
A) has had no impact on population growth rates
B) has increased population growth rates as it is safer to have children
C) has decreased population growth rates
D) has not occurred
E) none of the above

Answer: C

11) The change in population size due to birth and death rates alone
A) is the natural rate of population change
B) is not reasonable to include in population models
C) cannot be calculated
D) is the adjusted rate of population change
E) is often used to minimize a populations impact on the environment

Answer: A

12) Stronger programs for population reduction, such as those in Bangladesh, Tunisia, and Zimbabwe, were successful because
A) public demand was driving implementation
B) political ideology of the ruling elite was driving implementation
C) corporal punishment was driving implementation
D) C and D
E) None of these programs were successful.

Answer: B

13) The Cairo, Egypt, Conference in 1994 was a milestone conference on
A) alternatives to adoption
B) environmental responsibility
C) population and development
D) role of government in developing fiscal ideology
E) none of the above

Answer: C

14) One goal of the Cairo, Egypt, Conference in 1994 was
A) designing environmentally safe manufacturing
B) designing technology for replacing natural resources
C) improving treatment of women
D) improving the treatment of impoverished males
E) improving farming to require fewer workers for harvest

Answer: C

15) Developing nations

A) contained 70% of all people in 1960

B) contained 80% of all people in 1999

C) will contain 98% of the next billion people added to the global population

D) B and C

E) all of the above

Answer: E

16) The impact of humans on the environment depends on

A) religion

B) number of people

C) how those people live

D) B and C

E) all of the above

Answer: D

17) In 1999, the richest one-fifth of the world's people possessed __________ times the income of the poorest one-fifth

A) 5 B) 12 C) 32 D) 52 E) 82

Answer: D

18) As a result of consumption patterns by the wealthy, 80% of the world has been forced to share __________% of global resources.

A) 14

B) 34

C) 54

D) 74

E) This has never been estimated.

Answer: A

19) Mortality is on the rise in many developing countries due to

A) limitations on water

B) limitations of food

C) disease

D) lack of housing

E) mortality is not rising

Answer: C

20) Demographic changes resulting from increased mortality in developing countries include

A) changes in elderly populations

B) changes in the number of children aged 1–5 years

C) decreases in the number of college–age students

D) B and C

E) Mortality is not rising.

Answer: D

21) Life expectancy in countries in areas such as southern Africa

A) is on the rise

B) is starting to fall

C) has fallen dramatically compared to expectancies of the 1950s

D) is beginning to stabilize due to population control

E) cannot be estimated due to poor communication skills

Answer: C

22) AIDS has impacted the demographic transition by

A) removing the youngest and most productive members of society

B) removing teachers

C) undermining the ability to transition to modern technologies

D) all of the above

E) AIDS has not impacted demographic transition in any country.

Answer: D

23) Declining death rates due to increased food production and improved medical care while birth rates remain high is characteristic of the

A) industrial stage

B) postpartum stage

C) transitional stage

D) demographic stage

E) none of the above

Answer: A

## True/False Questions

1) When the TFR drops below 2.1, the size of the population will shrink, in the absence of immigration.

Answer: TRUE

2) Levels of poverty alone dictate TFR.

Answer: FALSE

3) There is no relationship between population growth rate and per-capita national income.

Answer: FALSE

4) Globally, the rate of population growth is still increasing.

Answer: FALSE

5) In developing countries, access to contraception decreases reproductive rates.

Answer: TRUE

## Essay Questions

1) What is China's policy on population control? How is it enforced? Why was it initiated and how is it controversial?

Answer: China's burgeoning population and its industrial and agricultural development were eroding the nation's soils, depleting its water, leveling its forests, and polluting its air. The government decided to institute a population control program that precluded large numbers of Chinese couples from having more than one child. A system of rewards, punishments, and social stigmas were used to enforce the one-child limit. The policy is controversial because it limits personal freedom to decide the number of children that a person may have.

2) Explain human population growth in terms of carrying capacity. How does this differ from organisms that exist in natural ecosystems? Is population growth for these organisms in the manner of human populations a problem?

Answer: Organisms in ecosystems are limited by carrying capacity, which is the maximum population size that a given environment can sustain. Some believe that the idea of carrying capacity doesn't apply to the human world because humans aren't passive with respect to their environment. Human beings create resources, find potential stuff, and human intelligence turns it into resources. Environmental scientists argue that not all resources are replaceable by others when depleted. The problem with human population growth is that higher population sizes will decrease the quality of life.

3) What is the model used for representing the total impact on environmental results from the interaction of three factors? What is the fourth factor that could be added to this? Give a simple explanation for each factor, and describe what it means in terms of human impacts on the environment.

Answer: The full equation is I=P+A+T. The terms are as follows: I= total impact on the environment by a population of individuals; P= population — the value for the size of the population; A= Affluence — the value for the relative standard of living or greater per-capita resources consumption that accompanies greater wealth; T= technology — changes in the availability of technology can either increase or decrease impact depending on whether the change makes resources more or less sustainable The fourth factor that could be added is S for sensitivity, to denote how sensitive a given environment is to these pressures.

4) What is a demographic transition? What are its four stages? State why each stage is important and what the consequence is for population growth. Do all countries go through the demographic transition?

Answer: A demographic transition is a theoretic model of economic and cultural change proposed in the 1940s and 1950s to explain the declining death rates and birth rates that occurred in Western nations as they experienced industrialization.

The first stage is a stable pre-industrial stage of high birth and death rates.

The second stage is a transitional stage characterized by declining death rates due to increased food production and improved medical care. Birth rates are still high as citizens have not yet grown used to the new economic and social conditions so there is a surge in population growth.

The third stage is the industrial stage. Widespread industrialization creates opportunities for employment outside the home. Children become less valuable. Birth rates begin to fall.

The last stage is a stable post-industrial stage of low birth and death rates.

All countries do not go through the demographic transition. Transition may be different in developing countries as they industrialize or in countries that place greater value on childbirth or grant women fewer freedoms. Resources may also limit the ability to attain an equal standard of living in all countries.

5) The impact of humans on the environment differs among countries. Define ecological footprint and differentiate between the ecological footprint of a developing country and the United States. Support or challenge the statement "the population problem does not lie entirely with the developing world."

Answer: An ecological footprint is the cumulative amount of land and water required to provide the raw materials the person or population consumes and to dispose of or recycle the waste that is produced. The ecological footprint of an average U.S. citizen is significantly larger than the average resident of a developing country. The population problem does not lie entirely with the developing world, as in the developed world consumption is rising faster than population, and some scientists have suggested that increasing consumption poses a larger environmental problem than increasing population. This is because while sooner or later an expanding population will run into its limits of growth, there is no theoretical limit to consumption. In the face of demand for luxury products and the all-too-human desire not only to use these products but to flaunt them as status symbols, consumption could conceivably rise without limits.

# *Chapter 8* Agriculture and Soil Formation, Degradation, and Conservation

## Matching Questions

*Match the following.*

1) Lands used for grazing livestock
2) Alternating bands of different types of vegetation planted across a slope
3) Unconsolidated material derived from rock
4) An individual layer of soil
5) The layer below the litter layer in an idealized profile
6) The movement of material from one place and deposition in another by wind

A) erosion
B) leaching
C) parent material
D) A horizon
E) horizon
F) eluviation
G) soil
H) dirt
I) profile
J) shelterbelts
K) O horizon
L) rangeland

1) L 2) J 3) C 4) E 5) D 6) A

## Short Answer Questions

1) Briefly, what was the lesson of the farmers in southern Brazil?

   Answer: Eliminating plowing through no-till farming reduces erosion.

2) What are the two main agricultural sources that provide our food?

   Answer: Croplands and rangelands

3) Briefly, why is industrialized agriculture necessary today?

   Answer: It is necessary because not everyone is a farmer, and farmers are required to produce large quantities of food on large amounts of land.

4) Briefly, what are the three types of weathering and how do they differ?

Answer: Mechanical weathering — weathering by wind, rain, etc.
Chemical weathering — chemical interaction of water, atmospheric gases, and other substances with parent material.
Biological weathering — breakdown through activities of living things.

5) What is the basis for soil textural determinations? What are the specific components that determine soil texture?

Answer: Soil texture is determined by the size of particles. The relative proportion of sand, silt and clay determines the soil texture.

6) Differentiate between splash, sheet, rill, and gully erosion.

Answer: Splash erosion occurs when rain striking the soil surface breaks aggregates apart.
Sheet erosion is when surface water flows downhill and removes topsoil in uniform layers.
Rill erosion takes place when surface water runs along contours into rills or small channels.
Gully erosion is when gullies are formed by water enlarging rills to form larger channels.

## Fill-in-the-Blank Questions

1) Soils that are not inverted by plowing for agriculture are said to be __________ farming systems.

Answer: zero-till, no-till, zero-tillage

2) __________ is the complex plant-supporting system consisting of disintegrated rock, organic matter, air, water, nutrients, and microorganisms.

Answer: Soil

3) The practice of planting vast areas with a single type of crop is known as __________.

Answer: monocropping or monoculture

4) The cross-section of soil as a whole, from the surface to the bedrock, is known as the __________.

Answer: soil profile

5) Soil with an even mixture of all three particle sizes is known as __________.

Answer: loam

6) The artificial provision of water to support agriculture is known as __________.

Answer: irrigation

## Multiple-Choice Questions

1) The practice of cultivating soil, producing crops, and raising livestock for human use and consumption is
   A) agronomy
   B) agriculture
   C) agroeconomics
   D) agroecology
   E) agrology

   Answer: B

2) We lose 5–7 million ha of productive cropland per year to
   A) forest removal
   B) erosion
   C) cropland use
   D) over irrigation
   E) all of the above

   Answer: E

3) During most of our species' 100,000–year existence and until about 10,000 years ago, we depended on
   A) agriculture
   B) hunting
   C) gathering
   D) B and C
   E) all of the above

   Answer: D

4) Agricultural practices where the members of a farming family produce only enough food for themselves and do not make use of large–scale irrigation, fertilizer, or large teams of animals is called
   A) intensive traditional agriculture
   B) subsidence agriculture
   C) subsistence agriculture
   D) advanced organic farming
   E) reduced tillage agriculture

   Answer: C

5) Industrialization

A) had no impact on agriculture

B) is necessary today

C) replaced oxen with faster means of cultivation

D) B and C

E) all of the above

Answer: D

6) Organic matter includes

A) living microbes

B) dead microbes

C) decaying materials

D) B and C

E) all of the above

Answer: E

7) The base geological material in a particular location is

A) parent material

B) bedrock

C) soil

D) lithosphere

E) stratolith

Answer: A

8) The breakdown of large rocks into smaller pieces is termed

A) mineralization

B) weathering

C) laterization

D) erosion

E) deposition

Answer: B

9) Leaching

A) can harm plant growth

B) is caused by movement of water downward through soil

C) removes nutrients from soil

D) can cause problems in surface or groundwater

E) all of the above

Answer: E

10) The E horizon is the

A) illuvial horizon

B) eluvial horizon

C) organic horizon

D) top soil

E) parent material

Answer: B

11) The zone beneath the A horizon where leaching has deposited materials is called the

A) O horizon

B) B horizon

C) C horizon

D) E horizon

E) Leaching does not result in mineral deposits.

Answer: D

12) Soil texture determines

A) soil porosity

B) rate of infiltration by water

C) amount of oxygen available to biotic soil components

D) ease of cultivation

E) all of the above

Answer: E

13) Soil structure is characterized by

A) The amount of sand, silt, and clay

B) Number of horizons

C) pH

D) arrangement of sand, silt and clay into aggregates

E) all of the above

Answer: C

14) pH influences

A) Plant growth

B) Nutrient availability

C) Cation availability

D) B and C

E) all of the above

Answer: E

15) The loss of more than 10% productivity in arid areas to erosion, soil compaction, forest removal, and an array of other factors is called

A) climatization

B) global change

C) desertification

D) salinization

E) stratification

Answer: C

16) The United States agency charged with slowing soil degradation is the

A) Soil Aggregation Service

B) Agricultural Standards Agency

C) Conservation Integration Service

D) Soil Conservation Service

E) There is not a U.S. agency charged with soil degradation, only private firms funded by farmers.

Answer: D

17) Shelterbelts are

A) rows of trees or other tall perennial plants

B) windbreaks

C) a technique to reduce wind erosion

D) B and C

E) all of the above

Answer: E

18) The buildup of salts in soils as a result of overirrigation is

A) salinization

B) leaching

C) weathering

D) erosion

E) evaporation

Answer: A

19) Green manure is a(n)

A) chemical fertilizer

B) organic fertilizer

C) accumulation of fresh vegetation

D) B and C

E) all of the above

Answer: D

20) Compost includes
A) animal manures
B) fresh vegetation
C) crop residues
D) a mix produced from decomposition of materials
E) all of the above

Answer: D

21) The consequences of overfertilization include
A) blue-baby disease
B) eutrophication
C) air pollution
D) stomach cancer
E) all of the above

Answer: E

22) The Conservation Reserve Program pays farmers to
A) grow crops such as corn and beans
B) stop cultivating highly erodible cropland
C) plant trees and grasses
D) B and C
E) all of the above

Answer: D

## True/False Questions

1) Feeding the world's population under the constraints of current land-use patterns means that we must increase the efficiency with which we produce food rather than the amount of land farmed.

Answer: TRUE

2) Successful hunting and gathering allowed for our ancestors to develop large more permanent camps.

Answer: FALSE

3) Climate, latitude, and elevation have much greater influence on a region's ecosystems than soil does.

Answer: FALSE

4) Soil profiles in all ecosystems contain O, A, E, B, C, and R horizons.

Answer: FALSE

5) Organic fertilizers can cause environmental damage even if used properly.

Answer: FALSE

## Essay Questions

1) What was the green revolution, and what was its role in altering Ehrlich's predictions? What practices were involved?

Answer: The green revolution was an intensification of the changes brought by the industrialization of agriculture, a change in agricultural practices that dramatically increased the crops per acre of farmland between 1950 and the 21st century. New practices involved devoting large areas of identical crops specially bred for high yields and rapid growth; heavy use of pesticides, fertilizers, and irrigation water; and sowing and harvesting on the same piece of land more than once per year or once per season. This altered Ehrlich's predictions by increasing food production on existing farmlands.

2) Define the term soil profile. What are the influences on the development of a soil profile, and how do profiles differ?

Answer: The process of soil formation can lead to characteristic aspects of soil structure. Once mechanical, chemical, and biological weathering have produced a layer of smaller particles between the parent material and atmosphere, wind and water begin to move and sort them. Organisms migrate in and move them as well. Eventually, distinct zones and patterns appear. Soil profiles differ from location to location due to variations in parent material, climate, and other factors.

3) Describe the United States' Dust Bowl and the lesson learned.

Answer: Homesteaders cultivated the native prairies of the Great Plains of the United States. In this area, prairie grasses had prevented erosion. Farmers planted wheat and raised cattle. In the early 1930s, a drought exacerbated the ongoing impact of humans on soils and resulted in wind erosion of millions of tons of topsoil. Impacts of soil entrained in the atmosphere were detected as far away as New York, where black snow and rain fell. The lesson was that soil conservation had to be a priority to protect our ability to produce food in this country. The Soil Conservation Service was created.

4) Discuss the practices used by farmers to protect their soils.

Answer: There are numerous practices used by farmers to protect their soils. Crop rotation, alternating the kind of crop grown, can return nutrients to the soil and represents an alternative to letting fields lie fallow, which can expose soils to erosion. Contour farming protects soils against erosion by shaping agricultural fields in a manner that decreases the water running down a hillside. Intercropping is the planting of two types of vegetation in the same field either overlapping or in alternating rows. It provides a more complete land cover by decreasing bare areas between rows. Shelterbelts provide windbreaks that slow ground wind speed across a field. No-till or conservation tillage decreases the plowing of soil and provides less exposure of soils to wind and water for erosion. Finally, use of irrigation can prevent wind erosion, though used incorrectly, it can cause water erosion. The final way to protect soils is to prevent salinization or the salt buildup on the surface that often accompanies overirrigation.

5) Discuss how specific land-use management strategies such as management of rangeland and forest can result in degradation of soils.

Answer: As long as livestock populations do not exceed a range's carrying capacity and do not consume grasses faster than they can replace themselves, grazing is sustainable. When overgrazing occurs, it exposes soils to erosion by wind and water. Native vegetation has a difficult time growing, causing a positive feedback that increases erosion. Overgrazing can also lead to compression of soils, which damages soil structure. Forestry practices such as clear-cutting can lead to severe erosion due to the sudden exposure of soil to wind and rain. Road building to access trees also causes erosion and compaction.

# *Chapter 9* Agriculture, Biotechnology, and the Future of Food

## Matching Questions

*Match the following.*

1) A disease caused by lack of iron in the diet

2) Organism used in the most widespread biocontrol efforts

3) A term for the lack of sufficient calories in a diet

4) The process by which one plant fertilizes another one of its own species

5) An organism that contains DNA from another species

6) Agriculture that uses lower amounts of fertilizer and pesticides than traditional agriculture

A) *Fusarium solani*

B) *Bacillus thuringiensis*

C) malaria

D) pollination

E) undernourished

F) anemia

G) malnutrition

H) low-input agriculture

I) marasmus

J) *Rhizoctonia*

K) biocontrol agriculture

L) transgenic

1) F 2) B 3) E 4) D 5) L 6) H

## Short Answer Questions

1) How did we increase food production during the 1960s?

Answer: We increased food production by devoting more energy to agriculture; planting and harvesting more frequently; increasing the use of irrigation, fertilizer and pesticides; increasing the amount of agricultural land; and developing more productive varieties.

2) Define the terms "pest" and "weed." Why are these definitions subjective?

Answer: A pest is any organism that damages crops that are valuable to us. A weed is any organism that competes with our crops. The definitions are subjective because they are defined by our economic interest.

2) Define the terms "pest" and "weed." Why are these definitions subjective?

Answer: A pest is any organism that damages crops that are valuable to us. A weed is any organism that competes with our crops. The definitions are subjective because they are defined by our economic interest.

3) Describe the use of biological control for battling pests.

Answer: This strategy uses crop pests rather than chemicals to control pest densities. An organism that eats a crop pest is released into a crop; it eats the crop pest, decreasing the density of the crop pest without chemicals.

4) What is the basic concept of sustainable agriculture?

Answer: Sustainable agriculture is agriculture that does not deplete soils faster than they form. It is farming and ranching that do not reduce the amount of healthy soil, clean water, and genetic diversity essential to long-term crop and livestock production.

5) What was the concern associated with the genetic stock of maize in Mexico, and why was it controversial?

Answer: The concern was that the genetic stock of maize in Mexico was contaminated with transgenes from GM maize stock. It was controversial because the research was suspect, though some suggest that whether it has occurred or not, a transgenic invasion is likely to happen soon.

## Fill-in-the-Blank Questions

1) Today, policymakers face the challenge of producing enough food to feed people over the long run. This is a goal of __________.

Answer: food security

2) __________ is the lack of sufficient nutritional elements the body needs.

Answer: Malnutrition

3) The practice of integrating biocontrol and minimal chemical use is called __________.

Answer: integrated pest management

4) Food-growing practice that uses no synthetic fertilizers, insecticides, fungicides, or herbicides is termed __________.

Answer: organic agriculture

5) The __________ suggests that we should proceed with caution where genetically modified organisms are present until the ramifications of our actions are known.

Answer: precautionary principle

## Multiple-Choice Questions

1) Crops made with genes extracted from other organisms are

A) genetically diluted

B) genetically engineered

C) genetically spiked

D) genetically mutated

E) not possible

Answer: B

2) Pesticides become less useful over time because

A) farmers use less per application because pests are fewer

B) pests can evolve in response to chemical applications

C) resistance is acquired by larger and larger numbers of individuals

D) B and C

E) all of the above

Answer: D

3) Pollination can occur by

A) water

B) wind

C) insects

D) animals

E) all of the above

Answer: E

4) Pollination of agricultural crops is mostly by

A) water

B) wind

C) insects

D) animals

E) all of the above

Answer: C

5) Insecticides kill

A) organisms that can act as biocontrol agents

B) pollinators

C) pests

D) B and C

E) all of the above

Answer: E

6) DNA that is patched together from the DNA from multiple organisms is called
   A) split DNA
   B) genetically devised DNA
   C) recombinant DNA
   D) patched DNA technology
   E) This process does not provide a practical approach, so it is not done.

Answer: C

7) DNA is introduced into organisms by
   A) fertilizer additions
   B) gene gun
   C) plasmid
   D) B and C
   E) all of the above

Answer: D

8) Transgenic organisms are produced through
   A) microtechnology
   B) biotechnology
   C) scientology
   D) bacteriology
   E) agrotechnology

Answer: B

9) The Cartagena Protocol on Biosafety
   A) regulates the creation of GM foods
   B) outlines regulations on international trade of GM foods
   C) was signed by the United states
   D) B and C
   E) all of the above

Answer: B

10) The Zambian government did not accept U.S. food aid in 2002 because
   A) they did not want charity
   B) of environmental concerns regarding GM foods
   C) their neighbors didn't
   D) they had few people at risk of starvation
   E) all of the above

Answer: B

11) In contrast to ancient agriculture, modern agricultural practices depend on
   A) crops with little genetic variety
   B) crops with high genetic variety
   C) soil seedbanks
   D) pollination by wind
   E) high rates of inbreeding

Answer: A

12) Wild relatives can provide cultivars that are
   A) resistant to fungal pathogens
   B) resistant to viral pathogens
   C) more resistant to drought
   D) all of the above
   E) none of the above

Answer: D

13) Aquaculture
   A) includes fish farms
   B) can increase incidence of disease
   C) can increase food security by increasing food production
   D) all of the above
   E) does not work and has been abandoned

Answer: D

14) In order for the number of humans to increase, we had to
   A) alter ecosystem stability
   B) increase our carrying capacity
   C) alter population structures
   D) increase environmental resistance
   E) decrease our biotic potential

Answer: B

15) Wheat production was increased in developing countries by
   A) increasing erosion rates
   B) increasing rates of leaching
   C) breeding varieties of wheat better acclimated to local growing conditions
   D) using transgenic species
   E) all of the above

Answer: C

16) The green revolution
   A) decreased yields
   B) resulted in higher crop yields
   C) resulted in environmental damage
   D) B and C
   E) all of the above

Answer: D

17) Seed banks are important for
   A) cash deposits for developing countries
   B) protecting monoculture productivity
   C) protecting genetic diversity
   D) loans to developing countries
   E) providing farmers with the current year's GM crops

Answer: C

18) Today's food security problems are a result of
   A) production
   B) distribution
   C) education
   D) fertilizer use
   E) none of the above

Answer: B

19) Biological control can have unintended consequences when
   A) genetically engineered organisms are introduced
   B) agricultural crops invade local vegetation
   C) the biological control agent becomes invasive and affects local ecosystems
   D) the biological control agent is altered by breeding with crop plants
   E) there are no unintended consequences

Answer: C

20) Decreases in alfalfa production occurred because
   A) fertilizer use killed the pollinator
   B) pesticide use killed the pollinator
   C) tillage killed the pollinator
   D) B and C
   E) all of the above

Answer: D

21) Honeybee populations, such as the European honeybee, that are necessary for pollination are endangered due to

A) pollution

B) parasites

C) habitat destruction

D) introduced species

E) all of the above

Answer: B

22) In the United States, transgenic plants

A) will never be sold

B) are labeled before they are sold

C) account for half of soybean, cotton, and wheat crops

D) cannot be planted

E) none of the above

Answer: C

23) Concentrated animal feeding operations can contribute to

A) air pollution

B) groundwater contamination

C) surface water contamination

D) B and C

E) all of the above

Answer: E

24) It is more energetically efficient to eat

A) primary producers

B) herbivores

C) carnivores

D) B and C

E) all of the above

Answer: A

## True/False Questions

1) Today almost 80 million people do not have enough to eat.

Answer: TRUE

2) Less than 25% of the world's people live on less than $2.00 per day.

Answer: FALSE

3) Sixty-one percent of U.S. adults are overweight and 27% are obese.

Answer: TRUE

4) Genetic modification of organisms by humans is an ancient exercise.

Answer: TRUE

5) Consumption of meat products has decreased as the vegetarian lifestyle has become popular.

Answer: FALSE

## Essay Questions

1) What was the green revolution, and what impact did it have on developing countries? Discuss the impact of the green revolution on the environment.

Answer: The need for higher quantity and better quality of food for the growing human population led in the mid-and late 20th century to the green revolution, wherein scientists in the developed world created methods and technology to increase crop output per unit area of existing cultivated land. In developing countries, this greatly increased agricultural production. Environmentally, this was positive because it decreased the need for new areas for cultivation and reduced rates of deforestation. Unfortunately, it also increased the use of water, chemical fertilizers, pesticides, and fossil fuels, increasing pollution, salinization, and desertification.

2) What are the arguments for and against genetically modified crops? Discuss both the scientific and political debates.

Answer: The proponents of GM crops stress continuity with the agricultural past, arguing that there's little reason to expect that today's GM food will be any less safe than the selectively bred food of the past. Critics point out that the new techniques differ from traditional breeding techniques because they mix species, create species in the lab not the field, and deal with novel gene combinations not possible in nature. The political debate involves labeling and an individual's right to know what is in the food they consume. Industry has a large financial stake in seeing the continued use of GM foods. Critics argue that we should adopt the precautionary principle with GM foods.

3) Explain the statement "the closer our food sources are to the sun as a direct source of energy, the more people the planet can support" in terms of the laws of thermodynamics and the biomass pyramid.

Answer: Meat is farther from the sun than plant material. Consuming meat decreases the amount of usable energy that is obtained directly from the sun because animals must first consume plants before they are eaten by humans. Every time energy moves from one trophic level to the next, as much as 90% of the useful energy present in the lower trophic level is lost. This is because the second law of energy states that entropy increases as one goes from one level to the next and energy is lost as heat or light at each transfer. For this reason, people who rely heavily on meat as a source of food energy are less energy efficient than ones that rely on vegetarian diet. The biomass pyramid echoes this, as each trophic level contains less biomass (energy) than the lower level.

4) Why is variety in crop plants important for "food security"? How is this threatened by GM food crops? What is the United States' position on GM products? How does this differ from the position of other countries?

Answer: Varieties contain genes that, through conventional breeding, might confer resistance to disease, pests, inbreeding, and other pressures that challenge modern agriculture. Monocultures of industrial agriculture place all our eggs in one basket, so that any single catastrophe could potentially wipe out multiple crops. Wild relatives contain genetic diversity that may have ready-made solutions to unforeseen problems. The U.S. position is that GM foods are an acceptable food crop. Other countries refuse to purchase or accept food or seed crops that are GM. The European Union has been extremely outspoken against the use or trade of GM foods.

5) What are the dangers associated with pesticide use? How can biocontrol and use of crops with high genetic diversity be used to decrease the amount of pesticides used?

Answer: Pesticides are toxins that can harm humans. Pesticide use has increased to lower crop loss due to pests and increase yield. Increased use results in resistance developing in pest populations. When this occurs, the type of pesticide used has to be altered so that pests can be controlled. Increasing the toxicity of pesticides is often the solution. Biological control can decrease pest density by introducing enemies of the pests to the field. This decreases pest numbers without chemicals. Increasing the genetic diversity of the crop can also decrease pest numbers because pests may not be able to consume all genetic varieties in the crop. This will result in higher yields through reduction of pest populations.

# Chapter 10 Toxicology and Environmental Health

## Matching Questions

*Match the following.*

1) The degree of harm a substance can inflict
2) Toxicants that cause cancer
3) Chemicals that cause harm to unborn young inside a mother's body are called
4) High exposure to a chemical over a short period of time
5) An organism that transfers a pathogen to a host

A) acute
B) tumerous
C) carcinogens
D) mutagens
E) vector
F) antigens
G) toxicity
H) teratogens
I) toxicological
J) oxidants

1) G 2) C 3) H 4) A 5) E

## Short Answer Questions

1) How did contaminants impact reproduction in alligators in Florida lakes?

Answer: Environmental contaminants mimic hormones and interfere with the functioning of the animal endocrine (hormone) systems. The alligator endocrine systems were disrupted during development of the egg.

2) How have artificially produced chemicals played a role in giving us the standard of living we enjoy today?

Answer: Without these chemicals, we would not have the industrial agriculture that produces our food, many of the medical advances that protect our health and prolong our lives, and modern materials and conveniences.

3) List the properties that determine the rate of degradation of toxicants.

Answer: Temperature, moisture, sun exposure, and chemistry of toxicant

4) Explain how biomagnification occurs.

Answer: When one organism ingests a toxicant, the toxicant becomes concentrated within its tissues. When the next organism feeds, it eats multiple organisms at the lower trophic level, consuming quantities of toxin with each feeding. Thus with every step up the food chain from primary producer to top predator, concentrations of toxicant increase.

5) What are epidemiological studies, and what is their value?

Answer: They involve large-scale comparisons among groups of people, usually contrasting a group known to have been exposed to a toxicant with a group that has not. They allow for the risk of exposure to a toxicant to be determined.

6) How is the precautionary principle used in environmental health?

Answer: Substances, such as potential toxic substances, are assumed to be harmful until shown to be harmless.

## Fill-in-the-Blank Questions

1) The science that examines the effects of chemicals on humans and wildlife, __________, has become increasingly important during the past century.

Answer: toxicology

2) The catalyst that helped spur the entire environmental movement in the United States was the publication of the book __________.

Answer: *Silent Spring*

3) The issue of airborne transport of pesticides, __________, can be severe if pesticides are applied on windy days.

Answer: pesticide drift

4) Toxicants, such as organic compounds, may build up in an animal, in a process termed __________.

Answer: bioaccumulation

5) Rachel Carson's 1962 book *Silent Spring* brought the pesticide __________ to the attention of the public.

Answer: DDT

6) The study and practice of __________ assesses environmental factors that influence human health and quality of life.

Answer: environmental health

## Multiple-Choice Questions

1) In the United States, more pesticides per unit area are applied by

A) city workers for park grounds

B) homeowners to lawns

C) farmers to agricultural fields

D) All apply pesticides equally.

E) These statistics are not available.

Answer: B

2) Substances that pose health risks include

A) natural chemical substances

B) synthetic chemical pesticides

C) chemical herbicides

D) B and C

E) all of the above

Answer: E

3) The message of Rachel Carson's 1962 book *Silent Spring* was that

A) humans allow groundwater tables to rise by overirrigation

B) artificial pesticides are hazardous to the health of people and animals

C) organisms are being lost from ecosystems due to clear-cutting

D) pesticide use should increase to intensify agriculture and slow habitat destruction

E) our understanding of chemical toxicity is complete and fear of chemical use is unnecessary

Answer: B

4) Carcinogens may be difficult to identify because

A) they are the least common toxicants

B) there is a long lag time between exposure to the agent and disease

C) they are rare in nature

D) B and C

E) all of the above

Answer: B

5) Toxicants that cause harm by affecting the immune system include

A) neurotoxins

B) allergens

C) teratogens

D) hormones

E) antibiotics

Answer: B

6) The book *Our Stolen Future* was important because it

A) provided evidence supporting the use of synthetic chemicals

B) supported organic farming as the only possible alternative

C) focused on the impacts of endocrine-disrupting chemicals on humans

D) provided evidence against Rachel Carson's book *Silent Spring*

E) started the environmental movement

Answer: C

7) The distribution of toxicants

A) is entirely random

B) reflects use patterns

C) reflects geology

D) B and C

E) all of the above

Answer: D

8) Toxicants in soil can

A) leach to the groundwater table

B) be carried into rivers and streams when soils erode

C) be entrained in the atmosphere through wind erosion

D) all of the above

E) not be moved once they become part of the topsoil

Answer: D

9) PCB contamination can lead to

A) neurological problems

B) penis abnormalities

C) low birth weight

D) smaller heads at birth

E) all of the above

Answer: E

10) Natural chemical substances

A) are not a health risk to humans

B) include oil oozing from the ground

C) include radioactive radon gas

D) B and C

E) all of the above

Answer: D

11) The worldwide drop in sperm counts among men has been attributed to

A) DDT
B) endocrine disruptors
C) teratogens
D) radon
E) all of the above

Answer: B

12) Bisphenol-A is a problem because it is

A) an estrogen mimic
B) used in plastic manufacturing
C) used to fight cavities
D) an endocrine disruptor
E) all of the above

Answer: E

13) Transport of airborne toxicants, a specific problem in agricultural environments, is called pesticide

A) spray B) drift C) response D) attach E) air loss

Answer: B

14) The toxicity of a chemical is evaluated using animal models by creating a

A) dose analysis
B) dose-response curve
C) dose evaluation kit
D) wellness chart for affected animals
E) test site for naturally exposed animals

Answer: B

15) A high LD50 indicates a

A) low toxicity
B) high toxicity
C) high radioactivity
D) low radioactivity
E) toxic compound may be removed from toxins list

Answer: A

16) Interactive effects of toxicants

A) often result in synergistic effects

B) are easy to detect

C) are easy to evaluate if chemicals are known

D) B and C

E) all of the above

Answer: A

17) Asbestos

A) is a radioactive gas that seeps into houses

B) is a fibrous material that is ingested with grains such as those in bread

C) is an insulator that has dangerous fibers that get lodged in lung tissue

D) is only a problem in developing countries

E) will not seriously affect human health

Answer: C

18) The most dangerous indoor pollutant for children has been

A) pesticides

B) herbicides

C) lead paint

D) vinyl paints

E) laundry detergent

Answer: B

19) The impact of any environmental health threat can only be estimated if the scientist knows the

A) strength or toxicity of the threat

B) chances an organism will encounter it

C) frequency with which the organism encounters it

D) amount of substance to which the organism is exposed

E) all of the above

Answer: E

20) Pesticides in the United States are registered through the

A) FDA

B) EPA

C) USDA

D) FIFRA

E) none of the above

Answer: B

21) The Toxic Substances Control Act regulates

A) industrial chemicals

B) drugs

C) pesticides

D) food additives

E) all of the above

Answer: A

22) Persistent organic pollutants

A) are toxic chemicals that persist in the environment

B) bioaccumulate in the food chain

C) travel long distances

D) were the focus of an international conference in Stockholm

E) all of the above

Answer: E

## True/False Questions

1) The U.S. Geological Survey found that 80% of U.S. streams contain at least trace amounts of wastewater contaminants.

Answer: TRUE

2) Some threats to human health are unavoidable because they are wholly natural and part of the natural environment.

Answer: TRUE

3) Radon is a highly toxic radioactive gas that is introduced into homes by use of electrical power generated by nuclear power plants.

Answer: FALSE

4) Acute exposure to chemical agents is more difficult to detect than chronic exposure.

Answer: FALSE

5) Synthetic pesticides have been found in high concentrations in uninhabited polar regions.

Answer: TRUE

## Essay Questions

1) What are endocrine disruptors? Why do they work on pests? Why is this specific group of chemicals a problem for humans? Why have they not been banned?

Answer: Endocrine disruptors are toxicants that interfere with the endocrine system. They work on pests because they mimic hormones that direct reproductive events. Decreases in biotic potential of pests will decrease pest densities in agricultural fields. These are problems for humans because our reproductive system, growth, and development can also be impacted by hormone mimics. They have not been banned because scientific evidence for the problems they cause has been slow in coming.

2) Discuss the position of each of the groups that are involved in the debate over how much risk is posed by natural toxicants. State each position and how it relates to synthetic chemicals.

Answer: Ames maintains that the amounts of synthetic chemicals in our food from pesticide residues are dwarfed by the amounts of natural toxicants, making synthetic chemicals a minor worry. Restricting fruit and vegetable consumption over fears of synthetic pesticide residue will actually cause more damage to human health than the synthetic chemicals. His critics say that natural toxins are usually more readily metabolized and excreted by the body than synthetic ones, that synthetic ones persist and accumulate in the environment, and that synthetic chemicals expose people to risks in other ways than just ingestion of the food.

3) Explain how dose-response curves are developed and used to evaluate the effects of toxicants on human populations.

Answer: Dose-response curves are produced by giving toxicants to lab animals or other human model systems and measuring how much effect they produce at different doses. The data are plotted on a graph. Once data are plotted, scientists extrapolate downward to estimate the effects of lower doses on a large population of animals. The numbers are then extrapolated to estimate the effect on humans.

4) What area does the field of environmental health cover? Differentiate between indoor and outdoor environmental health issues. Give examples of each.

Answer: Environmental health assesses environmental factors that influence human health and quality of life, and seeks to prevent adverse effects on human health and on ecological systems essential to environmental quality and long-term human well-being. Outdoor health issues include pollutants, pesticides, and any variety of other toxic chemical that are found outdoors. Radon, asbestos, and lead paint are all examples of indoor environmental health hazards.

5) Explain how risk management combines science and other social factors.

Answer: Accurate risk assessment consists of decisions and strategies to minimize risk. Federal agencies are charged with accessing risk and considering findings in light of economic, social, and political needs and values. The costs and benefits of addressing risk in various ways are addressed with regard to both scientific and nonscientific concerns. While economic benefits are generally known, easily quantified, and of a definite and stable amount, health risks are hard-to-measure probabilities that impact a small percentage of people that will suffer greatly. For example, if a pesticide is used, people may suffer, but if it is not used, people may not have enough to eat. Both costs must be considered before banning the pesticide.

6) What steps are involved with assessing risk for a chemical substance?

Answer: There are two main steps. The first is determining whether a substance has toxic effects, and measuring dose-response effects of toxicant exposure. The second step is assessing the likely exposure that an individual will have to the toxicant including frequency, concentration, and time of exposure.

# Chapter 11 Atmospheric Science and Air Pollution

## Matching Questions

*Match the following.*

1) Weight per unit area produced by a column of air

2) The boundary between the lower atmosphere directly above the planet and the upper atmosphere

3) Circular air current with warm air rising to be replaced by cold air descending

4) Air mass with an elevated atmospheric pressure

5) Departure from normal temperature distribution in the troposphere

A) conduction current

B) high-pressure system

C) tropopause

D) water vapor

E) convection current

F) hurricane

G) thermal inversion

H) low-pressure system

I) relative humidity

J) atmospheric pressure

1) J 2) C 3) E 4) B 5) G

## Short Answer Questions

1) Why was London's Killer Smog of 1952 important?

Answer: It helped change the way the public viewed air pollution.

2) List the important atmospheric properties.

Answer: Pressure, temperature, humidity

3) List the six pollutants that are closely tracked by the U.S. EPA.

Answer: Carbon monoxide, lead, nitrogen dioxide, ozone, sulfur dioxide, particulate matter

4) Differentiate between primary and secondary pollutants.

Answer: Primary pollutants are emitted into the troposphere in a form that is directly harmful, and secondary pollutants are hazardous substances that are produced through a reaction of substances added to the atmosphere with chemicals normally found in the atmosphere.

5) How does indoor pollution in developing countries differ from indoor pollution in developed countries?

Answer: In developing countries, wood or charcoal is burned in residences with little or no ventilation. In contrast, in developed countries a large amount of indoor pollution comes from synthetic chemicals used for cleaning or pesticides or in manufacturing of furniture or electronics.

## Fill-in-the-Blank Questions

1) A departure from the normal temperature distribution in the troposphere is called a(n) __________.

Answer: temperature or thermal inversion

2) The boundary between two air masses that differ in temperature and density is called a(n) __________.

Answer: front

3) Humans have generated significant quantities of __________, materials added to the atmosphere that can affect climate and/or harm organisms.

Answer: air pollution

4) The term __________ describes a specific spot, such as a factory's smokestacks, where large quantities of pollution are discharged.

Answer: point source

5) Any solid or liquid particles small enough to be carried aloft are pollutants grouped as __________.

Answer: particulate matter

6) The most successful international effort to address any global environmental problem was the __________, in which nations agreed to cut CFC production in half.

Answer: Montreal Protocol

7) The local physical properties of the troposphere result in __________.

Answer: weather

## Multiple-Choice Questions

1) The largest contributor to atmospheric gases is

A) oxygen B) nitrogen C) sulfur D) ozone E) argon

Answer: B

2) The relative humidity is

A) the amount of oxygen in the atmosphere

B) the amount of oxygen a given volume of air holds relative to the maximum amount it could hold

C) the amount of water vapor in the atmosphere

D) the amount of water vapor a given volume of air holds relative to the maximum amount it could hold

E) none of the above

Answer: D

3) Weather patterns are largely determined in the

A) stratosphere

B) tropopause

C) troposphere

D) lithosphere

E) biosphere

Answer: C

4) Seasons are a result of

A) differences in air pressure

B) periodic variations in sun exposure

C) alterations to relative humidity

D) changes in day length

E) rotation of the planet around the moon

Answer: B

5) Planet–wide patterns of convection currents are called

A) weather currents

B) Hadley cells

C) hot air

D) El Niño events

E) troposphere

Answer: B

6) Natural sources of air pollution come from

A) metabolism of plants

B) decay of dead plants

C) salt from sea spray

D) B and C

E) all of the above

Answer: E

7) The dust storms that have large impacts on the Caribbean

A) provide nutrients and improve the water quality for the coral reef systems

B) are the result of natural processes

C) are the result of poor farming techniques

D) B and C

E) None of the above as the storms do not have large impacts.

Answer: D

8) Carbon monoxide is a problem because

A) it binds with hemoglobin, preventing binding with oxygen

B) it is produced by vehicle emissions

C) it is odorless

D) all of the above

E) None of the above as carbon monoxide is consumed by plants for photosynthesis.

Answer: C

9) Tropospheric ozone

A) is an odorless gas

B) binds with hemoglobin, preventing binding with oxygen

C) is produced through the interaction of heat and light with nitrogen oxides and other carbon-containing compounds

D) is a primary pollutant

E) is not a problem because it is necessary to keep UV radiation from the surface of the planet

Answer: C

10) Lead is a metal that enters the atmosphere at a particulate pollutant. This is a problem because it

A) is a precious metal and is being lost to the atmosphere

B) will cause the ozone hole to increase

C) causes central nervous system malfunction in humans

D) can become attached to radon

E) will be ignited when in contact with open flame.

Answer: C

11) Particulate matter

A) includes nitrogen oxides

B) may cause damage to respiratory tissues when inhaled

C) binds with hemoglobin, preventing binding with oxygen

D) only interacts with surface tissues of humans, causing mild irritation

E) is problematic because it decreases primary production by limiting the availability of sunlight for plants

Answer: B

12) Photochemical smog differs from industrial smog in that it

A) is an unhealthy mixture of air pollutants

B) has large quantities of soot

C) requires light for activation

D) consists of primary pollutants

E) none of the above

Answer: C

13) The problems created by CFCs include

A) ozone depletion

B) toxins accumulating in freezers

C) insulating foam structures that currently fill landfills

D) movement of toxins into lakes and rivers poisoning fish

E) There were no problems as CFC's are relatively nontoxic.

Answer: A

14) The impacts of indoor pollution are

A) greater than the impacts of outdoor pollution

B) amplified because of the time we spend indoors

C) amplified because of the synthetic materials manufactured and sold for use indoors

D) amplified because ventilation systems are closed to increase energy efficiency

E) all of the above

Answer: E

15) In developed countries, the two most deadly sources of indoor pollution are

A) pesticides and cleaning agents

B) synthetic furniture materials and radiation from electronic equipment

C) radiation from electronic equipment and pesticides

D) radon and cigarette smoke

E) pesticides and cigarette smoke

Answer: D

16) Bacteria and fungi can be included as
   A) contributors to indoor pollutants
   B) contributors to outdoor pollutants
   C) pollutants for people with asthma
   D) problems in degrading the ozone layer
   E) the cause of high pesticide use in the home

Answer: A

17) Acid precipitation contains
   A) carbonic acid
   B) nitric acid
   C) sulfuric acid
   D) B and C
   E) all of the above

Answer: D

18) Which of the following is not a consequences of acid deposition?
   A) loss of calcium from soil
   B) water that is acidic enough to kill fish
   C) rainwater that can damage skin cells or cause cancers
   D) widespread tree die-offs
   E) erosion of buildings

Answer: C

19) The Coriolis effect
   A) keeps the Earth from spinning too fast
   B) keeps the north/south patterns of air circulation in Hadley cells from translating into north/south surface winds
   C) results in ice and dark at the poles in winter
   D) keeps the wind circulating at constant speed around the planet
   E) all of the above

Answer: B

20) The mesosphere
   A) is the farthest extent of atmosphere from the planet
   B) is the hottest point of the atmosphere
   C) is the coldest point of the atmosphere
   D) has the greatest concentration of ozone
   E) is where weather patterns develop

Answer: C

21) An especially great temperature difference between a dry mass of cold air and a warm humid air mass will generate
   A) spring
   B) fall
   C) intense vertical conduction currents
   D) intense vertical convection currents
   E) intense horizontal conduction currents

Answer: D

22) The most obvious cause of industrial smog is
   A) burning trash
   B) fires for heating food
   C) ignition of volatile organic matter
   D) burning fossil fuels
   E) generation of nuclear power

Answer: D

## True/False Questions

1) A London governmental body estimated that only 20 city residents die prematurely each year due to vehicle emissions.

Answer: FALSE

2) The stratospheric ozone layer is important for reducing the amount of UV radiation hitting the surface of the planet.

Answer: TRUE

3) The majority of outdoor pollution comes from natural sources.

Answer: TRUE

4) Of the six major pollutants tracked by the U.S. EPA in 2001, only 6% of the population lived in counties where one of the six reached unhealthy levels.

Answer: FALSE

5) Australia's Commonwealth Science Council in 1999 attributed 14 times as many deaths globally to outdoor pollution as to indoor pollution.

Answer: FALSE

6) Control of indoor pollution was enforced as early as the 1970 U.S. Clean Air Act.

Answer: FALSE

## Essay Questions

1) Discuss the objectives and success of the Montreal Protocol. To what two factors do scientists attribute its success?

Answer: The objectives of the Montreal Protocol were to alter use of CFCs as they were contributing to a growing ozone hole that would increase the probabilities of getting skin cancer. The world community came together in 1987 to craft the Montreal Protocol, which has now been signed by over 180 nations. In this convention, nations agreed to cut CFC production in half. Today the production and use of ozone-depleting compounds has fallen 95% since the late 1980s, and scientists can discern the beginnings of long-term recovery of the ozone layer. For these reasons the Montreal Protocol and its follow up amendments are widely considered the most spectacular success story so far in addressing any global environmental problem. Environmental scientists have attributed this success primarily to two factors. One is the fact that policymakers engaged industry in helping to solve the problem, and that government and industry worked together on coming up with technological fixes and replacement chemicals. Second, the process after 1987 successfully followed an adaptive management approach, which allows for altering strategies midstream in response to new scientific data, technological advances, or economic figures.

2) How do interacting masses of air generate weather patterns?

Answer: Students should address the following: Most changes in weather occur when air masses with different physical properties meet. The boundary between two air masses that differ in temperature and density is called a front. The air behind a warm front rises over a cold air mass and then gradually cools and condenses to form clouds that may descend and produce rain. A cold front is the boundary along which a cold air mass displaces a warm air mass. The cold air, being denser than the warm, tends to wedge beneath the warm air, pushing the warm air upward, where it cools and expands to form clouds and potentially produce thunderstorms. Once a cold front passes through, however, the sky usually clears and the temperature and humidity drop. Opposing air masses may also differ in atmospheric pressure. An air mass with elevated atmospheric pressure, or a high-pressure system, contains air that descends. High-pressure air masses typically bring fair weather. In contrast, in a low-pressure system, air tends to move towards the low atmospheric pressure at the center of the system and spiral upward. This causes the air to expand and cool, and clouds and precipitation often follow.

3) How does the spatial relationship between Earth and the sun determine the amount of solar radiation that strikes Earth's surface? What is the role of solar energy in creating seasons?

Answer: The spatial relationship between Earth and the sun determines the amount of solar radiation that strikes each point of Earth's surface. Sunlight is most intense when it shines directly overhead and meets the planet's surface at a perpendicular angle. At this angle, sunlight passes through a minimum of energy-absorbing atmosphere and focuses on a minimum of surface area. Given Earth's curvature, this means that solar radiation intensity is highest near the equator and weakest near the poles. Because Earth is tilted on its axis (an imaginary line connecting the poles, running perpendicular to the equator) by about 23.5°, the northern and southern hemispheres each face the sun for one-half of the year. The seasons result from these periodic variations in sun exposure. Regions near the equator are largely unaffected by this tilt, experiencing about 12 hours each of sunlight and darkness every day. Near the poles, however, the effect is strong, and seasonality is pronounced.

4) Why is indoor pollution still such a large problem? How does our understanding of it differ from our understanding of outdoor pollution?

Answer: Recognizing indoor air pollution as a problem is still quite novel. The 1970 U.S. Clean Air Act did not even mention indoor air; rather, indoor spaces were assumed to be safe havens from outdoor pollution. Even smoke from indoor fires was long viewed merely as a nuisance, in the absence of data showing it to cause health problems. Indoor air pollution has a long history; humans have been heating and cooking in shelters for hundreds of thousands of years, and to this day, many archaeological sites bear soot stains as evidence of the smoky emissions of these fires. We know far less about indoor air pollution than we do about outdoor air pollution. There is no scheme in place to monitor indoor pollutants comprehensively, as there is for some outdoor substances such as the EPA's six criteria pollutants. What we know about indoor pollution so far has come mostly from individual independent studies, and not comprehensive and coordinated federal or international efforts.

5) What remedies can be found for indoor pollution? Compare solutions for developed and developing countries.

Answer: Students should discuss some of the following: Use of low-toxicity material and adequate ventilation are key to alleviating indoor air pollution in almost any situation. Using materials that are nontoxic and making sure the indoor environment minimizes exposure to trapped air are crucial. In the developed world, limiting use of plastics and treated wood where possible, and limiting exposure to certain products by keeping pesticides, cleaning fluids, and other known toxicants in a garage or outdoor shed rather than in the house are important. Other solutions include getting homes and offices tested for radon and keeping indoor spaces as well ventilated as possible so that concentrations of chronic contaminants can be minimized. Remedies for fuelwood pollution in the developing world include drying wood before burning (which reduces the amount of smoke produced), shifting to less-polluting fuels (such as from biomass fuels to fossil fuels like natural gas), and replacing inefficient fires with cleaner stoves that burn fuel more efficiently. Increasing ventilation by installing hoods, chimneys, or cooking windows can also be accomplished inexpensively and can alleviate the majority of indoor smoke pollution.

# *Chapter 12* Global Climate Change

## Matching Questions

*Match the following.*

1) Predominant greenhouse gas produced by fossil fuels
2) Produced by microbes decomposing matter in landfills
3) Non-C-based renewable resource
4) Most abundant greenhouse gas
5) Compound that contributes to atmospheric cooling

A) methane

B) nitrous oxide

C) solar energy

D) biodiesel

E) ozone

F) argon

G) carbon dioxide

H) sulfate aerosol

I) coal

J) water vapor

1) G 2) A 3) C 4) J 5) H

## Short Answer Questions

1) Define the term *greenhouse gas.* List four greenhouse gases that are anthropogenically produced and contributing to climate change.

   Answer: Greenhouse gases effectively absorb infrared radiation released by Earth's surface and later warm that surface by emitting energy. Examples include carbon dioxide, nitrous oxide, methane, ozone, etc.

2) List the three most important factors determining climate. Briefly describe the role of each.

   Answer: Sun creates light and warmth; atmosphere insulates the planet; and oceans store and transport heat and moisture.

3) What is the role of the precautionary principle in drafting climate treaties?

   Answer: When used for environmental legislation, the precautionary principle says that threats of serious or irreversible damage and lack of full scientific certainty shall not be used as a reason for postponing cost-effective measures to prevent environmental degradation.

4) List three methods currently used by scientists to study climate change.

Answer: Modeling, ice cores, and direct measurement of greenhouse gases are ways of studying climate change.

5) Discuss the role of the Energy Star Program in energy conservation.

Answer: The Energy Star Program promoting energy conservation was started by the U.S. Environmental Protection Agency. The program rates appliances for energy efficiency, allowing consumers to buy more energy-efficient appliances.

## Fill-in-the-Blank Questions

1) __________ is the term used to describe short-term atmospheric conditions.

Answer: Weather

2) The most potent naturally occurring greenhouse gas per molecule gas is __________.

Answer: nitrous oxide

3) The greenhouse gas produced by herds of cattle is __________.

Answer: methane

4) An increase in Earth's average surface temperature is referred to as __________.

Answer: global warming

5) The largest source of anthropogenic greenhouse gases in the United States is __________, followed by __________.

Answer: electricity generation; transportation

6) Gas bubbles trapped in __________ can be used to evaluate past concentrations of greenhouse gases.

Answer: ice

## Multiple-Choice Questions

1) Earth's atmosphere is best described as a

A) solid physical barrier such as the glass in a greenhouse

B) liquid barrier such as the ocean currents

C) thin layer of gases such as nitrogen and oxygen

D) continuous layer of clouds

E) none of the above

Answer: C

2) The increase in atmospheric greenhouse gases over the last several centuries is likely due to

A) fossil fuel use
B) natural processes
C) land-use change
D) large herds of cattle
E) all of the above

Answer: E

3) Earth's climate

A) has been stable over the history of the planet
B) is subject to change as a result of natural processes
C) is subject to change through human processes
D) has only been altered once through the evolution of green photosynthesizing plants
E) B and C

Answer: E

4) The atmosphere around Earth is warmed because

A) warm air cannot escape as in a greenhouse
B) molecules in the atmosphere are warmed by radiation and retain heat
C) fossil fuels release heat
D) plants absorb $CO_2$
E) all of the above

Answer: B

5) Carbon dioxide ($CO_2$) is

A) the most potent (per molecule gas) of the greenhouse gases
B) less potent (per molecule gas) than nitrous oxide
C) more potent (per molecule gas) than methane
D) not a greenhouse gas
E) B and C

Answer: B

6) Water vapor

A) is the most abundant of the greenhouse gases
B) is capable of absorbing radiant energy
C) promotes cooling when present in the atmosphere
D) is not found in the atmosphere
E) A and B

Answer: E

7) Milankovitch cycles

A) are cycles of climate change

B) are changes in Earth's rotation and orbit around the sun

C) are the Russian description of planetary seasonal cycles

D) describe the movement of ocean currents

E) describe the evolution of planets

Answer: B

8) North Atlantic Deep Water (NADW) refers to

A) the deep end of the ocean

B) water impacted by the sea-to-air transfer of heat

C) a treaty to decrease pollution transfers to ocean water

D) circulation patterns that result from the heating of cold ocean water in the Pacific

E) B and D

Answer: B

9) The exceptionally strong warming of the eastern Pacific is referred to as

A) global warming

B) La Niña

C) El Niño

D) Eastern Pacific Shallow Water

E) A and C

Answer: C

10) Coupled general circulation models

A) are useful for evaluating pollution levels above cities

B) are useful for evaluating gases trapped in ice cores

C) are designed to simulate climate change

D) involve atmospheric circulation patterns only

E) C and D

Answer: C

11) The Intergovernmental Panel on Climate Change

A) constructed the Kyoto Protocol

B) performed the research included in the climate change findings

C) is an international panel of atmospheric scientists, experts, and government officials

D) worked to determine impacts of pollution on the U.S. economy

E) A and C

Answer: C

12) The impacts of global climate change on forests will likely include

A) forests becoming more productive

B) increases in flammability

C) alterations in species diversity

D) loss of some forest types

E) all of the above

Answer: E

13) Tropospheric cooling is caused by

A) water vapor

B) sulfate aerosols

C) nitrous oxides

D) ozone

E) Cooling does not occur, only warming.

Answer: B

14) Keeling's Mauna Loa data on $CO_2$ demonstrated

A) seasonal changes in $CO_2$ levels

B) an increase in $CO_2$ since recording began

C) an increase in $CO_2$ as distance to a city decreased

D) that $CO_2$ levels have been stable over the last 40 years

E) A and B

Answer: E

15) Which of the following is not a greenhouse gas?

A) $CO_2$

B) nitrous oxides

C) water vapor

D) $NH_4$

E) ozone

Answer: D

16) The consequences of global warming on agriculture include

A) higher productivity

B) lower productivity

C) greater water and nutrient stress

D) all of the above

E) none of the above

Answer: D

17) Carbon reservoirs

A) have formed for millions of years on Earth

B) are readily lost from Earth's surface in the absence of humans

C) have never been stable, meaning that $CO_2$ exists in the atmosphere

D) cannot be lost to the atmosphere by human processes once stabilized on Earth's surface

E) will be lost before the end of the decade

Answer: A

18) The Kyoto Protocol

A) was intended to reduce emissions of six greenhouse gases to levels lower than those of 1990

B) required concessions from all countries involved equally

C) required increases in nuclear power generation

D) would have resulted in overall decreases in greenhouse emissions

E) all of the above

Answer: A

19) In legislation, the precautionary principle requires that

A) caution be used in handling hazardous wastes

B) in threats of irreversible damage, lack of full scientific certainty shall not be used to postpone measures to prevent environmental degradation

C) alterations to legislation be done in a way that maximizes environmental protection at the urging of scientists without recourse from the voting public

D) all alternative sources of energy be evaluated by the scientific community before marketing

E) none of the above

Answer: B

20) The use of public transportation is

A) widely available in all metropolitan areas

B) increasing rapidly in the face of concerns over climate change

C) subsidized by the U.S. government

D) the best option for decreasing the use of fossil fuels for transportation

E) all of the above

Answer: D

21) Fossil fuel combustion changes the composition of the atmosphere because it
   A) releases heat into the environment
   B) results in greater economic spending in developed countries
   C) releases carbon from long-term stable terrestrial sinks
   D) releases carbon from short-term biosphere sinks
   E) A and C

   Answer: C

22) Which of the following kinds of power can be used to fuel vehicles?
   A) electricity
   B) compressed natural gas
   C) biodiesel
   D) hydrogen fuel cells
   E) all of the above

   Answer: E

## True / False Questions

1) The greenhouse effect is a new term for describing the impact of humans on Earth's climate.

   Answer: FALSE

2) Coal use in the United States is too low to contribute to climate change.

   Answer: FALSE

3) Changes to global climate caused by anthropogenic disturbance have already occurred on Earth.

   Answer: TRUE

4) Maintaining large herds of cattle can contribute to climate change.

   Answer: TRUE

5) Ozone is a greenhouse gas.

   Answer: TRUE

6) All greenhouse gases have the same global warming potential.

   Answer: FALSE

## Essay Questions

1) Define greenhouse effect, global warming, and global climate change. How are these terms related and why might they be misused?

   Answer: See definitions in text. They are sometimes but not always interchangeable, which is why they are misused. Poor understanding of environmental science leads to poor use of words in popular formats.

2) Models such as the coupled general circulation models are used to understand climate change. What is the value of this type of model? Why don't researchers simply collect more data?

Answer: The value of using models is, among other things, predictive capabilities and forecasting different scenarios. Feedback mechanisms can be elucidated. Researchers cannot collect the vast amount of data necessary and can't collect certain data until environmental damage has already occurred.

3) In general, how certain are scientists that humans are causing global climate change? Describe the language used by scientists and some of the particular climate trends they have identified as changing. If the scientific community is convinced of the evidence, why is there still debate?

Answer: Scientists can only express conclusions as probabilities, so the 2001 IPCC report is written almost entirely in uncertainties. Scientists are in agreement that humans are contributing to global climate change, but the public interprets probabilities as uncertainty. The debate continues over how to address climate change in political and economic arenas. Particular climate trends include changes in surface temperature, snow and ice cover, rising sea level and warmer oceans, and alterations to precipitation patterns and intensity.

4) Using the environmental properties discussed in this chapter (atmosphere, ocean currents, pollutants), give specific examples of why protecting the environment often requires international legislation.

Answer: Global circulation patterns in atmosphere and ocean mean that chemicals released into air or water are the problem of all nations, not just those releasing the chemicals.

5) In the United States, transportation accounts for a large amount of fossil fuel use. What would it take to reduce the amount of fossil fuels we burn in our automobiles? Include examples of how public opinion interferes with accomplishing these goals.

Answer: A more efficient automobile, increased fuel efficiency, alternative fuels, hydrogen fuel cells, and public transportation are five factors that would help reduce the amount of fossil fuels burned in automobiles. Problems result from public resistance to limiting choices regarding personal transportation choices.

6) Some say that global warming is a good thing. Using evidence from the chapter, support or refute this statement.

Answer: The chapter provides detailed explanations of why the damage from global warming will ultimately outweigh the benefits. Details of alterations to agriculture, forests, and freshwater systems suggest that warming will ultimately cause more damage including direct impacts on human health.

# Chapter 13 The Oceans: Natural Systems, Human Use, and Marine Conservation

## Matching Questions

*Match the following.*

1) A region below the zone of surface water
2) Waters of similar density that are heated by sunlight each day
3) Flow of cold deep water toward the surface
4) Marine habitats that occur between the ocean's surface and floor
5) Symbiotic bacteria that make food for corals

A) euphotic
B) detritivores
C) bathymetry
D) upwelling
E) zooplankton
F) benthic
G) zooxanthellae
H) pycnocline
I) thermocline
J) pelagic

1) H 2) A 3) D 4) J 5) G

## Short Answer Questions

1) What was the impetus for establishing the Florida Keys National Marine Sanctuary?

Answer: The Sanctuary was established because overfishing, trash and sewage dumping, and boat groundings and careless anchoring were damaging the region's ecosystems, while its waters received inputs of pesticides, oil, and heavy metals from roads, residential areas, and farms on the islands.

2) What is a marine protected area?

Answer: It is a term to describe any portion of the ocean that is protected from some human activities but may be open to others.

3) What is meant by the term "world ocean"?

Answer: The oceans of the Pacific, Atlantic, Indian, Artic, and Antarctic oceans are all connected, comprising a single vast body of water.

4) What conditions produce the diversity found in the rocky intertidal zone?

Answer: The large variation in temperature, salinity, and water level gives rise to the wide variety of organisms that live in these areas.

5) What does it mean that we are "fishing down the food chain"?

Answer: It means that the size of fish declines with higher rates of fishing and we are shifting from large, desirable species to smaller, less desirable ones.

6) How have declines in fisheries been masked in recent years?

Answer: Fishermen have been traveling farther and fishing longer to obtain the same number of fish. Technological advances have also improved fishing efficiency.

## Fill-in-the-Blank Questions

1) The study of the physics, chemistry, and geology of the oceans is called __________.

Answer: oceanography

2) Intertidal or __________ ecosystems lie along shorelines between the farthest reach of high tide and the lowest reach of the lowest tides.

Answer: littoral

3) __________ are the periodic rising and falling of the ocean's height at a given location due to the gravitational pull of the moon.

Answer: Tides

4) When excessive nutrient concentrations give rise to population explosions of toxic algae, a harmful __________ may occur.

Answer: algal bloom or red tide

5) The term __________ refers to the capture of animals not meant to be caught.

Answer: by-catch

6) A concept called __________ has been used to manage fish by allowing maximal harvests of particular populations while keeping fish available for the future

Answer: maximum sustainable yield

## Multiple-Choice Questions

1) Which of the following is not true for salinity in the ocean?

A) varies from place to place due to evaporation and runoff
B) ranges from 3.3 to 3.7%
C) gives the ocean its salty flavor
D) There is higher than average salinity at the equator.
E) There is higher than average salinity in areas that are adjacent to deserts.

Answer: D

2) The dissolved oxygen in saltwater is produced by

A) plankton
B) diffusion from the atmosphere
C) production by photosynthetic bacteria
D) all of the above
E) none of the above

Answer: D

3) Layers develop in the ocean due to

A) differences in organisms that live there
B) sunlight penetration providing heat
C) increases in density of water as it becomes saltier
D) B and C
E) all of the above

Answer: D

4) About 80% of the ocean's water exists in the

A) surface zone
B) pycnocline
C) deep zone
D) thermocline
E) euphotic zone

Answer: C

5) Horizontal movement of water results in

A) vertical stratification
B) high heat capacity
C) currents
D) salinity
E) spatial segregation among layers

Answer: C

6) Downwelling is important because it

A) brings nutrients to the surface
B) transports fish
C) keeps pollutants low
D) provides an influx of oxygen for deep–water life
E) provides a current for conductive heat

Answer: D

7) The areas that underlie the shallow waters bordering the continents are the

A) pycnoclinic shelves
B) topographic shelves
C) continental shelves
D) bathymetric shelves
E) surface shelves

Answer: C

8) The base of the marine food chain in the pelagic zone is

A) zooplankton
B) phytoplankton
C) fish
D) detritus
E) tubeworms

Answer: B

9) Coral reefs are

A) biological treasure troves
B) composed of calcium chloride skeletons of corals
C) home to corals, invertebrate animals that belong to the phylum Cnidaria
D) home to symbiotic bacteria that produce food for living corals
E) all of the above

Answer: E

10) Mangroves are

A) large animals that float in Florida
B) trees with roots that form snorkels to attain oxygen
C) forests in temperate zone estuaries
D) forests capable of withstanding human disturbance
E) none of the above

Answer: B

11) The areas where rivers flow into oceans are called

A) mangrove forests
B) salt marshes
C) estuaries
D) the Everglades
E) littoral zones

Answer: C

12) The U.S. Oil Protection Act of 1990

A) required oil to be transported by air, not boat

B) restricted oil movement to land rather than sea

C) required that by 2015 all oil tankers in U.S. water be double hulled

D) required gas taxes that will pay for the Exxon Valdez spill

E) is not effective at altering national oil incidents

Answer: C

13) What does the term *groundfish* refer to?

A) fish that form the base of the deep-water habitats

B) various species that live in benthic habitats such haddock and flounder

C) various species that live in littoral habitats such as tuna and whitefish

D) various species that are found in estuaries

E) various species that are found exclusively in mangroves

Answer: B

14) Which of the following is not true of deep-water ecosystems?

A) Animals are adapted to deal with extreme water pressure.

B) Animals are adapted to deal with the dark.

C) They can house organisms that thrive on chemicals in the heated water.

D) They include tubeworms and shrimp.

E) none of the above

Answer: E

15) Sea otters act as keystone species in the

A) salt marshes

B) mangrove forests

C) kelp forests

D) deep ocean systems

E) coral reefs

Answer: C

16) The energy that corals use is derived from

A) consumption of glucose from passing animals

B) symbiotic bacteria that decompose tissues of dead animals

C) symbiotic bacteria that fix nitrogen

D) symbiotic bacteria that are capable of photosynthesis

E) photosynthesis that occurs in their chloroplasts

Answer: D

17) Which of the following is true of eutrophication in marine systems?

A) It can lead to algal blooms that kill fish.

B) It can aid corals by killing parasites.

C) It is rare and only occurs in bad weather.

D) It provides needed limiting nutrients.

E) It does not occur.

Answer: A

18) Energy production in the open ocean currently includes

A) turbines that have been developed that use tides to generate energy

B) collectors that have been developed to use sunlight that warms the ocean to produce energy

C) boats that collect thermal energy

D) buoys that generate a current based on sunlight

E) all of the above

Answer: A

19) Currently, the greatest dilemma facing marine systems is

A) pollution

B) oil

C) plastic soda can rings

D) overharvesting

E) abandoned fishing nets

Answer: D

20) Hypoxia and eutrophication in the Chesapeake Bay may in part be attributed to

A) loss of kelp to take up nutrients

B) loss of otters to maintain kelp

C) harvesting of oysters that previously would have filtered nutrients

D) harvesting of sea turtles that maintain urchin populations

E) overfishing salmon that maintain the entire system

Answer: C

21) Data suggest that 90% of which of the following were lost in the first decade of industrialized fishing?

A) sea otters

B) large-bodied fish and sharks

C) whales

D) the bait fish

E) the groundfish

Answer: B

22) Nearly all marine protected areas
   A) prohibit fishing
   B) are harvested by multiple means
   C) are protected from pollution by physical barriers
   D) are protected from changes in temperature
   E) none of the above

Answer: B

## True / False Questions

1) Approximately 40% of the planet's surface is covered by ocean.

Answer: FALSE

2) Into the mid-20th century it was common for coastal cities in the United States to dump trash into the ocean.

Answer: TRUE

3) The majority of the oil polluting our oceans is from large spills

Answer: FALSE

4) As much as 89% of the trash in the North Pacific is plastic.

Answer: TRUE

5) Marine reserves have been supported by both scientists and fishermen as ways to make fisheries more sustainable.

Answer: FALSE

6) Only one-quarter of the world's marine fish populations can yield more than they are already yielding without being driven into decline.

Answer: TRUE

## Essay Questions

1) Describe the disturbances that are currently threatening coral reefs. Include the damage to deep coral. Why are these systems unique, and what is threatening them?

Answer: Coral populations and coral reefs are experiencing worldwide declines. Many reefs have undergone "coral bleaching." Coral bleaching may result from increased sea surface temperatures associated with global climate change, or from the influx of artificial pollutants into area waters, although scientists have not ruled out natural causes. Coral reefs also sustain damage when divers stun fish with cyanide in order to capture them and sell them for food or for the pet trade, a common practice in waters of Indonesia and the Philippines. A few coral species thrive in cold, deep, unlit waters outside of the tropics, and build large reefs on the ocean floor at depths of 200–500 m. These little-known reefs, which occur in cold-water areas such as off the coasts of Norway, Spain, and the British Isles, are only now beginning to be studied by scientists, but already many have been badly damaged by trawling.

2) Discuss the importance of the services that ocean ecosystems provide for humans. Also discuss goods other than fish that the oceans produce for humans.

Answer: Students should discuss some of the following: There are two main services that are provided by oceans. The first is transportation providing affordable means of moving people and products over vast distances. The historical impacts of shipping on human culture and commerce are profound, accelerating the global reach of certain cultures and the interaction of long-isolated peoples. Shipping has had substantial impacts on the environment as well. The thousands of ships plying the world's oceans today carry everything from cod to cargo containers to crude oil. The second is extraction of goods and energy. Humans have also used the oceans as sources of commercially valuable energy. The oceans also hold potential for providing us with renewable energy sources. In recent decades engineers have developed turbines that can generate electricity by utilizing the ebb and flow of the tides. Another possibility is known as ocean thermal energy conversion. In addition to energy resources, people also extract minerals from the ocean floor. By using large vacuum cleaner-like hydraulic dredges, miners collect sediments and mineral deposits such as sand and gravel from deep beneath the sea. Also extracted are sulfur from salt deposits in the Gulf of Mexico and phosphorite from many offshore areas including several near the California coast. Other valuable minerals found on or beneath the sea floor include calcium carbonate (used in making cement), silica (used as fire-resistant insulation and in manufacturing glass), and rich deposits of copper, zinc, silver, and gold ore. Many minerals are found concentrated in manganese nodules, small ball-shaped accretions that litter parts of the ocean floor.

3) Discuss the impacts that humans are having on the ocean ecosystems.

Answer: Students should discuss some of the following: Oceans have long been made a sink for human wastes. Even into the mid-20th century, it was common for coastal cities in the United States to dump trash and pump untreated sewage onto mudflats and into embayments. Coastal dumping practices have left a toxic legacy around the United States, but marine pollution continues even today. Oil, plastic, industrial chemicals, sewage sludge, excess nutrients, abandoned fishing gear, all eventually make their way into the oceans. Pollutants such as additions of crude oil to the oceans are also a problem. The majority of oil pollution in the oceans comes not from large spills but from cumulative small sources including leakage from small boats and runoff from human activities on land. In addition, the amount of petroleum spilled into the oceans each year is equaled by the amount that seeps into the water from naturally occurring seafloor deposits. Pollution from petroleum products is extremely detrimental to the marine environment and the human economies that draw sustenance from that environment. Petroleum can physically coat and kill intertidal and free-swimming marine organisms, and ingested chemical components in petroleum can poison marine life. Plastic bags and bottles, fishing nets, gloves, fishing line, buckets, floats, abandoned cargo, and nearly everything else that humans transport on the sea or dispose into it can present problems for marine organisms and for people who depend upon the sea. Because most plastic is not biodegradable, it can drift for decades before washing up on beaches. Some marine animals, including seabirds, fish, and endangered sea turtles, can mistake floating plastic debris for food (such as mistaking clear plastic for jellyfish), and many die as a result. Artificial pollution from fertilizer runoff or other nutrient inputs can also have dire effects on marine ecosystems, as we saw with the Gulf of Mexico's dead zone. The release of excess nutrients into surface waters can spur unusually high growth rates and population densities of phytoplankton, causing eutrophication, in either freshwater or saltwater ecosystems.

4) Discuss how fishing practices can damage ecosystems. Include problems associated with driftnets, longline fishing, and bottom-trawling.

Answer: The removal of species at high trophic levels from marine environments, particularly those that act as keystone species, can have serious ramifications for marine ecosystems. Fishing practices can also harm ecosystems in other ways. Many practices catch more than just the species they target. By-catch accounts for the deaths of many thousands of fish, sharks, marine mammals, and birds each year. Boats that drag driftnets through the water capture substantial numbers of large animals such as dolphins, seals, and sea turtles, as well as countless nontarget fish. Most of these end up dying from drowning or from air exposure on deck. Similar by-catch problems exist with longline fishing. Besides catching nontarget turtles and sharks, longline fishing kills many albatrosses. Other fishing practices can directly damage entire ecosystems. Bottom-trawling crushes many organisms in its path, and leaves long swaths of sea bottom damaged, especially those areas with structural complexity, such as reefs, that animals use for shelter.

5) What concept has traditional fisheries management been based on? What approach do scientists think would improve current management techniques?

Answer: For decades, fisheries management has been based on scientific assessments and has sought to ensure sustainable harvests. Historically, fisheries managers have studied fish population biology and used that knowledge to regulate the timing of harvests, the techniques used to catch fish, and the scale of the harvest. The goal was to allow for maximal harvests of particular populations while keeping fish available for the future, a concept called maximum sustainable yield. If data indicated that current yields looked unsustainable, managers might limit the number or total mass of that fish species that could be harvested, or might restrict the type of gear fishermen can use. Numerous marine scientists and some managers now suggest a shift away from management of individual fish species and toward viewing marine resources as elements of larger ecological systems. This means considering the effects of fishing practices on habitat quality, on interspecific interactions, and on other ecological factors that may have indirect or long-term effects on populations.

# *Chapter 14* Fresh Water Resources

## Matching Questions

*Match the following.*

1) Porous, spongelike layers of rock, sand, or gravel that are capable of holding water
2) The world's largest aquifer is the
3) Any obstruction placed in a river or stream to block flow
4) Water with high concentrations of calcium and magnesium ions
5) A measure of the density of suspended particles in a water supply

A) soft water
B) hard water
C) dam
D) water table
E) Okabogee aquifer
F) aquifers
G) turbidity
H) aqueduct
I) Ogallala aquifer
J) particle density

1) F 2) I 3) C 4) B 5) G

## Short Answer Questions

1) Briefly, how has the quantity of water that reaches the Sea of Cortez from the Colorado River changed in the last hundred years?

Answer: In the past, the river's copious supply of water surged into the Sea of Cortez, nourishing one of the continent's greatest estuaries. Today, the withdrawals have turned the mighty river into a small stream that barely reaches the sea.

2) What is the spatial relationship between the distribution of water and people?

Answer: People are not distributed across the globe in accordance with water availability, and areas that are dense with people are often water–poor, leading to inequalities in per capita water resources among and within nations.

3) Ignoring human alterations to the landscape, what causes floods and what is their value ecologically?

Answer: Flooding is a normal natural process during times of high water due to snowmelt or heavy rain, and floodwaters carry nutritive sediments and spread them over large areas of the floodplain.

4) What are the goals of dam removal?

Answer: Restore riparian ecosystems, reestablish economically valuable fisheries, and reintroduce river recreation such as flyfishing and rafting.

5) Describe two ways that salt can be removed from seawater.

Answer: The first is by mimicking the hydrologic cycle, by containing ocean water, hastening evaporation with heat and then condensing the vapor, in essence distilling for fresh water. Another method involves forcing water through membranes to filter out salts, the most common process of which is reverse osmosis.

6) Why is too much plant growth because of eutrophication in a freshwater system a problem?

Answer: Algae that grow too rapidly can cover the water's surface, harming the deeper-water plants that depend on sunlight for survival.

## Fill-in-the-Blank Questions

1) When water is used for agricultural irrigation and is not returned to the aquifer or surface water body that it was drawn on, this is __________ use.

Answer: consumptive

2) Most aquifers recharge very slowly or not at all, making it easy to withdraw water, a process called __________, more rapidly than it can be replenished.

Answer: water mining

3) Overpumping of groundwater in coastal areas can cause __________ into aquifers, making water undrinkable.

Answer: saltwater intrusion

4) The best-known technological approach to increasing water supply by generating freshwater is __________, the removal of salt from seawater.

Answer: desalinization

5) The process of __________, or overnourishment, of the surface water and its plants by nutrient pollution occurs in freshwater systems.

Answer: eutrophication

6) The __________, or water cycle, interacts with all other biogeochemical cycles and the __________ is intimately linked with the biosphere, lithosphere, and atmosphere.

Answer: hydrologic, hydrosphere

## Multiple-Choice Questions

1) What percentage of total water is freshwater?

A) 15% B) 10% C) 5% D) 2.5% E) 1%

Answer: D

2) A rainshadow is a dry area on the

A) leeward side of a mountain

B) windward side of a mountain

C) crest of a mountain

D) summit of a mountain

E) footslope of a mountain

Answer: A

3) Water that reaches Earth's surface that does not evaporate can

A) be taken up by animals

B) run off

C) infiltrate the surface

D) B and C

E) all of the above

Answer: E

4) One-fifth of Earth's freshwater supply is in

A) ponds

B) the ocean

C) groundwater

D) estuaries

E) the tundra

Answer: C

5) An artesian aquifer exists

A) when there are several aquifers together

B) where granite overlain by sand is adjoined

C) when a water-bearing porous layer of rock sand or gravel is trapped between upper and lower layers of less permeable substances

D) when a well is dug through layers of sand

E) when a water-bearing porous layer of rock, sand, or gravel houses water

Answer: C

6) The greatest use of freshwater is
   A) drinking
   B) washing
   C) irrigation
   D) industry
   E) electrical production

   Answer: C

7) Which of the following best describe floodplains?
   A) region of land over which a river has historically wandered and periodically flooded
   B) flooded only when humans alter landscapes
   C) flooded when farming operations change the course of rivers
   D) region of land adjacent to a river
   E) region of land adjacent to a river that currently flooded due to complex human disturbance patterns

   Answer: A

8) We build dams to
   A) prevent floods
   B) generate electricity
   C) provide drinking water
   D) ease irrigation
   E) all of the above

   Answer: E

9) Wide-scale dam removal in this country
   A) began with the Edwards Dam on the Kennebec River
   B) will increase now that the Federal Energy Regulatory Commission is reviewing 500 dam licenses in the next decade
   C) is a consequence of the age of most dams
   D) will never happen due to interest in renewable energy sources
   E) all of the above

   Answer: E

10) Data indicate that present freshwater consumption in much of the world is
   A) sustainable
   B) unsustainable
   C) irrelevant, as water is not currently limiting
   D) only a problem in areas not on the coast
   E) increasing groundwater storage and decreasing surface water storage

   Answer: B

11) Why was irrigation of Soviet cotton farming operations a problem?
   A) There was governmental opposition that limited water access, killing crops.
   B) Irrigation water came from rivers feeding into the fourth-largest lake on Earth and resulted in major contamination of that source.
   C) It drained the Aral Sea and increased salt content of soils.
   D) It angered local resort communities that did not want farming in the region.
   E) It was, for the most part, not a problem.

Answer: C

12) Sinkholes result from
   A) flood damage
   B) building on floodplains
   C) overconsumption of water from aquifers
   D) poorly drilled wells
   E) substrates that become weak following rain

Answer: C

13) Which of the following will not contribute to water conservation?
   A) replacing faucets with low-flow faucets
   B) replacing hand washing with dishwashers
   C) replacing washing machines with washing by hand
   D) watering lawns at night rather than during the day
   E) All of the above will contribute to water conservation.

Answer: C

14) Gray water can
   A) be used with little or no treatment for irrigation
   B) be used with little or no treatment for industry
   C) be used for washing cars with little or no treatment
   D) only be used with high-cost water treatment
   E) all of the above

Answer: E

15) Which of the following is not one of the major pollutants of groundwater?
   A) natural sources of pollutants
   B) untreated sewage
   C) agricultural runoff
   D) petroleum
   E) All of the above are major pollutants of groundwater.

Answer: E

16) Dissolved oxygen is measured in water to determine

A) presence of viruses
B) presence of bacteria
C) aquatic ecosystem health
D) aquatic ecosystem density
E) degree of turbidity

Answer: C

17) The nutrient that most limits growth in freshwater systems is

A) carbon
B) nitrogen
C) phosphorus
D) ozone
E) calcium

Answer: C

18) The "blue-baby" syndrome that suffocates infants is a consequence of which substance in water?

A) E. coli
B) phosphates
C) nitrates
D) chlorine
E) carbon

Answer: C

19) Water pollution has

A) decreased in the last 30 years in the United States.
B) increased in the last 30 years in the United States.
C) remained constant in the last 30 years
D) not been addressed by legislation the way air pollution has
E) only been addressed in the last 10 years so changes will be seen over the next decade

Answer: A

20) Which of the following has not contributed to aquifer contamination?

A) natural sources, including, for example, arsenic and fluoride, dissolve into aquifers
B) pathogens entering through wells
C) hazardous waste disposal by pumping waste underground
D) leaching of excess fertilizers to aquifers from agricultural application
E) All of the above have contributed to aquifer contamination.

Answer: E

21) Which of the following are physical parameters are measured to assess water quality?
   A) turbidity
   B) taste
   C) odor
   D) temperature
   E) all of the above

   Answer: E

22) Which of the following best describes the ecological consequences of falling water tables?
   A) loss of bird species
   B) loss of mammals
   C) loss of permanent wetlands
   D) loss of lakes
   E) loss of agricultural irrigation water

   Answer: C

## True / False Questions

1) Only 5% of Earth's human population relies directly on groundwater for its needs.

   Answer: FALSE

2) The number of people facing water scarcity is expected to grow to at least 2.4 billion by 2025.

   Answer: TRUE

3) Automatic dishwashers use more water than washing dishes by hand.

   Answer: FALSE

4) The World Commission on Water in 1999 concluded that over half of the world's major rivers are depleted and polluted.

   Answer: TRUE

5) The Great Lakes hold almost 20% of the world's surface freshwater.

   Answer: TRUE

6) One in 10 people in the developing world is infected by intestinal worms.

   Answer: TRUE

## Essay Questions

1) What is meant by the statement, "We are truly 'replumbing the planet'"?

Answer: Students should discuss some of the following: In areas near surface water, people have found it far easier to make use of rivers, streams, lakes, and ponds by moving water from these sources to farm fields and houses. People have been moving water from where it is to where it isn't for thousands of years; archaeological evidence shows that many ancient civilizations depended on complex irrigation systems transporting water from surface bodies. The powerful empires of ancient Egypt were built on the Nile River and could not have flourished without intricate networks of canals dug to spread the river's water among the vast agricultural fields that grew food for the society's peasants and rulers alike. The Colorado River's water is diverted and utilized every bit as much today. Early on in its course, some water is piped through a mountain tunnel across the Continental Divide and down the Rockies' eastern slope to supply the city of Denver. More is removed for Las Vegas and other cities, and for farmland, as it proceeds downriver. When it reaches Parker Dam on the California–Arizona line, large amounts are diverted into the Colorado River Aqueduct, which brings water to millions in the Los Angeles and San Diego areas in a huge open–air canal. From Parker Dam, Arizona also draws water, moving it in its own large canals of the Central Arizona Project. Further south at Imperial Dam, the largest amount of water is diverted into the Coachella and All–American Canals, destined for agriculture mostly in the Imperial Valley. More large–scale diversion projects are in store. One of the biggest plans consists of an aqueduct to bring water from the Yangtze River in southern China to the Yellow River in northern China, where the arid climate and population pressure have caused the river to dry up in many places. With such massive projects that transfer water between major watersheds, we are truly "replumbing the planet."

2) Using the Three Gorges Dam on China's Yangtze River as an example, what are the benefits and costs associated with building dams?

Answer: Students should discuss some of the following: The reservoir will hold over 10 trillion gallons of water. It will generate hydroelectric power, enable boats and barges to travel farther upstream, and provide flood control. The power generation may be enough to replace dozens of large coal or nuclear plants. One of the costs of the Three Gorges Dam, aside from its $25 billion construction price tag, is that its reservoir will flood 22 cities and the homes of 1.13 million people, requiring the largest–ever resettlement project. The reservoir behind the dam will also inundate archaeological sites 10,000 years old, and will submerge productive farmlands and wildlife habitat. In addition, critics hold, the reservoir will slow the flow of the river so much that suspended sediment will settle and begin to fill the reservoir as soon as it is completed. Other scientists worry about water quality, saying that the Yangtze's many pollutants will be trapped in the reservoir, making the water even more undrinkable than it is already. Indeed, high levels of bacteria were found in the water as it began building up behind the dam, but the government plans to sink $5 billion into building hundreds of sewage treatment and waste disposal facilities.

3) How can agricultural irrigation practices be altered to decrease loss of freshwater?

Answer: Students should discuss some of the following: Farmers can use technology to improve efficiency in a number of ways, including lining irrigation canals to prevent leaks and leveling fields to minimize runoff. Furthermore, some methods of applying irrigation water are more efficient than others. We can increase irrigation efficiency by using low-pressure spray irrigation that sprays water downward toward plants and by using drip irrigation systems that target individual plants and introduce water directly onto the soil. Both methods reduce the amount of water lost to evaporation and surface runoff. In addition, choosing crops to match the land and climate in which they are being farmed can save huge amounts of water. Presently, crops that require a great deal of water, such as cotton, rice, and alfalfa, are often planted in hot and arid areas where irrigation is government subsidized so that the true cost of water is not part of the costs of growing the crop. Eliminating subsidies and growing crops in climates that provide adequate rainfall could greatly reduce water use in many parts of the world. In addition, the genetic modification of crops is resulting in some varieties that require less water.

4) Define water pollution, point source, and non-point source pollution. Which of the two (point source or non-point source) is easier to identify? Which is easier to legislate? Which currently poses the greatest threat to freshwater?

Answer: The term "pollution" describes any matter or energy released into the environment, whether from human activity or from natural sources, that causes undesirable impacts on the health and well-being of humans or other organisms. Water pollution can be emitted from point sources — single locations such as a pipe from a factory — or can consist of non-point source pollution arising from multiple cumulative inputs over larger areas such as farms, city streets, and residential neighborhoods. Point sources are easy to identify but sometimes difficult to regulate, especially if owners or supporters of industrial plants lobby politicians to pressure agencies not to enforce regulations. Non-point source pollution is difficult to pinpoint in terms of source and presents a different type of societal challenge, requiring public education and the willingness of citizens to change certain behaviors. It is non-point source pollution that poses the greatest threat to water quality in the United States, according to the EPA. Many common activities give rise to non-point source water pollution, including applying fertilizers and pesticides to lawns, applying salt to roads in winter, and changing automobile oil.

5) Describe the solutions suggested for freshwater pollution.

Answer: Students should discuss some of the following: Suggestions include legislation to restrict pollutant that enter bodies of water. These have been successful in the past. To prevent further damage, solutions will likely need to be preventive ones, and not simply ones of treatment and cleanup. For instance, a prominent expert on water and soils has said that solving the problem of groundwater pollution will require a complete overhaul of the way we live and dispose of waste, and not just an "end-of-pipe" approach of piecemeal cleanups. Indeed, prevention of pollution in the first place would seem to be the best strategy when one considers the other options for dealing with groundwater contamination: filter groundwater before distributing it, pump water out of the aquifer, treat it, and then inject it back in, repeatedly, and we can restrict usage of pollutants on lands above selected aquifers. A change in attitudes, behavior, or technology may be necessary to clean up our water completely, there are many things ordinary people can do to help minimize freshwater pollution. One thing is to exercise the power of consumer choice in the marketplace, by purchasing phosphorus-free detergents and other "environmentally friendly" products. Another is to get to know your local waterways and become involved in protecting them. Locally based groups, often going by names like "Riverwatch," enlist people to collect data and help state and federal agencies safeguard the health of rivers and other water bodies. Similar programs, such as Australia's Waterwatch and Streamwatch, are popping up in many countries throughout the world, as people stand up and demand clean water.

# Chapter 15 Biodiversity and Conservation Biology

## Matching Questions

*Match the following.*

1) The loss of species from the planet
2) Differences in DNA composition among individuals within a given species
3) Animals like tigers that need large amounts of land
4) The generation of new species
5) The connections that human beings subconsciously seek with the rest of life
6) An area that supports an especially great diversity of species

A) umbrella species
B) genetic diversity
C) speciation
D) hotspot
E) extinction
F) alleles
G) species diversity
H) keystone species
I) biophilia
J) community
K) ecocentric
L) extirpation

1) E 2) B 3) A 4) C 5) I 6) D

## Short Answer Questions

1) What lesson can be learned from the case of the Siberian tiger in Russia?

Answer: Tigers were originally part of the cultural fabric of the indigenous people. When the Russians invaded, they had no cultural traditions and hunted tigers to near extinction. The involvement of conservation groups may alter population dynamics of the tiger. The lesson is that humans must value biodiversity or it will be lost.

2) What is the definition of biodiversity?

Answer: The sum total of all organisms in an area, taking into account the diversity of species, their genes, their populations, and their communities

3) What is inbreeding, and why is it a problem?

Answer: Inbreeding occurs when parents that are too genetically similar mate and produce offspring. The offspring are often weak or defective, and if all individuals in populations are too closely related, the species may become extinct.

4) Provide several reasons why our estimates of species numbers are incomplete.

Answer: One reason is that some areas of Earth remain little explored, such as the ocean depths, hydrothermal vents, and the tree canopies and soils of tropical forests. Another is that many species are tiny and easily overlooked; these inconspicuous organisms include species of bacteria, archaea, nematodes (roundworms), fungi, protists, and soil-dwelling arthropods. In addition, many organisms are so difficult to identify that species thought to be one turn out to be two or more once biologists look more closely.

5) Briefly, what is the cause of the sixth mass extinction event, and why is it a cause for concern?

Answer: The sixth mass extinction event has been caused by human alterations to landscapes. It is a cause for concern because the current global extinction rate is more than 1,000 times greater than it would have been without human destruction of habitat.

6) The major causes of species loss spell "HIPPO." What does each of these letters represent?

Answer: Habitat alteration, Invasive species, Pollution, Population, and Overexploitation

## Fill-in-the-Blank Questions

1) Increases in species diversity result from the process of __________ and decreases through __________.

Answer: speciation, extinction

2) A(n) __________ occurs when an ancestral species gives rise to many species that fill empty niches, and each species adapts to its niche by natural selection.

Answer: adaptive radiation

3) Most extinctions preceding the appearance of humans have occurred one by one, at a rate that paleontologists refer to as the __________.

Answer: background rate of extinction

4) __________ is a scientific discipline devoted to understanding the factors, forces, and processes that influence the loss, protection, and restoration of biological diversity within and among ecosystems.

Answer: Conservation biology

5) All of the valuable processes that intact ecosystems provide for us free of charge are known as __________.

Answer: ecosystem services

6) Diversity generally increases as one approaches the equator. This pattern of variation is referred to as the __________.

Answer: latitudinal gradient

## Multiple–Choice Questions

1) According to E. O. Wilson, biodiversity refers to

A) genetic variants of a single species

B) individual species

C) communities of organisms

D) ecosystems

E) all of the above

Answer: E

2) A species

A) is a population or group of populations whose members share certain characteristics

B) can freely breed with one another

C) produce fertile offspring

D) B and C

E) all of the above

Answer: E

3) What scientists classify species using an organism's physical appearance and genetic makeup?

A) ecologists

B) taxonomists

C) geneticists

D) environmentalists

E) none of the above

Answer: B

4) The greatest diversity of organisms can be found in

A) plants

B) animals

C) insects

D) birds

E) equally in all categories

Answer: C

5) An event held in a particular area, such as a state park or a city, in which taxonomists and interested citizens team up and race to thoroughly survey every species is a(n)

A) enviro gala

B) TaxoFaire

C) bioblitz

D) diversity race

E) none of the above

Answer: C

6) The extinction of a particular population from a given area (but not the entire species globally) is called

A) extinction

B) extirpation

C) emigration

D) evolution

E) adaptation

Answer: B

7) The IUCN's Red List is

A) an updated list of species facing unusually high risk of extinction

B) a list of unidentified species

C) found only in ecologically damaged ecosystems

D) an identification list of known species

E) used by Congress to identify international failures at conservation

Answer: A

8) Changes in habitat have tremendous effects on the organisms that depend on them. These effects are

A) generally negative because organisms are already adapted to the habitats in which they occur, so that any change is likely to render the habitat less suitable for them

B) generally positive because organisms are already adapted to the habitats in which they occur, so that any change is likely to render the habitat more suitable for them

C) generally positive because the changes increase the habitat that is available for species to colonize

D) generally negative because the changes cause rapid extinction of most species present

E) none of the above

Answer: A

9) Extinction occurs due to

A) inbreeding

B) habitat destruction

C) introduction of species

D) B and C

E) all of the above

Answer: E

10) In general, successful introduced species face

A) increased environmental resistance

B) decreased environmental resistance

C) increases in limiting factors

D) increased competition from other organisms

E) decreased biotic potential

Answer: B

11) Scientists use the "O" of the HIPPO acronym to refer to

A) overconsumption of resources by people

B) overharvesting of species from the wild

C) overexploitation

D) B and C

E) all of the above

Answer: E

12) Biodiversity enhances food security because it provides

A) genetic diversity

B) protection against loss of pollinators

C) protection against loss of secondary predators

D) protection against pathogens

E) all of the above

Answer: E

13) Which of the following can only change local species diversity?

A) immigration and emigration

B) speciation and extinction

C) speciation and immigration

D) emigration and extinction

E) none of the above

Answer: A

14) Which of the following change global species diversity?

A) immigration and emigration

B) speciation and extinction

C) speciation and immigration

D) emigration and extinction

E) none of the above

Answer: B

15) Which of the following are facing the highest rates of extinction?

A) K-strategists

B) r-strategists

C) insects

D) B and C

E) all of the above

Answer: A

16) Removal of which of the following species will always result in the greatest changes in an ecological system?

A) competitive species

B) carnivore species

C) keystone species

D) producer species

E) decomposer species

Answer: C

17) The species most often vulnerable to human impact is the

A) top predator

B) keystone species

C) decomposer

D) B and C

E) all of the above

Answer: A

18) The field of conservation biology

A) developed in response to government intervention

B) was initially viewed as lacking objectivity

C) attempts to integrate an understanding of evolution and extinction

D) B and C

E) all of the above

Answer: D

19) Which of the following can be a keystone species?

A) decomposer

B) primary producer

C) herbivore

D) carnivore

E) all of the above

Answer: E

20) Ecotourism

A) is only a reasonable option in impoverished countries

B) decreases biodiversity by causing increased population in environmentally sensitive areas

C) increases biodiversity by providing income to impoverished areas that would otherwise be destroyed

D) B and C

E) all of the above

Answer: D

21) The area effect of the Equilibrium Theory of Island Biogeography suggests that

A) the number of species increases with the size of the island; all else being equal, larger islands contain more species

B) the number of individuals of each species decreases as the size of the island increases because competition decreases population sizes

C) the number of species decreases with increasing island size; all else being equal, larger islands contain fewer species

D) random factors affect the number of species on an island, so size affects the number of individual of each species

E) the larger the national park, the more it attracts tourists

Answer: A

22) The Convention on Biodiversity produced documents

A) that included an international treaty

B) designed to conserve biodiversity

C) that require biodiversity be used in a sustainable manner

D) that ensure the fair distribution of biodiversity's benefits

E) all of the above

Answer: E

## True/False Questions

1) Paleontologists estimate that roughly 99% of all species that have ever lived are already extinct.

Answer: TRUE

2) Resource conservation for protection of pharmaceuticals is overstated because only 25% of the people on our planet use biological resources directly in traditional medicine.

Answer: FALSE

3) DNA is currently being recovered from extinct species to be used in cloning.

Answer: TRUE

4) Extinction is a relatively new phenomenon as it only results from impacts of humans on natural species.

Answer: FALSE

5) Nongovernmental agencies are currently paying off countries' debts in exchange for promises to keep diverse areas under protection.

Answer: TRUE

## Essay Questions

1) What is the value of genetic diversity for species?

Answer: Species with more genetic diversity have better chances of surviving, because their built-in variation better enables them to cope with environmental change. Species with little genetic diversity are vulnerable to environmental change for which they are not genetically prepared. Species with depressed genetic diversity may also be more vulnerable to disease, and may suffer the effects of inbreeding, which occurs when parents that are too genetically similar mate and produce weak or defective offspring. Genetic diversity in our crop plants is important for protection of our food sources.

2) What is the value of biodiversity to humanity?

Answer: Students should include and expand on some of the following concepts. Biodiversity provides valuable ecosystem services free of charge. Biodiversity gives us natural classrooms. Biodiversity enhances food security. Biodiversity provides traditional medicines and high-tech pharmaceutical products. Biodiversity provides economic benefits through tourism and recreation. People value and seek out connections with nature.

3) What are the basic concepts identified by the Equilibrium Theory of Island Biogeography? How do they apply to terrestrial ecosystems?

Answer: This theory was initially applied to oceanic islands to explain how species come to be distributed among them. Since then, researchers have increasingly applied the theory's tenets to other types of islands, including islands of habitat—patches of one type of habitat isolated within vast "seas" of others. Several patterns are apparent from the theory of island biogeography and the real-life study of species on islands. One is that the number of species increases with the size of the island. Larger islands possess more species in part because more space allows for larger populations, and larger populations are less vulnerable to extirpation and thus have longer expected species survival times. Larger islands also present fatter targets for organisms to encounter if they are wandering lost. Finally, larger islands also may possess more habitats than smaller islands. The distance between an island and the nearest continent also affects species number on the island. These patterns hold up for terrestrial habitat islands, such as forests fragmented by logging and road building. Small islands of forest lose their diversity fastest, starting with those large species that were few in number to begin with. In a landscape of fragmented habitat, species requiring the habitat will gradually disappear from the landscape, winking out from one island after another over time.

4) Is extinction natural? Briefly, how has the extinction rate changed over the history of Earth? Why are extinction rates today different than in the past?

Answer: Students should discuss some of the following. Extinction is a natural process. Extinction rates have risen higher than the background extinction rate during several mass extinction events during Earth's history. Since 440 million years ago, there have been five major episodes of mass extinction. If current trends continue, the modern era may see the extinction of more than half of all species. While similar in scale to previous mass extinctions, today's ongoing mass extinction is different in two primary respects. First, humans are causing it. Second, humans will suffer as a result of it.

5) What is the Endangered Species Act? Describe two of its successes and explain some of the current controversies surrounding it.

Answer: The Endangered Species Act is the primary legislation for protecting biodiversity in the United States. It forbids the government and private citizens from taking actions (such as developing land) that would destroy endangered species or their habitats, and also forbids trade in products made from endangered species. The aim is to prevent extinctions, stabilize declining populations, and when possible, enable populations to recover to the point they no longer need protection. The ESA has had a number of notable successes. Following the banning of DDT and years of management programs, birds like the peregrine falcon, brown pelican, and bald eagle have recovered and been taken off the endangered list. Intensive management efforts with other species like the red-cockaded woodpecker have held formerly declining populations steady in the face of continued habitat degradation. Roughly 40% of declining populations have been held stable. While most Americans support endangered species protection, some have vocally opposed provisions of the ESA. Some of the resentment results from the perception that the ESA is focused only on single species, and values the life of an endangered species over the life or livelihood of a person. Most popular resentment toward the ESA, however, has stemmed from worries of landowners that federal officials will restrict the use of private land if threatened or endangered species are found on it.

# Chapter 16 Land Use, Resource Management and Creating Livable Cities

## Matching Questions

*Match the following.*

1) Our natural affinity for contact with other organisms

2) Where all trees in an area are cut, leaving only stumps

3) The impulse that protects enormous, beautiful, or unusual natural features such as the Grand Canyon and Mount Rainier

4) Tracts of land with exceptional biodiversity that couple preservation with sustainable development to benefit local people

5) The practice of classifying areas for different types of development and land use

A) zoning

B) deforestation

C) regional development

D) homophilia

E) clear-cutting

F) biophilia

G) idolism

H) classification

I) monumentalism

J) biosphere reserves

1) F 2) E 3) I 4) J 5) A

## Short Answer Questions

1) What is the role of the Chicago-Area Forest Preserve System?

Answer: To protect natural lands from development and preserve open space.

2) What is the single greatest societal change in the United States over the last century?

Answer: The shift from rural to urban living brought about by industrialization.

3) How does increased distance from natural areas as a consequence of urbanization impact humans views of nature?

Answer: It has caused us to feel isolated from nature, and made us less aware of where resources come from and how our choices affect the larger environment on which we depend.

4) Why does the government offer farm subsidies?

Answer: These subsidies exist because the vagaries of weather make profits and losses from farming unpredictable from year to year, which means that a system without some way of compensating farmers for bad years might not survive in the long term.

5) How can grazing be done sustainably?

Answer: Grazing can be sustainable if done carefully and at low intensity.

6) Briefly, what are the two sometimes conflicting goals that motivated the establishment and design of the early city parks?

Answer: Parks were meant to be "pleasure grounds" for the wealthy, who would ride the parks' winding roadways in carriages. On the other hand, they were meant to alleviate congestion and allow some escape for the many poverty-stricken immigrants who lived in America's cities at the time, park users more interested in active recreation like ballgames than in carriage rides.

## Fill-in-the-Blank Questions

1) __________ encompasses making strategic decisions about who should extract resources in what ways, so resources are used wisely and not wasted.

Answer: Resource management

2) The phenomenon of urban and suburban spread across the landscape has been given the name __________.

Answer: sprawl

3) Forest products have helped our society achieve the standard of living we enjoy today, but clearing and loss of forests, or __________, has altered the landscape and ecosystems of much of the planet.

Answer: deforestation

4) Forest Service scientists in some districts have become involved in extensive programs of __________, attempting to protect, recover, or restore whole plant and animal communities that had been lost or degraded.

Answer: ecosystem management

5) The professional pursuit called __________ attempts to design cities in such a way as to maximize their efficiency, functionality, and beauty

Answer: city planning

6) Much of today's farmland exists on the site of former __________ swamps, marshes, bogs, and river floodplains—that were drained and filled in.

Answer: wetlands

## Multiple–Choice Questions

1) What drives the move to the suburbs from cities?

   A) desire to have a garden

   B) more jobs are available in suburbs

   C) desire to live in cleaner, more parklike conditions

   D) concern over demographic transitions

   E) none of the above

   Answer: C

2) The greatest general problem with suburbs is

   A) high population density

   B) lack of resources

   C) they spread environmental impact over a larger area

   D) decreased water quality

   E) all of the above

   Answer: C

3) What was the purpose of the battle fought by the 3,000 residents of the Sonoran desert community of Tortolita, on the outskirts of rapidly expanding Tucson?

   A) to maintain low population density

   B) against strip malls and parking lots

   C) against annexation by two adjacent towns

   D) to maintain their peaceful town

   E) all of the above

   Answer: E

4) The majority of forests are found in

   A) savannahs

   B) taiga

   C) tropical rain forest

   D) B and C

   E) all of the above

   Answer: D

5) Southern forest plantations are currently managed as

   A) ecologically functioning forests

   B) row crop agriculture

   C) warehouses of biodiversity

   D) polycultures that enable stability

   E) hot spots of habitat diversity

   Answer: B

6) Which of the following causes the most damage?
   A) clear–cutting
   B) selective logging
   C) shelterwood
   D) B and C
   E) All of the above do the same damage.

   Answer: A

7) Habitat disturbance that occurs as a result of logging includes
   A) erosion
   B) increases in runoff
   C) siltation of waterways
   D) increased flooding
   E) all of the above

   Answer: E

8) Fire history in a given area is determined by
   A) density of vegetation
   B) charcoal in soil
   C) soil chemistry
   D) tree ring scars
   E) all of the above

   Answer: D

9) The Sarawak tribes
   A) were rewarded for allowing clear–cutting of their forest
   B) were left without resources when the Malaysian government allowed clear–cutting in their forest
   C) began an oil palm farm and made lots of money once the trees were removed
   D) failed to mount a protest in the face of destruction of their way of life
   E) were already extinct when the government moved in

   Answer: B

10) The swampland acts of the mid–1800s encouraged
   A) removal of swamp areas and establishment of agriculture
   B) people to invade the prairie region so that Indian tribes would be displaced
   C) protection of swampland as valuable ecological systems
   D) hundreds of thousands of people to move west
   E) biodiversity protection for all organisms

   Answer: A

11) Land uses such as forestry or grazing cattle are not problems, but

A) sheep are

B) overuse of resources is

C) eating low on the biomass pyramid is

D) B and C

E) all of the above

Answer: B

12) John Wesley Powell thought that parcels in the West would have to be 16 times larger than government-distributed parcels in the East because

A) there was more land out there and few people

B) the need to populate the area was so great

C) for farmers to succeed they would need to irrigate

D) the lands were too swampy and vast areas of their property could not be farmed

E) watershed districts were large

Answer: C

13) The first national park was

A) Yosemite

B) General Grant

C) Yellowstone

D) Sequoia

E) Mount Rainier

Answer: C

14) Which of the following gave the president authority to declare selected public lands as national monuments?

A) The Homesteaders Act

B) The Swampland Acts

C) The Wilderness Act

D) The Antiquities Act

E) The National Parks Act

Answer: D

15) Which of the following is not true of the system of national wildlife refuges?

A) was begun in 1903 by Roosevelt

B) is managed by the U.S. Fish and Wildlife Service

C) calls employees land stewards

D) is guided by Aldo Leopold's teachings that land is a community of life

E) None of the above; they are all true statements.

Answer: E

16) Some state governments oppose land set–asides because they

A) don't have any

B) have too much land in federal control

C) need money from the sale of the land

D) feel they are overlooked in terms of federal dollars

E) are not environmentally conscious

Answer: B

17) Land trusts are

A) government entities

B) private nonprofit groups

C) local or regional organizations that aim to preserve lands valued by members of a region where the trust is based

D) B and C

E) all of the above

Answer: D

18) Transboundary parks

A) do not occur

B) are very rare

C) cause international dilemmas

D) account for 10% of protected areas

E) will not contribute to peace

Answer: D

19) The SLOSS dilemma involves

A) habitat fragmentation

B) preserve design

C) biodiversity protection

D) reserve size

E) all of the above

Answer: E

20) Burnham's 1909 Plan of Chicago represented the first

A) attempt to address biodiversity concerns

B) thorough city planning program

C) effort to address urban sprawl

D) effort to design a freeway

E) effort to plan for agriculture in city areas

Answer: B

21) Large traffic problems can be addressed by

A) public transportation systems

B) rewards for carpoolers

C) taxes on fuels

D) taxes on inefficient modes of transport

E) all of the above

Answer: E

22) The role of zoning is to

A) promote urbanization

B) classify areas for different types of developing and land use

C) encourage rural practices in downtown areas without clashing with current use

D) run city governments like the federal government

E) all of the above

Answer: B

## True / False Questions

1) In the United States, 75% of the population are considered urban dwellers.

Answer: TRUE

2) Forests cover less than 10% of Earth's surface.

Answer: FALSE

3) Livestock graze more than one quarter of Earth's surface.

Answer: TRUE

4) Timber harvests are currently increasing in developing nations and decreasing in developed nations.

Answer: TRUE

5) Agriculture, including both row-crop agriculture and livestock grazing, covers more acreage than any other land use.

Answer: TRUE

## Essay Questions

1) Why do urbanized societies need stretches of uninhabited and undeveloped land?

Answer: Large stretches of undeveloped land outside of cities provide natural resources needed to support urban populations. This includes providing city dwellers with timber, food, and other resources. Areas of natural land of all sizes close and far from urban centers provide ecosystem services, including purification of water and air, nutrient cycling, and waste treatment. Natural lands provide escape from the stresses of urban life. They provide open space, greenery, scenic beauty, and places for recreation. They also provide habitat for wildlife, which serves to satisfy our natural affinity for contact with other organisms. In addition to the utilitarian reasons cited above, many people feel an ethical obligation to preserve wild landscapes and biodiversity for the sake of nonhuman organisms and/or the integrity of ecological systems.

2) How has the Smokey the Bear campaign damaged forest health? What is the importance of fire in ecosystem management? What is the cost of fire suppression for ecosystem health? What is the alternative to fire suppression?

Answer: Students should discuss some of the following. For over a century, the Forest Service and other land management agencies have suppressed fire whenever and wherever it has broken out. Yet ecological research now clearly shows that many ecosystems depend on fire to maintain themselves. Certain plants have seeds that germinate only in response to fire, and researchers studying tree rings have documented that many ecosystems historically experienced fire with some frequency. Ecosystems dependent on fire are adversely affected by its suppression; open pine woodlands become cluttered with hardwood understory that ordinarily would be cleared away by fire, for instance, and animal diversity and abundance declines in such cluttered habitats. In addition, fire suppression increases the likelihood of catastrophic fires that truly do damage forests, and that also destroy human property and threaten human lives. This is because fire suppression allows the buildup of years' worth of limbs, logs, sticks, and leaf litter on the forest floor—excellent kindling for a catastrophic fire. Such fuel buildup helped cause the 1988 fires in Yellowstone National Park, and thousands of other fires across the continent, and it is why catastrophic fires have become more of a problem than in the past. To reduce this fuel load and improve the health and safety of forests, the Forest Service and other agencies have in recent years been burning areas of forest under carefully controlled conditions. These prescribed burning programs have worked wonders where they have been applied, but require so much time and effort that a relatively small amount of land has been treated. In addition, these efforts have been complicated by public misunderstanding and by interference from politicians who have not taken time to understand the science behind the approach.

3) Who owns the majority of U.S. grazing land? Why have environmentalists and ranchers been at loggerheads? What threat has recently seen them aligned on the same side?

Answer: Most U.S. rangelands are federally owned and managed by the Bureau of Land Management (BLM). Ranchers are allowed to graze cattle on BLM lands for inexpensive fees, which many public lands advocates see as an inducement to overgrazing. Thus ranchers and environmentalists have traditionally been at loggerheads. In the past several years, however, ranchers and environmentalists have been finding common ground, as they team up to preserve ranchland against what each of them views in common as a threat—the encroaching housing developments of suburban sprawl. While developers will often pay good money for ranchland, many ranchers do not want to see the loss of the wide open spaces and the ranching lifestyle that they cherish.

4) What are the four traditional reasons for the development of parks and protected areas? What fifth reason has been added recently?

Answer: First is the belief that enormous, beautiful, or unusual features such as the Grand Canyon and Mount Rainier should be protected — an impulse sometimes termed monumentalism. Second, parks have been created at sites lacking economically valuable material resources; land that holds little monetary value is easy to set aside because no one wants to buy it. A third reason we have set aside parks is for utilitarian purposes. A watershed protected from development provides cities with clean drinking water and a buffer against floods. A fourth reason for the creation of protected areas has been their recreational value to tourists, hikers, fishermen, hunters, and others. To these four traditional reasons, a fifth has been increasingly prioritized in recent years: the preservation of biodiversity. Human impact alters habitats in myriad ways, and has led to countless population declines and species extinctions. A park or reserve is widely viewed as a kind of Noah's Ark, an island of habitat that can, scientists hope, maintain species that might otherwise disappear.

5) Who owns the forest land that is home to timber harvesting? Why was the national forest system established, what was its mission, and who specifically directed its development? How did the political climate in the United States aid the formation of a system that incorporated the theme of conservation?

Answer: Most timber harvesting in the United States takes place on private land, including that owned by timber companies, but some takes place on public lands, notably the national forests. The national forest system, managed by the U.S. Forest Service, covers over 8% of the nation's land area. The depletion of the eastern forests and the fear of a "timber famine" spurred the formation of the Forest Service in 1905, under Gifford Pinchot. Pinchot and others developed the concept of resource management and conservation during the Progressive era in American politics, a time of social reform when people had confidence that the application of science and education to public policy could greatly improve society. In line with Pinchot's conservation ethic, the Service aimed to manage the forests for "the greatest good of the greatest number in the long run." Pinchot believed the nation should extract and use resources from its public lands, so timber harvesting was from the start the goal of the national forests. But conservation meant planting trees as well as harvesting them, and the Forest Service would seek restrained use and wise management of timber resources, which are not renewable if not given time to grow back.

6) What part of American history makes it difficult for us to suggest halting deforestation in the tropical rain forest? How did deforestation proceed in the United States? Why is deforestation there different than it was here?

Answer: Students should discuss some of the following. Timber harvesting propelled the growth of the United States throughout its phenomenal expansion across the continent in the 19th century, and into the 20th. Chicago was built with timber felled in the vast pine and hardwood forests of Wisconsin and Michigan. Those forests were virtually stripped of their trees in the 19th century. This followed the clear-cutting of the forests further east, which had been largely replaced by small farms. Logging operations then moved south to the Ozarks of Missouri and Arkansas to harvest more wood for the growing nation. The pine woodlands of the South were logged and many of them converted to pine plantations. When the largest, most valuable trees had been removed from these areas, timber companies moved west, cutting the continent's biggest trees in the Rockies, the Sierras, the Cascades, and the coast ranges. By the mid-20th century almost no virgin timber was left in the lower 48 states. Many U.S. trends are being paralleled internationally, but some developing nations, such as Brazil, are in the position the United States faced a century or two ago, having a vast frontier to conquer. However, in these countries deforestation can proceed more quickly because of newer technology. Furthermore, much of the cutting is being done not by the people of those countries but by multinational corporations that export the products elsewhere.

# Chapter 17 Nonrenewable Energy Sources and Their Environmental Impacts

## Matching Questions

*Match the following.*

1) An environment that has little or no oxygen

2) Organic matter compressed under high pressure to form solid carbon structures

3) A gaseous by-product of microbial decomposition

4) Organic material being broken down anaerobically, but remains wet, near the surface

5) Energy from processed uranium

6) A renewable resource

A) geothermal

B) hydrogen fuel cell

C) nuclear

D) coal

E) petroleum

F) peat

G) anaerobic

H) carbon dioxide

I) aerobic

J) mulch

K) crude oil

L) natural gas

1) G 2) D 3) L 4) F 5) C 6) A

## Short Answer Questions

1) Why has the Arctic National Wildlife Refuge (ANWR) been a subject of debate?

Answer: ANWR has been the focus of debate for decades, as advocates of oil drilling have tried to open its lands for development, while advocates of wilderness preservation have fought for its protection.

2) What are the three main sources of energy that Earth receives?

Answer: All energy comes to Earth from three sources. The majority comes in the form of radiation from the sun, some rises from Earth's core as heat, and a much smaller amount arrives in the form of the gravitational pull of the moon and sun.

3) If not all materials that decompose become fossil fuels, how are fossil fuels produced?

Answer: Fossil fuels are produced only when organic material is broken down in an environment that has little or no oxygen, a condition described as anaerobic.

4) What is "Hubbert's peak"?

Answer: A prediction that global oil production would peak in 1995.

5) Why was the use of natural gas limited during the 19th century?

Answer: During much of the 19th century, technology did not exist to pipe gas safely over long distances, so the early uses of gas were necessarily on very local scales.

6) How does the burning of oil and coal contribute to acid rain and industrial smog?

Answer: The burning of oil and coal releases sulfur dioxide and nitrous oxides, both of which contribute to acid rain and industrial smog.

## Fill-in-the-Blank Questions

1) The amount of a given fossil fuel in a deposit that is technologically and economically feasible to remove under current conditions is termed the __________ of that fuel.

Answer: proven recoverable reserve

2) As much as two-thirds of the total oil deposit may remain in the ground after the __________, the initial drilling and pumping of available oil.

Answer: primary extraction

3) In __________, huge amounts of earth are removed by heavy machinery to expose coal.

Answer: strip-mining

4) A tree that falls in the forest and decays as a rotting log undergoes __________ decomposition because in the presence of air, bacteria use oxygen to break down remains.

Answer: aerobic

5) Solid, liquid, and gaseous energy products from the tissues of organisms are called __________ fuels.

Answer: fossil

6) That which can change the position, physical composition, or temperature of matter is called __________.

Answer: energy

## Multiple-Choice Questions

1) The world's most abundant fuel is

A) biodiesel

B) coal

C) oil

D) natural gas

E) methane

Answer: B

2) Prior to 1765 the resource that provided the greatest amount of energy for heating and cooking was

A) dung B) wood C) coal D) oil E) water

Answer: B

3) The debate over the Arctic National Wildlife area has occurred because

A) Gwiich'in, one of the native Alaskan groups, depend on hunting caribou and fear that oil-industry activity will reduce caribou herds

B) the Inupiat, one of the native Alaskan groups, see oil extraction as one of the few opportunities for economic development in the area

C) many scientists anticipate damage to vegetation and wildlife as a result

D) oil company scientists contend that drilling operations in ANWR would have little impact on the environment

E) all of the above

Answer: E

4) Which of the following energy sources are considered renewable?

A) fossil fuel energy

B) sunlight and tidal energy

C) geothermal energy

D) B and C

E) all of the above

Answer: D

5) Which fossil fuel is formed depends on

A) the chemical composition of the starting material

B) pressures to which the material is subjected

C) the presence or absence of decomposers

D) the time that has passed since the organism died

E) all of the above

Answer: E

5) Which fossil fuel is formed depends on

A) the chemical composition of the starting material

B) pressures to which the material is subjected

C) the presence or absence of decomposers

D) the time that has passed since the organism died

E) all of the above

Answer: E

6) For the United States, which of the following represents the use of fossil fuels accurately?

A) oil is used most, followed by natural gas, then coal

B) natural gas and oil are used more than coal

C) coal is used more than natural gas and oil

D) oil is used almost exclusively

E) None of the above as methane provides for most of our use.

Answer: A

7) Sending a sound wave into the ground (by exploding dynamite, thumping the ground with a large weight, or using an electric vibrating machine) and measuring its return to the surface at receiving stations is called

A) dynamite surveying

B) destructive surveying

C) seismic surveying

D) sonar surveying

E) This is not used for finding fossil fuel deposits as it is too destructive.

Answer: C

8) The entire pool of oil is not extracted from the well because

A) it is too destructive to the environment

B) it is more expensive than moving to another well

C) we do not have the technology

D) B and C

E) all of the above

Answer: D

9) The world's most-used fuel since the 1960s is

A) coal

B) natural gas

C) oil

D) nuclear power

E) solar

Answer: C

11) Considering the statement "Coal continues to be popular in the United States," which of the following is not true?

A) The country has such large reserves of coal.

B) Quality of coal varies from deposit to deposit.

C) Coal causes less environmental damage than other fossil fuels.

D) Coal is relatively cheap.

E) None of the above are incorrect.

Answer: C

12) In each type of coal, sulfur content varies depending on whether the coal was formed in an area of

A) oxygen

B) aerobic vs. anaerobic decomposers

C) freshwater or saltwater

D) the Midwest

E) greatly depressed temperatures

Answer: C

13) Natural gas was first discovered

A) around 100 A.D.

B) by Bunsen in 1885

C) during the 19th century by Plutarch

D) during World War I

E) none of the above

Answer: A

14) Deposits of natural gas are most numerous in

A) the Middle East

B) Russia and the United States

C) South America

D) Panama

E) Spain and Portugal

Answer: B

15) Natural gas is

A) trapped for use as energy from landfills

B) produced by bacteria during decomposition

C) more damaging to the environment than coal

D) A and B

E) all of the above

Answer: D

15) Natural gas is

A) trapped for use as energy from landfills

B) produced by bacteria during decomposition

C) more damaging to the environment than coal

D) A and B

E) all of the above

Answer: D

16) The most dangerous occupation is working

A) at a nuclear power plant

B) as a coal miner

C) as an attendant at a gas station

D) on an oil rig

E) as an engineer on a fossil fuel project

Answer: B

17) The United States currently imports approximately what percentage of its crude oil?

A) 80%

B) 60%

C) 40%

D) 20%

E) none

Answer: B

18) The greatest damage caused to the environment by oil extraction is

A) the drilling activities themselves

B) road construction

C) development of infrastructure

D) B and C

E) all of the above

Answer: D

19) Alaskans benefit from the trans-Alaska pipeline because Alaska's state constitution requires approximately 25% of state revenues associated with the oil industry to be placed into a monetary fund called the Permanent Fund, which

A) is placed into fuel company pockets to reduce environmental damage

B) pays for education of native Alaskans through scholarships

C) pays yearly dividends to all Alaska residents

D) is divided equally among the politicians in the state for running their office

E) all of the above

Answer: C

21) Nuclear power comes from fission of

A) helium

B) neutronium

C) uranium

D) strontium

E) all of the above

Answer: C

## True / False Questions

1) North America consumes over five times as much energy per capita as the world average.

Answer: TRUE

2) One-quarter of the world's coal is located in the United States.

Answer: TRUE

3) Nuclear power contributes to the problems of air pollution.

Answer: FALSE

4) Addition of oil to waterways is largely from large catastrophic spills such as the Exxon Valdez.

Answer: FALSE

5) Oil has been used longer than any other fossil fuel.

Answer: FALSE

6) In developed nations, wood still accounts for 20% of energy consumption.

Answer: FALSE

## Essay Questions

1) What was the "energy crisis" of 1973–74 in the United States? What caused the embargo? How did the United States respond to the embargo? What did it demonstrate?

Answer: Students should discuss some of the following: By 1970, domestic U.S. sources of oil had declined to the point that the nation was importing half of its oil, depending on a constant flow from abroad to keep cars on the road and machines running. In addition, at that time a greater percentage of homes and electrical plants were run on petroleum than today. Then, in 1973, opposition to U.S. support of Israel in the Arab–Israeli Yom Kippur War prompted the predominantly Arab nations of the Organization of Petroleum Exporting Countries (OPEC) to stop selling oil to the United States. The embargo created panic among Western oil companies and investors and caused oil prices to skyrocket, eventually rising tenfold. Fear of a long–term oil shortage and rising oil prices drove American consumers to wait in long lines at gas pumps. In response to the embargo, the United States government enacted a series of policies designed to reduce reliance on foreign oil. These included searching for additional domestic reserves (such as those on Alaska's North Slope), resuming extraction at sites shut down when their initial operation had ceased being cost–effective, capping the price domestic producers could charge for oil, and beginning to import oil from a greater diversity of nations. The government also established a stockpile of oil stored underground in salt caverns in Louisiana, called "strategic oil reserves," as a short–term buffer against future shortages. Currently over 600 million barrels of oil are stored in the strategic reserves. Combined with ongoing domestic oil production, the stockpile ensures enough fuel for several months in case the country experiences another shortage of foreign oil. The "energy crisis" of 1973–74 in the United States demonstrated how the price of oil can affect U.S. government policies and the energy–using habits of the nation.

2) How is oil conservation in the United States a function of economic need? Are the conservation measures enacted in the 1970s still in place? How have they changed? Why is conservation an argument against oil drilling in the Arctic National Wildlife Refuge?

Answer: Students should discuss some of the following. The policies enacted in response to events in 1973 included conservation measures, such as a mandated increase in the fuel efficiency of automobiles, a reduction in the national speed limit, and funding of research into non–oil–based energy sources such as solar power. Thirty years later, many of the conservation policies developed after the 1973 oil crisis have been abandoned, now that high costs and the immediate threat of shortages no longer serve as motivation. Government funding for research into alternative energy sources has decreased, speed limits have increased, and a bill to raise the mandated average fuel efficiency of vehicles to 35 mpg recently failed in Congress. The failure to improve fuel economy of vehicles over the past 20 years, despite the existence of technology to do so, has added greatly to U.S. oil consumption, because transportation accounts for 27% of U.S. energy expenditures and 67% of oil use, with more than half of this energy use by passenger vehicles. Many critics of oil drilling in the Arctic National Wildlife Refuge point out the vast amounts of oil wasted by fuel–inefficient automobiles, and argue that a small amount of conservation would save the nation far more oil than it would ever obtain from ANWR.

3) How does coal mining affect the environment? Discuss the processes and impact of removing coal.

Answer: The mining of coal can also have substantial impacts on natural systems. Surface strip-mining can destroy large swaths of habitat and cause massive soil erosion and chemical runoff into waterways of surrounding regions. Regulations in the United States now require mining companies to restore strip-mined land following mining, but impacts are severe and long-lasting just the same, and most other nations exercise less oversight. Mountaintop removal can have even greater impacts than conventional strip-mining. When tons of earth are removed from the top of a mountain, it is difficult to keep rock and soil from sliding downhill, where large areas of habitat can be degraded or destroyed and creekbeds polluted and clogged. Loosening of government restrictions in 2002 enabled mining companies to legally dump mountaintop rock and soil into valleys and rivers below regardless of the consequences for ecosystems, wildlife, and local residents.

4) Why is it that in most parts of the world local people don't benefit from the removal of fossil fuels from their local environment? Discuss the economics, politics, and environmental reasons that locals may not benefit.

Answer: In most parts of the world where the oil industry has extracted oil, local residents have not seen great benefits. To the contrary, in many instances they have experienced disruption and harm to their way of life. This has occurred repeatedly when multinational corporations have extracted oil in developing countries, paying those countries' governments concessions for access to the oil. All too often, the money has not trickled down to residents of the region from which the oil is extracted. Furthermore, oil-rich developing countries such as Ecuador and Nigeria often have few environmental regulations, and existing regulations may be infrequently enforced if a government does not want to risk losing the large sums of money associated with oil development. Some critics accuse multinational oil corporations of furthering environmental degradation and political repression in developing countries by funding dictatorships and by threatening to withdraw investment and development money if environmental protection regulations are enforced.

# *Chapter 18* Renewable Energy Sources

## Matching Questions

*Match the following.*

1) The atom that will be used as a renewable energy source in Iceland
2) Collect sunlight and convert it to electrical energy directly
3) A practice in which the extra heat generated in the production of electricity is captured
4) The kinetic energy of moving water
5) Organic substances produced by recent photosynthesis

A) hydropower
B) cogeneration
C) carbon
D) biomass
E) litter
F) dam storage
G) detritus
H) oxygen electric power
I) hydrogen
J) photovoltaic (PV) cells

1) I  2) J  3) B  4) A  5) D

## Short Answer Questions

1) What are the benefits of hydrogen electric power?

Answer: The process is clean; nothing is combusted and the only waste product is water.

2) Why is renewable energy use growing fast?

Answer: Renewable energy use is growing fast due to advances in technology and increasing concern over environmental impacts of fossil fuel combustion.

3) What problem may arise if the transition to renewable resources occurs too slowly?

Answer: If the transition proceeds too slowly, falling fossil fuel supplies may outpace our ability to develop new sources, and we may find our economies greatly disrupted.

4) What are the two main advantages of hydropower over fossil fuel use?

Answer: It is renewable and it is clean.

5) What does it mean that consumers can "vote with their wallets" to achieve energy conservation?

Answer: It means that consumers vote by purchasing energy-efficient appliances. Decisions by consumers to purchase energy-efficient products are crucial in keeping those products commercially available. By purchasing these products we are ensuring energy conservation.

6) What are the benefits of using offshore sites for collecting wind power?

Answer: Wind speeds over water are often greater than those over land. Wind speeds on average are roughly 20% greater over water, producing 50% more power through a turbine. Turbulence near the surface is also reduced, so turbine towers can afford to be lower.

7) What is meant by the statement that "reducing our energy use is equivalent to finding a new oil reserve"?

Answer: Effective energy conservation in the United States alone could result in saving 6 million barrels of oil a day. In actuality, conserving energy is better than finding a new reserve, because it lengthens our access to fossil fuels and also lessens impacts on the environment.

## Fill-in-the-Blank Questions

1) The most commonly used approach to solar energy collection is __________, in which buildings are designed and building materials chosen to maximize their direct absorption of sunlight in winter, even as they keep the interior cool in the heat of summer.

Answer: passive solar energy collection

2) The __________, first proposed in 1839 by French physicist Edmund Becquerel, is produced when light strikes one of a pair of negatively charged metal plates in the photovoltaic cell, causing it to release electrons.

Answer: photoelectric effect

3) We can harness power from wind by using devices called __________, mechanical assemblies that convert wind's kinetic energy, or energy of motion, into electrical energy.

Answer: wind turbines

4) __________ is one form of renewable energy that does not originate from the sun. Instead, it is generated from deep within Earth.

Answer: Geothermal energy

5) __________ is the practice of reducing energy use as a way of extending the lifetime of our fossil fuel supplies, of being less wasteful, and of reducing our environmental impact.

Answer: Energy conservation

## Multiple-Choice Questions

1) In the United States, movement from fossil fuels to alternate energy sources is
   A) an option for those who believe conservation is important
   B) an option for those who believe human health is impacted by smog and pollution
   C) an option for the elitists who believe fossil fuel dependence is suicide because it makes us vulnerable to the Middle East.
   D) necessary as supplies of oil and natural gas are not expected to last more than half a century
   E) necessary as oxygen production by trees is currently endangered by fossil fuel use

   Answer: D

2) The largest pool, worldwide, of renewable resources currently used is
   A) solar B) hydro C) biomass D) wind E) coal

   Answer: C

3) The fastest source of electricity generation using renewable resources is
   A) solar
   B) wind
   C) hydro
   D) natural gas
   E) coal

   Answer: B

4) Which of the following does not describe a use of biomass for fuel?
   A) provides heat energy as fuel
   B) burns to create steam for turning turbines in a magnetic field
   C) converts into liquid fuels to power automobiles and other engines
   D) can be co-fired with coal in power plants
   E) All of the above describe uses of biomass for fuel.

   Answer: E

5) Which of the following is not true concerning combustion of biomass for energy production?
   A) It is a renewable resource if managed correctly.
   B) It does not contribute to air pollution and elevated $CO_2$.
   C) It is the most-used source of energy in developing countries.
   D) B and C
   E) all of the above

   Answer: B

6) The amount of energy generated from hydropower sources depends on

A) the temperature of the water

B) the distance the water falls

C) the volume of water released

D) B and C

E) all of the above

Answer: D

7) Passive solar design techniques can include which of the following?

A) using heat-absorbing construction materials

B) installing low, south-facing windows to maximize sunlight capture in the northern-hemisphere winter

C) thermal masses made of brick or concrete may be strategically located so that in cold weather the mass receives a great amount of sunlight and can radiate this heat in the interior of the building

D) can involve use of certain types of vegetation planted in certain locations around a building

E) all of the above

Answer: E

8) Solar represents a minuscule portion of the U.S. energy production because of

A) technological limitations

B) lack of investment

C) lack of scientific interest

D) poor outlook for potential for this energy source

E) potential for pollution from this source of energy

Answer: B

9) A major disadvantage of solar power is that

A) cost is prohibitive even in developed countries

B) pollution is high

C) not all regions are sunny enough to provide adequate power with current technology.

D) there is a lack of knowledge on long-term impacts

E) all of the above

Answer: C

10) Prior to 1950 the use of windmills was for

A) energy generation

B) grinding grain for bread

C) pump water for irrigating crops

D) B and C

E) all of the above

Answer: E

11) Windmills are generally better placed

A) higher to minimize turbulence and maximize wind speed

B) lower to minimize turbulence and maximize wind speed

C) higher to minimize the number of birds that interfere with blade turning

D) lower to increase heat convection off the ground

E) none of the above

Answer: A

12) The fastest-growing source of electricity is

A) water B) coal C) solar D) wind E) peat

Answer: D

13) One problem associated with geothermal power is that it

A) may not always be truly sustainable

B) is limited to areas that have hot springs

C) can pollute the air

D) B and C

E) all of the above

Answer: E

14) Ocean energy sources include

A) chemoluminescent bacteria

B) tide energy

C) wave energy

D) B and C

E) all of the above

Answer: D

15) The largest problem with adopting new technology of renewable resources

A) evaluating impacts of use scientifically

B) start-up costs are high

C) long-term maintenance costs are higher than fossil fuels

D) technological advances have not been made in the last 30 years to meet needs

E) all of the above

Answer: B

16) The problem with electricity is that it

A) is dangerous if stored too long

B) cannot be stored easily in large quantities for use when and where needed

C) is not understood properly

D) will be replaced shortly with other sources of power for homes

E) none of the above

Answer: B

17) Fuel cell technology has been tested in the United States because

A) it was originally slated for use in cars by Ford

B) it has been used widely since the 1960s in NASA's spaceflight programs

C) the visionaries of the fuel companies saw the need to develop this technology

D) they wanted it for use in WWII

E) Incorrect; it has never been tested in the United States.

Answer: B

18) Whether a hydrogen-based energy system is environmentally cleaner than a fossil-fuel system depends on

A) the car driven

B) the source of the oxygen used for the process

C) how the hydrogen is extracted

D) governmental incentives for research

E) Hydrogen is always cleaner.

Answer: E

19) Hydrogen is used as fuel through

A) ingestion

B) combustion

C) chemical reaction

D) incineration

E) electrolysis

Answer: C

20) The waste product associated with the use of a hydrogen fuel cell is

A) carbon dioxide

B) water

C) heat

D) B and C

E) all of the above

Answer: D

21) Which of the following is an effective route to energy conservation?

A) increasing the amount of fossil fuels available for processing

B) making fossil fuels a renewable resource

C) using batteries for generation of electricity

D) adjusting human behavior by taking steps to reduce energy consumption

E) all of the above

Answer: D

## True / False Questions

1) Today's economies are powered by fossil fuels, with four-fifths of all primary energy coming from oil, coal, and natural gas.

Answer: TRUE

2) Renewable energy sources have received far less in subsidies, tax breaks, and other incentives from governments than have conventional sources.

Answer: TRUE

3) In the United States, 60% of rivers appropriate for dam construction already are dammed.

Answer: FALSE

4) The sun's raw energy is so strong that if only 0.1% of Earth's surface were covered with solar panels, we would have enough solar energy to power all the world's electrical plants.

Answer: TRUE

5) The energy content of a given amount of wind increases as the square of its velocity; thus if wind velocity doubles, energy quadruples.

Answer: TRUE

6) The amount of energy released in the energy-generating hydrogen fuel cell reaction is less than the average efficiency in the U.S. electricity system.

Answer: FALSE

7) The EPA estimates that if all U.S. households purchased energy-efficient appliances, the national annual energy expenditure would be reduced by $100 million.

Answer: FALSE

## Essay Questions

1) What are the benefits and drawbacks of biomass energy? Include information on economics and the environment.

Answer: Students should include information on some of the following. Biomass energy can be efficient in terms of both energy use and cost; biomass tends to be the least expensive type of fuel for combustion in power plants, and improved energy efficiency can lead to lower prices for consumers. Where waste residues from crops or timber products are used, it can be virtually free, since these by-products would otherwise be thrown out as waste. Where waste costs money to dispose of, using waste for fuel can save money. Liquid fuels made from biomass are competitive in price with petroleum gasoline. Alcohol can fuel cars, stoves, and heaters, while gasohol, gasoline containing 10% ethanol, is cleaner burning than conventional gasoline. In terms of environmental impacts, biomass energy has a mixed record. Unsustainable wood harvesting can lead to deforestation, soil erosion, and desertification, damaging landscapes for thousands of years, eliminating biodiversity, and impoverishing human societies dependent on an area's resources. Among the newer uses of biomass, however, one positive environmental effect is that capturing landfill gas reduces emissions of methane, a powerful greenhouse gas that contributes to climate change. A larger issue is that the combustion of biomass does not reduce emissions relative to fossil fuels to the extent that other renewable energy sources do. Because carbon is being burned, carbon dioxide and other gases are being released as they are in the combustion of fossil fuels, although in most cases the levels of emissions are lower. Growing crops for energy establishes monoculture agriculture on precious land that could otherwise be left fallow or used to grow food. Producing ethanol for energy provides farmers with additional markets for their crops, but yields only small amounts of ethanol per acre of crop grown. It is not efficient to grow high-input, high-energy crops merely to reduce them to a few gallons of fuel; this process is less efficient than directly burning biomass. Another problem is that many farmers apply petroleum products to their crops to increase their yields, meaning that a shift to ethanol as a fuel would not eliminate our reliance on fossil fuels.

2) In general, what has spurred the use of renewable energy, and what are the benefits of its use in environmental and economic terms?

Answer: Renewable energy use is growing fast, due to advances in technology and increasing concern over environmental impacts of fossil fuel combustion. Unlike fossil fuels, renewable sources are inexhaustible on time scales relevant to human societies, and will help alleviate air pollution and the greenhouse gas emissions that are driving global warming. Renewable energy can also bring economic benefits. Developing renewables can help diversify an economy's mix of energy, lowering price volatility and protecting against shocks like the 1973 oil embargo by lessening dependence on foreign fuel. New energy sources also can create new employment opportunities and sources of income and property tax for local communities, often rural areas passed over by other types of economic development.

3) What are the advantages and disadvantages of the use of solar power?

Answer: Students should discuss some of the following. The fact that the sun will continue burning for another 4–5 billion years makes it practically inexhaustible as an energy source for human civilization. Additionally, as described above, the amount of solar energy reaching Earth's surface should be enough to power our civilization once technology is adequately developed. While these overarching benefits of using solar energy are clear, there are also a number of benefits involving the technologies themselves. PV cells and other solar technologies use no fuel, are quiet and safe, contain no moving parts, require little maintenance, and do not even require a turbine or generator to create electricity. An average unit can produce energy for 20–30 years, with low operating costs. Solar power enables local, decentralized control over power. Individual homes and businesses, and isolated communities, can use solar to produce their own electricity, and may not need to be near a power plant or connected to the grid of a large city. This can promote self–sufficiency by reducing an area's economic dependence on other areas, and also reduces the need for extensive networks of transmission lines for electricity. In the developed world, those homes with two–way metering that collect solar energy for PV cell use and also are connected to the local grid, can sell electricity to their utility, and essentially make money from whatever solar power they produce but do not use. In developing countries, the advent and spread of portable solar cookers is an example of decentralization that is making a big difference. Solar cookers enable families to cook food without having to gather fuelwood, lessening people's labor obligations and helping reduce deforestation. In locations such as refugee camps, solar cookers are greatly relieving social and environmental stress. Finally, a major benefit of solar power over fossil fuels is that it does not pollute the air with emissions, and thus greatly reduces levels of greenhouse gases and pollutants released into the atmosphere relative to fossil fuels. Solar power currently has two major disadvantages. One is that not all regions are sunny enough to provide adequate power with current technology and a reasonable amount of equipment. While Earth as a whole receives vast amounts of sunlight, not every location on Earth does. Cities like Seattle might find it difficult to harness enough sunlight most of the year to depend on solar power. Other areas, like the southwestern United States, the Middle East, and many areas in Australia, Africa, Asia, and Latin America, receive plenty of sunshine for solar power. Daily or seasonal variation in sunlight can also pose problems for stand–alone solar systems if these do not have adequate storage capacity in batteries or fuel cells, or if backup power is not available from other energy sources. If solar power merely supplements electricity from a municipal electricity grid, then cloudy periods will cause no interruptions in power. The second disadvantage to current solar technology—as with other renewable sources—is the up–front cost of investing in the equipment. The investment cost for solar remains higher than that for fossil fuels, and indeed, solar is still the most expensive way to produce electricity.

4) What is geothermal power? What are the advantages and disadvantages of the use of geothermal power?

Answer: Students should discuss some of the following. Geothermal energy is generated from deep within Earth. The radioactive decay of elements amid the extremely high pressures and temperatures deep in Earth generate heat that rises to the surface through magma, and through fissures and cracks. Where this energy heats groundwater, natural spurts of heated water and steam are sent up from below. Terrestrial geysers and submarine hydrothermal vents are the surface manifestations of these processes. Geothermal power plants use the heat energy of natural hot springs to generate power. Rising underground water and steam are harnessed to turn turbines and create electricity. Although geothermal energy is renewable in principle (its use does not affect the amount of heat produced in Earth's interior), the power plants we build to use this energy may not all be capable of operating indefinitely. Like other renewable sources, geothermal greatly reduces emissions relative to fossil fuel combustion. Geothermal sources currently used produce no nitrous oxides or sulfurous gases, and only a sixth of the carbon dioxide produced by natural gas-fueled plants, while geothermal developments using the latest technology produce virtually no emissions. One estimate has each megawatt of geothermal power preventing the emission of 7.8 million lb of carbon dioxide emissions and 1,900 lb of other pollutant emissions from gas-fired plants each year. On the negative side of the ledger, geothermal sources, as we have seen, may not always be truly sustainable. In addition, the water of many hot springs is laced with salts and other minerals that corrode equipment and can pollute the air, so these may shorten the lifetime of plants, increase maintenance costs, and add to pollution. Like solar and wind power, geothermal power involves substantial development costs but low operations costs compared to fossil-fuel-fired processes. This is true for utilities, and also for residential heat pumps, so consumers need to understand that while up-front costs may be high, adopting the technology will likely save money in the long run. Finally, geothermal is limited to being used in the certain areas it occurs. Unless technology is developed to penetrate far more deeply into the ground than we can at present, geothermal energy will remain more localized than solar, wind, biomass, or hydropower. While places like Iceland are especially rich in geothermal energy sources, most of the world is not. In the United States, geysers exist in certain areas such as Yellowstone National Park, and hot water and steam exist underground in various locations in the western part of the country. Nonetheless, many more hydrothermal resources remain unexploited around the world, awaiting improved technology and economic and policy encouragement by governments.

5) Why is energy conservation in the United States so poor? How can it be improved?

Answer: Energy conservation in this country has only been effective when the price of energy use has soared beyond current costs. When energy is cheap, conservation is not an economic or environmental concern. Energy conservation can be accomplished in two primary ways. As individuals, we can make conscious choices to adjust our behavior by taking steps to reduce energy consumption, for example, by turning off lights and cutting back on using machines and appliances. Reducing personal use of power can be cost-effective for an individual or for a business, while it also helps conserve resources for society. We can also conserve energy as a society by making our energy-consuming devices and processes more efficient.

# Chapter 19 Waste Management

## Matching Questions

*Match the following.*

1) Any unwanted item or substance that results from a human activity or process

2) Incinerators that use the heat from the furnace to boil water to create steam that drives electricity generation or fuels heating systems

3) Anaerobic decomposition deep within the landfill produces

4) Conversion of organic waste into mulch or humus useable for enriching soil, by encouraging natural biological processes of decomposition in a controlled manner

5) A new approach to reduce waste production by modifying processing techniques and by finding new uses for materials previously considered waste

6) Liquids that seep through liners and leach through the soil underneath

A) combustor

B) industrial ecology

C) composting

D) waste

E) infiltration

F) landfill gas

G) mulching

H) technological advance

I) leachates

J) waste-to-energy facility

K) oxygen

1) D 2) J 3) F 4) C 5) B 6) I

## Short Answer Questions

1) How did the government attempt to solve the Manila garbage crisis?

Answer: The government created the Ecological Solid Waste Management Act, which required reduction of waste by increased recycling efforts.

2) In the 1980s, a solid waste crisis similar to that in the Philippines was brewing in the United States. How was it averted?

Answer: Since the late 1980s, recovery of materials for recycling has greatly expanded in the United States, allowing the pressure on landfills to be decreased.

3) What technologies have been developed to mitigate or eliminate incinerator emissions?

Answer: Filters remove particulate matter, and scrubbers spray plants with liquid formulated to neutralize certain acidic gases. In addition, burning garbage at especially high temperatures can destroy certain pollutants. Just as landfills are required to monitor their leachate, incinerators are required to test their emissions, and to make sure that the ash discarded into landfills meets safety standards.

4) Why is the United States often described as a "throwaway society"? Why is this not the case for all developed countries?

Answer: We are referred to as the throwaway society because so many of our goods are made to be used once and then discarded. Most Americans are so used to this model of one-time use, that we generally fail to realize just how unusual and unprecedented it is. For instance, in the United States people are accustomed to drinking from a soft drink bottle once and then discarding or recycling it. In most of the world, however, soft drink bottles are returned to the retailer once the buyer drinks from them, and those bottles are cleaned by the manufacturer and used over and over again.

5) Briefly, why are heavy metals particularly prone to bioaccumulate?

Answer: They are prone to bioaccumulate because they do not break down over time.

6) Why was the Comprehensive Environmental Response Compensation and Liability Act (CERCLA) enacted?

Answer: The Comprehensive Environmental Response Compensation and Liability Act (CERCLA) was enacted to hold polluters responsible for their waste and establish a federal program to clean up polluted sites.

## Fill-in-the-Blank Questions

1) In modern __________,waste is buried in the ground or piled up in large mounds. Unlike with open dumps, however, every effort is made to prevent waste from contaminating the environment.

Answer: sanitary landfills

2) __________, or combustion, is a controlled process of burning in which mixed garbage is combusted at very high temperatures.

Answer: Incineration

3) Preventing the generation of waste before it is formed is called __________.

Answer: source reduction

4) Ten states have __________ legislation that allows consumers to return bottles and cans to stores after use and receive a refund.

Answer: bottle bill

5) __________ consists of collecting used materials that can be broken down and reprocessed in order to manufacture new items.

Answer: Recycling

6) In the United States, __________ is considered neither municipal solid waste nor hazardous waste under the federal Resource Conservation and Recovery Act.

Answer: industrial solid waste

7) A federal program called the __________ was established to clean up sites polluted with hazardous waste from past activities.

Answer: Superfund

## Multiple-Choice Questions

1) The main challenge for managing wastewater is
   A) treatment of solid waste
   B) decreasing surf levels in ocean systems
   C) treatment of sewage
   D) B and C
   E) all of the above

   Answer: C

2) Industrial solid waste includes waste from
   A) consumer goods production
   B) mining and petroleum extraction
   C) agriculture
   D) A and B
   E) all of the above

   Answer: E

3) The majority of municipal solid waste is
   A) composted materials
   B) packaging
   C) nondurable goods
   D) B and C
   E) all of the above

   Answer: D

4) Which of the following has the smallest amount of per capita solid waste production?

A) Canada

B) Netherlands

C) United States

D) Germany

E) Impossible to determine as these statistics are not currently kept.

Answer: D

5) In sanitary landfills, the primary safeguard against groundwater contamination is to

A) locate them on slopes so water runs downhill

B) line the landfill with plastic and impermeable clay

C) line the landfill with cement

D) locate them away from groundwater

E) locate sanitary landfills on industrial sites where groundwater is not used for drinking or agriculture

Answer: B

6) Waste–to–energy facilities

A) are more efficient than burning coal

B) will never be used in this country

C) are incinerators that use the heat from the furnace to boil water to create steam that drives electricity generation or fuels heating systems

D) is inefficient as wasted haulage costs are expensive

E) cause incinerator companies to operate at a loss

Answer: C

7) What is the best solution to the solid waste problem?

A) increase the number of WTE facilities

B) increase the number of sanitary landfills

C) reduce the amount of material that enters the waste stream

D) reduce the cost of maintaining WTE facilities

E) increase the number of oceanic burial sites

Answer: C

8) The first bottle bills were

A) designed to provide glass for road construction

B) initiated in the 1990s

C) designed to cut down on litter

D) designed to provide incentives to industry

E) a consequence of landfill regulations

Answer: C

9) We are still at an early stage in the shift from an economy that

A) moves circularly to one that moves linearly

B) moves linearly to one that moves circularly

C) provides incentive for waste disposal rather than increased production

D) includes external costs to one that only includes internal costs

E) A and C

Answer: B

10) In terms of industry, waste production reflects

A) overall productivity

B) resources that are being lost in an industrial process

C) resources that are being gained in the industrial process

D) inefficiency

E) B and D

Answer: E

11) The larger idea behind industrial ecology is that

A) preservation of resources will cripple industry, resulting in decreased waste

B) human industries should function more like ecological systems

C) human industries should sell more raw materials

D) human industries are too advanced technologically to exist long term on this planet

E) preservation of resources is the only likelihood of sustainability

Answer: B

12) Reactive substances are those that

A) easily catch fire

B) corrode metals in storage tanks or equipment

C) are chemically unstable and readily react with other compounds, often explosively or producing noxious fumes

D) are harmful to human health when inhaled, ingested, or contact human skin

E) all of the above

Answer: C

13) Ponds or surface impoundments are used for

A) storing solid materials

B) storing composted materials

C) storing liquid hazardous waste

D) decreasing runoff from sanitary landfills

E) none of the above

Answer: C

14) In 1970, the Resource Recovery Act gave the federal government jurisdiction over
   A) industrial pollution
   B) waste management
   C) the development of recycling programs
   D) B and C
   E) all of the above

   Answer: D

15) Early in the history of industry, waste was
   A) practically ignored
   B) discarded into the environment under the assumption that it would be diluted
   C) discarded into the environment under the assumption that it would decay
   D) discarded into the environment under the assumption that it would disappear
   E) all of the above

   Answer: E

16) Our ability to shift from an economy that moves linearly from raw materials to products to waste, to an economy that moves circularly will be impaired until
   A) more recyclable goods are collected
   B) recycling is mandatory
   C) markets improve for using recycled goods
   D) B and C
   E) all of the above

   Answer: C

17) Much of our waste stream consists not of goods but of
   A) timber
   B) vegetable peels
   C) the materials used to package goods
   D) material discarded from clothing
   E) none of the above

   Answer: C

18) Source reduction, in this country, would include
   A) containers and packaging
   B) newspapers, clothing, and other nondurable goods
   C) tires and other durable goods
   D) furniture
   E) all of the above

   Answer: E

## True / False Questions

1) The single most effective approach to waste management is to reduce the amount of material that needs to be disposed.

   Answer: TRUE

2) Even after recycling, paper is still the largest component of municipal solid waste in the United States.

   Answer: TRUE

3) Waste generation has increased in the United States by more than 2.6 times since 1960.

   Answer: TRUE

4) Developed nations make far more efficient reuse of goods than do developing nations.

   Answer: FALSE

5) Current waste practices in the United States include the greatest proportion of trash being landfilled, with lesser amounts being incinerated, recycled, and composted.

   Answer: TRUE

6) The United States has gone in two decades from doing virtually no recycling to diverting 30% of all solid waste is away from disposal.

   Answer: TRUE

## Essay Questions

1) How can landfills also produce energy?

   Answer: Students should discuss some of the following. Combustion in WTE plants is not the only way to gain energy from waste. Deep inside landfills, bacteria help decompose waste in an oxygen-deficient environment. This anaerobic decomposition produces landfill gas, which is slowly released into the atmosphere. Landfill gas, which can contribute to smog problems and can be a health hazard, roughly consists of half methane, which makes up natural gas, one of our prime sources of fossil-fuel energy. For these reasons—both to reduce pollution and to gain income from the sale of natural gas—people have developed ways of capturing landfill gas.

2) What are the goals of waste management? What is the most effective way to meet these goals? How can this be accomplished?

   Answer: The goals of waste management are to dispose of waste safely and effectively and to reduce the amount of waste generated. Several approaches to meeting these goals have been developed over the years. The single most effective approach, however, is to reduce the amount of material that needs to be disposed of. Manufacturers can accomplish direct reduction of waste by increasing efficiency so that fewer by-products are produced. Citizens can also reduce waste by making the decision to consume less±to purchase fewer goods, to purchase goods involving less packaging, and to use those goods for longer. Reusing goods, for instance purchasing used items, is also a way to reduce the amount of material entering the waste stream.

3) What are the drawbacks of sanitary landfills?

Answer: Sanitary landfills have many drawbacks. Students should discuss some of the following. For one, despite improvements in liner technology and landfill siting, many experts believe that the probability that leachate will eventually escape from even well-lined landfills remains high. Liners can get punctured, and leachate collection systems eventually cease to be maintained. In addition, the dry state in which landfills are kept slows down the rate of decay. Bacterial decomposers that act to break down material thrive in wet conditions, so when landfills are dry, waste is slow to decompose. In fact, it is surprising how slowly some materials biodegrade when tightly compressed in a landfill. Even paper may survive intact for decades. Another problem with relying too heavily on landfills for waste management is that finding areas to locate new landfills has become increasingly difficult. Most communities do not want large landfills in their midst for aesthetic reasons and for fear of potential health risks. In North America, as a result of the NIMBY syndrome, landfills are rarely sited in wealthy, educated, and politically powerful neighborhoods, but instead are disproportionately sited in poor and minority communities. Besides the obvious injustice of this pattern, an uneven distribution of landfills also decreases efficiency by requiring that waste be shipped long distances from where it is produced to where it is ultimately disposed.

4) What is hazardous waste? What are the four criteria used by the EPA to define hazardous materials? Give a short definition for each category.

Answer: Hazardous waste is waste that poses a danger or potential danger to human health. Public awareness of hazardous waste has greatly increased in recent decades, driven by numerous highly publicized instances of toxic contamination at abandoned industrial sites across the United States and other nations. The EPA defines hazardous materials based on four criteria:

- Ignitability. Substances that easily catch fire (for example, natural gas, or alcohol)
- Corrosivity. Substances that corrode metals in storage tanks or equipment
- Reactivity. Substances that are chemically unstable and readily react with other compounds, often explosively or producing noxious fumes
- Toxicity. Substances that are harmful to human health when inhaled, ingested, or contact human skin

5) What are the main disposal methods for hazardous waste? List the methods and describe each briefly.

Answer: There are three primary means of hazardous waste disposal in the United States and most other developed countries: landfills, surface impoundments, and injection wells. Secure landfills are frequently used to store hazardous waste. The standards for landfills that receive hazardous waste are higher than those of ordinary sanitary landfills. Another method for storing hazardous waste, particularly liquid hazardous waste or waste in dissolved form, is in ponds or surface impoundments. To create a surface impoundment, a shallow depression is dug and lined with impervious material such as clay. Water containing small amounts of hazardous waste is placed in the pond and allowed to evaporate, leaving a residue of solid hazardous waste on the bottom. This process is repeated indefinitely. The third disposal method is intended to be a long-term disposal method that takes waste well out of sight and out of mind. In deep-well injection, a well is drilled deep beneath an area's water table. The well must reach below an impervious soil layer and must enter into porous rock. Once the well has been properly drilled, wastes are injected into it with the idea that they will be absorbed into the porous rock and remain deep underground, isolated from groundwater and human contact.

6) What are the benefits of incinerating trash? What are the drawbacks to incinerating trash? How have these problems been dealt with in most developed countries?

Answer: Incinerating waste reduces its weight by up to 75%, and its volume by up to 90%. The remaining material, in the form of ash, is generally disposed of in a landfill. However, simply reducing the volume and weight does not get rid of those elements in trash that are toxic. In addition, combustion can create new chemical compounds that can be health hazards. When trash is burned, many hazardous chemicals can be released in the smoke that is generated, from dioxins to PCBs to heavy metals. Early incinerators did not include mechanisms for mitigating air pollution, and therefore released toxic gases and particulate matter into the atmosphere. Such releases caused a substantial backlash against incineration from citizens fearful of the health effects of such facilities. Most developed nations now regulate incinerator emissions. The Philippines is the only nation to have banned the incineration of municipal solid waste completely, as part of its clean air legislation. Ironically, the ban, which so many environmental advocates support, is contributing to the waste problem by exacerbating the overabundance of garbage without a proper disposal site.

7) What are the three basic steps in the recycling loop? What is the step that needs the most attention if the recycling loop is going to work?

Answer: The first step is collection and processing of recyclable goods and materials after they have been used. Items collected through these methods are taken to facilities to be sorted and processed. In materials recovery facilities (often called MRFs), workers sort items into different types, often with the help of automated machinery. The facilities then clean the materials, shred them, and otherwise prepare them for reprocessing into new items. Once readied, these materials are used in manufacturing new goods. Collection and reprocessing of recyclables is not enough, however. Consumers and businesses must then purchase the products made from recycled materials if the recycling loop is to work and become economically sustainable.

# *Chapter 20* Sustainable Solutions

## Matching Questions

*Match the following.*

1) A word for the way material goods fail to bring happiness to affluent people

2) The equation that summarizes human environmental impact

3) Process by which people of the world's diverse cultures are increasingly communicating with one another and learning about and partaking in one another's diversity

4) Process of homogenization of the world's cultures, with certain cultures and worldviews displacing others

A) diversification

B) affluenza

C) influenza

D) nationalization

E) globalization

F) I=PAT

G) internationalization

H) I=PTS

1) B 2) F 3) G 4) E

## Short Answer Questions

1) How does the United Nations define sustainable development?

Answer: The United Nation defines sustainable development as "development that meets the needs of the present without compromising the ability of future generations to meet their own needs."

2) When environmental scientists speak of sustainability, what exactly do they mean to sustain?

Answer: They mean to sustain human civilization in a healthy state—and such sustenance is a requisite for improvements in development. In addition, they mean to sustain the natural environment, its species, and its systems, in a healthy and functional state.

3) Why are the phrases "humans and the environment" or "people and nature" a stumbling block for sustainability?

Answer: People cannot exist without the environment, so it is not as much of a dichotomy as the use of those terms suggest. People are part of nature and the environment so it should be humans within the environment. This constraint in our language has led to limitations in our thinking. Some philosophers go as far as to say that the perceived dichotomy between humans and nature is at the root of all our environmental problems.

4) What does true progress consist of?

Answer: An increase in human happiness, and not simply growth in material wealth. In the end we are, one would hope, more than simply the sum of what we buy.

5) Human processes of manufacturing have run on a linear model. Why is this a problem?

Answer: Ecosystem principles suggest that linear models are not sustainable. We could in theory make all our industrial processes sustainable if we could transform linear processes into circular ones, in which waste is recycled and reused as raw materials, as it is in nature.

6) Briefly, how could market capitalism become the optimal tool for achieving prosperous and sustainable economies?

Answer: Market capitalism could become the optimal tool for achieving prosperous and sustainable economies if external costs were built in.

7) How can the tax structure be changed in this country to make market capitalism the optimal tool for achieving prosperous and sustainable economies?

Answer: Currently, people are generally taxed for things that they desire (such as income and property) rather than things that they would like to discourage (such as overuse and waste of resources). This should be reversed.

8) What is the role of technology in societal growth, economic growth, and progress toward sustainability?

Answer: Technology enabled the population increases spurred by the agricultural revolution, the industrial revolution, and our advances in medicine and health. Technology has also extended, deepened, and strengthened our impacts upon Earth's environmental systems. However, technology also can help us develop ways to reduce our impact on the environment and achieve sustainability. That is, technology may have gotten us into this mess, but it is technology that can get us out.

## Fill-in-the-Blank Questions

1) It is __________ that enabled the population increases spurred by the agricultural revolution, the industrial revolution, and our advances in medicine and health.

Answer: technology

2) The precepts of __________ economics are based on the notion that economies should be made efficient and sustainable and that such efficiency and sustainability are within reach.

Answer: ecological

3) Populations may grow exponentially for a time, but eventually run up against limiting factors and level off at a __________.

Answer: carrying capacity

4) The labeling of products produced through sustainable methods is called __________.

Answer: green labeling

5) __________ is meant to sustain human civilization in a healthy state.

Answer: Sustainable development

## Multiple-Choice Questions

1) The first meeting to discuss the steps that needed to be taken to respond to the increasing degradation of the natural environment was in

A) Johannesburg, South Africa, in 2002
B) Stockholm, Sweden, in 1972
C) Kyoto, Japan, in 1997
D) Rio de Janeiro, Brazil, in 1992
E) New York, USA, in 1982

Answer: B

2) Agenda 21, created at the meeting in Rio de Janeiro, Brazil,

A) drew a roadmap for nations to take action to improve people's lives and improve environmental conditions in their own countries and internationally
B) eliminated transport of fossil fuels in ships other than double hulled
C) created burdens on countries to decrease pollutants to pre-1992 levels
D) was largely ignored by most countries
E) all of the above

Answer: A

3) Which of the following statements best characterizes the impact of environmental protection?

A) They hurt the economy by costing people jobs.
B) They create opportunities for new industries.
C) They increase the attractiveness of a region, drawing more residents and increasing property values and the tax revenues that help fund social services.
D) B and C
E) all of the above

Answer: D

4) Presently, goods and services are priced as though
   A) the extraction and use of "natural capital," or resources from nature, have large price tags
   B) the extraction and use of "natural capital," or resources from nature, are free
   C) we understand external costs
   D) C and D
   E) none of the above

   Answer: B

5) To be sustainable, a solution must work
   A) as long as a politician is in office
   B) in the long term
   C) in the short term
   D) locally
   E) C and D

   Answer: B

6) The United States, with less than 5% of the world's population, now consumes
   A) 10% of the world's energy resources and 20% of its total resources
   B) 30% of the world's energy resources and 40% of its total resources
   C) 50% of the world's energy resources and 60% of its total resources
   D) 70% of the world's energy resources and 80% of its total resources
   E) There is no way to provide an estimate of this value.

   Answer: B

7) Our consumptive lifestyles are
   A) a new phenomenon on Earth
   B) sustainable if we use technology properly
   C) consistent with the lifestyles of previous generations
   D) not impacting the environment due to environmental regulations
   E) not likely to impact the ability of developing countries to obtain natural resources

   Answer: A

8) Sustainable development is
   A) an oxymoron
   B) achievable with technology
   C) necessary for survival of the human species
   D) B and C
   E) all of the above

   Answer: D

9) Industrialization created, in part, the need for sustainable practices by
   A) improving our understanding of ecosystem principles
   B) increasing our appreciation of diversity
   C) causing humans to feel completely disconnected from the natural environment
   D) B and C
   E) all of the above

   Answer: C

10) Sustainable agricultural processes do not
   A) use genetically modified organisms
   B) degrade the soil
   C) use fertilizer
   D) use pesticides
   E) use organic fertilizers

   Answer: B

11) Humans have increased Earth's carrying capacity for ourselves with
   A) natural resources
   B) technology
   C) population growth
   D) the opposable thumb
   E) the inability to curb reproduction

   Answer: B

12) Producing responsible and constructive technology that can achieve sustainable solutions requires
   A) scientific research
   B) elimination of inferior technology developed through self-interest of large companies
   C) citizens cognizant of the pressure placed on politicians by "big business"
   D) public pressure for scientific funding
   E) all of the above

   Answer: E

13) Ecological economists suggest we can gain better understanding of economics and humans interactions with the environment if we view human economies as
   A) consumer driven
   B) preservation driven
   C) entities that function within natural systems
   D) entities that are devoid of ecosystem characteristics
   E) all of the above

   Answer: C

14) Which of the following will not lead toward sustainability?

A) wisely harnessing technology

B) reducing consumption

C) halting population growth

D) runaway consumer growth

E) All of the above will lead toward sustainability.

Answer: D

15) We could in theory make all of our industrial processes sustainable if we could

A) transform triangular processes into circular ones

B) transform linear processes into circular ones

C) recycle waste and reuse it as raw materials

D) B and C

E) all of the above

Answer: D

16) Many proponents of sustainability believe that encouraging local self-sufficiency is important for building sustainable societies because

A) it eliminates governmental influence on local practices

B) it forces citizens to look more closely at the global community

C) when people are tied more closely to the area they live in, they will value the area more and seek to sustain its environment and its human communities

D) more and more people are growing gardens

E) None of the above because proponents believe that encouraging local self-sufficiency will pose a threat to building sustainable societies.

Answer: C

17) Some argue that globalization will have a negative impact because

A) it entails multinational corporations attaining greater and greater power over global trade

B) it entails weakened central power as a result of homogenization

C) governments will gain more power

D) citizens will gain more power

E) all of the above

Answer: A

18) Policymakers enact environmental law because
   A) corporations and interest groups employ lobbyists to push politicians
   B) citizens vote
   C) citizens write letters
   D) citizens make phone calls
   E) all of the above

   Answer: E

19) There is ample reason to hope that we may achieve sustainability before doing too much damage to our planet and to our own prospects because of human
   A) consumption patterns
   B) ingenuity
   C) compassion
   D) B and C
   E) all of the above

   Answer: D

20) The lesson of Easter Island was that
   A) no man is an island
   B) conservation of resources is necessary for sustainable societies
   C) men do not comprehend resource issues until resources are gone
   D) women should play a larger role in government
   E) stone statues are important for sustainable cultures

   Answer: B

21) Our global society has greater potential to address concerns of sustainability today compared to previous societies because
   A) politicians today propose short-term solutions
   B) we have citizens who vote
   C) we have many thousands of scientists who study Earth's processes and resources closely
   D) of the Bill of Rights
   E) we value goods

   Answer: C

## True/False Questions

1) In developed countries, technology has begun to decrease human environmental impact.

   Answer: TRUE

2) Subsidies are currently designed to support sustainable practices.

   Answer: FALSE

3) Continued population growth is not sustainable, but continued consumption is.

Answer: FALSE

4) Hope for decreased population growth is provided by the demographic transition that many developed nations are passing through.

Answer: TRUE

5) Currently, market capitalism is not the optimal tool it could be for building sustainability, because external costs are not built in.

Answer: TRUE

6) To be sustainable, a solution must work in the short term.

Answer: FALSE

7) If the world population consumed as much as today's average U.S. citizen does, at least another two to three planet Earths would be needed.

Answer: TRUE

## Essay Questions

1) What was the goal of the 2002 World summit in Johannesburg, South Africa? Why was this location appropriate for this event? Provide an example to support your answer.

Answer: The goal was to hammer out agreements for how to move participating nations and our global society toward a goal of sustainable development. South Africa is in many ways a microcosm of the world and illustrates the global need for sustainable development. Students should provide evidence such as the following: The nation has extreme wealth and extreme poverty, and its wealth is concentrated among a small proportion of its citizens. It possesses urban metropolises filled with skyscrapers, cell phones, and computer networks, but also is home to hunter-gatherer tribes who still live largely by traditional means. It has areas of rich biodiversity and unique endemic species that are increasingly threatened by human impact. South Africa supports its economy with valuable natural resources like gold and diamonds, although these are nonrenewable and their trade has largely enriched a small number of people. The country has become dependent on international trade to supply products it needs, such as fossil fuels.

2) In terms of sustainability, why is a "lose-lose" scenario for the environment and for humans a problem for humans and not for the environment?

Answer: In a lose-lose scenario, in the very long term, it may be only humans who lose. If we destroy our environment, we destroy ourselves forever, but the environment will bounce back eventually. Biodiversity may recover in its numbers (although with a very different collection of organisms)perhaps 10 million years or so after a mass extinction, paleontologists estimate. Desertified landscapes and eroded and salinized soil will, after millions of years, eventually plunge back into the mantle and be reborn through plate tectonics. A severely disturbed atmosphere and warmed global climate will likely cool (although this is not certain). In the very long term, then, it is we who will be the losers if we destroy our environment, because once extinct, our species, like any other, will not return.

3) What accounts for the view that people's needs cannot be provided for and the environment protected simultaneously?

Answer: Part of this unfortunate misconception stems from the history and development of the environmental movement. The wave of modern environmentalism that swept much of the developed world in the 1960s and 1970s was a response to what many people viewed as rampant and unthinking human impact on natural systems. Early environmentalists were simply desperate to reduce what they saw as human depredation on the environment, in any way that they could. Citizen outrage inspired politicians to take action, and the easiest course of action was legislation, leading to a regulatory approach. Governments enacted laws and regulations that limited what businesses, individuals, and government agencies could do.

4) How can consumption be reduced while raising one's quality of life?

Answer: Consumption can be greatly reduced even while raising one's quality of life in at least three major ways. One is through improvements in the technology of materials and manufacturing and the efficiency of manufacturing processes. By improving technology and efficiency, industry can produce goods using fewer natural resources. Another way is by having a truly sustainable manufacturing system—one that is circular and based on the principle of recycling, in which the waste from a process becomes raw material for input into that process or into other processes of the same business or other businesses. Developing this type of sustainable system would allow consumption to be sustained at some maximum level indefinitely. A third way to halt runaway consumption involves the consumer rather than industry; it is that each one of us alter our behavior, attitudes, and lifestyle, and strive to make personal choices that minimize consumption.

5) Why are short–term solutions often offered to achieve sustainability? Why must sustainable solutions work in the long term? Why does the current political system inhibit our ability as a community to work on long–term solutions and how can citizens change this?

Answer: Policymakers in democracies very often act for short–term good, because in order to be re–elected they need to produce immediate, positive results. This has been a major hurdle for addressing environmental dilemmas, since so many are cumulative problems that worsen gradually and can only be resolved in the long term. Often the best long–term solution is not also the best short–term solution, a fact that explains why much of what human societies presently do is not sustainable. Often the costs for addressing environmental problems are short term but the benefits are long term, giving a politician little incentive to tackle them. For this reason, citizen pressure on policymakers is most important for issues that involve long–term effects.